Praise for *The Space Between Black and White*

"Esua's memoir embodies the saying that 'the personal is political'. This compelling, funny, honest autobiography traces Esua's rich and complex life with humour, letting her resilient spirit shine through. Esua's quest to answer the insistent question forced on her by society: 'Who am I and where do I really belong?' runs parallel to the great social justice movements of the late 20th century. From Women's Lib to Black Power and other forms of resistance, Esua has been at the forefront of social change for most of her life."

—Kate Morrison, author of *A Book of Secrets*

T0007070

The Space Between Black and White

A Mixed-Race Memoir

Esuantsiwa Jane Goldsmith

JACARANDA

TWENTY
in 2020
Black Writers, British Voices

This edition first published in Great Britain 2020
Jacaranda Books Art Music Ltd
27 Old Gloucester Street,
London WC1N 3AX
www.jacarandabooksartmusic.co.uk

A CIP catalogue record for this book is available from the
British Library

ISBN: 9781913090128
eISBN: 9781913090326

Cover Design: Rodney Dive
Typeset by: Kamillah Brandes

Printed and bound by CPI Group (UK) Ltd, Croydon, CR0 4YY

Contents

Contents

To our global Mixed-Race Community

For Joshua Kwesi and Abena Grace, our
wonderful children who have taught me so much

*Knowing who you are, where you're from,
and your beginnings,
is the only way you can find out where you're going,
and who and what you can become.*

Foreword

From the Pram to the Palanquin

I was an 'Only-One'. Illegitimate, fatherless, the only Brown kid on the block.

Brought up in the 1950s by a single mother in a White working-class community in Battersea, I was a rarity among my generation. Only about five percent of babies were born 'out of wedlock' at the time. Many of those babies were adopted or 'hidden' within families. Their mothers were sometimes disguised as their 'older sisters'.

But there was no disguising me. I was different.

The Black and Asian population of the UK was tiny in those days, only numbering around 55,000, and largely concentrated in particular neighbourhoods in urban areas. In Brixton, just a few miles from where I grew up, the Windrush generation had been putting down roots six years before I was born. My Grandfather took me to Brixton occasionally to visit his boss. Other than that, as a small child I rarely saw another Black or Brown face because communities were tightly-knit. People tended to work and shop locally, and socialise with family and neighbours.

There was a great deal of stigma associated with mixed relationships and their progeny. Famous mixed marriages, such as Ruth and Seretse Khama and Joe and Peggy Appiah, hit the newspaper headlines and generated much debate and significant hostility. The controversy surrounding the recent addition of a Mixed-Race member of the royal family shows that these issues are still very much alive even today.

In the 1950s, Mixed-Race babies were rare. In that climate, the fact that my White British mother insisted on keeping me, and my extended family took me and my mother in, was courageous in itself. Children like me were difficult to place in adoptive families. I was an anomaly, like an alien dropped from outer space. The visible half of my personal story was missing. My absent father, about whom I knew very little, left me without a Black role model or a narrative upon which to build my identity.

I grew up with no books or images of people who looked like me. Moving from Surbiton to Stafford to rural Norfolk, I moved in almost exclusively White environments where there was no-one to compare with me. In those environments, I was as Black as they come. When I looked in the mirror, it always took me by surprise. Later, travelling the world as a young woman, I experienced confused and diverse responses to my difference. This had

a profound effect on me, a complex feeling of simultaneously not belonging anywhere and belonging in two places,
which will be familiar to any member of our growing
diaspora today. My memoir is about a lifetime's experience
of inhabiting this space, showing how attitudes towards
Mixed-Race people evolved over six decades, during the
quest to find my place.

Outsider In

I had none of the cultural references of the Black people
I met as a young adult, and White people around me did
not share my experience of the racism and prejudice I
encountered. The Mixed-Race community is in general a
very young community in the UK, whereas my experience
spans over six decades. The few Mixed-Race babies of my
age were often brought up in care, and special orphanages
were set up to house such children—mostly the children of
African American Soldiers born after the Second World
War. Not many were as brave and fortunate enough, as my
mother was, to be able to bring up their children at home.

As a visible outsider in most groups, I was startled to
discover that I often processed experiences in a different way from my peers. I had a different perspective and
differently-wired responses, from most of the people I met.
Outwardly I was sociable and optimistic, while inwardly I
often felt second-class, unsafe, not always up to the job of
living life. It disrupted my relationships with my family

and friends, as well as my interactions with the world. It affected my choices as well as my ability to trust and to form deep and intimate relationships with others. I found my White heritage all around me, in society and the family I was brought up in, but without connection to my father's family and my African heritage, I felt lost. I carried a lot of anger and dread around with me, a hollowing-out inside. It was a largely hidden internal struggle, erupting now and then like a dormant volcano, in ways that seemed unconnected and mystified those around me.

From a very young age, Mixed-Race children often become adept at protecting our families, friends and colleagues from the reality of our experience. Monoracial family and friends are not always conscious or willing to acknowledge what is going on. 'I have a Mixed-Race cousin, sister, grandchild, partner, and it doesn't bother me, so why should it bother you?' 'You don't feel like that', 'You shouldn't feel like that', 'You can't have experienced that—we would have noticed!' 'You don't have a problem—just a nice sun-tan!' Having a Mixed-Race member of your family is not the same as knowing what it is like through lived experience. Family members may not be aware that certainty about their own racial identity prevents them from seeing a problem that their Mixed-Race relative is genuinely struggling with.

From my earliest years, I was keenly aware of the stigma of my difference and developed a heightened sense of justice. Put-downs and racist taunts undoubtedly hurt me and damaged my self-esteem. But despite some setbacks, I'm an optimist. I looked for creative ways to prove myself, and positive energy to fight back, build my resilience, survive and eventually flourish.

Sticks and stones may break my bones... but words will give me a nervous breakdown

Does it really matter what we are called and what we call ourselves?

It does matter when we do not have the words or concepts to describe ourselves, or our experience, except in negative terms or in comparison to other groups, and when words are used as a form of abuse. Mono-racial people don't need to struggle with the language in the same way. Whiteness, the default racial 'norm' in the Western World, comes with its own lexicon and associations of unearned power and privilege.

All terms for Mixed-Race seem to be an uncomfortable fit. In the 1950s we were labelled half-castes, half-breeds, mongrels, little-Black-sambos, mulattos, coloureds, wogs. We had a 'touch of the tar brush'. I did not have positive language to describe myself, and I found the names I was called wounding and stigmatising. I internalised them, which affected my sense of self-worth.

Whatever we call ourselves, racism, prejudice and discrimination doesn't go away. The language has changed through the generations, not without intense argument about the correct words to use. Last decade's terminology is often this decade's term of abuse. Nowadays, the terms bi-racial, multi-racial, Mixed-Race and dual-heritage (or multiple heritage) are often used interchangeably, although the term 'heritage' can signify cultural as well as racial heritage.

Not everyone of Mixed-Race heritage wants to identify as such. The term 'Mixed-Race' is controversial in itself—the concept of race is a social construct, and is therefore highly problematic. No words are perfect. The current preference for the term 'people of colour' (although I do use it myself) to signify non-white people of any description, is just as problematic, implying erroneously that White is not a colour and non-Whites form a homogeneous group. No single term could capture the multi-layered meanings we want to convey. As long as people use the terms Black and White, then we need a language that helps us describe the spaces in between. A new generation is finding the term 'Mixed-Race' empowering and validating, building solidarity between different communities, whether we are Mixed-Race Asian, African or Caribbean. I hyphenate 'Mixed-Race' to try and convey a sense of our distinct identity, rather than two or more races mixed.

Mixed experiences

How we identify varies according to personal experience, political perspective and historical and social context.

As individuals, Mixed-Race people are as diverse as any other group, and our experiences vary with age, sex, sexuality, gender, faith, ability or disability, geographical location, and whether we have been brought up in diverse or mono-cultural communities, or have dual or multiple heritages.

Given such diversity among Mixed-Race people, it is argued that we don't have enough commonality or shared heritage to be a community. However, we have significant shared experiences which are different from other sections of the population, which connect us and can bring us a sense of belonging. Whatever racial mix we are, racial ambiguity can have an effect on our sense of self and place in the world, including some of us who do not look obviously mixed and may present as mono-racial, whether Black or White. Mixed-Race people live in an unpredictable environment, which interprets us, makes assumptions about where we 'fit in', who we are, and assesses our relationships to our families and those around us, often getting it wrong.

In the last few years, my connection with our Mixed-Race community has enabled me to understand that my struggles are not unique. They are real, not imagined. Enduring racist abuse in childhood is commonplace, as is having our identity called into question on a regular basis by those 'did-I just-hear-that?' moments that persist into adulthood: 'Oh you *do* look well. Been somewhere hot?' 'I expect you like this weather!' 'You're not a *real* one, though, are you?' 'No, but where do you *really* come from?'

I don't mind being asked where I come from, by people who are genuinely interested. It can lead on to the most fascinating conversations. But questioning about Mixed-Race provenance can often be hostile, insensitive or dismissive, and occasionally just funny. These remarks can come at us every day, when we least expect it, especially in all-White environments. At a bus stop or in a supermarket queue, in a meeting or an interview, we are frequently called upon to explain and justify our existence, and reveal intimate and sometimes painful aspects of our lives to complete strangers.

The reality of Mixed-Race is complex, nuanced, multi-layered, challenging and sometimes confusing. Experience will vary depending on context and how we 'present'—even by our hair texture and depth of skin-tone. We can range from invisible to hyper-visible, from privilege to marginalisation, in an instant. Under potential attack, unsure what to expect in any given situation, Mixed-Race individuals develop more phobias than the average person. These phobias are often projections of our experience of shifting responses to our identity. (Although my fear of maths, described in Chapter 4, turned out to be an un-diagnosed case of dyscalculia, or 'dyslexia by numbers', it still added to my sense of inferiority and insecurity.) We navigate all of this every day, often developing a watchful alertness and hyper-vigilance in order to survive, an ability to rapidly adapt to changing environments and volatile situations, an adeptness at 'reading a room', and sensing people's verbal and non-verbal cues.

Divide and rule

There is currently a tendency to romanticise Mixed-Race as the good-looking, exotic, acceptable face of Black—a non-threatening fashion accessory, the 'bridge' between Black and White. This brings with it accusations of being 'coconuts'—Brown on the outside and White on the inside—aberrations, mongrels, fakes, inauthentic, carrying the stigma of non-pure blood, not to be trusted. Mixed-Race is dismissed as 'Shadism'. In reality, Mixed-Race people are an oppressed group facing a great deal of structural racism, but clearly we have some privileges and differences of experience compared to Black people and other non-White racial groups. There may be an over-representation of Mixed-Race people in some areas of White society compared with Black and Asian people, and there are undeniable privileges associated with being lighter-skinned. At the same time, these may come with the disadvantages of lack of access to a community and other family members with a shared experience. Sometimes the perception of 'privilege among the underprivileged' can lead to racism and rejection from both Black and White communities, and ostracisation from all other groups. In a binary world, we may not be Black enough or White enough, existing only in comparison with other groups.

Throughout history, powerful ruling classes have had a vested interest in dividing and scapegoating minorities, undermining our natural solidarity, and setting us up in competition with one another. This becomes more acute, and an act of deliberate policy, during times of political, social and economic crisis, such as those we are experiencing today. Race remains an emotionally charged issue and there is still a sense of discomfort and some unwillingness to engage with it, even though discrimination and prejudice are still deeply ingrained. People of colour may feel they will be charged with 'playing the race card' if they raise the issue; White people, that they will be accused of racism. Efforts to increase inclusivity can, paradoxically, result in perceived unfair bias in favour of minorities. Some may find it difficult to accept that they do not notice, or do not seem to care. They would rather minimise or dismiss the problem and blame the victim. White people of my generation in particular, born in the 1950s and 60s, were taught that the polite thing was not to see race at all, and treat everyone as though they are White.

But if you don't see race, you don't see racism. It goes unchallenged.

In the current climate of backlash against diversity and equality it can be hard to call out injustice where we see it, for fear of being labelled 'snowflakes' or 'victims'—not tough enough to live in the real world. However, there is a world of difference between calling out oppression and discrimination, which takes courage and confidence, and being defined and destroyed by that experience—the so-called 'victim mentality'.

All marginalised people can and do experience levels of discomfort, stress and conflict, from within and without. We all have the right to tell our stories so that people are empowered to understand and change. Not all experiences are equivalent or comparable. There are degrees and levels of oppression and discrimination, and we need to give voice to them to deepen our understanding. Social and political justice and equality should not be a competition; they are a universal entitlement.

Identity politics

The ambivalence towards the concept of Mixed-Race comes not only from its perceived divisiveness, but also because some say it is a distraction from the real struggle for equality, and it de-politicises race. It's dismissed as mere identity politics. At their most negative, identity politics can indeed be a destructive, divisive and exclusive force, giving rise to nationalism, racism, sexism, populism and xenophobia. But at its most positive, exploring identity can strengthen and empower individuals and groups, and give us the positive energy to generate solidarity and a deeper understanding of what it is to be human. The greatest transformational movements—the Women's Movement, Trade Unionism, the Civil Rights Movement,

Socialism—have been founded on a strong sense of individual and collective identity linked to a desire for social and political justice for all.

I was a teenager at a time when to be Black was a political statement, to ally oneself with oppressed peoples, and acknowledge a strong connection with Black and Brown people all over the world. That is where I found my political commitment, and my sense of self and belonging, and still do. For me, Mixed-Race is an important aspect of my Black identity and vice-versa. In the 1970s in the era of Anti-Apartheid and Civil Rights, I strongly identified as Black and proud. Like many Mixed-Race people of my generation, I sublimated my White heritage in the cause of political activism and collective solidarity, in which I still strongly believe. Coming out as Mixed-Race enables me to articulate my whole identity within our political movement.

Today, mainstream media, literature, advertising, business, politics and public life still fail to truly reflect the diversity of UK society, and the problem of alienation remains a big issue. Being pressured to choose an identity that does not fully express our whole nature causes pain and disconnectedness for individuals who don't fit into established categories. The pervasive concept of duality in Western culture is central to maintaining unequal and unjust power structures. There is a constant tension between fighting oppression as we know it and as it is constructed, based on binary models, and the lived experience of most of us humans, which is non-binary and fluid. As a Mixed-Race person, that tension lives in me. The concept of Mixed-Race does not depoliticise inequality. It shines new light on it.

Mixed-Race community

Mixed-Race is now Britain's fastest-growing minority population. Through the centuries, Mixed-Race people in majority White societies have been dismissed or defined by others in different ways. For example, historically in Australia, the Belgian Congo and Canada, Mixed-Race children were forcibly taken away from their families in indigenous communities because their White heritage was considered to make them a part of White society. Conversely, Mixed-Race children were in other cases considered Black or 'coloured' because of their non-pure blood, the so-called 'One Drop Rule', as in the United States or South Africa. We are told that there is nothing that unites us, and that we do not have a 'community', we do not 'fit', we are *Other*.

The 2011 census figures reveal that 2.3 million people in the UK identified as Mixed-Race. This may not have been a true reflection of the actual population, because only 30% of those of mixed parentage chose to define themselves in this way. The true figure is therefore likely to be much higher, especially among the younger generation, as mixed relationships become increasingly common.

Since the introduction of Mixed-Race categories in the Census in 2001, we have been able to track our growing community's distinct profile over nearly two decades. The emerging patterns for Mixed-Race categories differ significantly from other Black, White, Asian and minority ethnic profiles, in areas as wide-ranging as educational attainment, mental health, feelings of belonging, friendship groups, poverty levels, employment, police stop-and-search figures, patterns of bullying in schools, and experience of racism and discrimination. Mixed-Race people are more likely than any other group to be in single parent families, and there is a higher proportion of Mixed-Race children in care than other non-White groups.

Collection of data is important for service provision, representation and validation. It felt so liberating for me personally, after years of campaigning and ticking the box marked 'Other' on so many forms, to finally have my identity officially recognised.

Light touch

I have explored some of these themes through telling my story. This is an experiential book, not a theoretical one. The fusion of styles and genres reflects my developing sense of identity in diverse settings. I use my own voice in the present tense, without the benefit of hindsight, to tell the story at different stages of my life, introducing humour and a light touch to explore positive experiences, whilst taking the reader with me into some of the darker, more challenging episodes in my journey, owning up to my mistakes and where I got things wrong.

The title of my memoir comes from the closing paragraph of Rebecca Walker's book on Mixed-Race identity, *Black, White and Jewish: Autobiography of a Shifting Self*, in which she says, "I exist somewhere in the space between Black and white". I also use the phrase 'between Black and White' metaphorically, so the story will have meaning for any reader who feels they occupy that space 'in between'— in terms of sex, race, class, disability, sexuality, gender, mental health, faith and religion, geography, parentage, life experience, background or personality and all the other myriad differences that make up our gloriously complex humankind.

I have drawn on thirty years of personal journals, letters and dream diaries, family stories, and more than fifty interviews with my Ghanaian and UK parents, family members and friends. I carried out in-depth research using material from modern and contemporary sources: books, films, newspapers, radio, archives, websites, social media and online Mixed-Race communities. I have used terms current at the time in their historical context—such as 'coloured', 'half caste' and 'Gypsy'—placed in quotations to indicate they are terms that would not be acceptable or in general currency today.

It was a deeply personal challenge to find a voice and style to articulate my own experience, when there are few published Mixed-Race role models and so few literature tutors of colour. When I finally did find tutors of colour, it made an enormous difference to my self-confidence as a writer. I have long been inspired by Jackie Kay, Zadie Smith, Andrea Levy, Afua Hirsch and other Mixed-Race women writers who have broken the mould, lit up our lives, and shown us the way.

For me, writing is an exciting and energising process of evolution and revelation in itself, not just a technical activity. It is writing for liberation, as an individual, and collectively as a person of colour and of Mixed-Race. We tell our stories to create a body of voices, inspire more writers of colour to document the human experience, and offer up stories that are captivating for readers of all kinds.

The spirit in the story

Memoir shines a spotlight on a particular strand of life experience—in my case, my Mixed-Race identity. This focus has inevitably involved making hard choices and omitting some significant people, events and aspects of my life that are not directly relevant to my theme, even though they will always remain important and dear to me. Exploring your own life can be a painful as well as a joyful process. Like many memoir writers, I have lost many nights' sleep wrestling with the challenge of walking that fine line between honesty and remaining true to the spirit of the story, without hurting or embarrassing those I love, invading their privacy, or offending by omission.

That said, I have tried to stay true to my lived experience, whilst occasionally altering the timing, details and sequencing of events to fit the narrative flow and protect identities where necessary. I have merged some characters and events, for the sake of brevity and economy, although they are all based on real people and real-life events. I have changed the names of my characters, but retained the names of some well-known figures to place my memoir in its historical context. I found changing most of the names unexpectedly freed me to shape the characters in my book whilst protecting their integrity. My story is not theirs in the way they would have told it. It is uniquely my own story, in my words and from my own experience, told in the hope that it will resonate with others and perhaps reveal some deeper truths.

I wouldn't change it for the world...

The world is at a pivotal moment. Multiple identities and a sense of belonging are central to the rapidly changing, diverse, non-binary and fluid nature of our 21st-century world. A new, diverse generation needs support and encouragement to find and celebrate their multi-layered authentic selves in positive and nurturing ways.

I hope my book will encourage intergenerational and inter-racial conversation so that we can increase empathy, and recognise that we are stronger in diversity. Those of us who believe in social justice need to come up with creative and inclusive ideas to address the damage caused by marginalisation, austerity and globalisation; new ways of living in which we respect one another and are not in deadly competition for political spaces and resources on this planet. In an age when minorities are increasingly under attack, we must learn how to reach out to people who are different from us, listen openly, and find out about them.

There are real privileges inherent in the Mixed-Race experience—fluidity of identity, the ability to navigate many different spaces, along with increased adaptability, agility of mind and thought, sensitivity and responsiveness to what is happening around us. These qualities are not exclusively, or always, the preserve of Mixed-Race people. But conversations with others who define as Mixed-Race have enabled me to delight in discovering that we have access to spaces and perspectives that others may not have. Mixed-Race people tend to have more connections with different cultures and locations, and more multi-racial and multi-ethnic friendships than mono-racial groups. Our experiences provide a rich and fascinating seam of creative energy and exploration, which enables us to reach out beyond boundaries.

I am indebted to all who helped me with this book, and especially to our Mixed-Race community, Intermix, Mixed-Race Irish, Mixed Race Matters, Halu Halo, and my dear friends in Mixed Race Peeps, who have opened up for me a world of validation, understanding and celebration of our Mixed-ness. Meeting others with similar experiences has given me space to banish 'only-ness', and finally discover my 'tribe'.

Being Mixed-Race is about challenge, inclusion, social and political justice, equality, diversity and finding commonalities between us as well as delighting in difference.

This book explores my struggle with that identity, and the discovery of its joys.

I wouldn't change it for the world.

Prologue
The Other Other

Clapham Common, mid-November, 1957

"Can we stay just a little bit longer, Auntie Bel? Let me have a go now, please let me..."

November afternoon, raw, damp, cold, grey. Breath hangs in the air, mud squelches underfoot between trampled tufts of grass. A gang of older boys have been on the swings ever since we arrived, their scabby, grubby knees blue with cold beneath gabardine school shorts. Suddenly they streak off, laughing, just as it's time for us to leave for home. *Finally*, it's my turn. The wooden swing is cold and hard against the backs of my legs. The creaky to-and-fro motion makes me feel queasy. But I still want to have my go.

Auntie relents. "OK. Five more minutes. I'm chilled to the bone."

It's around five o'clock when we finally start for home. The bare trees fringing the Common dissolve into dark spiky shadows in the dusk. There's a dull sound of traffic coming closer as yellow lights appear, one by one, in the street and in the flats across the main road. I hate the cold. I can feel Auntie Bel's warm hand clasping my numbed fingers through my woollen mitten.

In the foggy half-light I can just about make out a family group moving slowly across the grass ahead of us. As we get nearer, I can see they are wearing the strangest clothes: long robes and trousers, glimpses of red, gold and blue, with short jackets, scarves and hats to keep out the late autumn chill. The woman is wearing a green-and-gold scarf around her head like a turban. They stand out in the fast-fading light, like a flock of brightly coloured birds. The smallest bird breaks away from the group and runs towards me—a little girl, about four years old, the same age as me. She has dark skin and Black fuzzy hair, like mine. We stop and stare at each other, spellbound, rooted to the spot. A sudden shock of connection, of recognition. I know you.

"Kumba! Kumba!"

I think it was Kumba, they called her. Something like that. Kumba ran off to join her family, and they moved off across the Common and out of sight.

It all happens so quickly, I can't quite believe what I have just seen. I try to run after her, but Auntie Belinda holds me back.

"We have to go home now," she coaxes. "Your Mum will be back from work soon, it's getting dark, and Nan will have tea ready."

Teatime. It always interrupts something really important, just at the wrong moment. I have stumbled on a secret—I am not the only one! I am not alone in the world. There are other Others. And more than that, 'coloured' people sometimes come in *whole families*—Mum, Dad and two children—not just one-offs like me. I feel strange—excited, scared, shocked, all at the same time—but also comforted.

I can't remember seeing any 'coloured' people before in real life, only once or twice on the telly at Auntie Molly's, singing and dancing with banjos, or in American films with big Mamas in the kitchen in starched white aprons, cooking up giant pumpkin pies for White folks' kids.

But *why* am I Brown? Why me, when everyone else I know is White? Like those boxes of pure white eggs you get at the grocer's, with one surprise speckled brown egg nestling among the china-white ones. An odd one out— an accident. How does that happen? What causes it? It's because of my Dad, that's what they say. But where *is* my Dad? Did he ever see me when I was a baby? Why did he leave? Does he ever think about me? Did he get called names, like I do? What does he look like? Do I take after him? Would he even like me if he saw me? Can I see a photo? Can I go to Africa?

I don't know if I can ask all these questions; it makes the grown-ups look uncomfortable. It's like treading on eggshells—brown *and* white. At nursery, or out shopping with my Nan, people sometimes ask if I come from a different place, but I have no idea where; I don't know what to answer. Timbuktu is the furthest, most mysterious place I ever hear grown-ups talk about. When someone goes missing, they say, "He could be in Timbuktu for all *we* know". No-one has ever told me where Timbuktu is, or whether anyone could possibly come back. Is it a real place? I like the sound of it. Tim-buck-too; the furthest place in the world. Somewhere in Africa—where my Dad came from.

Kumba. I like the sound of that too. I wish I had a name like that. But maybe I'm not allowed.

Chapter 1

Outside Child

When we got home from Clapham Common, I didn't tell anyone about Kumba. Grandad was already sitting in his armchair, coughing and wheezing and puffing on his pipe. He spotted me by the back door.

"Don't 'ang abart, you'll wet yer knickers, Janie."

The toilet is out in the yard, damp and cobwebby, with toilet paper that's hard and scratchy like greaseproof paper.

"Much nicer than newspaper, like we had when I was a girl," says Nan.

I always leave it to the last moment to go outside, especially when it's cold and dark, hopping from one foot to the other until I'm fit to burst.

There are six of us at home: Grandad and Nan, Mum and Auntie Bel, me and our mongrel dog Mush. The scullery is out the back, with Nan's clothes mangle next to the sink, along with the food safe where we keep the butter and cheese. The front room downstairs is always kept 'for best' when visitors come, so we are all in the little back room where Grandad sits in his battered old armchair by the window. We have our tea at the grey-and-white speckled Formica table, Friday night baths in the tin tub by the stove. The grown-ups have arguments about all sorts of things—clothes, politics, housework, Grandad's smoking, money, and the state of the shoe cupboard in the corner. The dog bolts out of the front door every morning. He lives his secret doggie life out in the streets of Battersea, but he is always pleased to see us when he comes home for his dinner.

Now that I've started big school, I spend a lot of time with my cousins, the Harleys, who live at the other end of the same road. Auntie Lucy is Grandad's niece. When we're not at school, we spend most of the time playing in the street. Life at the Harleys is noisy and boisterous. Buster, the eldest, is often in trouble, laughing and hollering as he slides down the bannisters, followed by Auntie Lucy chasing him with a rolling pin, taking the stairs two at a time. "Just wait till I catch you, you little sod!" But mostly he gets away with it.

The boys draw faces on little Lucy's dolls with blue Biro. Lucy is named after Auntie Lucy, but we call her "little Lucy" so we don't get mixed up. The biro can't be washed off; "little Lucy" howls in protest, but she soon cheers up when we blame the whole thing on Timmy's teddy.

"What's poor old Ted done this time?" Auntie Lucy laughs, as Buster the Judge finds him guilty and hangs him by a noose from the banisters "until he is a *dead* Ted."

Timmy does not seem to mind his teddy being hanged. He is much more easy-going than his sister. We make elaborate arrangements for Teddy's funeral, complete with choir and vicar and a shoe-box coffin. We ask all the grown-ups if they want to be buried or cremated. "Cremated," says Uncle Bernie firmly. "But only *after* I am properly dead, mind."

Afterwards Timmy and I get married, borrowing a net curtain for a veil. Then we look down each other's pants with a torch and a mirror until Auntie catches us. I like being here at the Harleys', the energy, the chaos, the crazy fun of it. Although I feel a bit overwhelmed sometimes, because they are all bigger than me, apart from baby Shirley. More confident, sure of themselves. Next to them, I am like a little brown weed. My Mum calls them 'The Harley tribe', and they know they belong.

*****

It's springtime, less than two weeks after my fifth birthday.

"Come and see, there's someone in here I want you to meet!" Auntie Bel calls out from the front room when I get back from the Harleys' house. Mum has already told me there is a big surprise waiting for me at home. Auntie Bel is sitting on the floor, looking tired but pleased and happy about something. Next to her is a baby's cot.

"Come and see—a new baby cousin for you," she says. But instead I stand upside down on the sofa. I always stand on my head whenever I don't know what to do, or I'm embarrassed, or even after dinner. It feels good to stand the wrong way up, my skirts covering my face. I can still see everybody but they can't see me. But the grown-ups say it will give me *'in digestion'*.

"Come on, get down, come and see," Auntie Bel insists. Now I'm on my feet again, the right way up, tiptoeing up to the cot. Inside there's a tiny new-born baby with a sprinkling of pale golden-ginger hair and a mark on his right cheek. Auntie Belinda is smiling.

"What do you think of him, Janie?"

I wrinkle my nose. Not sure. "What's his name?"

"Victor; he's named after Dad. We'll call him Baby Vic, so we won't get mixed up."

"What's that funny mark on his cheek?"

"Oh, that's just a birthmark. It doesn't hurt him, it'll fade after a while. They call it a strawberry mark. Looks like a strawberry, doesn't it?"

So, this baby doesn't have the stain on his skin like me. He only has a mark on his cheek that will fade after a while. I have a feeling he is going to turn my whole world upside down. I was the only child in the family, and now suddenly there's this new boy, and everyone is making such a fuss of him. Grandad will be very pleased. He always wanted a boy, but he got two daughters and a grand-daughter.

*****

It's Friday night at the Harleys'. As usual, money is tight at the end of the week, so we are having our favourite bread and sugar for tea. We help Auntie Lucy get it ready, taking turns to bash the sugar loaf with a rolling pin—the one she tries to thrash Buster with—until it's a mound of sparkling crystals. We pile the sugar onto a big dinner plate, then carry it to the table along with two loaves of sliced white bread, "which is the most *brilliant* invention since sliced bread!" Auntie Lucy chortles. A slab of soft yellow margarine next to the sugar, and that's it, we're off, self-service. Two loaves disappear in minutes, slapped on the sugar mound to pick up as many grains as possible. I have to be fast, but I'm a slow eater. My four cousins greedily eye the last bit of crust on my plate.

"What do ya think of your new baby cousin?" Auntie Lucy asks me above the hubbub.

"All right," I mumble, through a mouthful of bread. "It's like I got me own baby brother now. And I wrote him a poem."

"Not jealous then?"

"Uh–uh. Nope." They laugh. I s'pose I am—a bit.

After tea, my cousins are having their baths and getting ready for bed. Auntie pours heavy buckets of hot water into the big tin bath dragged out onto the kitchen floor. The bathing goes on all evening. First baby Shirley, then the kids, then grown-ups, their Grandad last, all using the same bathwater in turn, topped up with extra hot from the kettle. After that, long after I have gone home, Auntie says she washes the floor with a mop, using what's left in the bath, and tips the rest of the water—"By then, it's the colour of Mississippi mud!"—out into the yard to water the horseradish plants and the Michaelmas daisies.

She's a big woman, Auntie Lucy, and she works hard, her face red with sweat and effort. She swears like Grandad. She stops work every now and then to lean on the mop and brush her hair from her forehead with the back of her hand.

"Bugger this for a game of soldiers! One day I'm gonna get a bathroom with an indoor lav, in a little cottage in the country. That would make my bleedin' day, every day."

My cousins are all ready for bed by the time Uncle Bernie gets home from work at five-thirty in the evening. He doesn't like to have the kids around too long once he gets home on weekdays. He likes Auntie Lucy to himself in the evenings, so the kids are always in pyjamas when he arrives. The downside is, all four of them are awake again at half past five in the morning.

"You lot are up with the lark, thunderin' and hollerin' up and down them bleedin' stairs!"

Once my cousins are all tucked up in bed, I wait for my Mum to pick me up on her way back from work. At least I get to stay up later than all my cousins so I can spend time with my Mum when we get home. I also get a chance to talk to my Auntie and Uncle sometimes, on my own, when it's quieter. They always say what they think. They like to comment on what's going on in my house, so I find out lots of things. I realise that what seems like normal home life to me is quite unusual.

"What abart your Auntie Belinda's friends? They're a weird bunch, aren't they?" Uncle Bernie chuckles. "You can't always tell the men from the women. I don't think they even know themselves which is which! What about that posh friend of Bel's that comes round your house? Terri, that's it. Always wears slacks and those turtle-neck sweaters, and smokes cheroots, just like a man!"

"I reckon that's Uncle Victor, brainwashing them all with his communist ideas," Auntie Lucy laughs. He's so dogmatic with all his politics. He just encourages them all!"

"And what 'appened to your Mum's friend—Babs, Babs Hodgson? The one with the little coloured kid like you?"

Another coloured kid in the world, and I didn't know! Suddenly the memory comes back to me again—Kumba, the little girl I saw on Clapham Common before I started school, that afternoon when Auntie Bel took me up to the swings. So there are more of us! Not just me and Kumba. A little boy too! I am shocked and thrilled by this news. But I have never heard of Babs. Nobody has ever mentioned her. I wish her little Brown kid could come round to my house—I would let him have a go on my new scooter.

"'Ere, while you're waiting for yer Mum to arrive, you can watch *Popeye* on the TV, if you like," says Auntie Lucy. Just like Popeye, I have one eye on the TV and the other on the grown-ups. Auntie Lucy is sitting on Uncle Bernie's lap at the dinner table. He's squeezing her big breasts, which he fondly calls her 'Bristols', while she throws her head back and laughs her deep, rich laugh—they are cuddling and canoodling while he finishes his dinner, before he takes his bath.

"Look at our Janie, lookin' at us!" says Uncle Bernie with a wink. I am embarrassed that they've noticed. But I really can't take my eyes off them. I've never seen a man and woman behave like this. In our family, there are no men apart from my Grandad—and he and my Nan don't often touch, especially not in *that* way. I wonder if my African Dad and my Mum were like that…

At last Mum's here to take me home—it's only a few minutes' walk. Mum has a bad leg. She keeps it wrapped in bandages and she can't move her ankle. She can still walk, but not very fast. I wish I could ask her about the Brown boy I heard Uncle and Auntie talking about. But maybe I'm not supposed to know.

*****

It's Saturday morning during the summer holidays, and I'm impatient to show off my new scooter to the Harleys.

"Take your vitamins before you go," says Mum.

"But the Harleys only have one spoonful each. Why do I have to have *two* spoons of all the vitamins? It all tastes nasty, especially the cod liver oil. I *hate* it."

"The doctor says you have to have a double dose of

everything because he hasn't seen a kid with your skin colour before. He's not sure if you will get enough of the right vitamins, especially vitamin D, because there might not be enough sunlight here. That's it, hold your nose, swallow. All done, have a fruit gum. Not that bad, was it?"

It's a baking hot day. A heat-haze shimmers over the tarmac road and the sun burns the back of my neck. There's not a soul about, apart from those boys hanging around on the corner again. They always call me names—'woggie, darkie, Blackie, choccy, coon, who's been rolling in dog's muck?' How many names have they got for me? My tummy tightens, I try and scoot faster, but they call out those nasty, hateful things just the same. I lose my balance, trip up, fall over, and now they are laughing at me. I dust off my scraped knees, suck the graze on my hand.

"Where's your Dad? You 'aven't even *got* a Dad, 'ave yer?"

"Yes, I have! His name is Victor."

"'E's not yer Dad, 'e's yer grandad!"

"I know that. But I *call* him Dad, anyway."

I wobble off on my scooter again, eyes blurry with tears. Why do they pick on me for no reason when I'm minding my own business, enjoying my new scooter? All of a sudden, someone points out the stain on my skin, my fuzzy hair, and then everything is spoilt. I feel ashamed, angry, stupid, different, like there is something wrong with me.

My knee is bleeding by the time I get to the Harleys'.

I can't stand the sight of blood. It makes my feet go fizzy. Auntie Lucy wipes off the blood and dirt with cotton wool and puts a plaster on my knee.

"Wounded soldier. Just a graze. You'll be alright, you'll live," she says. "Just ignore those little buggers, they don't know any better. 'Sticks and stones may break my bones but words can never 'urt me'. That's what they say."

But it's the words that hurt the most. Those boys always pick on me, especially if there is no-one else about. And there's a boy at school who says I look like the golliwogs in the *Noddy* story the teacher reads to us. He sings "Baa baa Black sheep, have you any wool?" very loudly right in my face in the playground. Some of the kids ask if my skin colour washes off in the bath. They call me fuzzy-wuzzy, touch my hair, then pull a face, saying it feels like a *Brillo* pad. I have a knot in my stomach all the time, in case it happens again. It's not my fault. It's not fair.

"Be careful on that scooter outside," warns Auntie. "You go out with 'er Lucy, make sure she don't fall off again. And don't 'ang abart near the Penfolds' house—and don't go near the bomb site…" Her list of instructions tails off as we bang the front door shut.

The Penfolds are a 'Gypsy' family who live next to the bomb site, a few doors down. I sometimes hear the other kids call them 'gyppos' and say they are smelly and dirty. But I like them. I like people who are different, like me. We pass their house every day on the way to school. They are a large, lively, nice-looking family and there are always plenty of comings and goings in and out of their home. I don't know how they all manage to cram into such a small place. Sometimes their front door is ajar, and I can see into the passageway. It's full of old mattresses and planks of wood leaning up against the wall.

My favourite is Vicky Penfold. She goes to our school and she's about two years older than me. Slim and dark, with long tangled hair, graceful as a ballerina, she is out on the pavement now, entertaining the neighbourhood in the sunshine. Along with my cousins, I wheel my scooter up to have a closer look. Even the boys searching for old shells and bits of shrapnel on the bomb site stop to watch, and so do the neighbours opposite, leaning on their gatepost.

Little Simon, from next door to the Harleys', rolls up with his teddy in his dolly's pram. I feel sorry for him. He often gets teased, because boys are not supposed to play with dolly's prams. But all the same, he is brave because he never goes anywhere without it. I know how it feels, to be small and different. You never know when you are going to get picked on.

Today he needn't worry, because everybody's attention is focused on Vicky. First, she puts her arms above her head to form a graceful arc. Then she does a handstand, toes pointed skywards, walking on her hands all the way from the bomb site and back. Her grubby tattered skirts and petticoats cover her face, like a walking lampshade. Bending over backwards, she's off again, crab-fashion, despite the burning hot pavements. For the grand finale, there's a circle of cartwheels, followed by handstands, up and over and up again, her arms and legs a blur like a Catherine Wheel. She ends with a flourish and a bow, to wild applause from the crowd.

Just then, Vicky's Mum flings up the sash window in the front bedroom and sticks her head out.

"Oi, Vicky! You 'bin round the shop to git the bread yet?"

Vicky wipes her grimy hands on her skirt and races off in bare feet to the corner shop. She's got work to do. Show's over. I wish I could be like Vicky, but I've got nothing to show off about. People stare at me because I look strange and ugly, not because I'm an acrobat. They look at me, trying to work out what I am. And I don't know.

Uncle Bernie calls us in from the doorstep. He is just back from his work as a barman at University College. He finishes after lunch on Saturdays. As a joke, he always pretends not to know my name.

"Allo Joyce Janet Julia Jeanette Jemima Joan Jennifer…"

"Jane!" we all chorus obligingly.

"What yer done to yer knee, Janie?" He points to my plaster.

"Some boys called me names and I fell off my scooter."

My cousins laugh and my eyes prick with tears again at the memory of it.

"Don't worry," he says. "Our Janie's just got a touch of

the tar brush, that's all, like 'arry Belafonte."

They all laugh again. I don't know what a tar brush is—if it's a good thing or not. And I've no idea who Harry Belafonte is, though he has a nice name. I smile weakly and nod anyway.

*****

"You gone arse over tip on yer scooter?" says Grandad sympathetically, when I get home. He sits me on his knee. "Never mind Duck, 'ere's a threepenny bit for you. Go rahnd the corner and get yourself some sweets and some baccy for me. Tell 'em I'll settle up on the way to the Fox later."

"What's a tar brush, Dad?"

"Sailors use it, to paint their ships with tar to stop the water getting in."

I'm none the wiser.

"Do you know where my Dad is, Dad?"

"Nah, mate. I think he went back to Africa."

I miss my Dad, even though nobody talks about him, and I've never seen him. I don't even have a photograph. Even Grandad doesn't know where he's gone.

*****

A few Saturdays later, Auntie Belinda is all dressed up to go to Glyndebourne with her boss, who is a dentist.

She's wearing Cousin Susanna's ankle-length peach bridesmaid's dress as a ball gown, brought out from the back of the wardrobe. She clips on her mother-of-pearl earrings and gives us a twirl.

"You're certainly mixing with all sorts of grand people since you got that job as a dental nurse, Bel. Make the most of it, Duck. It's not often people like us get a chance to go to the opera, especially not a world-famous place like Glyndebourne. When we were courtin', I used to take Laura to the Grand Theatre, up the Junction, on our night out. Then I'd get 'alf-a-dozen oysters and a bottle o' milk stout for my future mother-in-law on the way 'ome."

I can see Grandad is pleased about Auntie Bel going to the opera—even though he says he's proud of being working class and refuses promotion every time they ask him at work, because he'd rather stay with the men, in the union, and not be one of the bosses.

Auntie Bel looks as pretty as a princess to me, with her soft blonde hair and white skin. I wish I had hair like hers. When people touch my hair, they say it feels nasty, like wire wool. It's very dry and Mum has to put lots of *Vitapointe* on it. I usually get my hair cut short at the hairdresser's, because the grown-ups find it hard to manage. Mum ties a crepe ribbon in my hair so it doesn't look so much like a boy's haircut. I was so jealous when my cousin Lucy was allowed to grow her hair long and wear it in a pony-tail with a fringe. Auntie Lucy made me a pony-tail out of black wool from her knitting basket, but it wasn't the same, not like real hair. I don't know anybody with hair like mine. It sticks up and out—it just won't lie in pretty waves or fall around my shoulders like the other girls' hair.

When I went back to school this term I got nits, and my cousins had them as well. Everybody got them, even some of the teachers. It was a disaster. Mum had to pour cold lotion on my hair every night and try her best to comb it with the fine steel comb. The comb wouldn't go through because my hair is too fuzzy. I was crying so hard that in the end Mum took me to the hairdresser to get it all cut off short.

But the hairdresser said, "You can't bring nits in 'ere!" So Mum just had to cut it herself and it was a bit ragged and looked worse than ever. As we were leaving, I told the hairdresser and all the customers, "When I grow up I am going to have my hair straightened and dyed blonde." All the women having their hair done and sitting under the dryers thought that was very funny. But I was serious. My hair is painful, even just brushing it hurts me. No one knows what to do with it, it's ugly. When I grow up, I will wear it straight and blonde, like Auntie Bel's.

*****

Christmas morning, baby Vic and I always have a pillow-case each, stuffed full of presents from all the family and neighbours, sometimes too many to fit in. Spinning tops, snakes and ladders and tiddlywinks, a kaleidoscope with all the colours of the rainbow, dolls' house furniture with red plush seats, a doll with hair that you can really comb, and a golliwog with stripy trousers, woolly hair and a big white smile. I feel sad for him. Sometimes the boys at school call me 'golliwog'. I want to look like Alice, my beautiful new doll with the blonde shiny hair—like the hair I will have when I grow up. There are so many presents, all wrapped in thin blue-and-red Christmas paper with snowmen and Santas on. I soon get too tired to unwrap them all, so Mum takes over.

"Gordon Bennet, Victor, would you Adam and Eve all this lot! These children with no fathers are over-compensated for," Uncle Bernie says to Grandad, eyeing the heap of presents.

Uncle Bernie and Grandad talk a strange language when they get together. Nan doesn't like Grandad's Cockney rhymes. She makes us all speak 'properly.' But I like hearing them talk. It's like a poem.

"We got our weasels and titfers on, cos we're off dahn the rubba-dub-dub for a King Lear," says Grandad, winking at Uncle Bernie, when I ask where they are going. "Don't tell yer Nan."

Their secret is safe with me. I don't understand a word.

Every Christmas we have a show at the Harleys' house and we all dress up and do a turn, singing and dancing and making up our own songs. The boys rig up a curtain in the back room for the performance. One Christmas the curtain fell down and we all got tangled up in it. Everybody said it was the best bit of the whole show. I always like it when it's my turn to perform, with my cousin Lucy. We're in matching outfits, singing *'Hey look me over, lend me an ear/Fresh out of clover, moor gate up to here'*. I like the feeling of butterflies in my tummy, the attention, all the comments and laughter from the grown-ups, and the clapping afterwards.

On Boxing Day, I'm allowed in the front room to play games with my new doll's furniture and my new doll, Alice. Blonde, beautiful Alice. Alice's father has gone home to Africa and she will never see him again. Her mother is dead, she has no brothers and sisters, and now she has to run away or be adopted. Alice is all ready to leave, with her new clothes and a bit of bread wrapped in a napkin, so she can steal away in the dead of night, alone and unloved, with nowhere to call home, while everyone else is sleeping...

It's all too much, too unbearably sad. I rush sobbing into the back room and into Mum's arms.

"Why don't you play more cheerful games? No need to make yourself cry like that, Silly," says Mum.

The stories make me feel a bit better. And a bit worse.

"Mum, why am I brown?"

"Because you're half African. Your father was an African."

"Where is he now?"

"He went back to Africa."

"Why?"

"He had to go back, he was a student here. When he

finished his studies, he went home."

*****

The next Saturday, I've just got back from next-door's birthday party. Eddie had jelly and cake and pass-the-parcel. I'm in my best party dress, with a balloon in one hand and a slice of Victoria sponge in the other.

"Come into the front room," says Mum. "There's somebody I want you to meet."

Not another baby, I hope. I give the cake and balloon to Nan to hold, race into the front room, then immediately stand on my head on the sofa. Upside down, below the hem of my dress, I can see Mum all dressed up in her best emerald green check wool dress and pointy green glasses to match, wearing earrings and lipstick. I can smell her Tweed perfume. A man with light brown hair and a nice face is standing in the corner of the room beside the window. He is smiling.

"This is Ernest, Jane."

"Is he your boyfriend?" I ask, from upside-down.

"I suppose you could say that," Mum says, nodding and laughing. "Get down, come and say hello."

"Is that your motorbike outside?" I ask him.

"Yes, would you like a ride on it? Next time I'll come earlier and take you round the block."

Round about my eighth birthday, Ernest says he wants to talk to me about something really important. He sits hands in his. "How would you and your Mum like to come and live with me in Surbiton? I have asked your Mum if she would like to get married," he says. I look at Mum first, and she looks pleased. She is smiling, so I say yes immediately.

I am so excited. This will be a wonderful new adventure. A new school, new family, new house, new Dad, maybe even new brothers and sisters. Of course, I am sad about leaving my friends and neighbours, and the Harleys, and Auntie Molly's family, and Nan and Grandad and Auntie Belinda and my baby cousin Vic. But they all say they are happy for us, and they will come and visit us in Surbiton, and we will have a garden with a lawn and a loganberry bush, and I can have a rabbit and some newts.

In some ways, I'll be glad to be leaving Battersea. I don't like those boys who call me names on the corner of the street and in the playground. And Grandad shouts at me sometimes and grumbles, especially when I start giggling with my cousin Lucy. He's not well and he won't get better. He can't breathe properly because he's got a disease called silicosis and it's made his lungs bad. He coughs and wheezes and spits out the gunge, and that makes him very grumpy. He says it's because of all the brick dust he was breathing during the war in the hot brick kilns. That's what's made him sick. His own Dad got the same thing. He got very ill and died of the brick dust as well.

When I tell Grandad I'm going to Surbiton, he says, "We'll be sad to see you go, Duck. We'll miss ya. But we'll all come and visit, and it will be a really great new life for you an' your Mum. You know I'll always be yer Dad, even if from now on you call me Grandad and you call Ernest 'Dad', so as not to get us mixed up."

I hope Mum and Ernest have a big wedding! I will be a bridesmaid, and I'll have a pink dress with rosebuds all over, gathered at the waist, with a satin sash. I'll have open sandals and white socks, and lace gloves fastened with a little pearl button at the wrist, like my cousin Lucy when she goes to church. And a little posy of pink flowers. Mum says I am going through my 'pink phase'. She hates pink. She says Auntie Molly forced her to wear it when she was a bridesmaid at her wedding and she's been against it ever since.

When I tell the Harleys about the wedding, I have their complete attention for once. They look impressed.

"Can *we* come?" asks my cousin Lucy.

"Of *course* you can! And I will ask Mum if you can be a bridesmaid too, and then you can wear the same dress as me."

"Pink!" says Lucy excitedly, "And can we get those stiff net petticoats that scratch and tickle your legs and make the dresses stick out?"

But to my horror, there is to be no wedding. Mum has planned a registry office ceremony, no guests, not even me. Two passers-by will be witnesses. I have asked my cousins and at least six of my friends at school if they want to be bridesmaids. What will I tell them? How to explain it? I practically *promised* them, we have planned the dresses and everything. And I have invited so many guests in the street besides, and now there's going to be no wedding at all. I so much wanted to have a *good* story to tell people about me. Now they think I am just a big fibber.

When the big day arrives and Mum and Ernest go off together to get married, I spend the day with my Harley cousins. At teatime they all sit around the table, singing *'Once upon a time there was—A LITTLE BROWN BULL!'* at the tops of their voices, like the Tommy Steele song, because I'm brown and Ernest's last name is Bull. I am crawling with shame while they sing at me.

I'm going to say goodbye to all this, leave everything I know for a new place where I don't know anyone at all. Mum and Ernest will be together, married. And I will have to explain where I come from and the colour of my skin and my fuzzy-wuzzy hair to a whole new set of people.

I am desperate to stand on my head.

Chapter 2

In Digestion

At school dinners, I have to sit on the bench opposite Stephen Chandler, the red-haired boy with the freckles. He calls me woggie, Blackie, fuzzy-wuzzy, nig-nog all through dinner-time. He sings it out like a nursery rhyme, and then asks me if I've been rolling in dog's muck. He is just like the boys on the estate in Battersea. There's no end to the names he knows to call me, and his friends think he's hilarious. And I hate the frogspawn pudding, it's salty with my tears which makes it taste worse. I've had enough. I'm going to tell the teacher about him.

While I tell her what's been happening, Miss Collier stands behind Stephen Chandler with her hands on both his shoulders. She tells me from above his ginger head to "just ignore him, dear, because otherwise it will only encourage him." As she walks away his face breaks out in a big toothy grin, and he whispers "golliwog" under his breath, loud enough for his friends to hear he's not done yet with his big sack of dirty names. I can see Gary laughing along with the others. Now he'll never want to be my boyfriend. He can see I'm the wrong colour.

I swallow back more tears, staring hard into my dish of cold gluey pudding. My whole body stings with shame, from the roots of my frizzy hair to the soles of my flat brown feet. I feel ugly, stupid, and angry at the unfairness of it all. Why should Miss Collier be standing on Stephen's side of the table? Why couldn't she put her hands on *my* shoulders? *I'm* the one that's upset. How am I supposed to ignore somebody who is pelting me with names like hailstones? I bet you anything it's because he doesn't like people making fun of his red hair. That's why he picks on me.

*****

It's been a horrible day. I'm still burning up with the hurt of it. I can't get it out of my mind, can't get to sleep. I told Mum about what happened when I got home from school and she said, "Why don't you come home for lunch instead?" I know she'd like the company, she's stuck at home all day with my new baby brother Tommy. She gets lonely. But I want to stay for school dinners. Not for the food, it's nasty—lumpy mashed potatoes, cold gravy, gristle stew, frogspawn pudding. I want to be in the playground and make friends and fit in at my new school. I want people to like me and play with me and forget that I'm Brown.

My bedroom is quiet and shadowy at night in the pink glow of my nightlight. Lying here in bed under the eiderdown, I can just about make out the dark shapes of the imaginary city I made after school. It takes up the whole floor. Blue chiffon scarves for the river, empty bath salt bottles for castle towers, shoeboxes for the shops, twigs from the garden stuck in lumps of plasticine for trees. Sometimes my games go on for days, still the sad stories about running away, being adopted, getting lost in the woods. Sometimes they make me cry. My blue-eyed dolls—Alice with her long yellow-blonde hair, and Carol with soft ash-blonde curls all nicely combed—are safely tucked up in bed beside me. My children are not going to look like them, that's for sure.

I wonder what I'm going to look like when I grow up. Could I get married and have babies? I have never seen anybody my colour in a white dress. I try to imagine myself in a kitchen cooking for my family, a grown-up woman in a nice blue dress and high heels like my teacher Miss Selby. In my imagination I'm standing by the sink, helping my children wash their hands before dinner. But how do I look, what do grown-up Brown women look like? How is my hair, what colour are my children? I have no idea.

It would be much easier if I were a boy. Boys get away with more. They can get dirty and they don't have to look pretty. Sometimes I pretend I'm a boy and play cowboys and Indians with my *Swapits*. The Indians are my only brown toys—but they say the Indians always lose the fight.

Suddenly I'm floating up near the ceiling, in the corner above the dressing-table. I can see myself lying there in my bed below, my fuzzy black hair peeping above the white bed-sheet. I gaze down at myself for several moments, from way up high above the picture-rail, not feeling frightened, just thinking I look sad and alone. Distant, as if I'm in a spot-light at the beginning of a play.

Then just as suddenly, I land back in my bed and back into my body with a thump. Now I'm scared. My heart is hammering. Did that just happen? It wasn't a dream because I wasn't asleep. The house is still and silent. My Uncle, my new Dad's brother, is in the bedroom next door. Mum is sleeping in the bedroom downstairs with Ernest and my new baby brother. I badly want to creep out of bed and go downstairs to be with them but I better not. I'm afraid of being in the dark on the stairs. They told me to stay in my own bed now I'm eight-and-a-half.

*****

I'm really looking forward to going to school today. I've got an idea. It's a really good idea. It will explain everything.

But in the playground at break-time my idea is not going down as well as I had hoped. Gary and Elizabeth are shuffling their feet, glancing at each other sideways to see who is up for it. Gary is bending down to pick at a scab on his scuffed knees, as if he is not really interested. He really wants to go off and play with the boys. And then the bell goes.

But by lunchtime things have shifted a bit. Gary

volunteers to play my Dad, and Elizabeth will be my Mum. She's got dark hair and she wears glasses so she reminds me a bit of Mum. Soon a few more kids are queueing up to claim a part in my new play. Pretty, sandy-haired Sandra is just right for my Auntie Bel, and she says "wonderful!" a lot, just like her. Now there's an argument going on about who's going to play my Nan and Grandad, and how to make their hair look grey like old people—maybe by sprinkling it with talcum powder.

"Anyway, what's this play about?" someone asks.

"The play is going to be about my story."

"But who will be the audience? We need an audience."

"The whole class ort ter see it," ventures Gary.

"—what, even the teacher?"

"Why not? She don't know the story—let's go an' ask her."

The school is an old red-brick Victorian building with turrets and a weathervane with a weathercock on it. It has separate entrances in the playground labelled 'Boys' and 'Girls', but we ignore them because all our classes are mixed. Miss Selby is pinning charts to the walls of the high-ceilinged classroom with all the times tables on them, from two to twelve, with a space next to each of our names. When we learn our tables, we get a star next to our name. Miss Selby is blonde and glamorous like Auntie Bel. She wears flowery perfume and blue eye-shadow. She has already told our class she's getting married in June, so she will have to leave this summer. I try to remember to put on my posh voice and speak like Sandra when I talk to her. At my old school in Battersea, the teacher said I talked nicely, but here in Surbiton they say I sound like a Cockney.

Miss Selby considers our idea for a moment, eyeing the three of us over her shoulder as she carries on pinning the chart to the wall. She's wondering if we're up to it.

"What's the play called?"

I hadn't even thought of that.

"The play is called… it's called… "Why I am Brown," I blurt out.

"And you wrote it all by yourself?"

"It's nearly written," I lie. Only half of it is in my head, and not a word of it is written down.

"All right," she agrees, "You can do it in the 'bring and tell' on Friday afternoon."

Back in the playground, there's great excitement. As the opening performance is only two days from now, rehearsals must begin right away, before second-sitting dinner. I'm finding it hard to tell everyone their lines as well as playing me, especially as I have to make myself small, crouching on all fours because I am a baby. My knees sting from scraping on the asphalt playground.

"But your Dad's a darkie," Gary points out. "How am I gonna make my face look Black?"

"Maybe Marmite," suggests Sandra helpfully, "or soot."

In the end we opt in favour of black paint from the art class. Far more realistic.

The characters in the cast are enthusiastic. They

demand more lines, more action, more facts.

"And then what happened?"

"… And then what did your Mum say?"

"… And what did your Dad say?"

"Wasn't your Nan annoyed when your Mum had a Brown baby?"

"How did your Dad get the baby into your Mum's tummy anyway? Did they kiss?"

"I ain't gonna kiss *nobody*," says Gary firmly.

"Well I know how they make babies, the man puts his thing…"

"Shut up Stephen, that's *disgusting*—and you know it's not true," Sandra cuts him off. "Anyway, you're not even *in* the play."

"Yes I am. I'm the dog."

I realise I have only the vaguest idea about my own story. I can't answer any of their questions, and I feel awkward asking Mum again, so I will just have to make a lot of stuff up to fill in the gaps.

*****

Friday comes and I'm sick with nerves. Supposing they all forget their lines? Supposing the audience just laughs, or boos, or Stephen calls me even worse names afterwards, even though I let him play the dog? I feel browner than ever, when I wanted people to forget about my colour. And getting me born is going to be tricky. Mum says babies have to come out head-first or they might die. It's a shame Miss Selby said "No black paint, it will take ages to get off Gary's face and his Mum won't be happy," so we have to imagine it. But she has found a cushion in the staff room for Elizabeth to stuff up her jumper to show she has a baby inside.

I wish I had a stand-up speaking part like the others. I don't appear in the first bit at all, because I haven't been born yet, and then I have to spend the next few scenes sitting on Elizabeth's lap making small baby noises. I'm the most important person in the whole thing and hardly anyone talks to me and I can't even say anything.

But now it's Friday afternoon, and the play is actually going quite well. Time is going by so fast, we are on to the final scene, waving my Dad off to Africa on a boat made up of rows of chairs in front of the blackboard.

"Goodbye Brown baby!" Gary calls to me grandly, with a wave of his hand. "I will come back soon and fetch you, because I am an African King and that makes you a *Princess*."

The audience claps a bit longer than they usually do. I think my classmates are beginning to see me in a different way. By Monday, even some of the other teachers have heard about the play. Mr Mason the Headmaster stops me in the corridor to say, "Well done Jane!"

*****

The play was an unexpected success. Stephen Chandler even asked me if my Dad was really an African King, and I said yes, I think so. I still get called names but not quite so much. Things are much better than last term, when I entered the Easter Egg decorating competition. Mum suggested I take a brown egg from the box and glue some of my own hair on top, and draw a face on it, and call it 'Self Portrait'. We made Eggie a lilac dress like mine, and I sat her in an egg-cup for a chair. I liked her because she was my colour and had real hair. My hair. But when she was displayed on the table in the school hall alongside all the other competition entries, I realised she was a big mistake. I was ashamed of her. I wanted to forget about being Brown and there I was, drawing attention to it again. What if Stephen Chandler saw her and started calling me names again? I wanted to steal her away and hide her, but I was afraid someone would notice and tell me off.

Eggie didn't win a prize. After school, the teacher gave her back to me and I threw her in the bin. Her head got smashed. Then I missed her, and I felt sorry—because she had my skin and my hair.

But now things are looking up because at the end of spring term the class voted me the Queen of the May! I think it was because they liked my play. Although St Andrew's is a Church of England school, every year there is a school procession to the church on May Day, and the girls dance around the Maypole, plaiting brightly coloured ribbons to the music of *Ye Olde English* country tunes. Mum calls it a 'pagan ritual'—"… it's nothing to do with Christianity, it's a fertility dance!" But she doesn't mind because she says she is an atheist. Usually it's pretty blonde girls like Sandra who get chosen to be May Queen in each class, and wear a garland of spring flowers in their hair. I didn't think I'd have a chance. The Virgin Mary part in the Christmas Nativity play always goes to the pretty blonde girls too. I always get the part of one of the three Wise Men.

"You can play Balthasar, the Black one," said Miss Selby. "You'll look really good dressed up in the robes and the crown will stay on your head without clips because your fuzzy hair will keep it in place." I played one of the three wise men in my last school in Battersea too. "Forever typecast!" Mum laughed.

But now this is my big moment. Queen of the May! I will ride on a float, and I will get the outfit I've always wanted—a new dress, candy-striped and dotted with pink roses, tied with a pink satin sash, with a stiff petticoat underneath that sticks out like a brush and tickles and scratches my legs. How am I going to stop my flower garland sinking into my hair?

But the week of the May Day festival is the very week my family have planned a holiday to the Isle of Wight. Despite my tears and tantrums, I'm going to miss the coronation. In the end, Dad promises to bring me back for the day, so I can be there.

*****

"Mum, is it true what Stephen said at school, you know, the way babies are made?" I wave my hand uncertainly in the air in front of the area between my legs. "You know, where the man puts his thing."

Mum laughs. She looks as if she's wondering how to explain it.

"Yes, of course it is. Didn't you know that?"

I hesitate. I'm dying to ask more questions, but it's obvious I'm already supposed to know all about it, so I feel a bit stupid. And shocked! Those games I played with my cousins—doctors and nurses—I thought kids grew out of that. I had no idea the grown-ups were playing the same sort of games, only worse. How disgusting—but how interesting! That must be how I got brown.

"Mum, did my Dad get to see me before he went back to Africa?"

"No."

"Why not?"

"Ummm… he left about… about six weeks before you were born. He had to go, otherwise he might have missed the boat."

*****

Mum and I are sitting at the dinner table, making badges out of bottle caps for my new club I am organising in the playground at school. We are trying to agree on my middle name at the same time.

"No, *not* Christabel!" Mum says. She laughs and pulls a face. "Any name as long as it's a family name. One of your Aunties' or Grandmas' or Great-Grandmas'. There's Louisa, Laura, Mary, Molly, Abigail, Amy, Joan, Emma, Belinda, Grace—lots of lovely names to choose from. Let's make a list."

I want a sparkly name like Christabel, not like plain Jane. Jane Eyre. Calamity Jane. "You were named after my favourite author, Jane Austen," says Mum, "but you can pick a second name."

I stop working on the badges to look at the names on the list, thinking hard.

"Belinda! Like my beautiful Auntie!" We look it up in the dictionary of names. It means 'beautiful'. I try it out and write it down—'Jane Belinda Bull'. It sounds like another person, not like me at all. Like a pretty blonde girl with white skin and eyes of blue.

"That sounds good," Mum approves. "Jane Bull is a bit too short, but with a longer middle name like Belinda, it balances out nicely." It's decided.

"We'll be going to the adoption court in Kingston on Tuesday so you can take the day off school, and we'll take Tommy with us. We could go out to lunch afterwards if you like, and then we can have a look round Bentalls in the shopping centre."

*****

This is going to be an exciting day. I'm going to get my new name. I'm wearing my best white sandals and my new pink candy-striped dress. I finally got my pink dress! The Family Court in Kingston is in a huge old building, with tall windows, very grand. The corridors smell like wax polish and musty old papers. It will be a very different 'me' that steps out of that Courthouse later.

We have to wait on the bench in the hall with the high ceiling and vaulted roof. I am sitting on the polished wooden bench next to Tommy in the pram, swinging my legs back and forth impatiently. A man in a suit comes out of one of the rooms to talk to us, and he is speaking with Mum and Dad in very quiet and serious tones. It looks as if there is a problem. They talk for ages and now it sounds like they are arguing.

Finally, Mum explains it to me. "We can't do it, Jane. The man says that for Ernest to adopt you, I would have to give you up first, and then Ernest and I would have to adopt you together. You wouldn't want that, would you? I don't see why I should adopt my own child. And they say that then Ernest would become your legal guardian, not me!"

"Can't you both adopt me?" I plead as she marches off. Mum can walk really fast when she needs to, in spite of her bad leg.

"No, unfortunately that won't work unless I give you

69

up first. I didn't give you up for adoption when you were born, and I'm *certainly* not going to do it now. It doesn't make any sense. Let's go!"

Mum is really upset. I feel so disappointed after the big build-up. But I'm confused. Why should Mum have to adopt me? She's my real Mum. It doesn't make sense, just like she says. I went in there as Jane Goldsmith and I have come back out again as Jane Goldsmith. No new name, no new me. I don't really know who the old me is either. I can't give me up without knowing who I am. People keep asking me where I come from and why I'm a different colour from the rest of the family. I still don't have an answer.

I can't stop crying about it now. Auntie Bel is coming from Battersea on the train to comfort me.

*****

I saw one of the teachers slap a boy round the face today for being cheeky. I was so shocked. I have seen teachers smack children with a ruler before. I got the ruler once myself. The whole class had to line up, hold out both hands close together, while the teacher whacked us across the palms, just because we all got our homework wrong. My hands went red and swollen and I felt the sting for several minutes. It made the tears come into my eyes. I shook my hands in the air and then rubbed them, and cradled them under opposite armpits to nurse the hurt, and hug myself better, like the others did. But it didn't take away the sting.

Inside I was burning with the unfairness of it.

When I went to school with the Harleys, in Battersea, they used to punish the older boys in that school with the slipper; the big boys said you had to go to the Headmaster's office and he would put you over his knee and hit you on the bum hard several times. Some boys used to put socks or a scarf down their trousers. They were tough, they thought it was a laugh, a badge of honour. I was horrified, because nobody ever hit me at home.

But at my old school I had never seen a teacher hit a child round the face before. I am so upset about it, I have made up my mind to speak out when I get into school tomorrow. I'm going to tell that teacher that you should *never* hit people, especially not round the face. It's cruel and dangerous.

But in the end, when I got to school, I was too scared to say anything.

*****

"Mum, you know that thing you were saying, about the blood? Well it's happening, I've got it. I've just seen it on my pants!"

"Oh, you *clever* girl!" says Mum, getting up from the breakfast table to give me a big hug. "Congratulations! This is a really important day. I noticed a couple of months ago that you were beginning to develop. Your body is changing. I thought I'd better explain about it, so that when it actually happens, it won't be too much of a surprise. Sounds like I was just in time! I have some towels and a belt, just a minute…"

I follow her into her bedroom where she rummages around in the top drawer of the dressing table. "You've started very young, it might be difficult for you to manage these things at first. But you'll get the hang of it, don't worry. We'll go out tomorrow, as it's Saturday, and I'll take you round the shops and buy you your first pair of stockings and suspenders, and a pair of those blue sandals, the ones you said you like. It's a celebration!"

I feel special, pleased, happy. Ten years and ten months old, and I'm already beginning to grow up. I want to tell everyone.

"You don't need to say anything, it's a private thing really," says Mum. "You can tell Auntie Bel, but generally people don't talk about it."

"Why?"

"Because it's personal. But it's not a bad thing—you'll soon get used to it."

Once a month Dad burns the towels in the grate, mine and Mum's together, so it's not that much of a secret. Dad knows it's happening too.

The girls in the playground are impressed—and excited.

"Oh yuk! Does it smell?"

"Will it happen to us?"

"Does it 'urt?"

"Can we see the blood?"

"Ewwww, it sounds disgusting!"

"Don't worry, when it happens your Mum will take you out and buy you presents, to celebrate. And it's not too bad, it doesn't really hurt much," I lie. I don't like the cramps you get the day it starts. I often forget it's coming and get stuck without pads.

When I got caught out at school, the teacher said, "We don't keep any spare towels, it's very unusual for girls to start their periods at primary school. It's probably because people your colour tend to develop earlier. You're one of the tallest in the class too, aren't you? You must be nearly 5 foot!"

But in the summer term, a new girl called Lynne started at the school. She's blonde-haired and blue-eyed, and much taller than me, and she has already started her periods. The teacher went out and bought an emergency pack of sanitary towels "just in case."

"My Mum calls it 'the Curse,'" Lynne says. "How come your Mum gave you presents when you started? Is it a tradition where you come from?"

"Yes, I suppose it must be," I agree. How else to explain it? But it all seems to be a big load of trouble and effort every month, just to get babies. Mum is having another baby in January. The periods stop, that's how you tell. I hope it will be a girl. Then I can tell *her* about the periods when she gets older. Boys are lucky. They don't have to go through all this.

*****

Before we start secondary school, everybody in my class has to do the Eleven Plus exam to see which school we're going to. Mr Mason calls me out of the class during reading time.

"Jane, your results have come through and you're *border-line*. That means you have nearly enough marks to get into grammar school. They want to see you for an interview on Thursday. There will be a panel of three teachers from other schools. They will ask you some questions and see if you deserve to be awarded a grammar school place."

On the day of the interview, I'm wearing my dark green drop-waist pinafore dress and my gold-coloured Beatles brooch. I'm very nervous, but Mr Mason is waiting for me in the corridor to reassure me.

"Good luck Jane," he says. "Would you like me to keep your Beatles badge for you? Best not to wear it in the interview."

I take it off reluctantly and hand it to him—I was hoping it would bring me luck.

The interview is in Mr Mason's study so he has to wait outside. There's a man and two women sitting behind his desk. They are all wearing glasses, and I feel small and unimportant sitting in front of them in the big high-backed chair.

"What are your interests when you are not at school? What kind of music do you like? What kind of books do you read?"

"I like the Beatles… and I like reading the Beatles monthly fan club magazine." I can see that Beatlemania does not impress them so I add, in a rush, "…and I like keeping ants in a jam-jar in my garden and seeing how they make tunnels and carry their eggs. Umm… and… I like learning about different kinds of dinosaurs and why they got extinct, and ancient Egyptian Mummies and hieroglyphs, and big Whales and the way they travel thousands of miles every summer with their babies to feed in the Arctic… and I like writing my own comic books with my friend Lizzie. We make up all the stories and do the drawings and the word bubbles, and then we make lots of copies by hand for our friends… and… ummm… I wrote a play. It was about my story, why I'm Brown. I performed it in front of the class, when I was in Class 1, and they clapped." I'm racking my brains to try and think of anything else.

Now they are looking at each other the way grown-ups do, eyebrows raised, lips pursed, nodding slowly, glancing at each other sideways, as if to say, "Not *bad*, considering."

Now they're asking me a maths problem, about what time is it when 10 men dig five holes in the ground, and I just feel hopelessly lost. It's nice to get the extra attention, but now I'm confused, and I am so glad it's all over. I can't do sums. I collect my Beatles brooch from Mr Mason. That's the end of that.

But apparently it isn't. Next day Mr Mason says that I have passed!

"But there aren't enough grammar school places in this area for girls," he explains, "so you'll be going to a grammar stream in a secondary modern school."

My clever friend Lizzie will also be in the grammar stream at the secondary modern school. I'm sure she's a lot cleverer than me, but her birthday is in September, so she is a year older than most of the children in our class. This apparently counts against her so she doesn't get a place in a grammar school either.

Mr Mason says it's a scandal. "What a system! If you were boys you'd go straight to grammar school," he says crossly. "There are plenty of places, even for '*borderline*' boys. But they ration out the places for the girls, because there are just not enough grammar places for all the clever girls in our schools. It's a shambles, it's not fair. Anyway, you girls must do your very best in the Grammar stream. You go and show them what you're made of."

*****

My secondary modern school in Tolworth is in a new building, much bigger than the Church school, with lots of plate glass windows. I have to get there by bus. Mum tells me I won't be there for long. "At half term we are going to move to Stafford, so you'll only be there a few weeks."

It's very warm for September and it hasn't rained for

a while, so there's a lot of dust blowing about in the wind among the fallen russet-gold leaves. I don't like windy weather. We are supposed to be running three times round the games field, but I'm soon struggling to breathe, and the games teacher is getting impatient. She urges me to keep up and run faster. I'm sure she thinks I'm faking it because I hate games. I can feel my chest tightening, I can't breathe out, and finally my knees buckle under me. The grass feels cool and soft and the ground feels reassuringly solid underneath me. The teacher comes over, looks down at me sprawled out on the grass, and calls a couple of the other girls to take me to the nurse in the medical room. It's a small room smelling of antiseptic, shelves stacked neatly with labelled boxes, and a narrow bed in the corner covered with a starched white sheet.

The nurse is a kindly middle-aged woman. She sits me down on a chair beside the first-aid cupboard. "I think you probably had a mild asthma attack, dear, brought on by the dust. Have you had one of those before?"

I shake my head. "But I do get hay fever in the summer—that sometimes makes me a bit wheezy... but I have never had this before." I suddenly feel tearful. That empty feeling of loneliness and fear welling up inside me.

The nurse says, "Don't worry dear, it's not serious..." But she can see I'm distressed, so she asks "Is there anything else bothering you?"

How to explain? At my new secondary school everyone

is asking those unanswerable questions again: where do you come from? why are you Brown? why are you a different colour from the rest of your family?

I study my image in the mirror in the new bathroom at home, and I don't recognise myself. It is as if I have landed from outer space on an alien planet. People look at me with narrowed eyes that say, "You're from somewhere else, you're not from here."

And then there's the move to Stafford in a few weeks, when I'll have to go through being a new girl all over again. How to explain all this to the nurse, someone I've only just met?

"It's just that... It's just... I don't know who my Dad is, and it makes me feel lonely being the only Brown girl in the school."

"Where's your Dad from, dear?"

"Africa."

"Oh, I see, I thought you were a little Spanish girl when I first saw you! We don't get that many people like you in Surrey. Why don't you ask your Mum about it?"

Mum has already arrived to take me home. I can hear her voice at the end of the corridor, talking to my teacher.

"Jane, what on *earth* is the matter, I could hear you crying right along the corridor!" she exclaims, wheeling my new baby sister and brother in the pram and peering through the half-open door of the medical room. "What a drama, just like your Auntie Bel when she was your age, all these tears. What's up?" Turning to the nurse, she asks,

"What's happened? Is she all right?"

"Nothing serious. Started wheezing on the games field, probably just a mild asthma attack because of all the dust. But you'd better get her checked out by the GP." She pats my shoulder. "You go home with your Mum and rest, come back tomorrow, after you've seen the doctor."

I was hoping the nurse would say something to Mum about my Dad, but she didn't mention it. Maybe she didn't think it was important.

Chapter 3
High School, Low Points

1966

Thursday 11 January 1966

My Dear Diary,

It's over a year now since I arrived in Stafford. We have already moved twice since we came here. First an old cold brick house in Cambridge Street with an outside toilet—Mum loved it, she likes 'original features'. But we only stayed there for six weeks. Winter was coming, and it was too cold for the two babies. My sister Molly was only nine months old, and my brother only eighteen months older. So the Council moved us to this modern estate down the road from school, with a proper indoor bathroom and toilet. I can see the school building from my bedroom window, all plate glass and pastel panels. Even though I live two minutes away, I'm always late. "We'll put you in the High School," they said. "Plenty of grammar school places for girls here, not like Surrey." Shame. I hate the place, and everyone in it, especially the chemistry teacher, Miss Singleton. Sharp nose, thin lips, a steel-grey helmet of hair—she must have been wearing that bob since 1922.

Today's chemistry lesson started with her usual *Diatribe Against the Spectre of Communism.*

"I have lived through two world wars and I warn you, Communism is still the greatest threat we have *ever* faced. We could be taken over by an evil regime which murders and tortures people and takes away their freedom, and it is up to your generation to fight it with every breath in your body... " Blah blah blah, and on and on she goes as usual. Her voice sounds like she has a mouth full of marbles.

I thought, this is it, I am going to screw up all my courage. There was an uneasy silence when I raised my hand. No-one interrupts *the Tirade Against Communism!* It stopped Miss Singleton dead in her tracks. She paused mid-sentence to glare at me with those bulging eyes of hers. She terrifies the life out of everyone just by looking at them.

"Yes, Jane Goldsmith?"

And I said, "Please Miss, my Grandad was a Communist."

Stunned silence in the class. I bet they thought—*this is going to be the best chemistry lesson ever!*

"Your *Grandfather?*"

"Yes, Miss. He believes human beings are equal, and we should all get what we need from the government and

give what we can, no matter what race, creed, or colour…
That's what he told me."

I could see her hesitate. I could tell she was thinking,
this is all going way off the point. "Your family is from
Kingston, Jamaica. I'm talking about the threat to us here
in Europe. *In England.* The Cold War."

"I was born in Kingston, *Surrey*, Miss, not Kingston
Jamaica," I explained. She's not the first person to have
made that mistake. "My family comes from England—
they are all the same colour as you."

You could have heard a pin drop.

"Come and see me after class," she said finally, "Girls.
Page 57, sulphuric acid, read the paragraph—in *silence*!—
while I come around and light your Bunsen burners."

My stomach was doing somersaults for the rest of
the lesson, thinking about what she would say to me
afterwards.

"Jane Goldsmith. Now that the rest of the class has
gone, you may come up to my desk. You say your Grandad
is a Communist."

I told her he *was* a Communist. He and his mates
started up the Communist Party, Battersea branch, in the
1920s.

"You say *was*. Is he still living?"

"Yes, he still lives in Battersea but he left the Communist
Party years ago."

Her eyes narrowed. "So—he saw the light."

"No Miss, he's a socialist and he says he still believes

in all the principles. He's an atheist, but he thinks everyone should be free to believe in God and follow the religion they want. So he disagreed with the Communists on religion being the opium of the people... Also, I think there was a letter..."

"A letter from your Grandad?"

"No, a letter in the newspaper... in the *Daily Mail* I think he said. S'posed to be from the Russians. Saying that Communists in England should take over the government here, like they did in Russia. But Grandad says he will always be loyal to his country, so maybe that's why he left the party—"

"—Ah, the famous Zinoviev Letter!"

So, she'd heard of it too! She knew I wasn't making it all up.

"Maybe that was it, I can't remember the name, Miss. But Grandad told me that afterwards some people thought that letter in the newspaper might have been a fake, made up, to make people hate the Communists even more. I—I don't know..."

That was when I realised I had gone too far. I'd be in for double detention for suggesting she'd been taken in by a fake letter.

Miss Singleton paused and looked me in the eye. "My fiancé died in the Second World War. My father died in the First World War. I know what a terrible price people have to pay for war. Your generation really cannot imagine."

"I'm sorry, Miss Singleton. I didn't know..." I lowered my eyes at that, looked down at my scuffed school shoes with the holes in the soles. I felt *really* bad, embarrassed. Her boyfriend died. Her Dad died. My Dad just disappeared, and I feel bad enough about that. When you hear people's stories you see them differently—even teachers.

"You seem to be very well informed for a young girl your age."

I was surprised when she said that. I feel completely ignorant compared to grown-ups who know all that stuff, like names of prime ministers and politicians, dates in history and suchlike, but I said: "I'm really interested in politics, Miss. I listen to my family talking and we watch that TV series on the BBC, you know, *the Great War*, about the First World War. I wish we could learn more about politics in school. Much more interesting than... than..." I was going to say chemistry but I stopped myself, just in time.

"Now that would be *very* dangerous. Politics should be kept out of school, we should not poison young minds..."

Keep politics out of school—when she's the one who keeps on bringing it up!

"What lesson do you have now?"

"English, Miss. With Miss Berman. The new American teacher."

"Well you'd better run along then—and apologise for being late. Tell her I detained you after class."

Friday 18 February 1966
My Dear Diary,

Today I had the most terrible shock! I was kept behind in Maths this time. Didn't do my maths homework. Columns of numbers make me feel sick and always set me off in a panic. So, I was late for the start of English again. We are taking it in turns to read aloud from the *Diary of Anne Frank*. It was getting a bit boring because Anne couldn't go anywhere, she was hiding from the Nazis. I was looking forward to getting to the end of the book, so we'd find out what happens to her when the war ends and she can finally get out of hiding—then it would get more interesting.

Annie Smethers was reading the last page of the diary when I arrived in class. It stopped abruptly. Just like that.

"What happened then, Miss?"

"I'm afraid she didn't get to write any more. The Nazis took her to a concentration camp called Bergen-Belsen. Most of her family died there. She and her sister got sick with typhus and they died too. A lady who was in the camp gave the diary to Anne's father after the war, and he had it published. She was about your age when she died… a dreadful tragedy… I'm sure she would have been a famous writer if she had lived."

I walked around all day in a daze.

How could this happen to Anne Frank? I had no idea it was going to end like that. It's just too much to bear. A 14-year-old girl, only a year older than me, hunted down and locked in a concentration camp to die, because she was different. How could grown-ups have let this happen? They think they have the right to be in charge, they give us the impression they are responsible and they know everything. How can we ever trust them with the world if they are capable of this kind of unspeakable horror?

That programme about the Holocaust we watched on the telly. Chalk-white bodies shovelled into deep soulless pits. Human beings reduced to taut skin stretched over bags of bones, hollowed-out eyes filled with emptiness and despair. It haunted me for weeks, kept me awake long into the night. What if they come for me? If people like the Nazis ever come to power in Britain, who would hide me? Who would my people be? At least Anne Frank had her family, they were all Jewish. I'd be all on my own. I don't know anyone who looks like me.

There's an angry terror in the pit of my stomach that won't go away, even though I draw my knees up to my chest and cry it out in bed at night. I feel completely alone in the world. When I'm grown up this won't be allowed. I will be a famous writer too. A journalist. I'll write about this kind of thing and stop it happening. I will fight injustice with every breath in my body…

Monday 14 March 1966
Diary,

I have an idea! I am fed up with learning useless boring

Latin war chants at school—*bloom bloom bloom, blee blow blow, bla bla bla, blorum bliss bliss.* What does it mean, what's the point? We could learn about politics in school instead, and then we could discuss how to vote, how to stop wars from happening, how to stop prejudice and injustice, how to treat each other as equals. I asked our form teacher Miss Clarke today if we can use the notice-board at the back of the classroom and bring in lots of cuttings each day from the newspapers about interesting things that are happening in the world. Then we can discuss the topics in form-time on Friday afternoons. Miss Clarke said yes, she is interested in this idea. At least she is willing to give it a try.

Wednesday 18 June 1966
Diary Dear,

It's Paul McCartney's birthday! I made him a lovely card in the shape of a scroll, like the Dead Sea Scrolls, and I made it look like parchment by burning the corners with a candle. It looked fab. But I forgot to put any stamps on it, so now he'll never get it. The politics noticeboard died a death too, after only a few weeks. It went really well at first—a few interesting articles about the war in Vietnam, the Moors murders, Chi-Chi and An-An the giant Pandas' romance, Labour winning the General Election, the Beatles at Number One with 'Paperback Writer'. But someone put up a clip from the *News of the World*, about a vicar in a sex romp, and after that everyone was seeing how many rude stories they could get away with.

By Friday, Miss Rake the Deputy Head marched in and decreed the noticeboard be closed forthwith and all articles taken down. "This material is totally unsuitable for High School girls…" Blah blah blah. She is such a square. Why do parents read the *News of the World* anyway if it's so bad? It's their fault. That's the end of politics in class.

Monday 5 September 1966
Oh Dear, Diary!

This morning on the way to school, it was so windy, my stupid hat blew off and flew across the road, so I ran after it, picked it up and stuffed it in my school bag. It's difficult to balance on top of my kind of hair, it won't stay on, and it squashes it, so when I take it off my hair is hat-shaped. Everyone was laughing at me, I felt such a fool. Then this new Prefect comes up to me, all puffed-up with her own importance, and tells me I should be wearing my hat. *Stupid* hat! I threw it on the ground, stomped on it and kicked it into the long grass by the path. Everyone cheered and clapped.

The punishment for not wearing your hat and stomping on it and being rude to a Prefect is to walk around the perimeter of the games field three times after school, wearing the stupid hat. So, there I was, in the gathering dusk, doing this stupid punishment, wearing this stupid hat that's crushed and kicked and covered in mud. Wishing I was dead. And it's only the first day of term.

Monday 10 October 1966
Diary Dear

On the way home every day, I always pass those secondary mod girls, standing on the street corner opposite our house—smoking fags, skirts hitched up at the waist so they just about cover their bums, long white socks, long straight hair scraped back in ponytails with a thick fringe at the front, swearing, laughing, chewing gum, talking about boys. They don't have to do Latin. They look happy. I wish I could be one of them, I wish they were my friends. They live nearby, on our estate. I could hang about on the corner with them. Why do we have different kinds of schools anyway? It worked fine when I was in the secondary modern school in the grammar stream in Surrey. Some of the High School girls are so posh, so stuck-up. Linda P. lives in the country on a farm and has a pony. *A pony!* I am allergic to the country. They stare at me even more there. And it makes me sneeze. At high school, we have to wear uniform with skirts below the knee, woolly tights, sensible shoes, gabardine coat, and the dreaded velour hat. The summer uniform is just as bad— navy gingham dress, Panama hat, navy cardigan, sandals. I feel so stupid and worthless in that ugly stuff.

Tuesday 15 November 1966

Dear, Dear Diary

I had another really good idea today! A sit-in in protest about the uniform, like the students do on the news!

As soon as the bell rang for break, we barricaded all the desks in front of the classroom door and waited for Miss Rake, the Deputy Head, to arrive for the elocution lesson. Everyone was jumping up and down with excitement. I was afraid someone would hear us and put a stop to it before we were ready.

Miss Rake is under five foot—she is even shorter than me. We could only just see the top half of her face through the glass panel in the door.

"What's all this nonsense?" she shouted through the glass. "Get those desks away from the door immediately, girls!"

We looked at each other, then obeyed.

In she stormed, red-faced with rage.

"Who's the ringleader?"

Everyone looked at me and backed away.

"*Jane Goldsmith*. Thought so. What's all this about?"

I took a deep breath.

"Please, Miss Rake, we don't want to wear beige woolly stockings any more. We want to wear long white socks. Like the ones Pattie Boyd wears in *A Hard Day's Night*."

Everyone murmured and nodded in agreement.

"All you girls put the desks back where you found

them, open your books and sit quietly until I return. I do not want to hear *another word*. As for you, Jane Goldsmith, you come with me."

Outside the classroom she let me have it, in her high-pitched scrapy voice, like a cracked violin.

"This is not *St Trinian's*. This is a High School. You are not to stir up your classmates in this way. When you are an adult, if you are lucky enough, you will be in a responsible job and you will have to obey the rules, whether you like it or not. That's why we have rules in school. It's an important discipline to learn that you must do as you are told and fit in with the way the world is."

I was thinking, *no I won't. I'll change the world and change the stupid rules*. But I said, "Yes-Miss-Rake-sorry-Miss-Rake-I-won't-do-it-again-Miss-Rake."

"And don't just keep saying sorry and then misbehaving again. We are going to see the Headmistress this time. This is *serious*."

Turns out Miss Dickson was also serious. She pressed her fingertips together in a pyramid just in front of her lips, like she always does before preparing to give you a lecture.

"I'm very disappointed in you. All this nonsense just for the right to wear long white socks—such a trivial issue. What have you got to say for yourself this time, *Jane Goldsmith*?"

I don't like the way teachers keep hurling my name at me these days, as if it's some kind of accusation.

"If it's a trivial thing, Miss Dickson, please can we wear the white socks? Seeing as it's a trivial issue—not that important either way?"

I thought that was smart. But she came back at me.

"It is not a trivial issue to barricade yourself and all the other girls into the classroom. Supposing somebody had an accident? It really is *too* bad of you."

"But it wasn't only me, Miss. The whole class was in on it…"

I thought maybe she'd see the unfairness of picking on me alone. But instead she said, "You were the ringleader. And this is not the only issue we have had concerning you in the last few weeks."

Uh-oh. The stomping on the hat issue? The Communists? The political noticeboard that got out of hand?

"Mr Roberts has made a complaint about your behaviour in Religious Studies."

So that's it. Yawn.

"I only asked the meaning of a word in the Bible, Miss Dickson."

"Yes, and that word was *circumcision*. You know exactly what that means. You were deliberately embarrassing Mr Roberts in front of the class, and you can see that it's very difficult for him as a male teacher in a class full of girls."

I was really struggling not to laugh. There is nothing like the excitement, the suspense, the sheer exhilaration, of being in trouble. The main point of it all is to get found out. Spice up my totally boring life. And she hadn't finished yet.

"I hope to see you taking your studies more seriously in future. It's time you settled down to work and set a better example to the class. Sit outside my office in the corridor for the rest of the morning and think about what I have said."

Pity I missed the elocution lesson. It's usually my only chance to shine. Well-spoken in Battersea, a Cockney in Surrey, I am fêted in the Midlands for my southern vowels. I stand up and read out passages in elocution which the class is forced to repeat, exactly the way I say them, and they look so envious and resentful. The only Brown girl in class telling everyone else how they should speak! It's such a laugh, being different in a good way for a change. But in the playground, I make sure I talk like them, so I fit in. Otherwise I'd be in for it.

Sitting in the corridor outside Miss Dickson's office turned out not to be too much of a punishment. By the time the bell rang for the next lesson, everyone had heard about the sit-in. Some girls went by with their noses in the air, but one of the fifth-formers grinned at me and winked as she passed me in the corridor. I'm a celebrity. And it's all my own work.

Friday 16 December 1966
Bad news, Diary.

No long white socks. Despite my best efforts, we are still stuck with the beige woolly tights. The only way you can show your personality, wearing that kind of hideous gear, is through your hairstyle. I see these girls at our school with their long straight blonde or red hair, like Pattie Boyd and Jane Asher. They iron it carefully every day. I cannot hope to compete with them, no matter how much time I spend straightening my hair with rollers at the weekends. They stare at me with my fuzzy hair and brown skin, with that questioning look. *"What are you and where do you come from?"*

Five hundred girls in school, and no other kid who looks like me. I don't want to be in High School or Grammar School, I don't want to be clever. I want to be groovy. Auntie Bel says looks aren't everything. Maybe they aren't if you look like her. Pretty blonde hair, blue eyes and white skin. The eyes looking back at her are full of admiration. In my dressing-table mirror I see a reflection I don't recognise. Brown skin and fuzzy hair, thick lips and wide nose. This is me. I am ugly and worthless.

Do I take after my Dad? If I ever saw him, would I recognise him? I wonder if he was bad, like me? I wonder if he was sad when he left me? I wonder if he ever thinks of me… Will he ever come back and get me? Would he understand how I'm feeling right now? Did he ever feel like I do, when he was here all those years ago? Did he get called names, did he feel different? How could he have left me here to face this all on my own?

1967

Thursday January 5 1967

Okay, Diary, it's true the sit-in and the noticeboard idea didn't work out last year, but now I have a much better idea. I wanna be a writer, like Anne Frank; a paperback writer. I will use big words like dichotomy and peripatetic—all the words my Mum knows, so I sound clever like her. When we play the dictionary game I pick out long complicated words in the Oxford dictionary and Mum knows the meaning of every single one. It is impossible to catch her out. She says it's because she did Latin.

My stories will be about girls with white skin and long straight hair down to the waist. Famous girls, like Pattie Boyd and Jane Asher and Maureen and Cynthia, the Beatles wives and girlfriends. Lots of romantic, sexy, exciting stories. I finished the first one over the Christmas holidays and I have loads more stories in my head.

I was worried at first that nobody would want to read what I'd written. But as soon as I showed them in the playground, the girls were interested. Linda P. took the first one about Jane Asher and Paul McCartney to read at home. I can't wait to see what she thinks of it.

Friday January 13 1967

Diary, it's a success! Linda P. came back without the book last week, with big dark circles under her eyes. She said, "I've lent it to Annie Smethers, it's really good! I read it under the covers with the torch till one in the morning! When you gonna write the next one?"

Tuesday 28 February 1967

Sorry, Dear Diary, hardly got time to write you these days. We moved again to another house, this time a brand new one. The third move in three years—and another set of neighbours to stare at me and wonder what happened. Was I adopted, found on a doorstep, mail-ordered from Freeman's catalogue? Now my books are in big demand, I can't produce them fast enough. They all have to be hand-written in exercise books, in neat print. I really have to concentrate when I write, I can't make a mistake or change the story—it's in biro so I can't rub it out.

When I walk into school these days, I don't hear them whisper "There's that Brown girl, where does she come from? Why is all her family White? Bet she never gets a boyfriend!" Now they say, "There's that girl who writes the stories. Has she got a new one for us?"

My readers can only keep each story to read overnight, because there is a queue of people waiting. Even the fifth-formers want to read them, the big girls with the long

straight hair. The two Lindas—Linda P. and Linda N.—
help me keep track because there is only one copy of each
book. They write everybody's names down on a list when
they borrow them, and they are helping me to make copies
of the most popular ones. That will make things easier.
One has already gone missing. I'm upset because it's the
only copy. I hope it'll turn up.

Monday May 8 1967
Diary, guess what!

I was working on my fourth book in the English class today,
concentrating hard, writing carefully and fast. Everything
was quiet, everyone was poring over their desks studying
boring poetry. When I am writing, I get lost in the story,
escape into another world. I don't notice time passing. I
saw a shadow fall over my notebook. The shadow belonged
to Miss Berman. Last time I looked up, she was on the
other side of the classroom. But suddenly she was right
there, standing next to my desk, looking very stern.

"*Jane Goldsmith*, you know you are supposed to be
making notes on the imagery in Wordsworth's 'I Wandered
Lonely as a Cloud'. Give me that exercise book and carry
on with your work. See me after class."

My classmates were on my side this time. They were
fed up with golden daffodils. They are all waiting for
the new story I am writing about Ringo, and how his
girlfriend Maureen persuades him to make up with Pete

Best (the Beatles' old drummer) before she agrees to marry him.

After class Miss Berman flicked through my unfinished novelette, lips pursed, scanning the pages and thinking, making me more and more nervous.

"This is quite good, y'know," she said in her American drawl. "I believe this is yours too?"

She fished around at the back of her desk drawer—and held out my missing manuscript! I thought, *where did she get that from*? It was the one where Pattie Boyd tells George she won't give up her modelling career just to go out with him.

"These are very well-written… although you could try varying the subject matter sometimes. What do you want to be when you grow up?"

I said, "A writer or a journalist, Miss. Writing about politics."

"Well then, this is a very good start. Keep on writing. But not in my class. In my class it's Wordsworth's daffodils poem."

She handed the books back to me. What a relief! That was close. If she'd given me another detention, I'd have run out of evenings to stay behind—I'd be in school for life. I need time to write my books.

Saturday 10 June 1967
Diary, this is dire.

This year the school trip is to Nigeria. Nigeria, of all places! Everyone is really excited about it. All my classmates who have signed up for the trip get special lessons about West Africa instead of doing games. It's a nightmare. They will end up knowing more than I do about the part of the world where my Dad comes from. Almost everyone in the class is going. Pam, the girl with the calliper—the one who had polio—she's going. And so is Ahmad, the girl whose Dad comes from Iraq. It's not as if I'm the only one who is different. But still, I can't bear the thought of going. I have a different kind of difference. A difference that connects me to West Africa.

I told Mum I'm not going because I hate school and I can't think of anything worse than spending the whole of my summer holiday with the teachers. But that's only partly it. The thing is, Nigeria is too far and too close. It stirs up all sorts of feelings in me. There's a part of me that is West African. What if I meet my Dad there? I want Mum to explain it to me. She shows me Nigeria on the spinning globe; it's not far from Ghana, where my Dad comes from. But I want to know where Ghana is on *my* map, on the map inside me. I am afraid to go, even though Mum encouraged me and said she would pay for my ticket and pocket money. Now it's too late to book anyway. That ship has already sailed.

Wednesday 19 July 1967
Dreary, Diary.

When I got home from school, Mum was flaked out as usual in the front room with the kids in the armchair, all piled up on top of one another, sleeping off another exhausting day. It's a lot for Mum to cope with—two toddlers all day—what with her bad leg and everything. It's my job to clear up the toys strewn all over the floor and bring Mum a cup of tea and give the kids a drink of orange squash. I have to help out a lot with babysitting and housework and putting the kids to bed. I don't mind helping. But things are really beginning to get on top of me. I just feel miserable some days, or full of rage, with a big screwed-up knot in my stomach. And sometimes just a big gaping aching space inside.

I hate being the only Brown girl in a school of five hundred. I stick out. My skin is all wrong and my hair is all wrong. It's hard to find a moment to talk to Mum and Dad about it. When I tried to explain what's wrong to Mum, she said, "The teachers can spot you from miles away, they can always see when you're among a group of girls who are misbehaving, that's why they pick on you—you look different. It would be the same if you had bright red hair. Your trouble is, you're a White girl in a Brown girl's skin."

But that's not all there is to me, I know it. I am more than that. There is an African girl inside me too. I am living a life like no-one else I know, inside or outside school. A half-life, with the missing half plain for all to see. Sometimes it's the *only* thing people see.

Mum said, "Well I know what it's like to be different. It's not as bad as having a bad leg like mine. I couldn't dance or run or play games or wear short skirts when I was your age. I'd rather have your skin than my leg." It must have been awful for her, I feel for her, I really do. And hard for her to talk about it too. We hugged each other after that. She was brave, having me, in spite of all the things people must have said. Being different has affected both our lives in different ways.

Tuesday 19 September 1967

When Dad came home from his anti-Vietnam War meeting, which he goes to every Tuesday after work, he asked me, "What's up? You been in trouble at school again?"

I burst into tears and he put his arms around me and held me until I calmed down. Then he said, "I didn't like school much when I was your age, but looking back, it's amazing how quickly school days pass. Soon you'll be out in the big wide world, which gets much tougher."

I started to cry again. I was sobbing so hard I was out of control. It was all pouring out of me. "But you weren't '*coloured*', were you? You weren't different. This feels like it's gonna go on forever and it won't stop." He patted my back kindly, and made ssshhhh-ing noises. I stayed there, resting my head on his shoulder until the feeling started to go away.

"Ahhh, don't cry, it's not your fault."

Thursday 5 October 1967

I tried talking to Miss Berman, the English teacher, about how I'm feeling. She's always been really understanding. But when it came to it I just cried some more, sitting on the desk in her classroom.

"What's wrong? Has someone been mean to you?"

"It's because I'm the only coloured girl in the school and I feel lonely. I have no one to talk to about it. There's this big gap in my life and I can't explain it."

"What about your Dad? Is he American?"

"No, he's African and I've never met him. I have a Stepdad. He's good to me but I still feel bad inside."

"You are not alone, believe me. Where I come from, in the States, there are lots of people your colour. Have you ever heard of Martin Luther King, the one who made the famous speech which begins 'I have a dream, that one day people will be equal?'"

I nodded. I saw it on the news in Surbiton before we moved here.

"He's part of the Civil Rights Movement. My family are Jewish. We all used to be active in the movement when I was in the States. Like you, we are all angry about injustice, we want to make a better world. One day maybe you'll get a chance to go to the States and meet some of them. In the meantime, take heart. I can see that you are a very special person. It takes a lot of courage to speak out at your age. You may think you're not getting anywhere, but I can tell you, you make some of the pupils and even the teachers in this school think about things in a different way, and that's important. Don't give up."

That made me feel better, Diary.

1968

Friday 21 June 1968

Got this new diary for Christmas, haven't felt like writing in it until now. So much bad news: Martin Luther King assassinated, that man Enoch Powell who looks a bit like Hitler making a speech about Rivers of Blood. It makes me shiver just thinking about it. Lots of stuff on the news about the Civil Rights Movement that Miss Berman told me about. Coloured people rioting in the streets. Reminds me of seeing all those people shot down in the streets in Sharpeville in South Africa on the news when we lived in Surbiton.

All I see nowadays is people being called 'trouble' and gunned down in the streets, as if there's a war on people with Brown and Black skins. It seems like the world is not a safe place for us; as if there is something wrong with people with my skin colour, something bad, not as good as White. Grown-ups talk about it as if it has nothing to do with me, as if having a Brown skin doesn't affect me.

I'm upsetting my family as well as my teachers. They are all on about me being a troublemaker at school and being miserable at home. I sit in the corner meditating to 'Fool on the Hill', trying to pretend it's not happening.

"It's a teenage phase, it's her hormones!" they say. "She'll get over it."

As if you get over being this colour. It's for life.

Thursday August 8 1968

Holidays in Wales. It was my little brother Tommy's Birthday Picnic today.

We were parked at the top of a Welsh mountain looking down on the spectacular view of the valley below. Rolling hills, fields dotted with sheep and tiny white and yellow wildflowers. I was sitting in the front seat in the Morris Traveller with Auntie Belinda, watching Tommy, Molly and Vic laughing, rolling down the hill on the grass in the sunshine, Mum and Dad setting out the picnic in the field. A perfect family day out.

I felt like death.

"What is *wrong* with you, Janie?" Auntie Bel said. "It's getting impossible to have family holidays with you these days. You sit in the car with your head in your hands all day, looking so depressed. It just puts a damper on the whole thing. What is your *problem*, for God's sake!"

How to explain what I'm feeling inside? A pit of emptiness, a void, a chasm where my Self should be. I can't name it or say it, but it seeps into everything, it blots out the sun. It does not pass, it will not pass, because I can't pass as anything or anybody.

I can't see myself anywhere; in the streets, in the magazines, in my family, among my friends. I can't see my own reflection. I only see other people's reflection of me. "There's Helen Shapiro and Shirley Bassey," they reassure me. "And the Supremes. And the Black-and-White Minstrels." But Helen and Shirley are impossibly glamorous figures, decked out in sequins. And the Black-and-White Minstrels are fakes. I see them all on the telly, but I am nowhere. I can't even sing. What can *I* be? Where are the ordinary brown girls, doing ordinary things? Every day, I wake up and try to prove myself and fail.

How to explain all this to Auntie, in a way that make sense...

"Boys don't like me," I said. "My hair is all wrong. I'm the wrong colour. Last week we went to the disco, wearing the silver dresses, the dresses we saw on *Top of the Pops*—me, Linda P., Linda N. and Annie Smethers. You can get a kit to make them, you know, the ones that look like they're made of silver foil. So I'm all excited about the dress and everything, but when we get there, I'm the only one who doesn't get a dance. The boys think I look strange, I see them staring at me."

Auntie Bel said what they all say. Don't-cry-it's-not-your-fault. But I'm beginning to think it is. Then she said, "Tell you what, I've got an idea. What you need is a bit of adult time, doing something you really like, without the little kids around. Come down to London for the weekend, August Bank Holiday. I'll perm your hair and straighten it—everybody feels better when they have pretty hair... and then I'll take you out shopping in the King's Road, and lunch, a real treat, just you and me together."

That has really cheered me up, Diary.

Bank Holiday, London, 31 August 1968

A tall Brown-skinned man in a chocolate-brown fedora and smart tailored suit crossed the road with us opposite Peter Jones yesterday.

"Excuse me, young lady, my name is Mr Mahesh Patel, may I ask what part of India you come from?" An easy mistake to make. Auntie had just been helping me straighten my hair. It looked black and glossy, lying softly against my cheek, not a frizz in sight. I was so thrilled to get this man's attention, but I never know how to reply to this question. Where do I come from? Impossible to say.

Auntie Bel came to my rescue. "Her father is African." He seemed a little disappointed, raised his hat, said "I beg your pardon," and disappeared up Sloane Street in the opposite direction.

After that, we went and tried on lots of floppy hats in the King's Road.

Thursday September 5 1968

Hello Diary. I asked Mum if we can get tickets to *Top of the Pops* when it comes to the Birmingham studios. We always watch it together every Thursday night on the telly, to find out what Pan's People are wearing. Then we go upstairs and raid the wardrobe and see what we can make out of our old dresses and bits of fabric. Mum always has loads of great ideas. She has knitted me an Op Art Dress and a lime-green bikini. She knew how much I wanted to be at the live *Top of the Pops* show, and at first she was very keen on the idea and said I could go. But now she's been talking to Linda P.'s and Annie Smethers' parents, and they say they've heard it's a 'meat market'. All the parents are being warned to keep their girls away, because they get touched up and preyed on by the older men.

It's not fair. I can handle it, I'm fourteen, not a child. I like going to Birmingham, and now I've missed out on the whole trip. I like shopping in the new Bullring Centre. It's the only time I get to see lots of Brown faces—Asian families mostly, from Birmingham, Wolverhampton, Leicester and Nottingham. I know they aren't like me, they don't come from where my Dad came from. But it's good to see them all the same, Brown-skinned people, in whole families, just doing ordinary things. I like the clothes they wear, their bright colours and their sparkly bangles.

It seems as if Stafford is the only Midlands town that hasn't got any Brown people. At least, I have hardly seen any. Mum and Dad get cross with me for staring at my own reflection in car windows and shop fronts. Other people can stare at me all they want, and I'm not supposed to mind. But if I stare at myself, I'm being vain. Truth is, the only Brown face I see around here is in my own reflection. I want to see what other people are staring at. Is it okay? Am I okay? Do I look okay?

Wednesday October 9 1968

Things are looking up, Diary!

Jilly and I were hiding out in the cloakroom yesterday, bunking off games again. Although she's two years younger than me, Jilly knows all the tricks. "When old Sexy comes looking for us, what we do is crouch down behind the coats like this and hold another coat underneath so it hides our feet," she told me. We call Miss Sexton the games mistress 'Sexy', but actually she's the exact opposite. She has beefy legs and a hairy moustache.

Miss Sexton walked right past us and stopped for a moment exactly where we were crouching. We hardly dared breathe… and then finally we heard her footsteps retreating down the corridor, back to the sports hall. Jilly and I burst into fits of giggles and then went over the wall to have a fag. Jilly said, "Hey do you want to come to my party on Saturday?" Jilly is the youngest of four, and it's really her older brothers' and sister's party, but they said she could invite a few of her friends. "My brother Georgie saw you in town last weekend wearing your orange coat, and he fancies you, he really wants me to invite you."

Georgie has noticed me! He's the same age as me and I have often seen him around town and thought he was out of my league. The Blaines are a well-known family around here, glamorous and sophisticated. My Stepdad sees their Dad at the anti-Vietnam war group meetings on Tuesdays. They have a huge house with a swimming pool on the edge of town. The older Blaines must be nineteen or twenty. They are hippies and rumour has it they're into pot and LSD.

Saturday 19 October 1968

I'm so nervous, Diary.

The Blaines' party fills me with excitement and dread. The boys at parties usually can't make me out. I feel awkward, like an outsider.

"Do you like Blues or Soul?" they interrogate, screwing up their eyes. Giving the right answer to this question is very important. It makes the difference between being 'in' or 'out'.

"Blues, of course."

"Okay. Maybe you can come with us then."

I hear them say that Soul music is for 'those coloureds dancing about'. Not serious music. Blues, on the other hand, is all clever, cool White boys on guitars—Eric Clapton, John Mayall, Keith Richards. Whereas I like Soul *and* Blues. Why should I have to choose? I have to tell them I like Blues, and then I go home and dance to my favourite Soul and Motown records in secret in my bedroom—*"Your Love is Lifting me Higher"* by Jackie Wilson, over and over again. It makes me feel happy.

Mum said, "Those boys are so *ignorant*! What do they know? American Negroes invented the Blues as well as Soul. And Gospel. And Jazz. And Calypso, like we had in the '50s. All the best music is what Americans call 'Negro music.'"

I looked up 'Negro' in the Encyclopedia. Mum and Dad have just bought a whole set, dated 1863. They like antiques. It says some people mistakenly think Negroes are equal to White people, but there's no evidence to support that view. I feel like tearing out the page and burning it. Miss Berman told me the Transatlantic Slave Trade was abolished in 1807, but she reckons some people in England forget slavery was still going on in America long after, even when that Encyclopedia was written.

The run-up to Saturday night is unbearably exciting. I am scared Georgie Blaine will change his mind and just ignore me when I get there. I don't know what I'm going to wear. All the pictures in the magazines and on the dress patterns are of White girls with straight hair. It's hard to picture myself in those outfits.

Monday 28 October 1968

You should have seen me!

I wore my halter-neck tangerine mini-dress. I made it myself from a dress pattern I got in the market. It looked great with white cutaway Lulu boots. Mum helped me make a matching hairband, and big white hoop earrings, and I had the BIGGEST beehive I could manage, with a straightened fringe. The whole outfit was finished off with tangerine lipstick and lots of spangly bangles. Pale lipstick doesn't look good on my brown lips. It's made for pink lips. But this is as good as I could possibly ever look, Dear Diary—unless I was a different colour.

I drifted through the Blaines' spacious living room in a cloud of Aqua Manda, as if I was floating through heaven. The room was all decked out with the latest rugs and furniture from Habitat, opening out onto the swimming pool through the open French doors. *A swimming pool!!!* It was the poshest place I have ever seen.

And there was Georgie Blaine standing on the patio by the pool, smiling, holding out his hand to greet me, with 'Satisfaction' blaring out on the speakers...

Chapter 4

Ice and Fire

A line of cars is crawling single-file along the main road up ahead. Our school bus is at a standstill, stuck in a snowdrift in a narrow country lane. We haven't budged for the last half-hour.

Stationary. Like my life.

Things didn't go so well with Georgie Blaine. We had fun at the beginning, hanging around town on Saturdays, or dropping in on a squat nearby to see Sue and Matt, friends of Georgie's older brother and sister. They had big squashy cushions on the floor and old carpets at the windows. We puffed at the ashy remains in the hookah pipe left over from the night before, listening to T Rex on the record player, watching people coming and going in hippy hats and patchwork jackets. They didn't seem to mind us hanging around. They sent us out to fetch sausage rolls and fags.

Naturally, I told my friends at school what a high old time I was having on Saturdays, and soon word got around. The police found out, and all the squatters disappeared overnight. Georgie and I were forbidden to see each other again. People said I'd gone off the rails, but the truth is, I never wanted to be on track. I'm desperate for life and everything it has to offer. Sex, drugs, rock-and-roll, politics, independence, fame... I am sick of being treated like a child. I'm fifteen, I have big stuff to discover, things I will never learn in school. Such as, who exactly am I?

Dad was furious when he found out I'd bunked off Games again.

"That's it. You're just not serious about your education. No point putting off moving back to London—"

"—But Dad, I'm not even taking O-level PE—"

And I hate the smell of sweaty gym shoes, the clack of jolly hockey sticks, and the communal cold showers, where I am not just Brown but Brown and *naked*, among all those stark-White bodies... and afterwards my skin goes pasty-dry and my hair goes frizzy.

After the bunking-off-Games episode, Dad got a job as a health inspector at County Hall in London, and a few weeks later Mum, Tommy and Molly joined him there. Mum was happy to be going back home. London! But what to do with me, in the middle of exam year?

So here I am, on a school bus, stuck in a snowdrift on the Norfolk-Suffolk border, miles from anywhere.

Sarah Flowerdew sits next to me, as rosy apple-cheeked as her surname, her moon-shaped face framed by short light-brown hair and a wispy fringe. She speaks in a thick Norfolk lilt, and she has a habit of wrinkling her nose and blinking, head to one side, when she's puzzled. She seems particularly puzzled by me.

"*Stafford*—that explains it. I reckoned you was a cockney with a bit of a northern accent. How come you've moved over here in the middle of your O-level year?"

"My Dad got a new job in London so the whole family moved back there," I explain. "They couldn't find a school for me that did the Cambridge Board exam in London, so I came here to Diss Grammar. I'm only staying six months, until the exams are over. Then I'll be going back to London to join them."

"Such a lot of changes! New teachers, new friends... how're you s'posed to settle in and catch up in such a short time?"

"Yeah, it *is* quite hard," I admit. I don't mention that it's much harder to walk into a school of five hundred and be the only Brown face. "This is the fifth school I've been to, and it's the first secondary school that's mixed, so I'm not used to having boys around..."

Boys call me names. The girls seem to ask me more questions.

"... Plus, the books you are doing in English Lit are all different. I was doing *Hamlet* and you're doing *Romeo and Juliet*. But the way you do French is much better. We had to do a lot of boring grammar exercises in Stafford, whereas you do the 'look-say' thing here—you get to speak the language. But I'm still trying to get the hang of the language lab..."

I can never get the hang of Maths anywhere I go. Columns of numbers make me sick to my stomach, dizzy with fear, like an evil spell. Various theories have been proffered to account for this: *girls are no good at maths anyway, she's just not trying hard enough, she's creative, better at arts subjects.*

My Maths teachers seem to take it personally, concluding that I have taken against their subject for no good reason.

"You're a perfectly intelligent girl, Jane Goldsmith, you are just lazy. Two percent out of one hundred for your Maths mock exam—and you get the two marks for spelling your name correctly. Absolutely not good enough. You need to make one hundred percent more effort."

Mathematically, I believe that should be ninety-eight percent more effort. But my Maths teachers have added me up all wrong. It's not laziness. My terror of numbers is a phobia, like my pathological fear of the dark, of spiders, and dogs, heights and car crashes. A dread that no amount of maths lessons will cure. The world is a dangerous place. I dare not tell anyone about the weird and ominous thoughts that go on in my head.

Sarah, on the other hand, is very good at Maths—it's her best subject. She nods when I ask if she has always lived around here. I'm not surprised. She's a proper wholesome country girl—practical, no-nonsense, she even smells earthy.

"We live on a farm—my Great-grandad's farm. We

still have the old windmill there. Oi quoite loike it…"

I listen carefully to the way she speaks, so that I can perfect it later. An accent is easy to fake—unlike skin colour or hair. Speak like the locals and you fit in faster—though not too much like them, or you may be accused of 'taking the mickey'. Not everyone here is as friendly and congenial as Sarah.

"What's it like, living on a farm?"

"Well, Oi 'specially loike lookin' after our 'orses, but it can be a bit boring, always being in the same place. And this is the worst win'errr we've had for years. Moi two older brothers, Colin and Moikey, were out in the field with moi Dad at first loight this morrrnin', diggin' lambs out of the snow…"

I like the way she says 'win'errrr' and 'morrrnin'. But I can't imagine anything more horrendous than digging a sheep out of a snowdrift. I'm a city girl through and through.

"Wow. That must be *amazing*. I've never lived in the country before. I'm staying with my cousins, the Harleys, about a mile from the village. I used to spend a lot of time with them when I was a kid, when we were in London. We lived in the same road and we all went to school together. Auntie Lucy always said she dreamed of living in a cottage in the country, but nobody thought she was serious…"

"But Oi still don't get it. 'Ow come you're living here with your cousins, why didn't your parents wait till you'd finished your exams to move to London?"

"I suppose my Mum was desperate to get back home, she wasn't happy so far away in Stafford, she missed her London family. But to be honest, I reckon my parents and teachers gave up on me, they got fed up with me... Maybe the *real* reason I was sent here is that I was too much for them all to handle—getting into trouble, you know—bunking off lessons, boyfriends, smoking pot, hanging around with people living in a squat, that kind of thing. One time, the police had to be called. I think they thought I might be taken away by social services if they didn't do something drastic..."

I've already said too much. But I badly need to just tell someone the story, to join up all the things that have led up to this. I look to see her reaction. She opens her eyes wide. "Gosh!"

"Yep, I was a *bad* girl! So, they sent me here to straighten me out in the country."

"As it worked then?" She wrinkles her nose again, head cocked to one side.

I pause to consider. "Maybe it *has* worked, come to think of it. I miss my family, especially my little brother and sister, Tom and Molly, but they all drive up from London to see me most weekends—though I doubt they will make it this weekend in this weather. But anyway, the point is, I've decided I really am gonna study hard now."

"Thass good, that'll make your Mum and Dad 'appy."

"Well I'm not doing it to make my parents happy. It's because my cousins all left school at fifteen to get a job—all except for Shirley, she's only twelve, she still goes to the secondary mod. The Harleys think education is a waste of time, especially for girls. Best go out and earn some money as soon as you can, so you can save up and get married, that's their philosophy… so I thought, 'I'll show 'em'."

"You really loike to do the opposite of what everyone else thinks!" she says, impressed. "There aren't many people loike you at our school… is your Dad from Jamaica?" Wrinkled nose again. I can tell she's been dying to ask me that ever since I arrived here.

"No. Not Jamaica. Surbiton. He's my Stepdad. I don't know my other Dad. I have never even seen a photo of him."

"*Really*, you never even met 'im! That must be weirrrd… Don't you miss him, don't you ever wonder what he looks loike?"

"You can't miss what you never had," I lie.

"Well you do have an in'erestin' loife. I bet you'd get bored if you lived 'ere all the toime. It's quoiet in Norfolk… Still, at least if moi O-level results aren't any good, I can always stay and work on the farm…"

The other passengers are definitely getting bored—and rowdy and impatient. We have been stuck in this snowdrift for at least three-quarters of an hour now, and it's getting hard to hear ourselves talk above the hubbub. A boy leans over the back of our seat and demands, "Oi wanna feel your 'air—I never felt fuzzy wuzzy 'air before."

"Yeah, let him feel it!" his friend urges. It's obviously a

dare. He's been put up to this.

Despite careful combing at six o'clock this morning, and copious amounts of *Vitapointe*, the cold damp weather has made my hair a mass of frizz.

"Don't touch my hair!" I plead, cringing into the back of my seat, hands clasped protectively over the top of my head.

But he leans over anyway and grabs at a handful of my hair, then recoils in horror. "Ewww, it feels *disgusting*, loike a greasy Brillo pad!" which prompts howls of laughter from his friend. My credibility with Sarah, which I have been carefully nurturing during the journey thus far, is now in shreds.

Just then a triumphant whoop goes up from the bus. The snowplough has finally arrived. Twenty minutes later, the road in front of us is cleared and we all pile out while the driver and a couple of men from neighbouring houses shovel the snow away from under the wheels. We get caught in the crossfire as the boys take the opportunity to stage a ferocious snowball fight around us.

The bus driver revs the engine to ease the bus out of the rut. The wheels spin furiously and spray us all with filthy grey sludge. Wet, cold, hungry, elated, we clamber back on board, finally on our way again, to join the line of crawling traffic along the main road. A watery lemon sun breaks out ahead, lighting up the softly undulating snow-covered fields. When we finally arrive at school it has started snowing hard again.

The place is deserted apart from the janitor.

"Closed early," he says. "So everyone can get 'ome afore dark. It'll be a whoite-owt to-noight."

Another ear-splitting holler goes up from the bus at the news that we are going home. Joy! All the way to school and back with no lessons in between. Let off the bus briefly for the toilet, we thrust our tongues out to catch the fat fluffy white flakes falling from the sky—the only refreshment available, the contents of lunch boxes having been devoured long since.

It's 1.30 in the afternoon. We've been on the road since early morning. In mid-February the nights should be getting lighter, but the sky is sickly yellow-grey with snow, as if dusk is already closing in. The bus turns around in the schoolyard, wheels scrunching in the slush, to begin the whole journey again in reverse.

*****

More than an hour later, I'm deposited in the centre of the village, watching Sarah's pale face at the window dissolve into the dusk as the school bus pulls away, leaving me alone at the crossroads. I have caused quite a stir since my arrival here in Walby. When I arrive here at 7.30 in the mornings to catch the bus, the place is bustling with folks setting out for school and work. People stop to stare at me, even opening their leaded casement windows to watch me pass, in spite of the freezing weather.

"Don't moind them. They've never seen one loike you except on the telly," Sarah explains, as I swing into the seat next to her.

This afternoon, the village scene could not be more different. The place is deserted. The man who stands at the crossroads shouting and singing all day long at the top of his voice—unkindly referred to as the 'village idiot'—has long since left for home.

Everything is silent, the kind of muffled silence you get when the world is covered in a blanket of snow. The village is like a picture-perfect decorated Christmas cake—church, pub, post office, a handful of little thatched cottages with a square of yellow light in each downstairs window— thickly spread with a foot of glistening icing. A trail of footprints is barely visible beneath the freshly fallen snow.

I pause a moment to steel myself for the miserable, never-ending trudge back to the cottage, lugging my heavy bag of schoolbooks. The way is flanked by flat frozen fields on one side and copses of bare trees hanging with icicles on the other. On the slippery open road, a gusty biting wind races across the fields, nearly knocking me off my feet, tearing at my school scarf, searing my face with tiny shards of ice. Everywhere is bleak and heavy with snow, not a living soul in sight. No houses or cars, no pavements or street lights, just an eerie whitish glow reflected off the snow.

Trust the Harleys to set up home a mile away from the middle of nowhere.

My torch is useless in this weather. I have to lean into the wind to make any progress. A small brown townie, battling the elements, marooned on an alien ice-planet. One false slip and I could be flat on my back like a stranded beetle. Every pore in my skin is screaming to get out of here. I hate the cold, I hate the wind, I'm terrified of being alone in the dark in the countryside, where malevolent spirits lurk in the trees. Up ahead of me, the light from the cottage is a solitary tiny golden beacon in the flat feature-less landscape. It never seems to get any closer.

Finally I'm propelled through the cottage door in a whirl of snowflakes, chilled to the bone, toes and fingers frozen, into the welcoming warmth and light of the sitting room. Bomb the Jack Russell terrier is ricocheting off the furniture as usual with the excitement of any new arrival. The dog's full title is Lance Corporal Bombadier Charlie Farnes Barnes. Bomb for short.

Auntie looks up from her ironing.

"You're early!" she exclaims. "'Ow was school?"

"Didn't get to school. Spent the whole day on the school bus in a snowdrift," I reply thickly, my nose numb with cold, "… and when we finally got there, school was closed."

"Yer poor old soldier… Sit yerself dahn and I'll put the kettle on. We'll 'ave a nice 'ot cuppa and a custard cream."

I sit gratefully by the fire and hang my steaming wet socks and gloves to dry on the fireguard, listening to Auntie busying herself in the kitchen and the homely sound of her coffee percolator—the one treat she allows herself in the afternoons while she irons a mountain of shirts and listens to the afternoon radio play.

"Don't put yer bare toes too near the fire," she warns from the hatch in the kitchen, "You'll be complainin' of chilblains next. Remember we used to put your feet in your own wee in the potty when you 'ad chilblains as a kid? You'd be screaming the place dahn."

Reminded of this weird and embarrassing childhood remedy, now to be avoided at all costs, I quickly withdraw my feet, put my knees up to my chest, and stuff my frozen toes into the hem of my brown school jumper. At least the uniform at this new school is not navy blue, it's a dull shade of mid-brown. Brown jumper, brown skirt, brown blazer, brown shoes, brown skin. I look like a potato.

Warm spicy aromas of percolating coffee drift in from the kitchen. Beyond the little leaded windows, snowflakes swirl on the uplift of the wind. The four-hundred-year old-cottage is really two tiny cottages knocked into one. Uneven floors, wooden beams, and a rickety staircase at either end leading up to the bedrooms. It is the first house the Harleys have ever owned. When the family moved here from London, Uncle Bernie officially named it 'Ourn Cottage'. He delights in telling everyone who asks, "It's called Ourn Cottage 'cos it ain't *yourn*, it's *ourn*," in his deep rich baritone voice. The locals have no idea what he's talking about, as Cockney is not widely spoken around here.

"There's a coupla letters for you on the mantelpiece—from Stafford, by the looks of the postmark."

One is from my boyfriend, Danny Blumenfeld. I started going out with him after I broke up with Georgie.

"Dear Sweet Baby Jane,

Snow still driftin' over there in the old countryside? It's dead around here without you… When are you back in London? I plan to come visit over the summer after the exams are over… Miss ya like crazy, Lady Jane…"

He seems cheerful, upbeat, a bit more like his old self. A few months before I left Stafford, he had an acid trip that went badly wrong, and ended up in hospital for several weeks. When he came out, he was just not the same Danny as before. It knocked the spirit out of him, it was heart-breaking. I knew others who took LSD with no ill-effects, but all the same, it really scared me to see him like that, at only fifteen, a shell of himself.

The other letter is from Annie Smethers, lamenting that everyone is being boring and studying for O-levels at the High School. *"… It's not the same without you, not half as much fun! I wish you could come back here… It sounds like a wilderness where you are. But at least you'll be in London come summer, you lucky thing! I'll be down to visit…"*

I miss my friends, I miss my family. But I'm not sure about going back. Creating a bad reputation is altogether a different thing from *living* with one, especially when the sickening feeling kicks in that it's all been a big mistake. I got fed up with them all, and they got fed up with me. Best to jump ship and build a bad reputation somewhere else, from scratch.

But where? Not back in Stafford. Not miles away from anywhere in Norfolk. London will be more of the same. Walking into yet another new school, having to explain where I come from to another sceptical audience, with no real information to hand. "*Get over it, it's not that bad*," say all the people who can blend into the crowd whenever they please. People who don't have to explain themselves on a daily basis. *What are you? Where do you come from? Originally, I mean?*

I don't come from anywhere and I don't belong anywhere. There's nowhere that doesn't see me as a stranger.

"Anyway, I'm glad you're back early," says Auntie, appearing with the tray of coffee and biscuits. "Everyone is still at work and Shirley's not back from school yet. I 'ope she ain't stuck in a snow-drift an' all. I thought as I've finished the ironing, I'd do yer miniskirt. It just needs hemmin'. When we've 'ad our coffee, I'll measure you up and you can show me what length yer wan' it."

I sip gingerly at the scalding brew, letting the steam defrost my cheeks as the lifeblood returns to my numbed blue fingers wrapped around the hot mug. "Thanks a million, Auntie."

"So, you didn't make it to any lessons today?"

"No, so luckily I missed double biology. There are only six of us girls in the class and that biology teacher, Mr Pinter, puts us all at the back. He says girls can't do science so it's a waste of time teaching us. If any girls put their hands up he always pretends not to notice."

"...'E probably thinks the girls will be gettin' married and 'aving babies, so it's much more important for the boys to get the science education—then they can support the family."

"What's the point of girls going to school at all then? I was quite good at biology at my last school. Apparently, the girls here always get the best marks, in spite of Mr Pinter. Anyway, Grandad says that girls should *never* be dependent on a man—they should always earn their own living."

Auntie Lucy rolls her eyes. "We're all fond of yer Grandad, 'e's a very clever bloke... But 'e's so *dogmatic*, and 'e fills yer 'ead with some very strange ideas—and yer mother's, too...'e really wanted a son, that's the problem..."

"Well it's a problem for *me*... I'm different and everyone can see it. I'm the only Brown girl around here, and I'm the only one in school. Every time I go into the village everybody stares at me. Shirley said yesterday one of the girls in her class said, 'Who's that *Black* girl living with you?'"

"Well I'll tell our Shirley people should mind their own sodding business!" exclaims Auntie, laughing.

Then she puts on her serious face.

"I *knew* it was gonna be 'ard fer you, being different, soon as you were born. You see what trouble people get into if they don't stick to what's normal? Yer Mum made a big mistake—the coloured boyfriends and everythin'—but we all stuck by her 'cos she's been through a lot in 'er life, she's had a tough time. Terrible business, that was, when she caught that infection in the 'ospital. It was s'posed to be a routine op. And yer Mum only ten years old—we nearly lost 'er..."

When I was a kid, I always enjoyed Mum's stories about her year in hospital during the war. She made it sound so much fun, the things the other kids got up to. It was only later I heard that most of the children were seriously ill, and half of them died on that ward. Mum was in a coma for four days. After a year in hospital, her leg was permanently damaged. My poor Mum. I feel a surge of homesickness. I do miss her. She is amazing, really, the way she turns even the darkest of times into great stories.

Auntie rakes the embers in the grate and throws on another couple of logs, flinging a shower of sparks up the chimney. Small flames lick the damp wood as it hisses and spits, letting off a thin jet of steam.

"When yer Mum got pregnant, yer Nan was the one who insisted she went into the unmarried mothers' 'ome to 'ave ya. She didn't want yer Mum to bring you 'ome, you know 'ow she feels about 'coloured' people. And she was worried about 'ow yer Mum would cope. But when it comes dahn to it, we're all family..."

Half-formed thoughts, snatches of information—the questions I dared not ask—are tumbling out and taking shape as she speaks. My mind is racing to take it all in, leaving yet more questions unanswered. So, Mum had other coloured boyfriends apart from my Dad, and yet I don't know any brown people! And why did my Dad leave? Was it because of my Nan's attitude? Did Auntie ever meet him?

Auntie leans back in her chair.

"No duck, none of us ever clapped eyes on yer Dad. Anyway, thass all in the past. The main thing is, not to walk around with a chip on yer shoulder. People don' like that. It will make you unpopular. Yer Mum broke all the rules when she 'ad you. By rights—it's 'ard to say this—but really, you should never 'ave been born…"

I am shocked at the baldness of this statement, tears pricking behind my eyes, swallowing hard to hold back my emotions. There is only one thing worse than wishing you had never been born; and that's your Auntie telling you that, by rights, *you should never have been born.*

So that's it. I have to take all the torment and name-calling and hair-pulling and *where-are-you-froms* and unanswered questions, and smile and laugh at golliwog jokes and pretend I don't care. Because if I get upset about it, people won't like me, they'll think I'm just making a fuss.

"Don't trouble yer Mum with too many questions, it's not fair on 'er. Yer best bet is to fit in as much as possible.

All these boys you're 'angin' round with, for instance—that ain't good, you'll be getting a name for yerself round 'ere..."

It seems that other people don't call anyone names. We misfits mysteriously acquire names for ourselves. Nobody's fault but ours.

"What boys?" I say innocently.

"Whatcha-ma-call-'im, some posh name—Pickersgill, Oliver Pickersgill, thass it—rich family with a big farm. And the other one, suicidal Sid, the miserable one."

We both laugh. Good job she doesn't know what's really going on.

I remember first meeting Sidney when I was newly arrived at the school a month ago. A strange, striking-looking boy—bulbous turned-up nose, cauliflower ears, small, slightly crossed, deep-set pale blue eyes, fair hair sticking out at all angles... and a stammer. I empathised with Sidney immediately. There was an aura of sadness and resignation about him. He was often the butt of his class-mates' jokes. They called him *piggy-wiggy*, and a lot worse. I could see it ground him down, made him stoop slightly as he walked.

He soon sought me out to tell me we should stick together, "... because—you know—we both get bullied 'cos we both have the same p-p-problem."

And then he swept his hand awkwardly in front of his face to indicate what he meant. I was horrified. I had felt sorry for him, but he evidently felt the same about me, and cast us both in the same bracket. Misfit. Picked on.

Outcast. Ugly.

"But seriously, Jane, you better get 'itched before you're twenty," Auntie breaks into my thoughts. "Otherwise, the rate you're goin', you'll be makin' the same mistake as your Mum. Stick to the rules and you can't go wrong. Girls should be virgins until they get married."

Too late for that. This is 1969 after all. And I wouldn't want to marry anyone who wanted to marry me.

She fishes a tape measure out of her sewing box and holds the pink mini-skirt up against my hips.

"Now, where d'you want the 'em?"

"Just here." I indicate the top of my right thigh.

"Thass only twelve inches from the waist!"

"Yes, but it's a *hipster*, Auntie, so it starts lower down."

"You girls are wearin' your skirts 'alfway up your arses these days," she grumbles, inserting a pin in the exact spot I want it. "You'll be flashing your knickers every time you bend down in this."

"But what about your Timmy?" I venture. "He's allowed to go off with all the girls in the village, and he's the same age as me." The double standard concerning virginity has got me riled.

"Well he's a bit of a lad, our Timmy, but any'ow, boys will be boys… They need to sow their wild oats, so they know how to make their wives 'appy!" She looks up at me sideways from her stool to give me a half-grin through a mouthful of pins.

This seems ridiculously unfair to me. And impossible.

"But Auntie, if all the girls are virgins, who would the boys practise on—to sow their wild oats, I mean?"

There's a girl in the village who enjoys herself in exactly the same way as Timmy, and they all smirk behind their hands and call her *the village bicycle*—everyone gets a ride. She is 'soiled goods'. He is 'sowing his oats'.

Auntie grunts with irritation when I expose this flaw in her argument. She continues her pinning, not sure how to answer.

"Well," she says finally, "I'm perfectly 'appy bringin' up my kids and keeping house. Best job in the world. There's such a thing as being too clever—you think far more than is good for ya. You're a rebel, just like yer mother and yer grandfather. It's best not to dwell on some things, just accept life the way it is."

I have no intention of doing that. I'm a rebel, after all.

Auntie upsets me terribly sometimes—I'm still smarting from the idea that I should never have been born. It's making me want to stay alive, just to spite everyone. But she speaks her mind. She says things that other people are only thinking. She is at least prepared to talk honestly with me about how I feel about the colour of my skin.

Funny, I have never heard her having these kinds of conversations with her own children about how they feel. Maybe because she's their Mum, she expects them to stick to her advice and not ask so many awkward questions. I reckon *she's* the boss in this house at any rate, though she says Uncle Bernie is. She does a lot for me, come to think of it. She has taken me in when everybody says I'm out of control. And maybe I upset her too, questioning everything she believes in. This is her whole life—the cottage, her kids, looking after her family day in, day out. I don't want to seem ungrateful. But it's not for me.

The skirt is finished off with a thin black patent-leather belt, and I'm delighted with it. A perfect fit.

The others are coming home now, bursting through the door in a whirl of snowflakes. The cottage is soon full of light and life and muddy footprints. Amongst the chaos of raucous laughter, teasing, arguing, swearing, and thumping up and down the rickety wooden stairs, the dog is going berserk to the shouts of *Bomb! Bomb!* as if he were about to explode at any moment. It's like it used to be years ago, when we all lived in Battersea on the Shaftesbury Estate.

The warm savoury smell of home-made sausage-meat pie and gravy wafts through the house. The table is laid for seven. Auntie and Uncle, my three cousins (Buster having left home to join the army), Farve—their Grandad, and me.

"Allo Joyce Janet Julia Jeanette Jemima Joan Jennifer... is that a new pink belt, or a skirt you got on there?" Uncle Bernie quips as I slide along the bench next to cousin Lucy. He still likes to pretend he's forgotten my name. Everyone is ravenously devouring the food and moaning about the weather. Lucy has far more important things on her mind than my skirt.

"The Stradbroke disco's been cancelled this Saturday because of the snow. I was 'oping to go with Trevor—"

"—You're always thinking about your bleedin' Trev!" Uncle Bernie cuts in irritably, "What about the farmers? All those sheep will have to be dug out of the snow, right at the beginnin' of the lambing season."

"Never mind loves, in a month or so the whole place will be transformed with spring flowers on the road to the village," says Auntie, eyes lighting up at the prospect, her voice taking on a wistfulness quite unlike her usual strident tones. "Yer walk to school will be a dream, Janie— all yer favourite colours… carpets of purple bluebells under the trees, yellow, blue, and white crocuses on the grass verges. Just you wait, it's a sight for sore eyes. And the dawn chorus in spring, now that's *really* somethin' to wake up to. I've never regretted moving 'ere from London."

"It's still a bloody long walk to the village. You're the only one that doesn't have to do it every morning, Mum," says Cousin Lucy, matter-of-factly. "And it's always so windy, so *flat*."

This evening I'm preoccupied. I'm not interested in joining in the conversation, loud voices tumbling over each other, competing to be heard. For once, I don't care about the Stradbroke disco or the tempestuous weather.

"You're quiet tonight, Janie. Cat got your tongue?"

I can't wait for the meal to finish, the table cleared, washing up done, the floor swept. Only us girls are told to stay and help, while Uncle Bernie, Farve and Timmy go off to watch TV. My mind's in turmoil. That book by the French woman—Simone de something-or-other. I'm sure it's somewhere up in my bedroom. A boy gave it to me in Stafford—I think he thought it was a dirty book because it had a drawing of a naked woman on the cover.

As soon as I can, I make my excuses, saying I've got homework to do. I race upstairs to rummage in the bottom of the wardrobe. Found it! Simone De Beauvoir, *The Second Sex*. I only read a few pages the first time around, and I was incensed. I asked Mum why the author thought women were so bad.

"She doesn't think women are bad!" Mum exclaimed. "She's making a point that the world thinks women are not as good as men. She doesn't agree, she's sticking up for women, saying we shouldn't have to put up with it—that's the whole point of the book."

Still, I gave up on reading it at the time. It mystified me. Why would anyone need to write a book like that? It's quite obvious women are more powerful and cleverer than men. All the women in my family—Mum and Auntie Bel, Nan and her sister Auntie Molly, Auntie Lucy—are in charge of everything. They could run the country.

I never knew the wind had so many voices. The sound is almost human—wailing, shrieking, moaning, like a woman in pain, whirling around the little cottage all night as if it would tear it apart from the rafters. I was on fire. I kept reading that book by torchlight under the blankets, to the sound of the howling tempest outside, until my neck ached, the ice formed on the inside of the casement window, and the snowplough came through at first light.

It finally dawned on me. Now it all makes perfect sense. It explains everything. Or almost everything.

Thank you, Auntie Lucy! I know who I am now, and it's the best feeling ever. Aged fifteen and three-quarters, I'm a women's libber.

Chapter 5
Shades of Meaning

Back in London in the summer of '69, searing hot days turn into sticky, breathless nights, heavy with pollen and insects. The city is suffocating in the heat, the Stones are playing in Hyde Park, Brian Jones is dead. My six-year-old sister Molly and I cling together in the big brass bed in our new house, wide-eyed in darkness, straining to hear unfamiliar sounds—bumps, creaks, buzzes, scrapes, strange stirrings, making our pulses race and innards somersault. The French windows are wide open to catch the slightest breeze, but every tiny movement of the curtain terrifies us more. "D'you reckon this place is haunted?" Molly asks out of the darkness.

We are like squatters in someone else's house. Sight failing, Mrs Hetherington, the previous owner, has recently moved into a residential home. Before we moved in, the house-clearers came for all her saleable items, leaving behind a treasure-trove of her personal belongings.

Abandoned dust-covered curios lie in every room: a soft olive-green woollen shawl that I have taken to wearing with my hippy hat; carved wooden boxes containing assorted pieces of 1920s costume jewellery; tattered silk and velvet curtains, heavy dark-wood furniture, earthenware pots and chipped enamel jugs. Faint white rings and grey shadows lie beneath every ornament and behind every picture frame. None of them have been moved for decades.

Mum is marshalling the whole family to help with the big clean-up. "I don't know why the hell the house-clearers didn't take all this stuff and clear the whole place out while they were about it..." she complains. "All the same, there's some wonderful stuff among all this..."

We are constantly distracted by new discoveries. Mrs Hetherington's daughter-in-law was a Jamaican artist and potter, and some of her paintings still adorn the walls—harbour scenes alive with Brown-skinned people, sun on water, vibrant turquoise and orange hues. I want to step inside one of these captivating paintings, feel the sun on my neck and arms, dress in those clothes, be surrounded by Brown people like me.

*****

At my new school, Clapham County, there are more Brown faces. At last I'm not the only one. In the lower forms, there are a few West Indian girls, and in my class in the lower sixth there are Rosa and Angelica whose families are from the Philippines, and Nina from Jamaica.

Our English teacher Miss Winters urges us to expand our minds, make the most of not having exams this year. She is taking our English group to the matinée every Friday afternoon, in the cheap seats, so we will see every play in the West End by the end of term. I stand expectantly in the queue with my new classmates to see *The White Devil*, clutching my orange Penguin paperback, *Three Jacobean Plays*. The play features a feisty Black woman, a servant girl called Zanche, who taunts her torturers: "I am proud death cannot alter my complexion/For I shall ne'er look pale."

So, there must have been courageous and witty Black women characters in London even in the seventeenth century! There are so few stories and images of young Black and Brown-skinned women in my world. I am hungry for more, to understand how I will look and be seen, what I might be capable of, what I might become; women I can identify with, who come from the 20th century.

The tall auburn-haired girl next to me smiles, interrupting my thoughts. I'm instantly captivated by her green-brown eyes, and the smattering of light brown freckles on the bridge of her nose. She looks stylish in a peacock-blue maxi-skirt and kaftan. As sixth-formers, we no longer have to wear uniform.

"I'm Maddie—short for Madeleine. Are you new?" Her voice is warm and gentle, with a crackle, like shot silk.

"Jane—just started this week. Doing History, English, Religious Studies…"

"Is that a Norfolk accent? Or is it West Country?"

"Umm… No… I spent a few months in Norfolk with my cousins, must've picked up the accent a bit. I'm from here originally—London. I've just been away for a few years, been living all over the place… "

"Well thank God I have somebody interesting to talk to at last!" she grins, looking me up and down approvingly. "We can sit up in the gods together and make mischief every Friday!"

I have discovered a soulmate, a kindred spirit. I have fallen in love with Maddie. Copper-brown hair, tall, sophisticated, clever, fun, with an hour-glass figure, ginger-freckled milk-white skin, soft peachy lips, cupid-bow mouth, full milk-white breasts. She is everything I want and wish—hopelessly—I could be. She makes me feel like no-one else can—a heady concoction of danger and excitement. And yet we are a team, warriors against the world, a pair of outsiders, pacesetters, troublemakers, subversives.

On Saturday night we hit central London, looking for adventure, a couple of 16-year-olds enjoying our first delicious taste of freedom. Arm in arm, delighting in each other's company, among the neon lights. We can't afford real drugs, so we feign troublesome coughs and pick up two bottles of Collis Brown cough linctus from a chemist on the Strand. Then we collect a bottle of cider and a packet of Peter Stuyvesant from the off-licence. We dance among the pigeons in Trafalgar Square, try on floppy hats in the Chelsea Drugstore, and sit on the steps of Eros, amid discarded chip wrappers, paper cups and cigarette butts, to share a drink and a spliff with the down-and-outs and tourists.

By 1am—elated, dazed, famished, out of money, but still looking for more adventure—we find ourselves festooned with garlands of marigolds at the Hare Krishna temple, chanting interminably with legs crossed and one eye open, hungrily surveying the rapidly congealing banquet. We are longing for the gods to be at peace so we can gorge ourselves on cold vegetable curry, before returning to our irate parents, who must be wondering where we've been all night.

Maddie invites me home, and introduces me to her brother Andrew—slim, gentle, beautiful, artistic—a male version of Maddie, and only two years older, with shoulder-length wavy brown hair. He accompanies her on guitar, as she sings Donovan songs in her rich, warm, lilting voice.

Andrew invites me to the theatre to see the musical, *Hair*. It is the dawning of the Age of Aquarius, so of course we fall in love. With long strong slender fingers, he is practical as well as creative. He helps me decorate my bedroom with dark-green patterned paper, builds a new kitchen for Auntie Bel single-handed, and makes studded leather belts to sell to my school-friends, using off-cuts of leather hide that he gets from work. Best of all, he tailors me a soft black leather skirt, slit to the thigh, fastened at the hip with a row of gold buckles. I team it with knee-high black boots, ivory satin shirt, carefully straightened hair and wide-brimmed hat. Parading up and down the King's Road with Andrew and Maddie, alongside all the beautiful people, I am finally beginning to enjoy being in my own skin.

*****

On Friday afternoon, I hurtle downstairs on my way out to meet Andrew, running late as usual. Molly is just home from school, and—through the half-open door—I can hear her talking to Mum in the kitchen. I'm about to shout goodbye, but something in Molly's tone of voice makes me stop.

"Mum, is it true that Jane is a different colour from us? Why is she different from the rest of the family?"

Mum is at the sink, with her back to me, washing up.

"Of course she is! Haven't you ever noticed that before?"

There is a pause. This is clearly a complete revelation to my six-year-old sister. Judging by Mum's reply, she is supposed to know all about it already. I can see the look of incomprehension on Molly's face.

"But Mum, where does she get it from, the colour? In the playground this morning, one of the big girls asked me, who was that coloured lady who picked me up from school yesterday. I didn't know what she was talking about at first. Then I thought, she's talking about Jane. I told her, Jane's my big sister, she's not a coloured lady!"

"Jane's half African, that's why."

"But that girl said Jane must have been adopted, or else she's my half-sister—otherwise she'd be the same colour. That's not true, is it? What's a half-sister? I thought she was my whole sister."

"Jane has an African Dad, that's all."

The conversation is awkward, stilted. Mum doesn't like talking about it. The notion of a half-sister appears to be a totally unfamiliar and perplexing concept for Molly. It's taken a conversation at her new school, with a girl not much older than her, to point out the obvious. I feel for Molly. I have often been in her shoes—desperately seeking information and being left with unanswered questions.

I have to go. Andrew will be furious that I'm late again, this time because I've been mending the hem on my white, flowing, home-made Yoko Ono trousers, made from a bed-sheet. I was feeling great just now, all dressed up, excited at the prospect of a night on the town. But the conversation between Molly and Mum has left me uneasy. Should I have talked to Molly about it, as her big sister? Did I let her down? But I have very little information myself.

Less than two years older than Molly, my little brother Tom is outside playing in the street with our neighbour's son, Mikey Parks. As soon as I get to the front gate, Mikey calls out "Allo choccy-face-coon!"

Some things never change. I am still being called names in the street by nasty little boys. Tom is looking to see my reaction; whether I will respond to Mikey's insults. I am his big sister. Am I going to stick up for myself? I wish I could just ignore it. I am so much older and more sophisticated now, and I have a boyfriend who thinks I am attractive. But it still embarrasses me, makes me feel 'lesser'. I don't know how to handle it, much less help my siblings work it out.

*****

I tell Mum I read Simone de Beauvoir's *Second Sex* while I was in Norfolk staying with Auntie Lucy, and now I'm a Women's Libber. It turns out that Mum has been a Feminist all along. We are a mother-and-daughter team in the vanguard of the revolution. The extended family roll their eyes with a mixture of boredom and exasperation when the two of us get started, but we are undeterred. They say we are unfair to men, but haven't men been unfair to us for centuries?

"*Us!* Who's *us*?" queries Dad. "You're not even a woman yet, you're only sixteen." I burst into tears and rush to my bedroom. Later he comes in to apologise. "I didn't mean to upset you."

It's all right. I feel awkward sometimes, tongue-tied, unable to argue my point, overwhelmed with emotion. Mum is so knowledgeable, clever and well-read. I wish I could speak fluently like her, feel confident and sure of myself. I desperately want to make a witty, compelling speech at the debate in the boys' school this term—take the audience by storm, and revel in the applause. But words stick in my throat, and when challenged, I burst into tears. I need to prove I can do it, so people see past my colour, and recognise that I'm as good as anyone. Then I can *be* someone in my own right, somebody tangible, recognisable, real.

*****

"I don't do dates," says Miss Shaw. "Can't remember them. And anyway, they're not that important."

A ripple of admiration goes around the class—a history teacher who has no time for dates!

"But *you* will need dates for the exam, so you'll have to look them up yourselves and learn them. And what's important is the *impact* these historical characters had on the world—the changes they brought about."

After class, I hang back; I need Miss Shaw's help.

"Miss, I'm going to take part in the annual debate with Emmanuel School. I'm proposing the motion, *'Anything men can do, women can do better'*. I need some ideas about women who have succeeded in a man's world."

In truth, I am sick with nerves about the debate, but I am going to make myself do it and learn how to speak and argue in front of a big audience—without bursting into tears. I am going to prove myself.

"Not a problem, there are *lots* of examples from every

era, in every sphere of learning, politics, culture—we just have to look for them."

Miss Shaw warms to her theme, spreading her hands out flat on the desk as she does when she has something important to explain. She is my favourite teacher; I confess I have a crush on her. A heavy-featured woman with cropped brown hair (Nan might call her 'plain'), she's full of energy, wit and vitality. Her passion for history lights up her face and the room as she talks.

"Two of our most successful and influential monarchs of all time were women—Elizabeth the First and Queen Victoria. If you're looking for warrior queens, there's Boadicea, of course; nursing—Florence Nightingale; the Civil Rights movement—Rosa Parks, who refused to sit in the seats designated for Blacks on the segregated bus... Women have made formidable tyrants too—how about Catherine the Great of Russia? She had so many lovers and still found time to build an Empire... and great revolutionaries—Rosa Luxemburg, for example. How far back do you want to go? Among the ancient Greeks there's Sappho. She lived on the island of Lesbos—that's where we get the word 'lesbian'. She was a brilliant, cultured poetess... Mustn't forget Cleopatra, of course, if we are talking about the ancient world... and, more recently, the Pankhurst family, campaigning for votes for women..."

"Miss, could you slow down please?" My fingers are stiff and my arm aches with the effort of scribbling notes as she picks up speed, racing back and forth across the centuries.

"Sorry, my apologies, of course, I'll slow down a bit…" She closes her eyes to aid concentration. "Politics—Indira Gandhi, Golda Meir; modern art—Barbara Hepworth; Renaissance art—Artemisia Gentileschi…"

Miss Shaw knows so much. There's a whole world to discover out there. I am both hungry and daunted.

Finally, she reopens her eyes. "How long do you have for your speech?"

"Ten minutes."

She laughs. "I should have asked that at the beginning! Not long enough to cover all that. You'd better choose two or three good examples from different historical periods—I'll help you. One day I'll write an encyclopaedia—*The Rise and Fall of the World's Women*—to show just how much women have achieved against all the odds, and the world hasn't even noticed. It will be a very thick book—probably several volumes! What do you want to read when you go to university?"

I notice she says *when*, not *if*; she actually believes I have what it takes to get there.

"I'd like to read history, and then be a writer, or a journalist. Or even a newsreader on television."

"Excellent—there are hardly any women news-readers on the telly, and none your colour. And I am *delighted* you want to read history. We need more women reading history, writing history and above all, *making* history. Of course, most history books are written by men.

It's time we told our side of the story... Without understanding our past, how can we make any sense of the present, or even *think* about what might happen in the future?" she concludes, grandly.

This makes perfect sense. And then a thought occurs to me. "Miss, do you think that applies to your own *personal* history as well? I mean, like my own history—I don't know it. I don't know my father. I feel as if half of me is missing—the half of me that shows. I think I could forget about it if I wasn't 'coloured'. But almost every day someone asks me where I'm from, and I can't answer. So I can't... sort of... make any sense of *me*, really. Sometimes I feel completely lost..."

Miss Shaw ponders this for a moment. "Yes, yes, I think you're right. That's a very good point. I hadn't really thought of it that way before. It must surely apply to an individual's story every bit as much as it does to society's story... Good luck with the debate. I'm sure we'll win."

We *did* win. And now I know I can do something, thanks to Miss Shaw. I can make a good speech.

*****

Our English teacher, Miss Winters—earnest, dainty, blue-eyed and bird-like, every inch the young Cambridge graduate—hands out an impossibly long reading list: Shakespeare, Austen, the Brontës, Dickens, the complete works of Oscar Wilde, and the plays of the Ancient Greeks.

"The Greeks believed in many kinds of love," she enthuses, "not just sexual love, but also love of friends, playful affection, longstanding, patient love, love for the human race, love of one's teacher, love of oneself…"

Brilliant! Why stick to Eros when there is so much more love on offer?

"… and of course, there's love of books," she continues. "You'll be learning from each other too, girls. I want each of you to bring in your favourite book, for the whole class to read and discuss—for you to inspire each other, tell us why you love it…"

There's a ripple of excitement around the class. For me, it's got to be Emily Brontë's *Wuthering Heights*; dark, stormy, passionate, intense. Like life. Finally, I am getting a real education, and I can even play a part in choosing what's on the curriculum. It's so different from my schools in Stafford and Norfolk.

Debbie is sitting in front of me in the English class as usual, long straight white-blonde tresses reaching halfway down her back. She runs milk-white fingers through it, chewed fingernails twisting and flicking, forever fiddling with her hair. It distracts and fascinates me at first, but by half term it is as irritating as hell.

In the lower sixth common room during lunch break, Debbie pauses her beloved Leonard Cohen album for a moment to make a sensational announcement.

"I'm leaving school at the end of this term," she says excitedly. "It's all set, I've been to see Miss Vine about it.

I've seen a pair of snakeskin boots in the King's Road—thirty quid—and I'm gonna get them! And I'm taking Leonard Cohen with me!"

"Well that's no way to say goodbye!" Maddie says wittily.

Thirty pounds—an unbelievable sum. How will she ever afford it? And how can she throw her education away for a pair of snakeskin boots?

"I'm gonna save up," she responds gleefully. "I've never been that bothered about A-levels really. I've got a job in Arding and Hobbs bargain basement, up the Junction—where you got your herringbone maxi-coat, Jane."

After school, I join Maddie, Jackie and Debbie on the top deck of the number 19 bus, for a pilgrimage to the Boot Shop on the King's Road, to feast our eyes upon these *Objects of Desire*. The shapely snakeskin boots are displayed centre-stage on a glass pedestal in the window: intricate black-and-white grain, black block heels, square toes, a tiny silver buckle glinting just below the knee.

I've been reading the book of Genesis in Religious Studies, and I'm captivated by the relationship between Eve and the serpent—and why on earth Eve should get blamed for all the sins of the world. I am filled with lustful longing for these snakeskin boots, snaking around my resolve, threatening to throttle my hopes and dreams. My reflection hovers in the window just above the boots. I rest my forehead against the cool glass for a moment, eyes closed.

What am I thinking of? I will not give in to temptation. I will not eat of the 'forbidden fruit'. I already have my eyes on a much bigger prize—to prove myself. To prove I'm not just an aberration, a Black bastard abandoned by her father, 'who should never have been born' as my Auntie Lucy said. Forget the frivolous footwear. My ambition is to get my hands on the fruit of the entire tree of knowledge. Then I will be *worth* something. The first in our family ever to go to university. Finally, people will take me seriously. *Nothing* must get in my way.

*****

Outside the clinic, the dazzling sun lights up the world just to spite me. A crushing weight of dread and fear presses under my ribcage so I can hardly breathe. Andrew puts a reassuring arm around me.

"It will be okay. We will look after this baby together. We can get married, we'll manage, don't worry…"

But I can't bear it. I'm not ready for a baby… and I'm a Women's Libber, I don't believe in marriage.

"Look, let's go and see the Beatles anyway. You've been looking forward to it… It might take your mind off things for a while, give us time to think…"

Andrew hails a taxi to Leicester Square. The streets of London are rolling by outside the window, as if in slow motion. Throngs of revellers enjoy a baking hot Saturday afternoon, in their T-shirts, mini-skirts and bell-bottoms, spilling out onto the sizzling pavements in Covent Garden, eating ice cream and chips. Laughing, strolling, chatting, without a care in the world, full of life and colour.

Inside the cinema, it's warm, dark, womb-like. A thousand thoughts are teeming in my head. Am I full of life, or not? Is this my own life, or someone else's? The life I want, or a life I don't want? I'm dreading telling my parents when they get back from holiday. What will they think of me? Why would I go and throw it all away? On screen, even the Beatles are falling apart. The world has gone mad, everything is upside down, no-one wants to *Let It Be*.

I retreat to my bed, head under the covers, the safest place I can find.

"Jane, what is it?" I can hear Mum's voice close by and I can sense all three of them—Mum, Dad and Auntie Bel—clustered anxiously around the bed. Auntie Bel tells them what's happened. Finally, I lift my head to face them.

"Seventeen. *Seventeen!*" Dad keeps repeating, shaking his head, pacing up and down the bedroom. "I thought you wanted to go to university. You set your sights so high…"

"I *do*, I still *do* want to go!"

There's a heavy silence, the implications churning over in our heads.

Mum takes a seat on the chair, by the wash basin.

"Oh dear… Well, I guess you should have thought of that before you took such a risk. You're just going to have to grow up and have this baby. You can stay here at home with us. We'll support you..."

"But I can't, I just can't bear it, Mum!" I pull the covers over my head again. It's like a death sentence. I am such a failure. I'm wishing I was as strong and full of courage as my Mum must have been when she had me. I can't begin to imagine how she must have felt, all those years ago in the 1950s, sent away from home, not much older than me, carrying an illegitimate Brown child with no father.

And here I am in 1970—not being kicked out of home into an unmarried mothers' home, but with the loving support of my family, my boyfriend ready to stay with me. There's the Pill, and abortion is safe and legal. I have no excuse. So many choices, and yet so hard to make one. People still look down on 'girls in trouble' as if we have brought it all upon ourselves, as if the boys are not equally involved. As if this is not the most natural normal thing in the world, to be young and pregnant and have babies. The world should surely make space for us.

What is *wrong* with me? I just know I can't go through with this.

A memory flashes through my mind, of the promise I made to myself outside the shop window, when I was worshipping the snakeskin boots. I was mistaken. If I ever make it, I will not be the first person in my family to go to university. My African father went to university, here, in London. I am suddenly, painfully aware of what is causing me this overwhelming grief. I know this is forbidden territory. But if I don't get some answers now, in this crisis, I never will.

"I can't have this baby because... until... I don't know who I am, Mum... I can't have a baby until you tell me about my father. My African father. I just need to know about him... just need you to tell me... "

Who was he? What was he like? Why did he leave? Where did he go? Is he alive or dead?

Same questions.

Still no answers.

Mum hesitates, caught off-guard at this turn in the conversation.

"If you think a child has the right to know about its father, then *you* can tell this baby all about its father when it grows up."

She hugs me, and leaves the room. Maybe she can't handle any more just now—so many emotions stirred up, long-buried, deeply painful, unprocessed. The experience is too close, raw, agonising.

I curl up into a ball again, in a foetal position. Empty, a no-body, with something inside that isn't me, inside a person I don't know. I feel bad for Mum, it's not her fault. My father left us and he doesn't get all these questions, agony, heartache. But he's not here, I don't know where to find him, and I don't have anyone else I can ask.

My Stepdad sits on the bed beside me, gently patting the bedcovers. He has been a real father to me since I was eight years old.

"I don't know anything about your natural father,

Jane... All I know is, your Mum would never have had you if she didn't love him. To carry you into the world and show you so much love, to be prepared to bring you up all on her own—she must have loved him very much."

His words are soothing, comforting. They must have cost a lot for him to say.

If only they were true.

It isn't the right time for me to have a baby, to be a mother. Right from the beginning, I just knew I couldn't go through with it. There is so much else I need to do with my life before that happens, so much I need to sort out about *me*—who I am, how I fit into the world.

*****

Mum and I sit in the Middlesex Hospital car park together, talking it through, before I go in for my pregnancy termination. Abortion was only legalised two years ago. I'm lucky to have this choice, and to know it's safe. We feel very close just now. I am so grateful she is here, supporting me.

"It doesn't feel right or real, being pregnant, Mum. Just terrifying. I need to find myself before I can have a baby."

"You're making the right decision for *you*, Jane, remember that. After it's all over, you can put it behind you, go back to school, fulfil your ambitions to go to university. You don't need to tell anyone about this." We hug each other before we go in.

We are very different, Mum and I. I need to talk through whatever is happening to me, whereas she is a much more private person. I am desperate to ask her more about my father. It's difficult to explain the connection— why it's so important to me at this moment, when there's so much else to preoccupy us—but it's what I really need to talk about right now.

Chapter 6

Busted

Handsome, six-foot-three, with a booming voice to match, the Doctor cuts a dashing figure towering in the doorway of the waiting room, doing his usual stand-up routine.

"You people never come to visit me except when you're sick! How inconsiderate—I could catch some nasty disease, the state you're all in!"

The tiny waiting room is always full to bursting with snotty noses, bad backs, blinding headaches. If you don't arrive early for morning surgery, you'll be lucky to get a seat.

His comedy act rarely varies.

"… you lot always turn up at once, on the dot of ten, just when I'm busy. I suppose you want to see a doctor. Wait. I *am* the doctor. Now we'll be here all day! Let's see, how many have we got this time…"

He counts loudly in German, jabbing his forefinger at each patient in turn.

"*Eins, zwei, drei, vier, fünf, sechs…*" His accusing finger hovers in the air in front of me. "Why are *you* always sex?

I'll see you about that later. Now then, who's first?"

The patients shift uneasily on the uncomfortable, hard wooden chairs. No-one wants to go first. We are all too sick, or simply not feeling up to it. It's a well-known fact that the Doctor is at his most boisterous for morning surgery. Patients often listen uneasily to the muffled sounds emanating from behind the closed door, the Doctor's raucous laughter punctuated by shrieks and nervous giggling from his hapless victims. He has a reputation for being particularly 'good with kids'. He instructs children who have just had their tonsils removed to lift their arms above them, whilst he whips up their jumpers over their heads and tickles them mercilessly under the armpits as they croak, writhe and twist, desperately trying to escape their improvised straitjacket. Parents are powerless to intervene. No one dares contradict or remonstrate. He's the Doctor after all, he knows best, a pillar of the establishment, a jolly old physician.

My turn. Six weeks ago, Mum and I came to see him to ask for a referral for my pregnancy termination. He was dismissive of the pleas and distress of a desperate seventeen-year-old pregnant schoolgirl.

"I'm afraid I can't help you. I am completely anti-abortion and I fought against that law being brought in two years ago. Dreadful idea. Immoral. You're obviously one of these girls who is incredibly fertile, you get pregnant as soon as you blink. Abortion just encourages people like you. I hope you'll be more careful next time. As far as

I'm concerned, you're having this baby. I'll work out your due date and book you into St George's for delivery."

I left his surgery in tears.

A week after the abortion, arranged through the British Pregnancy Advisory Service, I came back to the doctor's surgery, full of trepidation. My breasts had become swollen and painful. I made sure to put on a front-fastening top in case the Doctor was tempted to whip it up and pin my arms above my head for the customary bout of tickling.

"So, you went ahead and did it anyway, did you? And now you're in trouble. Come on, let's have a look then… Oooh, no bra! How daring!"

He chuckled and squeezed my nipple. A tiny drop of milky fluid appeared.

"There, you see, you young girls think you can get rid of a pregnancy with impunity. But your body thinks differently—it's preparing for motherhood."

"But nobody warned me this would happen…"

"I have to say, lactation is rare so early, when you were only twelve weeks gone. Bad luck. But it's natural, all the same."

I wanted to say I didn't regret my decision, I made the right choice for me. I was distraught when I discovered I was pregnant. I was simply not ready for a baby. But this new development came as a shock. I was unprepared, tearful, vulnerable.

"Now I suppose we'll have to clear this up. We don't want you getting an infection."

He took out his pad and scribbled a prescription.

"Take these tablets—that should deal with it. Come back in a week and we'll see."

I went home and cried.

A week later, I'm back to face another of the doctor's gruelling, judgemental examinations.

"How are they then, your little ones? Let's have a look... much better?"

"They are still a bit tender..."

"They *would* be. Let's have a feel."

Things happen fast. I am caught completely by surprise. He pulls me towards him, spins me around and sits me on his lap, my back hard up against him, his breath in my ear. Cupping my sore breasts in both his hands, he squeezes so hard, tears spurt from my eyes as the pain shoots through my chest, up my neck and down my arms. The more I writhe and struggle on his lap, the tighter his hold, the louder his laugh, the more he seems to be enjoying it. I have no breath to scream. Strangled noises of protest come out of my mouth—not unusual sounds in this doctor's surgery. When he finally lets me go, I stagger to the door, clutching my open top, and hurtle through the waiting room past the straggle of startled patients still waiting to be seen.

I hear him booming "Next!" as I bang the door shut and race down the path.

It's not far to our front door, but it is miles—miles of rage, violation, humiliation. Too much, too horrible. This time he has gone too far, when I'm at my most hurt and most vulnerable. I arrive home, gasping, tearful, in pain.

"Mum! You'll never guess what he did to me—the Doctor…"

"That man! He's going to get struck off one of these days if he carries on like that—"

"Shouldn't we complain? I mean, he can't just get away with it, can he? We should say something…"

Mum is thoughtful, uncertain. "I don't know. Trouble is, that Doctor has a lot of clout around here. He's a big cheese at the tennis club and the local societies. He's got powerful friends. He seems to be very popular—the neighbours recommended him. He'd be a difficult person to take on, especially since we've not long moved here. And you are still recovering. Goodness knows what people would start saying about us, about you—things we would want to keep private, put behind us. You know how anti-abortion he is."

It's true. He's punishing me, when I am exhausted and hurting and can't do anything about it. I have been a bad girl, I broke the rules. People would probably say I asked for it. He thinks he can do what he likes to the only brown girl on the estate, girls like me who get pregnant in the blink of an eye. Who would care? Who would believe me anyway?

*****

What with all the goings-on in my life I've flunked my A-levels, of course. I haven't got the right grades to get into university. I wonder if I'm ever going to make it at this rate. I'm always messing things up, always 'borderline'. Not even a pair of snakeskin boots to show for it.

My teachers are very keen for me to have another try. There are so many people living in our house—Mum, Dad, sister Molly, brother Tom, Auntie Bel, Cousin Vic, and our disabled cat Josie. It's hard to find anywhere quiet to study. So, it's settled… I'm moving in with my grandparents again after all these years, on the Shaftesbury Estate, returning to my first childhood home (not counting the unmarried mothers' home) to study for my retakes.

It's peaceful here now, compared with the old days—more than a decade ago—when we were all living here together.

Times have changed. Nan has had the whole place repainted in magnolia. There's a two-bar electric fire in the dining room where the coal stove used to be, and in the scullery, a fridge and spin dryer have replaced the food safe and the clothes mangle. An upstairs bathroom was installed a few years ago. Built in the late 19th century, all the houses on this working-class estate were originally built with outside toilets. There's even a new sofa and a black-and-white television in the front room, where Grandad can watch his Westerns.

Grandad and I have time to talk, now the others aren't around. He is self-educated, having left school at thirteen.

"I used to read all sorts of books when I came 'ome for me dinner at midday—the Communist Manifesto, the complete works of Shakespeare and Dickens, Jane Austen, Oliver Goldsmith. I've even read the Bible from cover to cover. Not bad for a working-class atheist!"

Grandad and I share a great interest in religion, despite our lack of religious faith. Religious Studies is one of the A-level subjects I am re-taking this year.

"All them crackin' stories in the Old Testament—myth, mayhem and ancient history," he muses. "Fascinating. You should respect people's faith, no matter what religion they are... That's where I took issue with the Communist Party."

Grandad shows me his framed 50-year trade union membership certificate, proudly displayed in the alcove, next to the sitting-room fireplace.

"I'm all for workers' rights, as you know," he says. "They offered me promotion at Morgan's Crucible Company many times, but I wanted to stay with the men, not be with the bosses... Did I ever tell you we used to 'ave a mayor in Battersea who was your colour? 'E was in the Socialist Party like me, then 'e went Labour. Stood as an MP at one point, as I recall... John Archer was 'is name. Bajan father, Irish mother, one of the first Black men to get elected in Britain, just before the First World War, and 'e was active all through the 1920s on Battersea Council."

John Archer. A man who looked like me—'half-and-half'—and achieved great things. A pioneer, a politician, who believed in all the things I believe in—equality, socialism, justice—living right here in Battersea, where I grew up. This is part of my history. I'm thrilled at the thought that I wasn't the only one. As a child I had thought I was a species of one, apart from hearing about a friend of Mum's who had a Brown boy like me—although I never met him.

I was loved, I was brought up in a loving family—that much I knew. But there is a difference between being loved, and feeling you *belong*. In 1947, six years before I was born, nearly five hundred Jamaicans disembarked from the *Windrush* to settle in nearby Brixton. I read about it in the Library. By the mid-1950s, there were still only around twenty thousand Black people in the UK. But as a kid on this estate, the changing face of Britain had passed me by. As for me, I had more than my fair share of stigma to contend with, alone. Only about five percent of children were born out of wedlock in the '50s. Being the half-caste, illegitimate child of a disabled working-class single parent, there was no escaping it. Around these streets, I was a rarity, and I stuck out like a sore thumb. I often felt lost. Bewildered.

"I've never heard of John Archer before."

Grandad can see my eyes light up.

"Yeah, John Archer, met 'im a few times… good bloke. Got a lot of racial prejudice while he was campaignin'. But after 'e was elected, I remember hearing 'im speak at Battersea Town Hall, saying the world will look to

Battersea and say the greatest thing we've done is show that there's no racial prejudice 'ere. We recognise Black and White men as equals, for the work they do, not the colour of their skin."

"... And Black *women*, too, Grandad."

Grandad looks at me wryly. "Yeah, Auntie Lucy told me you were a pain in the arse when you were staying with her in Norfolk, you an' yer bloody Women's Lib. She was well fed up with it by the time you left, she was—"

"—but it's interesting that John Archer got a lot of racial prejudice," I hastily change the subject—"... and then in his speech he said there wasn't any prejudice in Battersea..."

And three decades after John Archer's time, in the 1950s, I was still being called names in the streets around here.

"Well maybe he meant among the people like us, who elected 'im, *we* weren't prejudiced, at least. Anyway, *Showboat*'s on TV now, let's watch."

But we know the film so well, we carry on talking all the way through it. Paul Robeson is our family hero—a great supporter of the Civil Rights movement, Communist sympathiser and frequent visitor to the Soviet Union.

"Paul Robeson says they shake 'is 'and and treat 'im like a human being over there in Moscow," Grandad muses. "We saw 'im in *Othello* at the theatre when he played here in London. In those days, it was a big scandal when 'e kissed Peggy Ashcroft on stage—a Black man kissing a

White woman! Didya know 'e lived in Lambeth while 'e was performing 'ere, near my Mum's place, because 'e wasn't allowed to stay with the White cast?"

"Did Granny Goldsmith ever meet him?"

"Yeah, she did Duck, and she was always on about it! She was a chorus dancer before she married my Dad, and then they both used to do the warm-up act on stage before the main act—jokes and sketches, that sorta thing. She always loved the theatre, my Mum, she liked meeting the big stars."

Grandad's mind is still razor sharp, his memory acute. But his body's in a bad way. He's only in his mid-sixties, but he's pretty much confined to his armchair now, and wheezes and coughs like an old man. I feel angry and powerless when I think how industrial disease has disabled a strong, fit, intelligent, principled man like him. Ruined his life, with no compensation.

"Silicosis done away with my Dad, and it will most likely kill me an' all—breathin' in all that brick dust in the 'ot kilns during the war, seven days a week."

"Didn't the doctor say you should give up smoking and drinking? I know it seems harsh, when those are the things you enjoy most."

"I s'pose I could give it a try. I dunno. Life wouldn't be the same without me baccy and me beer. I always 'oped one day there'd be a classless society, and the workers would own the factories and run the whole system—health, education, transport, the economy, the lot. I doubt I'll live to see that day now. But I'm curious about the future. I'd like to stay alive just to see what 'appens next, Duck…"

Nan is calling us upstairs. "Are you two still talking down there? That film finished ages ago and Jane has to get up early to study tomorrow."

*****

On my way back from the library, I stop to look at a newly-opened shop on Lavender Hill. The Jamaican proprietor, busily arranging his window display, dashes outside to greet me.

"Wha gwann, beautiful lady? Are yuh mi new neighbour?" he says hopefully.

"Um… no… I'm just staying here for a while, studying at my grandparents'…"

"'Ang on a minute, I got sometin' for yuh…"

He disappears inside and emerges with a large white plastic bag full of samples. I back off, miming refusal, but he insists.

"Tek it, tek it, no hobligation a-tarl," he beams.

Inside the bag there's a whole treasure trove of goodies—skin-lightening lotion and skin-bleaching soap, hair straightener, hair-relaxing cream. A few years ago, I'd have given anything for such a store of delights. But now, who needs these dangerous, noxious products, promoting a false idea of White Western beauty, to which we cannot possibly aspire?

I've discovered Black Power.

"I see… Then you juss might be lookin' for an Afro… go visit my friend Whitey up the 'ill. Tell 'im mi sent yuh."

The sign above the door says *Hair Paradise*. It's written in elaborate script, featuring tropical birds perched among fruits and palm trees. The hairdresser is one of the most extraordinary-looking people I've ever seen. He can't be much under seven feet tall, pale honey-yellow skin, bleached-white eyebrows and eyelashes, short curly ginger-blond Afro, startling blue eyes, a mass of dark freckles over the bridge of his nose, and unmistakably African features—a strong full-rounded nose and lips.

"Welcome to *'Air Paradise*! The name's Karl—Karrrrrl with a 'K'." He purrs his name with a deep rich Caribbean lilt, like warm molasses.

"You wan' cut an' blow-out, right? You jus' in time to see my re-furr-bish-ment," he says proudly, emphasising all four syllables, sweeping a hand around his salon—blue peeling paint, ill-matching, frayed bits of lino on the floor, a single dim cobwebby lightbulb hanging from the ceiling; and a framed portrait of Emperor Haile Selassie taking pride of place on the wall. He is surrounded by tattered posters of Bob Marley, Eldridge Cleaver, Marcus Garvey, Nina Simone, Angela Davis and Malcolm X. A veritable *Who's Who* of Black Power, along with myriad faded posters for bygone gigs in Kingston town.

"My *makeover*," he insists, seeing my puzzled expression and pointing to a brand-new Hollywood-style black-and-silver hairdresser's chair, placed carefully in front of a tall mirror framed with lightbulbs. Rows of hair products—waxes, lotions and sprays in every colour of the rainbow—are displayed neatly on illuminated shelves next to the mirror. The new chair and the mirror are a dazzling contrast to the surrounding dilapidation.

"C'mon in, c'mon in," he urges. "Our first lady customer."

It seems I'm also his only *paying* customer too. There are three young guys inside, lounging on battered chairs and upturned crates, smoking roll-ups. "These 'ere are my friends—Winston, Martin, Malcolm X."

"Yo, Waa Gwaan?!"

They nod, grunt and raise cans of beer in greeting. "Not the famous Malcolm X. Our very own Malcolm X," he laughs.

Karl fastens a waterproof apron around my neck, washes my hair with thick apple-scented shampoo, then vigorously massages my scalp with copious quantities of coconut conditioner.

"Yuh got beautiful 'air," he says approvingly, running the tips of his long honey-coloured fingers gently through my damp curly strands. His touch is gentle, feather-light.

I'm delighted. "Nobody's ever told me that before."

"Well it's true. Wha ya puttin' ahn? Yuh relaxin' it?"

"No, it's completely natural. I just put hairdressing on it every day because it tends to be dry."

"Whe yuh com fram?"

Difficult question, without explaining where my parents come from.

"Mum English. Dad African, from Ghana."

"*Aha!* Mixed 'air, it don' need relaxin'. Soft texture. But can be dry, a true. This climate no good for Black skin and 'air. Tropical an' 'umid suit us best. You need to hoil it every day, 'air an' skin, see wha' mi sayin'?" He reaches for a gigantic jar of raw shea butter from the shelf.

"Specially me, bein' a White-Black, skin tend to crack. We Blacks come in all shades and sizes!" he laughs.

Settling me under the steamer, he continues, "Albinos like me get a 'ard time in Jamaica, you know. People think we cursed. That's why I got out o' there. I was called Whitey, yellow man, devil-boy, as a kid. They call me *Outside Child*, the name they give to any pikney that's part of the family but don't quite fit, you get mi?"

Outside Child. Like me.

"Now *ev'rybody* try and look like us light-skinned Blacks, with the bleach an' the skin-light'nin' creams!" He rolls his eyes. "Now your 'air nice and soft, all ready for the blow-out..."

He leads me over to the splendid new chair and raises it up to his height, pumping the lever with his foot until my legs are dangling high above the frayed lino and my head is under his chin. He sets to work with a hairdryer and oversized Afro comb.

"Ting wi' dis kind o' mixed 'air, it change texture every day accordin' to the wedder, the time o' day, and the way yuh *feelin'*. Can be 'ard to manage, true. But can be an asset. Afro 'air can tell yuh about politics, de climate, de fashion, de date in 'istory even. Few years back, mi used to do relaxin' an' straight'nin' all day long. Mi got toxi-fied by all dem chemicals. Some ladies—and quite a few gentlemen—got no 'air a-tarl now, and only in their forties. It aaall burned off and fell out. Ain't no Black woman mi ever met didn't 'ave a complicated relationship with 'er 'air. Now we got Black Power, our 'air is gonna *stay* beautiful, believe you me."

I've never had a proper conversation with anyone about my hair before. Most people I meet comment on my hair, but no-one has ever been able to advise me on what to do with it. Before this, I've had no access to any of the specialist hair products and hairdressers that are beginning to appear in London, let alone the kind of expert knowl-edge and political analysis Karl offers. Managing my hair seems like a daily battle that I always lose. Even now, complete strangers still think they have the right to feel it, pat it, stroke it, poke it, pull it—and often recoil with distaste.

The Best of the Wailers is playing fuzzily on the paint-splattered record player in the corner. "Take this 'ere Bob Marley. He's half-half like you. Mum Jamaican, Dad Scottish. They gave him a 'ard time in the ghetto 'cos 'e 'alf White. An' now look, 'e's a Black hero all over the world."

"At the end of the day, Black is a political concept, it's not about the shade of your skin," Malcolm X suddenly interjects. "We all belang to the Black nation, we all fightin' for our freedom. X stands for the African name they took away from me when my ancestors were sold into slavery…"

I wonder if women can do that too. 'Jane X'—now that's a thought.

"It's what you *do* with your Black power that counts," Martin joins in, pushing heavy dark-rimmed glasses up to the bridge of his nose. "You gotta talent, you show the world what you can do. Take Karl 'ere. He's an artist. Topiary for the 'air!" he grins.

Karl works meticulously, first with the electric trimmer and then with the scissors, fluffing out each strand with his Afro comb until my hair is as light and airy as a puff-ball and as round and symmetrical as if it has been drawn with a protractor.

"Would yuh care for some creamy Jamaican ponch— made to my own special recipe?" asks Karl's reflection in the mirror opposite me.

I'm thinking this must be a reference to some new kind of hair product.

"No, just a bit of hair lotion, thanks."

They all laugh uproariously at this, at my expense—and for a bit too long, I think—except for Winston. He doesn't say much, just nods and smiles through broken teeth.

"*Ponch*, Jamaican ponch," Karl explains, purposely emphasising his rolling Jamaican accent. "Hey, Winston, go out back an' bring us all a taste o' the good stuff."

Winston, carefully adjusting his oversized knitted

Rasta hat over his unruly dreadlocks, disappears unsteadily through the beaded curtain. He returns with five tall glasses of warm coffee-coloured liquid, each with a magnificent rounded foaming head—the consistency of hair mousse—with what looks like chocolate flakes sprinkled on top.

"Oh, I see, *punch*, thank you." I am conscious that I am pronouncing it 'parnch'. I have lost my Norfolk lilt and got my Sarf Larndon accent back at last!

I sip cautiously.

"Delicious. What's in it?" They all nod and smile knowingly at this.

"Well lemmee see, it's my secret recipe… " Karl rolls his eyes to the ceiling to aid concentration, holding the Afro comb aloft to tick off each ingredient with a flick of his wrist: "A lotta Guinness, a dash o' milk, a likkle bit o' cream, and a sprinkle o' magic…"

I have never tasted anything like it—rich, herbal, bitter, creamy, intoxicating. The glasses are filled and refilled. We are laughing together, enjoying the conversation and the company while Karl continues his artistry. My head feels as light and relaxed as the mood… I am floating way off the ground. I strongly suspect these are not chocolate flakes.

Finally, the hairdryer is silenced, the combs and scissors stowed, my neck and face brushed clean of loose hairs, apron whisked away. Karl lowers the chair gently and swings it round with a flourish, to gain the approval of the assembled company.

"Mi dun, darlin'!" he declares.

"Bee-you-dee-ful! Jus' like Sista Angela."

"Rispek! Glad to see you wearin' your Natural with pride, Sista," nods Malcom X, "... makin' a statement about who ya are an' what ya believe in."

Winston says nothing—just nods and grins, clenching his fist in the Black Power salute.

I float out of the salon elated, high as a kite—and a little bit stoned.

"It's that likkle sprinkle o' magic on top of the ponch done the trick!" Karl laughs, waving me off. "Inna Lataz."

Suddenly I feel so good in my own hair. Every follicle radiates from my head in a soft shimmering Black halo. Before I go back to Nan and Grandad's I am going to glide about Clapham Junction for a while to show off, as if I own the place, just until the magic wears off and my eyes get back in focus.

At the bottom of Lavender Hill, outside Arding and Hobbs, I bump into Debbie—Debbie from the English class with the Leonard Cohen songs and the chewed fingernails and the long blonde hair. I haven't seen her since she left school. We greet each other like long-lost friends.

"Did you ever get those snakeskin boots?"

"Umm... yeah... Don't really wear them that much— they pinch a bit. Nice *hair*, Jane!" Finally, a girl with long straight blonde locks says I have nice hair.

When I get home, Grandad is less impressed.

"Gawd, what the bleedin' 'ell you done with yer barnet,

mate?" As poetic as Karl, in a different way.

A few months later I arrive at *Hair Paradise* for my usual fortnightly cut-and-blow-out, looking forward to a tall glass of warm punch with a sprinkle o' magic, and a good dose of Black power. To my utter dismay and disappointment, the place looks desolate—doors and windows all boarded up and scrawled over with multi-coloured graffiti. My first and only Black friends have disappeared, just like that, and there's no forwarding address to return the battered copy of *The Autobiography of Malcom X* I am clutching in my hand.

A notice nailed to the door bears a brief, forlorn message: *"Gone away."*

Evidently, they have been busted.

Chapter 7
Fish Out of Water

It's hard to tell when sunset ends and sunrise begins. About midnight, the orange disc dips toward the horizon, setting the sky ablaze in a riot of yellow and crimson. Clouds turn peachy, the lake is molten gold. The sun comes to rest just above the horizon—then almost imperceptibly, it begins to rise again, an orange haze marking the few moments it takes for one day to dissolve into the next.

That's when it's time to go fishing.

Out on the lake the water is crystal-clear and you can see way down into the depths. The silent twilight is magical, otherworldly. We stop in deep open water, the lake surface dead calm with the occasional flip and flash of a jumping fish. A scene of absolute peace and tranquillity. The Koskinen boys are out on deck, lean tanned bodies glistening with sweat, hauling up the catch in vertical fishing nets lowered there the night before.

Suddenly all hell breaks loose as the nets hit the deck in a frenzy of leaping fish like a lava of quicksilver. We are reeling and writhing, skating and sliding, cannoning into each other on the bloody slimy surface, to the sound of shouting and swearing and the thwacking of wooden cosh on fish-head.

The others are adept at it, smacking and thwacking and then quick as a flash, flinging the fish into deep buckets on deck. I am terrified of tackling live fish as big as a tea-trays. The first time I looked a fish in the eye, it looked straight back at me. Much as I adore eating them, I couldn't bring myself to do it. I flailed my arms around, acting tough, my cosh whirling above my head, feigning pursuit of my hapless targets as they flip-flopped frantically across the deck and slipped gently starboard-side to freedom.

The sounds and sights of attack all around me are unnerving, it puts me on edge. I feel thwacked on the head by life itself. I have travelled as far as the top of the world but I haven't left my skin or my scars behind. Back in the middle of nowhere, like I was in Norfolk, the only brown person around, with thoughts and memories still teeming in my brain: my abortion, what happened in the doctor's surgery, missing my Dad, my abysmal A-level results, Andrew and I breaking up… my *alone-ness*, which is different from loneliness. The feeling of being an *only-one*.

I never really talked about all this at the time; there was too much going on. Andrew really wanted the baby. His Dad was dying of cancer, and he badly needed some hope to cling on to, and I think perhaps Maddie did too. I was studying for my A-level exams, and I had to keep going. That was why I had made my choice, after all—so that I could go to University. So that I could find *me*.

"You're letting them get avay!" Ivari shouts at me.

"Oh sorry, sorry, I'm not very good at this," I shout back above the din.

I have failed miserably at the fish-thwacking job.

Back on shore, the boys set to work, digging a pit the size of a baby's bath. They light the fire with brushwood while Mr Koskinen wraps the giant of the catch in layers and layers of newspaper like an enormous pass-the-parcel, tips the bundle onto the white-hot embers in the pit—and whoosh!—our supper goes up in flames. A wretched blackened smoking fish-shaped package is all that remains. I am mesmerised, appalled—and expectant.

Fifteen minutes later, the charred layers are peeled back, the fish-skin falls away with the newspaper, to reveal a perfectly-cooked sweet-fleshed smoky white fish beneath, which we eat with our fingers, washed down with bottles of chilled beer from the crate, whilst another fishy parcel is put to the embers. I'm ashamed that I'm not brave enough to kill what I so enjoy devouring; but comforted to see that good things may come out of the ashes, just when you think all is lost. Ivari says these fish—*Silvu* and *Moiku*—can't be found anywhere else in the world apart from this lake in Eastern Finland. Rare fish indeed, in such an idyllic setting.

When Mum suggested I ditch the idea of being an au-pair in France, I was dubious at first. Be adventurous, she said, everyone goes to France. Go somewhere different.

Finland. This place is different, all right. And so am I.

The two eldest Koskinen boys, Pekka and Ivari—a year older and a year younger than me—came to welcome me at Helsinki airport. We spent a few days sightseeing there before coming to Kesalahti. I could see I wasn't quite what they were expecting an English au-pair to look like.

"You're from *England*, not Amerrrica?" As if I had got confused.

Helsinki is very different from multicultural London. I didn't spot another Black or Brown person. A couple of young people held up a clenched fist at me and shouted "Black Power!" and "Free Angela Davis!" I felt like a celebrity—a little bit of stardust from my heroine rubbing off on me. We stopped off at a waterfront café near the harbour, where three boys a little older than me—probably students—were eating at the next table. They glanced over at us several times.

Finally, one of them turned around and leaned across the back of his chair, sporting a *Free Angela Davis* badge on his T-shirt, and said in perfect English, "We're talking about the Black Power movement in your countrrry, and how angrrry we are that people like you are treated so badly—we see it on the news. Here in Finland we love people your colour. We want to support your movement—how do we show our solidarity?"

They thought I was Black American too. I didn't know what to say. I never know what to say, without going into some long story about my disappeared African Dad and my single mother. I disappoint people. I'm a fraud. I can't be what they want me to be, and I don't have the words to tell them who I am.

*****

From Helsinki we travelled by train to Eastern Finland, to the family's log cabins in the forest at the edge of Lake Puruvesi.

"Our family built these houses with vood from the forest," Ivari explains. "My two younger brothers and my Mum and Dad don't speak any Englis at all. You'll be helping my Mum with the chores, and teaching Englis to the younger two. Our family has been running the motel in the village, for over twenty years. Sometimes you might have to help out in the restaurant when it's busy. It's the only place around here that has a licence to sell alcohol within a hundred kilometres, so you can imagine our Saturday night dances are verrry popular—people come from miles around."

From my bedroom window I can see the lake through the pines and birches. Lake Puruvesi is the purest lake in Finland. After a swim, I stop at the shore and scoop up the clear water in my hands and drink it. The resinous tang of the forest is everywhere, indoors and out, permeating my clothes and hair.

I thought, Scandinavia—bound to be cold—but I don't

need all these jumpers I packed. It's the hottest summer on record here. Lying naked on my bed, my body gently marinating in the scent of pine and sweat, I dare not open the windows because of the giant mosquitoes. I am already covered in suppurating bites. In the land of the midnight sun the earth never cools, the light never fades, and nothing sleeps. There is a ceaseless hum of daytime noise all through the night—buzzing insects, birdsong, rustling of small animals. I can't sleep for more than an hour or two at time in this din. I'm afraid of being alone in the dark, but I didn't realise how much we humans rely on it being dark and quiet to get to sleep, and the space between dark and light to track the passing of time. I guess people here are used to it.

I have heard there are giant elks silently stalking these woods. I haven't seen any, but I saw the head of a dead one mounted on a plaque in a restaurant—a hunting trophy. It was bigger than the stags in Richmond Park, antlers like horizontal trees, drooping top lip, doleful eyes staring accusingly down its nose. They seem like mythical creatures but they must be real. I had smoked elk ham for dinner at the Koskinen's restaurant at their motel. A single round slice of dark-pink fine-grained succulent flesh, large as a dinner plate, not a trace of fat, served with pickles and black bread piled up in the centre.

The Koskinens love their forest, they are at home here and they find their way around effortlessly. But I am afraid of the woods, teeming with malevolent spirits—trees whispering behind my back, strange rustling in the bushes, the sudden crack of a branch in the silence, startling me out of my wits. When we go blueberry and mushroom picking in the forest, I always make sure to stick with our group, for fear of getting lost. I have no sense of direction. I habitually go the wrong way, and eventually the wrong path becomes so familiar, I recognise it, so I take it every time.

When I finally drift into fitful sleep I dream of satyrs with elk horns like wings, tapping on my window, speaking to me in Finnish, inviting me to come to the dance, and then getting lost in the forest. I wake suddenly, heart thumping. People say I look happy and lively. I've had to adapt fast to new situations and people, make friends quickly, be ready to try new things, move on after a few months. But inside I am fearful, alert, always prepared for something bad to happen. The world seems a hostile place. I don't always feel safe.

*****

I am trying to teach Mrs Koskinen a few phrases of English every day while we are doing the washing up.

"Yestooday, stooday, stoomorrow."

This is as far as we've got without dissolving into fits of giggles. She is inventing her own hilarious language with its own perfectly consistent grammatical rules. We have plenty of time to laugh. She has a giant dishwasher as large as the lake; in fact, it *is* the lake. We plunge the pots into the shallow water by the shore and wait—but not for long. Within minutes, thousands of tiny silver fish have devoured the remains of our meal, scraping our pots sparkling clean, no need for detergent. Then the fish start on our feet, giving us a free pedicure as we dangle our legs into the water from the jetty, my short brown legs next to Mrs Koskinen's long strong veined ones.

I tried to learn some Finnish this afternoon so I can see how hard it is for her to get her tongue round English. The sounds are like nothing I've ever heard before— strange magical musical notes. It's like no other European language, apart from Hungarian and Siberian, so they say. I'm learning the colours—*punainen* is red, *sininen* is blue; *vihrea*, green, *keltainen*, yellow, *valkoinen*, white, and *musta*, Black. It would be a challenge even for a good linguist. I repeat the words everywhere I go—in the forest collecting mushrooms for the restaurant, down by the lake doing the washing up, by the back-door stacking wood for the fire. I don't know if I'll ever be able to get the hang of it.

On the plus side, I have learnt to swim properly while I've been here. It's easy because the lake is so warm, calm and shallow near the shore. Yesterday Mrs Koskinen came down to the jetty, pointed to me in the water, and said, "You are fis ." I couldn't have felt prouder of both of us. But she still says "Stoomorrow."

*****

We went to the village disco in Kesalahti on Friday. It reminded me of the village discos I used to go to when I lived with the Harleys in Norfolk, when I was fifteen—boys strung out along one side of the hall chatting with their mates, trying to look cool, looking sideways at the girls in little groups laughing and talking about them. But this time I walked in with a group of good-looking Koskinen boys—the three eldest and one of their cousins. I was the only Black girl there, so of course I got stared at, but things soon warmed up. Everyone crowded onto the dance floor eyeing each other up, Aretha Franklin on the turntable, belting out R-E-S-P-E-C-T.

Half an hour or so into the dance, there was a sudden kerfuffle at the entrance. A group of about twenty young people burst into the hall, bringing a surge of energy with them, like an electric charge. Extraordinary-looking people, the women dressed in red, gold and black skirts and headscarves, frilled lace blouses, gold hoop earrings setting off their dark skins, dark eyes and blue-black shining hair. The men looked almost as colourful as the women, in wide-brimmed hats, floral patterned shirts, knee-length leather boots, and embroidered waistcoats.

They brought their own instruments—a violin, two fiddles, and an accordion—and immediately started up impossibly fast music, the women whirling around the room, full skirts twirling from their waists like spinning tops, the sequins on their shawls glinting, their hands weaving above their heads like flamenco dancers, and the men clapping, whooping and stamping in time. The whole effect was breath-taking—fast, furious, frenetic.

I was spellbound. I felt a strange kind of connection with these people, I don't know why. Their music, their clothes, their hair, their dark skins—because they were outsiders, maybe. But it seems I was the only one enjoying the spectacle. There was a lot of muttering and dark looks among the rest of the crowd. The only word I could make out was *Mustalainen*. I asked Ivari what it meant, and he said it means *Blacks*. Of course. *Musta*. Black. I just learnt that word. "Roma. Gypsies!" he continued, by way of explanation. "These people often cause trouble. Fights and stuff. They don't vant them here, they're not velcome—things could get ugly." Sure enough, the next minute, there was a stand-off between the Roma men and some of the disco crowd. It seemed they were being thrown out, though they weren't doing any harm as far as I could see. The music stopped abruptly, and there was a scene—pushing, shoving and shouting. I felt scared and edged towards the back of the hall with the Koskinen boys.

It was over so fast. They left after a few minutes, and the energy and excitement left the hall with them, as suddenly as it had swept in. People drifted back onto the dancefloor, Aretha was back on the turntable. It unsettled me. Not everyone gets Respect. Some kinds of Blacks are more welcome than others.

*****

Mr Koskinen is as short as me, nut-brown and wrinkled from the sun, and bald, so he wears his flat cap in all weathers. His family trekked from Estonia to Finland in 1941 during the winter war—thirteen brothers and sisters making the gruelling journey, struggling for months through the snow. He's very proud of his Estonian roots and gets very upset if anyone mistakes him for a Finn.

His family of refugees settled only a mile from where they eventually established the Russian border. Mr Koskinen took us in the car to show us. There is a clearing in the forest fringed with pine and birch to mark the border, and no fence to keep people out. We played at putting one foot in the USSR and the other foot in Finland, and sang the Beatles' 'Back in the USSR' as loud as we dared. It seemed a strangely dangerous and thrilling thing to do. Although there was nobody in sight, I had the feeling someone could be watching us.

Afterwards we drove towards the Arctic Circle to pick cloudberries for the restaurant table, to make jam and liqueur and decorate fruit salads. Cloudberries grow wild in small bushes about a mile each side of the Arctic Circle, and they resemble giant raspberries. I was determined not to repeat the failure of the fish-thwacking fiasco. I worked hard all afternoon, picking the reddest juiciest cloud-berries to put in my bucket, but the Koskinens were dismayed when they saw the results of my labour. The fruits ripen from red to golden-yellow, so I'd picked all the sour hard unripe ones. How was I to know? I'm useless in the country.

*****

The day before we left for Leningrad and Moscow, there was a letter from Maddie, telling me she'd married an American she met only three weeks ago. She told me that Andrew had also got married. He hadn't known Aisha for more than a few months, surely? When Andrew and I made love for the last time, I knew in his heart he had already left me. The next day he caught the plane for America. He wanted to emigrate, start a new life. Afterwards, Maddie and I went home and watched the moon landing on the TV. Everything so hopelessly far away.

I re-read Maddie's letter again on the coach, written in turquoise ink in her exquisite copper-plate handwriting. I feel deeply jealous at the news that both she and Andrew have found new love. And bereft, remembering the old days—not so long ago in fact—when we three swanned up and down Knightsbridge and the King's Road together, Maddie and me in our hippy hats, and Andrew taking all those glamorous photos of us. I loved them equally. I feel I have lost them both.

It's the end of an era. Maddie and I at opposite ends of the Cold War, either side of the Iron Curtain. I bet the food is better in the States. It's served up lukewarm here— white fish, potatoes, cauliflower and white cabbage on white plates. Strange how unappetising an all-white meal looks, even if you are eating it in a hotel dining room that looks like a ballroom in a Tsar's palace—Baroque on speed.

The Koskinen family have brought suitcases crammed with clothes and goodies to distribute among their extended family still living here in Leningrad. The only way they can smuggle them in is by joining an official tourist party and filling suitcases disguised as holiday luggage. I am their decoy. I can do the tourist circuit whilst the rest of the Koskinens look up their family.

A group of gorgeous young German students join our coach party. They call me '*Lady Chain*' after the Rolling Stones song. Later that night, Franz visits me in my hotel room with a bottle of Vodka. He's like a frisky young colt, gambolling about the room, leaping on and off the bed, dark fringe flopping over startling blue eyes. He pauses momentarily to admire the contrast between my nut-brown skin and the Whiteness of his own—"Kaffee und Sahne!" and then he's off again. "Ya, another act, Lady Chain, another act!"

Sex-starved after nearly six months in a remote Finnish village, covertly admiring the elder Koskinen boys' lean tanned bodies, I'm charmed and excited by Franz's boisterous enthusiasm for love-making. But by three o'clock in the morning, I wish the boy would control his enthusiasm, keep still and just hold me a while, so I can drift off to sleep in his arms. I'm tired, and we have a full day's sightseeing in Leningrad ahead.

The next day we are at Peter the Great's Palace, stunning golden equestrian fountains glinting in the sun. This being Soviet Russia, the guides tell you how many workers it took to build each monument and how many died or were injured during construction. A sobering thought, an important part of the history. No wonder they had a revolution.

I doze off on the way back on the coach, when I should be looking out of the window, drinking in the sights. Not enough sleep last night. Franz is too much of a distraction. But I needed someone's arms around me, some affection. I'm homesick.

Having devoured Dostoevsky on the long coach journey to Leningrad—*Crime and Punishment*, *The Idiot*, *The Brothers Karamazov*, *The Double*—I'm now ploughing through Tolstoy's *War and Peace* to get me in the mood for Moscow. It's exciting to recognise the places in the novels as we drive through the streets. Maya Angelou also loved these Russian writers best. Something about the intensity of the way they convey their oppressive sense of alienation really speaks to Black people.

First impressions of Moscow—it's like stepping onto a film set for a 1930s movie, built for giants. Cars with running-boards, old buses in cream and red, vast city streets lit by elegant gas lamps; magnificent buildings on a monumental scale built by the Tsars; the wide river full of boats and ferries, ornate bridges and gardens. Every square featuring colossal statues to the founding fathers of the revolution—Lenin, Stalin, Marx. Grand hotels with chandeliered interiors built to accommodate thousands of guests, with luxurious ballrooms decorated in gilt and marble.

Yet the people on the streets are clad in drab shabby clothes for the most part, contrasting oddly with the opulent architecture, and we are followed everywhere by a crowd of scrawny kids begging for chewing gum and jeans. They clench their fists sideways and wiggle their thumbs up and down, mystifying us all. Some kind of secret solidarity gesture? The tour guide explains they are asking for retractable biros—the last word in luxury items around here. You can't seem to get much else. GUM in Red Square—the Harrods of Russia—seems desolate and empty compared with Arding and Hobbs in Clapham Junction.

Everything we hear at home gives the impression that Russia is a cold, grey, soulless monolith of a place, and the Russians are ready to drop a bomb on you if you so much as sneeze. But shopping aside, Red Square is so vibrant—all those fairground turrets atop St Basil's cathedral, and the golden onion domes peeping from behind the warm red-and-white walls of the Kremlin—in need of a lick of paint here and there, maybe, but still colourful. I'm in awe, standing for a long moment outside Lenin's tomb. The socialist dream. Such a perfect idea. From each according to her ability, to each according to her need. What could possibly go wrong?

A couple of young African students from Ethiopia are standing beside me in Red Square also admiring Lenin's tomb—Kalid and Jemal. They speak good English and tell me they experience a lot of racism here, people calling them names, refusing to sit with them or serve them, sometimes even being spat at by children. But they're determined to make the most of the opportunity to get an education. I'm shocked by their stories and not a little disappointed, as I had the impression the Russians welcomed Black people. My Grandad told me he'd heard they gave Paul Robeson the warmest reception when he visited. My heart goes out to them, so far from home in a place they find so hostile.

They invite me back to the University with them the next evening to meet some of the other students. I'm excited and terrified about venturing in there. It's a forbidding-looking prison-like building, resembling a layered wedding-cake in the Stalinist architectural style, high up on the hill overlooking the bend in the river. We have to pass through the high arched doorway, with grim armed guards all around us. I have no pass, and I imagine someone my colour will stick out like a sore thumb. I thought we would never get away with it, my heart was pounding, but I was surprised to see a few other African students around, as well as myself and my companions.

Now I have been successfully smuggled in, I am equally terrified I might never get out again. It crosses my mind that I might end up in some Gulag in Siberia. We climb endless flights of stone stairs and finally arrive at a door to one of the small student rooms. As it opens I can see about twenty students, Russian and African, crammed into the tiny space. They have been waiting for us. They stand up and applaud as we walk in. I feel close to tears.

"We are not all Rossians," they correct me. "We are Ukrainians, Armenians, Georgians and from other parts of the USSR." They want to know about the West, what it's really like, the student sit-ins, and the protests of '68, Women's Lib, Black Power, Angela Davis, the Civil Rights Movement, the Beatles, the Stones, the left, right and centre of politics. I tell them about homelessness in the UK, the class divide, the strikes, the recession, the anti-apartheid movement. They seem to be interested in freedom of ideas and information, not in ditching socialism. We talk about the advantages and disadvantages of living under Capitalism and Communism—it seems like utopia to me, to have a guaranteed job, housing and childcare and practically free transport on a metro that looks like the corridors in St Peter's Palace. But I have to admit, the food, the cold and the lack of freedom would be dire.

They have put on a cold buffet of pickled fish, reindeer sausage, sauerkraut, beetroot, black bread, white radish, Russian potato salad, bottles of beer and vodka, laid out on a small table in the corner, far surpassing anything I've eaten since I have been here. I can't imagine what it took for them to put on such a spread at short notice. It's a party atmosphere, lots of laughter and politics, a warm celebration of East-meets-West-meets-Africa. We decide we would all like to live in a world which has the best of all three.

I came back to the hotel woozy from raising a glass of

vodka to toast each new turn in the conversation. It was the vodka that gave me the courage to walk back through the security guards on the way out, star-struck after the most extraordinary night of my life. If university is anything like this at home, I have to get there or die.

*****

It seemed as if the forest was on fire as we drove back into Finland, but it turned out to be flashes of flaming bronze-and-scarlet birch leaves in among the pines, the first signs of autumn.

There are two small log cabin saunas on the beach by the lake, and they are in use most days. I had never had a sauna before I came here, and now I'm addicted. At this time of year, early September, the sauna gets hotter as the lake gets colder. The oldies go in stark naked, flailing their strong suntanned wrinkled bodies with birch twigs. I don't know why they do it; it just blasts me with gusts of stifling, burning hot air, like repeatedly opening an oven door in an already unbearably hot kitchen. I have to cover my hands under my opposite armpits to stop my fingernails from burning. I can only bear the heat for a few seconds at first—it's 140 degrees in there!

My hair is always a problem. If I leave it, it becomes a mass of dried frizz, the texture of the birch twigs they beat themselves with. I tried putting curlers in but the heat was so fierce, it melted the plastic spikes of my rollers into my hair, and Mrs Koskinen spent half an hour carefully cutting them out for me with scissors. My hair is much shorter now and my Afro is ruined—there are no Black hairdressers here like Karl around to rescue it.

All the unmarried young people have to wear swimsuits for modesty in the sauna when it's mixed, but when we are only women together we all go naked—Mrs Koskinen and I, a couple of holidaying cousins and a visiting Aunt, and two of the off-duty waitresses from the restaurant, my brown skin, theirs tanned. I go darker in the sun, I tan very easily. Without clothes, I look as if I am wearing a beige bikini. We race naked into the near-freezing water to cool off after the unbearable heat of the sauna, and back again, many times in quick succession, until finally something miraculous seems to happen. The body somehow gets acclimatised and I can stand completely naked on the jetty, feeling the icy tingle of the first snowflakes on the heat of the blood beneath my skin. I've never felt so alive, elated, aware of every sense, every cell in my body. A fish out of water—but warm-blooded and still breathing.

*****

The midnight sun has been replaced by starstudded nights. Last week it seemed as if a line had been drawn across the sky, one half orange-and-gold sunset, the other half inky-blue, crammed with constellations. I can see why they call it the Milky Way; from here it's like a spilt milkshake. Now, only a week later, the night sky has turned completely dark. There's no moon, so you can see by starlight. I have never seen so many stars—they are illuminating the sky like a bright silvery electric beam.

Some people say that when they look up at a sky full of stars, they feel small. Not me. What a piece of work I am, a small Brown girl at the top of the world, marvelling at a celestial firework display! Lying on my back on the beach by the lake this evening, I could see the shooting stars, silently zip-zip-zip across the sky, scores of them, every second. Mum warned me there would be a spectacular meteor shower visible from here—a rare cosmic event, according to Patrick Moore. Otherwise I would have assumed the sky in Finland was always alive like this at this time of year. How lucky I am to be here to see it, the best view on the planet. I hope it's a good omen. Still no word about my A-level results.

I've booked my passage home from Helsinki, departing on 25 September, going by boat and train through to the Hook of Holland, stopping in Denmark, Sweden and Norway. I'm nervous but excited about travelling on my own. They say there are lots of students going back by boat at this time of year. I should be able to meet up with people my age on the way. I'll be sad to leave. I have had the most unforgettable experience here. But I can't wait to be home.

The day before leaving for Helsinki to catch the boat, I finally receive a letter from Mum saying I have missed

Leicester University's offer of a place by one grade, and she is chasing them up to see if they will still take me. Borderline again, not good enough for anything. I feel sick to my stomach. What am I going to do if I don't get in after all this? I've aimed for the shooting stars... but maybe the whole universe is racing away from me at the speed of light, way beyond my grasp.

Chapter 8

Off, Off, Off!

The Queen's Hall is packed with students craning their necks to get a good view. A stocky red-haired figure climbs the steps onto the stage. It's a disadvantage being so short. I can hardly see a thing at the back. A fair-haired student, about my own height, gives me a hand up onto a chair. We wobble precariously, clutching each other, giggling, trying to find our balance.

"Oim Mary-Ann. You're jost in time."

One of the taller students standing next to us steadies our chair so that we can find our feet.

"Hi everyone, I'm Jake Morgan, President of the students' union. I just want to say one or two words at the start of your university adventure. I 'ope you're going to have a fantastic time 'ere at Leicester, it's a great university with a real sense of community—all the buildings for your lectures and tutorials are here on campus, so you can meet students studying other subjects, get to know lots of different people. And of course, there's Victoria Park right next to us, which is the best place to meet up when the weather gets warmer. Most of you will be in Halls of Residence in your first year, on different sites, where you'll have your own community, and you'll 'ave elected officers there who will make you feel at hoome...

But University is not just about gettin' a degree and drinking in the Hall bar. It's a once-in-a-lifetime chance for you to explore life, start to make sense of the world. I 'ope you will find yourself here in Leicester, fall in love 'ere, but best of all—get involved in your students' union. This building, the Percy Gee, is where everything 'appens. It's where you'll get your political education, share your ideas and your ideals, expand your 'orizons, explore what's going on in the world outside, beyond this campus. Come to our general meetings, get involved in the grants campaign, join the student societies. Get immersed in the whole of what university life has to offer. Get a *whole* education."

I'm mesmerised by Jake's speech. A new world is opening up for me: politics, passion, friendships, love, knowledge, being part of the student movement. Jake up there on the stage, addressing the students in his soft Lancashire lilt with such effortless confidence, receiving the applause—I wish I could do that. I wish I could hold a whole roomful of people's attention, with something to say that's really important—something that will stay with them, make them think, change the way they look at things, right from the start of their student career.

Mary-Ann and I are off to the Freshers' Fair straight

after the speech to join the Anti-Apartheid Society and the Women's Lib Group. Mary-Ann joins the Communist Party of Great Britain Marxist Leninist Party too—the CPGBML—"The one with the longest set of initials!" she announces triumphantly. But I can't decide. Workers' Revolutionary Party? International Socialists? Communists? Labour Students? Young Liberals? A perplexing array of choice, many of them led by earnest spotty middle-class White ex-public schoolboys, pretending to be working class. They are ignorant or ambivalent about my twin passions, Women's Lib and Black Power. I'm going to have to think about it.

Clare Hall is the only all-women's hall, with three hundred residents. I am the only Black girl, apart from Aisha who is mixed Indian. The accommodation is in grand converted Victorian and Georgian family houses, strung out along the length of Elms Road, behind tall hedges, housing fifteen to twenty students in each.

Number thirty-four, white-painted in the Georgian style, with a sweeping gravel driveway, is home to fifteen of us, the first-years sharing twin rooms. I share a spacious attic bedroom with sloping ceiling with my room-mate, Jean. Joan and Jenny are in the identical room across the corridor. People are constantly mixing up our names. Jean Joan Jenny Jane. That old joke of Uncle Bernie's, pretending to forget my name, has followed me all the way to University.

But we four Js could not be more different. My

room-mate Jean is the opposite of the '70s student image. Her look is a throwback to a different era. Fluffy blonde hair, curvy hourglass figure, wafty perfume and a *Happy-Birthday-Mister-President* voice, squidgy as a cotton wool ball. She never goes out without full make-up. Joan, on the other hand, has more than a little of the Goth about her. A slim raven-haired English literature student, she paints her face with matt white foundation, red lips, and heavy black mascara. She has a peculiarly mannered diction, as if she is performing in a play. Jenny Hennigan is a pretty, working-class, brown-haired chemistry student from Sheffield, with an engaging smile that shows off her dimples. She says "ay-up" in every other sentence.

They are all eighteen-year-olds, fresh out of school. I feel very much the senior member of the group. No-one else has been a pregnant teenager, high in a hair-dresser's, cloudberry-picking in the Arctic Circle, or getting frisky with Franz in a Moscow hotel. I doubt any of them know what it's like to be an *only-one* either. I'm disappointed that my housemates don't seem to share my passion for politics. I suspect they think Karl is one of the Marx Brothers. Whereas in fact he was my hairdresser, who taught me the politics of Black hair. But the other three J's soon become my family, an antidote to the macho culture of the students' union.

The Rattray building is the hub of the Hall, housing the refectory, the Common Room, and most importantly, the bar. The Warden, Miss Audrey Grayson, is an eccentric, ex-Girton bluestocking—a diminutive woman with a booming, cut-glass-and-gravel voice. She *actually* wears blue stockings. At her welcome address to our group of around a hundred female Freshers, she informs us that there are to be no fire drills in Hall—"because it would reveal how many young men are living in this all-women Hall." And she confesses that she purposely assigned Jean, Jane, Joan and Jenny shared rooms, to enjoy the ensuing confusion over our names. "And you must all call me Grayson," she concludes. "Not Miss. Or Mrs. Or Mr. Just Grayson." I suspect they must have called each other by their surnames in the 1920s when she was an undergraduate, like the men did, and she has never changed.

My room-mate Jean's Dad runs a successful printing business in Crawley, and for her eighteenth birthday he has gifted her a brand-new bright red soft-top sports car to nip about in at Uni. The male students and lecturers are salivating, falling over themselves to go out on a date with her.

"I always tell them I can't, because I'm collecting you from your women's lib meetings."

"That's really good of you Jean—but you don't have to."

"My pleasure—I say that to get rid of them anyway, I'm not interested. I have a boyfriend back home. We are getting engaged."

Jean has brought lots of giant posters of sunsets with her from her Daddy's printing business, and we paper the walls of our shared attic room with fiery orange-red pictures of sun on water, from floor to ceiling. From the vantage point of my bed, I imagine I am back in Finland in the midnight sun on the lake. We sell the rest of the posters to our friends in Hall and spend the proceeds in the bar drinking bottles of Newcastle Brown—although Jean prefers Babycham—listening to Roxy Music's "*Let's Get Together*," basking in student life.

Mary-Ann drops in to have a drink with us from her self-catering apartment in Mary Gee Houses next door. "Your Jean is a stereotype in stilettos, all to herself," she whispers, while Jean is up at the bar getting in the next round.

It's true, Jean looks as if she could be a spoilt Daddy's girl with nothing between her ears, the epitome of what the Women's Lib movement is fighting against. But in fact, she is one of the kindest, most generous people I have ever met. Sadly, I don't think she'll last out the year. Her mother has just left her father for another man, and Jean's Dad is heartbroken. He is on the phone every night imploring her to come home.

*****

Christina welcomes us to our first consciousness-raising meeting. "This is Mary-Ann and Jane, our new first-years, and this is Penny, Katie and Sylvia who runs the *Our Bodies Ourselves* sessions. They call me Tiggy, short for Christina."

We are trying to get comfortable and look poised on

giant multi-coloured beanbags on the floor—not an easy thing to pull off, when the polystyrene filling keeps moving around. After a while we just sink into the middle and can't get up. A tasselled Indian macramé lampshade hangs from the ceiling, made from coarse brown string and large orange wooden beads, casting criss-cross shadows on the walls. Multi-coloured moth-eaten Indian rugs are strewn about the floor, and there's a poster of a giant clenched fist in the middle of a female symbol on the wall next to the tattered brown velvet curtains. We sip thoughtfully on our mugs of tepid instant coffee, small undissolved globules of powdered milk leaving a thin greasy film floating on the surface.

Tiggy sits forward on her beanbag, round-shouldered, her arms folded across her breasts, half-cradling and half-hiding her chest, blinking rapidly as stray blonde hairs from her fringe fall into her eyes. "Let's talk about conditioning again this week, where we left off last term. We said we would come back to our experiences in early childhood. Who wants to go first?"

"I've been thinking about this. Toys are a big factor in our conditioning," Sylvia begins, stirring her coffee with a biro—Tiggy is out of teaspoons—and taking a sip from her chipped coffee mug. Sylvia is the oldest, doing post-graduate nursing. "For example, you can't build or make anything out of dolls. They just reinforce the idea that girls are essentially passive, maternal, destined to look after everybody else. They try to tell us it's instinctive, but it's drummed into us from a young age that we have to be little angels."

"I always had Barbies for Christmas—then I realised, aged thirteen, that I was going to turn into one," Tiggy agrees. "I've always 'ated my big boobs and my fair wispy hair. People don't take you seriously."

"We didn't have many toys at all, growing up in Belfast," Mary-Ann joins in. "I was one of six kids, four of them boys, Catholic family. We fought over everything we were given. The boys made toy guns out of sticks, coat-hangers, anything they could foind basically. It's a violent male chauvinist society. The gun culture is everywhere, you can't escape it in Narthern Oireland."

"My brother and I always played with my dolls together. It's not a boy or girl thing," Penny volunteers.

I have a sudden unexpected flashback to my pink bedroom in Surbiton, looking at my dolls, Alice and Carol, and then having that out-of-body experience—suddenly transported way up on the ceiling, looking down on myself, feeling isolated and distant. Tears are pricking behind my eyes.

"I *loved* my dolls!" I suddenly blurt out. "I wanted them to look like me, so they could be my family. But they were white and blonde. The only brown dolls I had were Native American Indian dolls in traditional costume, made of hard plastic—they were more for display. You couldn't cuddle them and pretend they were your babies. I'd have settled for any doll that looked like me."

There's an embarrassed silence. I have evidently stopped the conversation in its tracks.

"I don't think any of us have experienced anything like that," says Tiggy tentatively, shaking her head, winding up for the evening.

"A few announcements before we go. We've invited Sheila Rowbotham to come and speak next month on *Women's Liberation and the New Politics*. She's a Marxist Feminist, I've heard her speak in London, what she says about women's oppression in the home is really exciting. We've booked the School of Ed meeting room so hopefully we will get a serious crowd and we won't be bothered too much by the Rugby Club trying to get in and disrupt everything. Oh, and I nearly forgot—if anyone wants to come to the National Women's Liberation Conference, sign up here for the coach, and remember you have to bring a sleeping bag."

I am still shaken by my sudden childhood memory as we collect our coats from the hall.

"You all roight? What brought all that on?" asks Mary-Ann.

*****

Tiggy approaches the microphone, arms folded in front of her as usual, in a vain attempt to hide her chest, blinking rapidly from behind her fringe. The audience immediately erupts before she's even opened her mouth to speak.

"Get yer tits out!"

"Get 'em off!"

"Off! Off! Off!"

Tiggy valiantly attempts to make herself heard above the din, but to no avail. The Rugby Club have scheduled a strip show for Rag Week and the Women's Lib Group want it cancelled, because it objectifies and demeans women. Tiggy doesn't get a chance to be heard above the noise and the heckling, the wolf-whistles and cat-calls, the shouting and stamping. She mouths to the Speaker to "*do something*" but he just bangs his gavel feebly, shrugs his shoulders and grins at her. Only a first-year, I am shocked by this reception. Is this what we have to put up with? No wonder so few women ever speak at union meetings.

After this abject humiliation, the Women's Libbers regroup at lunchtime in the students' union coffee bar in the basement of the Percy Gee Building, at our usual unofficial Women's Lib table in the corner. We are enraged and appalled at the way Tiggy has been treated.

"That was a total fiasco. From now on, we should boycott this place and have all our meetings at my place."

"But that will mean they've won!" I counter. "We have every right to be in the students' union and be heard at general meetings. We've paid our subs like everyone else. We're being treated like second-class citizens here, in our own Union. We *can't* give up without a fight."

"We'll come down here to the Grapple and Strip Show this evening," Mary-Ann suggests. "We'll stage a protest, and just stop it from happening. Direct Action."

"What's a Grapple and Strip anyway?"

"Naked women, mud-wrestling each other."

Not good news. I have a bad feeling there will be a lot of mud-slinging all round tonight.

Sure enough, the protest turns out to be a fiasco too. Only a handful of us turn up with banners and we are stopped at the door by the bouncers, so we have to make do with chanting outside. Tiggy and Mary-Ann manage to sneak in round the side door and try to rush the stage, but the strippers are infuriated that we are trying to ruin their show; they are doing their job and they want to get paid. Moments later, Mary-Ann and Tiggy are ejected ignominiously through the front entrance, visibly shaken, spattered with mud.

"That woman in the G-string told me to fuck off, did you hear?" Tiggy says indignantly. "She called us interfering student bitches and said we were just getting in their way. She said, 'Why should we care about being sex objects if we get paid for it?' I was terrified, she had muscles like this, I tell you…" she cups her hand around her upper arm to demonstrate.

Jean can only fit three of us in her sports car to give us a lift back to Hall, but at least there's room for most of the placards in the boot. She is good-natured about the mud Mary-Ann is smearing on her upholstery, and sympathetic about the failure of our protest.

This Women's Lib stuff is turning out to be much more

complex than I'd thought. It's not the strippers we're fighting. We should be on *their* side, our sisters who have to earn their living taking their clothes off. What a job. It's the sexism in the students' union that's the enemy.

I have an idea.

The next day I march into the Percy Gee to table an emergency motion: *This House is Against Sexism.* In the bar back at Clare Hall, my housemates help me design posters to be displayed all over the campus, advertising the big debate.

The day of the meeting, the Queen's Hall is rapidly filling up. There's going to be a really good turnout. I am about to give the performance of my life and I am literally sick with nerves. My innards are turning to water, and I've got intense griping pains in my abdomen. I'm having an emergency motion all of my own, just before I'm due to go on. I need a toilet, fast. Why did I ever think of doing this? It's a completely different kettle of fish from the annual debate with the Emmanuel Boys' School in Wandsworth. Ten minutes later, as I emerge from the Ladies (to cries of *where the hell have you been, Jane!*), the Queen's Hall has filled to bursting point. Students are spilling out of the doors and into the entrance hall, and more are arriving every moment, so they rig up some speakers in the foyer for the overspill.

In the hall there is uproar. The Rugby Club guys are in their usual position, leaning over the balcony, shaking their fists, leering, jeering, grinning, stomping, and shouting

what they are convinced are witty insults, bellowing *Off,*
Off, Off! even before we are ready to start. Luckily, I am
flat-chested so they are not demanding to see my tits.
Excitement is mounting, along with the cacophony.

Finally, I approach the microphone. Phil has to adjust
it so that it's short enough for my height, prompting more
mayhem and hilarity from the audience. I instruct the
Speaker, who chairs the debates, not to start the clock. I'm
not going to start until there is silence. I plant my feet on
the ground, slightly apart, and face them down, more than
eight hundred students. Finally, the hubbub dies down,
there's a sudden hush, and I begin.

"Sisters, Brothers, Comrades,

I am so glad there is such a big audience for this
momentous debate in the history of our Union. Although
I suspect a lot of you are here—especially the Rugby
Club—because you saw the first three letters of the word
sexism and had a very different idea about the subject of
this debate…"

I look up at the balcony at the Rugby Club and pause
for the audience to laugh and applaud. This is it! They are
listening. They are laughing not *at* me but *with* me; and the
Rugby Club are lapping up all the attention.

"… Let me enlighten you about the meaning of this
word, *sexism*. It's a new word for something that's been
going on for millennia. In this very room last night there
was a stripple and grap—no, I mean a gripple and strap,
no, hang on, a strapple and grip…" I falter, deliberately,

and there is uproar again. I turn to the Speaker once more, shaking my head. "Stop the clock, don't start again until everybody is quiet." But I'm grinning, they are laughing, again, not at me, I hope—but at the joke. I feel totally in control now. "... You see, the words are unspeakable. The *behaviour* is unspeakable!"

"... Sexism means not treating women like human beings but treating them like sex objects. Nothing wrong with that, you may think. But actually, it's all part of the oppression of women, why we don't get a good deal in any direction. We haven't even got equal pay into law yet. We have the intelligence to get to university, but we don't get the kind of jobs, the promotion and opportunities that men have. If we complain, we're just accused of having no sense of humour..."

"... Now you Rugby Club," I jab my finger up at the balcony, "you may argue that you have a right to have strippers in this place because you are members of the Students' Union. Just because it's for charity, you think you can get away with *anything* during rag week. Shame on you! Think about the women here last night, having to earn their living as strippers because they don't have the same career choices as men. Why the hell would you want to take your clothes off for the Rugby Club if you had an alternative at the same rate of pay?" Another roar of approval from the crowd.

"Nobody pays us for streaking across the pitch stark naked!" counters the rugby captain, Chris Marlowe, grinning broadly as his team-mates clap him on the back.

"We'd pay *not* to see your ugly tackle, Mr Marlowe," someone rescues me from the audience, to hoots of laughter, allowing me time to recover.

"You think it's just a bit of fun to shout *Off! Off! Off!* when a woman comes up here to speak? But we have the right to free speech as well. The very presence of strippers in our Union undermines us, it robs us of the confidence to speak out and know we'll be heard…

"Call yourselves revolutionaries, Socialists, rebels? Sexism is the deadly weapon used by our oppressors to divide us. Is our students' union on the side of the oppressors, or do we support Women's Liberation?" Another huge roar goes up from the audience. They know whose side they *ought* to be on, at least. But I haven't finished yet.

"This motion will make sure this kind of thing *never* happens again, that when we women walk in here we will be listened to, taken seriously, treated with respect. We deserve that, every bit as much as you men do. We are fighting for our freedom. Are you with us?

I urge you to vote for this motion and banish sexism from our union—*forever!*"

A sudden surge of energy and elation courses through me as I raise my clenched fist above my head. There's a fraction of a second's pause, and then—yes! Everybody is up on their feet, clapping, shouting, stomping their approval. I realise I have gone well over my three minutes, but the Speaker has lost count, he just shrugs his shoulders. He can see there's no stopping me. The audience is on my side.

"Speeches against? Abstentions?" he asks, when the cacophony has subsided. "No? Thought not, after that performance. Nobody would dare! Okay then, let's go straight to a vote. All those in favour, raise your hands."

All the hands are shooting up. I can see the crowd spilling in through the door and out into the foyer also have their hands raised.

"Carried Nem. Con." Bang goes the gavel, I turn around to Fran, in her usual place on the platform next to the Speaker, taking the minutes. She grins at me and writes "Standing Ovation—loud and sustained applause," in the red Minute book. We won.

Nearly a thousand students turned up for my maiden speech, counting the ones in the foyer outside. The news spreads fast. I am an unexpected celebrity on campus.

"Great speech, Jane!"

"Congrats!"

"Fantastic build—up!"

"Do that at every Students' Union meeting—much better than the boring old crap we usually get!"

"Hey, Jane, you're so short! You look so much taller on stage!"

"Oh, I missed it, I was in the lab!"

I urgently need the toilet again and the downstairs one will be crowded, with everyone pouring out of the Queen's Hall, so I make for the one on the first floor next to the Redfearne bar. Racing along the empty corridor upstairs, from the far end I can see Chris Marlow, my nemesis, Captain of the Rugby Club, six foot five inches tall, fresh-faced, curly auburn hair and freckles, and the wickedest grin. He reminds me of that boy who called me woggie in school dinners. Too late to turn back now. My heart is thumping as I approach him at a gallop.

"I have to admit that was a pretty good speech, *Ms Goldsmith*," he says, grinning, as he stops me with an enormous hand on my shoulder, "even if we did shout *off! off! off!* Just a bit of fun."

In the coffee bar there's an excited buzz around the table where the all-male group of Black students gather. Ray grabs my arm. "See what you just did for the women? Now we want you to do that for Black Students."

But some of my Women's Lib sisters are not so sure this is a victory for the movement. "We shouldn't be talking to these men and demanding entrance to their rotten patriarchal institutions. Bunch of male chauvinist pigs, all of them."

Mr *politics-not-personalities* Martin is likewise unimpressed.

"But are you a *Socialist*, Ms Goldsmith?"

I know this is a trick question. Soul or Blues? Socialist or Feminist? Black or White? One or the Other. You cannot be both. Are you fake or are you for real? Pick a side.

"Of course I'm a Socialist, Mr Martin. And a Feminist too."

Unlike the White boys in their Left caucuses—if in doubt, just quote Marx—Feminists have to speed-read *The Female Eunuch* one week and then start making policy on sexism the next. This is the biggest thing for women since the Suffragettes. We have to make it up as we go along, invent new language, new concepts. It's not been done before. Dale Spender says patriarchy infects the very words we utter—no trivial matter.

Life doesn't get much more exciting than this, and everyone wants a piece of me. I have multiple constituencies which expect big things of me—the Black Students, the Socialists, the Women Students, the Feminists, and the students in Hall. I'm treading new ground with no-one to show me how it's done. How does a Black female student leader go about things? I have no role models.

But I'm on a high for days afterwards. Even my tutors have heard about The Speech. Coming out of the paternoster lift on the sixteenth Floor of the Attenborough Tower, where most of my tutorials are held, I bump into Jack Runcie, my tutor in American Studies.

Paternoster. Our Father. I pray every time I get into it. The Paternoster lift is a conveyor-belt of constantly moving cubicles, up-ended joined-up coffins, open on one side. There are only three such lifts in existence in the whole country. Just my luck that I am required to use one several times a day. I suffer from acute vertigo and I have been terrified of it since my arrival. Most people glide on and off between floors with ease and grace. I always manage to fluff my exit, tumble off and drop all my textbooks, a look of panic on my face. As usual I barely manage to retain my poise.

"I hear you made a great speech on Women's Lib yesterday in the Students' Union, Jane," says Mr Runcie, my tutor, in his trans-Atlantic accent, helping me collect my books from the floor. "Congratulations! You'll be pleased to know we are discussing Sojourner Truth's role in the abolitionist movement in next week's tutorial."

"Then you better change the title of your course, Mr Runcie—'the Black *Man* in America from Slavery to Civil Rights'. Sojourner Truth—ain't she a woman?"

"Very witty, yeah, yeah, her famous speech. Listen— I've been meaning to say to you—I know you are a great success in the Union and it means a lot to you, Jane, but don't let it take over your life. You still need to study hard, you're capable of getting a very good degree."

But this feels like the real deal to me. A political education. Not studying it. *Living* it.

*****

We are all prepared. Hands washed, nails scrubbed, mirrors, towels and torches at the ready. Tiggy's front room is heavy with excitement and expectation. We are sitting on five beanbags, arranged like the petals of a flower, in a circle around the box of Kleenex in the centre.

Sylvia, who is studying Postgrad nursing, opens the

session. "I promise you, this is going to be one of the most exciting experiences of your lives, sisters. A revelation! But first let's get acquainted with our equipment."

She introduces us to Bessie, a plastic model of a female torso from upper thighs to breasts. "I 'borrowed' her from the teaching lab," she explains. "Got to get her back home as soon as they open up tomorrow, before anyone notices she's missing."

She pats Bessie affectionately where her shoulder should be, and then dismantles her innards one by one, handing out the multi-coloured pieces around our circle: uterus, ovaries, fallopian tubes, pointing out the vagina, cervix, labia and clitoris, lovingly describing their form and function.

"Now we are going to see right inside ourselves," she says gravely. "Sadly, a rare privilege, when it should be ours by right. Not many women get to see themselves, own their own bodies. It's really important for our wellbeing to know what looks normal and healthy for our own body, and the range of differences there are in women. But the first thing is, we all have to promise not to talk about it to anyone else—who was here, what went on, right?"

We nod solemnly.

"Good. If the Rugby Club get a hold of this, we're finished. They already think we're a coven of lesbian witches—whether we *are* lesbians or not."

"I think we should take that as a compliment. Nothing wrong with lesbian witches. I've been called a lot worse names than that," I point out.

There's a ripple of laughter. Evidently none of them have been called racist names.

"Only doctors ever see this usually," Sylvia continues. "It's one of the most important places in a woman's body and yet few of us know what it looks like. To see inside yourself. It's metaphorical—spiritual as well as physical. It is truly liberating...

"First, let's get comfortable, prop yourselves up on your bean-bags so you can get a good view, put your towels underneath you, remove the bottom half of your clothes, shine the torch onto the mirror, that's it. If you feel your cervix with your finger first, it feels just like the tip of your nose, right at the back there."

It's awkward at first, holding the mirror and trying to find the spot, but once we get the hang of it, there are gasps of delighted discovery.

She hands us each a transparent plastic speculum and shows us how to insert it with the gel and see right up into the cervix. We examine ourselves and each other one by one.

"Katie has her period, you can see it there, just a trickle—you don't mind, Katie, you okay? And Jane you have had a termination so the opening is a slightly different shape, can you see? And I've had two kids, so mine is bigger."

I feel the emotion welling up inside me, owning my own body, my past, my experience, sharing with my sisters, acknowledging our different shapes and histories, with no judgement, just unconditional acceptance.

Sylvia is right, it is truly liberating. We hug each other, elated and excited about what we have just seen and learned, bonded by a unique shared experience.

"Don't forget, if men want to see themselves, they just look down. We women look up. It's symbolic."

In Jean's car on the way back to Hall, Jean is impressed when Mary-Ann and I enthusiastically regale her with the highlights of our revelatory evening, instantly forgetting our vows of confidentiality.

"You two have such *interesting* adventures!" she exclaims, turning into our drive after dropping Mary-Ann off at the Mary Gee Houses.

"Why don't you join in with us next time, Jean?"

"Me? Too shy. I like to keep that sort of thing private. But I like hearing about it."

*****

Jake Morgan, President of the Students' Union, and Richard Martin from the International Socialists, are gathered at the front of the Queen's Hall near the stage, chatting with the student union officers. It's the first time since my speech that I've attended an event as a student union activist. I feel more confident, important, one of the otherwise all-male gang. We are waiting for our guest speaker Dennis Skinner to arrive, to give a speech about the impending Miners' Strike over pay.

"It all comes down to the class struggle," says Jake.

Flushed with confidence after the success of my speech, I interject: "Yes, that's true Jake, absolutely agree. But I think in the students' movement, we have a real opportunity to look at different forms of oppression and how our students experience it, depending on whether we are women, Black, disabled or working class—or even a mixture. It's really important that we include everyone."

He narrows his eyes, unused to being challenged by a short brown woman in an Afro.

"I fail to see how you have experienced any kind of oppression whatsoever, in *any way*, Jane Goldsmith. I, on the other hand, am working-class."

I'm absolutely taken aback at this public put-down. I have had people shout racist comments at me since my earliest memories. I have been told that I can't do this and I must do that because I'm female. I was born to a disabled single mother on a working-class estate. I am a bastard—I don't even have the legal rights that most people have. He knows *nothing* about me. Why should this turn into a competition anyway? I'm crushed, just when I have plucked up the courage to address him as an equal.

This is not the first time this has happened to me. There's evidently a difference of opinion among people on the Left about the impact of my speech.

"Politics, not personalities, *Ms Goldsmith*," says Richard Martin from the International Socialists.

"You only say that 'cos you've got no personality Mr Martin," I quip, rallying a little after Jake's comments.

"You only say *that* because you've got no politics, Ms Goldsmith."

"I've got the *best* politics—Women's Liberation. Socialism. Anti-racism. Class consciousness."

"Everything is class. Class oppression is the root of all other oppression. Once we have the revolution, everything will be solved."

"Class is central, but there can be no true revolution without Women's Liberation," I come back at him. I have studied Sheila Rowbotham well. "What's the point of a revolution where you go all the way round the circle and end up back in the same place, with White men in charge? Patriarchy is the root of all oppression; before Capitalism we had Feudalism—still rich White men in charge."

My mouth is dry, my heart is thumping against my chest. Girls don't usually talk back. I've rattled him. Now I can banter with the big boys. I am learning to adopt their laconic, sarcastic tone. They learn their repartee from each other, leaving us defenceless. After their endless put-downs every day, I go home and write down what I would have said if I'd been quick enough and brave enough. Now I'm starting to be both. I have been stockpiling smart responses.

"Anyway," Jake comes in again, "you Women's Libbers are just a bunch of middle-class ladies. All you do at your meetings is look up each other's fannies."

Jake has delivered the killer blow. Someone has talked.

Someone has rumbled us.

I haven't thought about how to reply to that one yet. I remember Sylvia saying that men size each other up surreptitiously every day in the urinals without ruining their political and social credibility. When women do the same, to understand our own bodies, it's dismissed with a smutty joke.

*****

In spite of my tussles with the boys I have been elected as one of the official delegates to the National Union of Students conference in Margate. I slip out of the conference session with Calvin McDougal, one of my fellow delegates. Making good our escape from the interminable procedural wrangling, we head for the shellfish stall on the rainy, windswept beach. Chilled to the bone, flirting outrageously, we slurp a dozen luscious plump peak-season oysters laced with lemon juice and pepper.

"Did you know that oysters are an Afro-disiac?" he asks, reaching out to stroke my hair.

"No—don't touch my hair!" I protest, weaving around him, dodging his *double-entendres*.

Calvin is a sailor, on sabbatical from the Royal Navy, doing a Masters in politics. He wears a pale blue cummerbund and black tails when he escorts me to Students' Union receptions. He works on a nuclear submarine, and he tells me interesting anecdotes about life on board, whilst

I accuse him of being the epitome of evil. One day he will have the end of the world on his conscience.

"What does your commanding officer think of you becoming a political activist?"

"It's all part of my education."

"I think you're a spy."

He grabs hold of my wrist, pulls me to him and tucks me under his heavy regulation navy greatcoat, pressing me up against his warm body, shielding me from the wind.

Back in the foyer of the Winter Gardens, Mary-Ann has been looking for me everywhere.

"Where the hell have you *been*? There's an emergency session, two students escaped from Chile. Come on, it's standing room only."

The NUS president, John Randall, is on stage, introducing the Chilean students as we walk in at the back, and we have to stand on tip-toe to see. I spot Trevor Philips at the front. He is the only other Black student I can see in a hall of over a thousand delegates.

Roberto speaks in Spanish, translated by an interpreter.

"On 11 September General Salvador Allende's democratically-elected Government of Popular Unity was overthrown by General Pinochet. I was working with a group of students in a poor Santiago neighbourhood, volunteering in a community clinic, on the night of the coup. The first we heard was the sound of low-flying planes and gunfire, and then we realised bombs were falling on the presidential palace. Then the soldiers appeared, rounding people up and taking them away. I was shot through my left arm as we were arrested.

They took us to the football stadium, which they have turned into a place of blood—four hundred people were shot in only six days, executed by firing squad. They divide people up into groups—Indians, working class, students, and lead them from the changing rooms out into the stadium, twenty at a time. Unspeakable things are being done to the people of Chile: beatings, rape, torture with electric shocks and burns, water-boarding, throwing people against concrete walls head-first; all in the name of defending the country against democracy and socialism, with the full blessing and aid from the United States and Britain."

There is a stunned silence in the hall as Roberto's testimony unfolds. We have all read about Chile, attended solidarity meetings and protest rallies. But hearing the story of a nineteen-year-old student, a similar age to us, who has been through it all, brings home the full horror.

Alejandro takes up the story. "We are the lucky ones. We managed to escape. They are wiping out the leaders of a whole generation of working-class people and students in Chile. We are honoured and proud to have been allowed to address this conference. We are asking the NUS to support the Chile Solidarity Campaign, call upon the Heath Government to welcome refugees from our country here, bring in a total trade embargo against the Pinochet regime…

Aluta Continua!"

The hall erupts into a standing ovation, and then John Randall our President says the message of Chile is that we are all victims of this atrocity. Human rights is everybody's business, the world must react in solidarity and in outrage. After the unanimous vote in favour, I stagger from the conference room with Mary-Ann and out onto the Grand Parade. We hold each other up, weeping hysterically into the wind and rain.

What gets into people—that they turn into monsters? I remember having this same visceral feeling of rage and despair when I first heard about the Holocaust, when I was fourteen. I feel as if I have been punched in the gut.

Later, I go into the ladies' toilets and chuck up all the oysters into the pan.

*****

Back home for the Christmas break, I'm at the Maloneys, babysitting again, earning some money before the University term starts. The Maloneys are a lovely Irish couple, living above their off-license. I had a part-time job as a children's Nanny here whilst studying for my A-levels. Mrs Maloney races up the narrow stairs from the shop, red-faced, looking more flustered than usual.

"Jane, that was your Mum on the telephone—it's your Grandad, he's been taken ill, he's at the hospital, they say all the family needs to get there quick. Here, take this money for a taxi, you go… Leave all that, I'll see to the girls."

Nan, Mum and Dad, Auntie Bel and Cousin Vic are there already, standing in a forlorn and anxious huddle in the corridor. I give Mum a desperate, questioning look. "Heart attack," she whispers hoarsley, hugging me, tears flowing. "Only a matter of time, they say."

Now that I've arrived, the doctor asks us all to come in and say goodbye. Grandad's skin is paper-thin, blue-veined, transparent. As I bend to kiss him, his forehead feels stone cold and damp on my lips. He can't talk, but he smiles faintly and gazes at each of us in turn with red-rimmed watery blue eyes, with a look of complete recognition and serenity.

"We can't hold out much hope, I'm afraid, but we are going to try an emergency tracheotomy, to see if that helps him to breathe," says the Doctor. "It means making a hole in his windpipe, and feeding in a tube, so it's best if you all leave while we do this procedure."

Outside in the corridor again, Mum and Auntie Bel are talking urgently in low whispers, worried about whether this is the right thing—doing something so invasive when there is so little hope. Perhaps better to leave him in peace. But a moment later, as he emerges from the room, I can tell from the Doctor's expression that it's all over.

"So sorry. The silicosis—too much strain on his heart."

I can hear someone howling along the corridor, a strange sound like an animal in agony echoing from far away, drawing gradually nearer. The sound is coming from me. Vic and I cling to each other, distraught. We have both lost a father as well as a Grandfather. One who was always there for us, from the very beginning, even when our fathers abandoned us. Grandad said he wanted to know what was going to happen next. That was the point of being alive. And now he is not here to witness it. It feels as if the bottom has fallen out of our family's world.

If Grandad's premature death is a tragedy, then his funeral is a travesty. The Anglican vicar delivers the service in a thin, soulless, whiny sing-song voice, devoid of feeling or sentiment. A meaningless religious monologue—even though our dear departed Grandad was a staunch atheist all his life. The Reverend is a long-serving minister from our local church, but he evidently never bothered to find out anything about Grandad, despite meeting him several times at family funerals.

He makes not one mention of Grandad's humanist principles, his love of life, his interest in people and politics. His lifelong commitment to trade unionism, Socialism, anti-racism and egalitarianism. His passion for literature, the theatre, and for his amateur painting. His love of sport and horse-riding and Paul Robeson's music. His courage in battling industrial disease, so that he spent his last years literally fighting for every breath. His formidable intelligence, dogmatic personality, his humour and his kindness. So much you could say about the man who was Brother, Father, Uncle and Grandfather to all of us.

How to ruin a noble death.

To the Reverend, Grandad is just another departed soul on the crematorium Paternoster. This vicar has *no idea*, no conception, of what we have lost, what the world has lost. No-one should have to die, especially not Grandad. I am angry and bereft. I howl all the way through the service, louder and louder, the more Grandad isn't mentioned.

I want to scream *Off! Off! Off!*

On the way out, I hide behind Mum and Auntie Bel to avoid having to shake the Reverend's hand. Outside in the frosty air, for once Uncle Bernie doesn't pretend to forget my name. "Chin up, Janie. He was a great man, yer Grandad. He would've seen the funny side." He puts a comforting arm around my shoulder. "We'll go back to the Estate and have a good old piss-up and a sing-song, like the old days. Yer Grandad would approve of that. We'll see 'im off in style."

My mother and me in
the unmarried mothers'
home, 1953

Me and 'Auntie Bel,'
1954

At nursery school,
1954

With my
grandfather and
dolly, 1955

With 'The Harleys' in their back yard, 1956

On my new scooter, 1957

School friends, 1958

In Surbiton with mum and new stepdad, 1961

Student political activist with Afro, 1970s

Volunteering in Tanzania, 1977

First meeting
with my father,
1990

The photo Dad
gave me the
night we met

My father (back row right) with my Grandmother the Queen Mother (seated centre) and his four brothers

Dad visiting us in London Christmas, 1997

My inauguration as Queen Mother, 2009
from L to R: Son, partner and daughter

Carried through the
village in the palanquin,
2009

Chapter 9

Skin Deep

I stroll along the street among short Brown people, blending in a little. Calvin, with his blond hair and white skin, is the one who looks more out of place. We pass colourful vegetable stalls selling green ochra, glossy purple brinjal, orange-brown sweet potato, white mooli, and bunches of dark green curry leaves. The aroma of spices and incense wafts out from the curry emporia, amidst the intermingled sounds of a plethora of languages from the Indian sub-continent—Gujarati, Hindi, Bengali, Punjabi, Urdu, and even a smattering of Swahili from the most recent arrivals, Ugandan Asians. Belgrave Road, Leicester. A little India.

Calvin is going to buy me a sari to wear at the end-of-term reception. Sunita unrolls scores of silk and satin saris, with an expert flourish, onto the green baize platform, each one more sumptuous and vibrant than the last. Finally, I choose one in a magnificent deep green, embellished with silver embroidery, and select a pair of dangly silver filigree earrings to contrast. I feel a million dollars in this gear;

glamorous, floating, regal.

At the University reception, however, the verdict is mixed.

"I didn't know it was fancy dress tonight," says Jake derisively, looking me up and down with that curl of disdain on his lip.

I have been humiliated enough by similar put-downs about the way I dress. This time I have rehearsed my riposte in advance.

"So why have you come all dressed up as a penguin then, Jake?" I ask, pointing to his black suit and bow tie. Without his customary jeans, he looks as incongruous as I do.

Not everyone is so unforgiving about my new look. Pam, the manager of the Students' Union shop, introduces me to her husband, Sam.

"Yes, I know, Pam and Sam, we always get those comments," she laughs. "And no, our children are not called Spam and Ham, before you ask..."

"I do like your sari," says Sam. "That beautiful green is a magnificent contrast with your skin tone."

An unusually precise compliment, but still, I'm flattered—and grateful.

"Sam has taken up painting now he's retired," Pam explains, noticing my slight puzzlement. "Actually, he wants me to ask if you'd be willing to let him paint your portrait."

"Yes, that's right... I'm very keen to do portraits, and

I've never had the chance to paint someone your colour before… It would usually be about six sittings for a portrait, an hour each, at my home studio. I always paint from life, I don't use photos."

"You'll never be able to sit still for a whoole hour," Jake remarks over my shoulder.

In fact, I look forward to the sessions at Sam's studio. I can't talk, can't move an inch. There's plenty of time to sit and think, without interruptions; a welcome change of pace. It gives me time to grieve for Grandad, to think about my family, my childhood.

"He's made you look as if you're about forty, and about six feet tall, very regal and mature!" Mum jokes, viewing the finished artwork when she brings my sister Molly and brother Tom up to Leicester for the Easter holidays. "It will be the opposite of Dorian Gray. You'll grow into it as you get older. Wouldn't it look nice hanging up in our hallway?"

Mum offers to buy the portrait from Sam for £25.00, an arrangement that pleases him greatly. "As long as I can borrow it back for exhibitions," he says.

Now he wants to paint me nude. "A portrait of *your-self*," he says, euphemistically. "Pam doesn't mind. She'll be here all the time, popping in and out with the tea, and we'll turn the gas fire up for you, keep you cosy."

This is an interesting one for a Women's Libber. Am I being objectified? Or made into a work of art? And what's the difference? Is it any different from grapple and strip? And when you're naked, are you really *yourself*, as Sam coyly puts it? I have always had trouble, knowing who my 'Self' is. To be naked in my own skin.

Despite the *Black is Beautiful* movement, the idea is still ingrained in me deep down. Black is ugly—black leg, black mark, black magic, dark deeds; White is beautiful and pure and makes even bad things better—white wedding, white lie, lily-white, white-wash, fair point. I remember Sad Sidney in Norfolk, saying we should stick together because, basically, we were both ugly. I have seen that look of rejection in many a young man's eyes. I am just not the right shade of pretty.

I have hidden my skin colour behind my clothes since childhood—progressing from pink dresses to purple dungarees and green saris. In my teens, my favoured fancy dress costume was to turn up as Al Capone, complete with man's suit, trilby hat and pencil moustache, my brother's plastic machine gun secreted inside my little sister's violin case. I reasoned that if I couldn't be attractive as a woman, I'd go as a man. I looked good and I felt good. But the other fourteen-year-olds in Stafford had no idea how to react to a brown-skinned cross-dresser.

What would it be like, to be a nude model? To take all my clothes off and be completely Brown in front of a White man, nearly three times my age, who would stare at me for long periods and then reflect my image back to me in oils? Would I recognise myself through his gaze? And how many women my colour have I ever seen completely nude? I can't think of any. I've decided to give it a go. Perhaps it would be like seeing my own cervix for the first time. Liberating.

I feel a tingle of nervousness mixed with arousal when he leaves me alone to undress and strike a pose on the couch. I've only taken my clothes off in front of someone else for the usual reasons—to make love, to be medically examined, or because I have a relationship so intimate that I can shed all inhibitions along with my outer garments. This is all new for me. I don't know how to act at first. I'm self-conscious, even a little embarrassed.

But as soon as Sam takes his usual place behind his easel, I feel an unexpected sense of tranquillity, safety, and relaxation I've rarely experienced before. At home in my own body for a change, drifting away, like a meditation… the resinous tang of oil paint infusing the warm air, and the faint sssh, ssshp sound of paint-brush on canvas. I am so unused to silence. It makes the hairs at the back of my neck prickle and my feet fizz. It is a kind of therapy, an antidote to the frenetic pace of the Students' Union. The weather is so hot, we soon dispense with the heating as the weeks go by. The studio window is wide open, letting in a cooling breeze that gently stirs the net curtains.

The gaze I am accustomed to is often one of puzzlement. Who are you, with the brown skin and the fuzzy hair? And those clothes? Where do you fit in? Where do you come from? I mean, *originally*? And yet now I'm here, stark naked, holding myself open to Sam's deep and penetrating gaze. I can't see his work taking shape. I can only see his eyes glancing at me frequently from behind the easel, taking in my whole body, for colour, texture, light, shade and form. The only thing required of me is to be still, which sets my mind completely free.

When Sam starts to fill in the background with colour, we can chat.

"I hear from Pam that you've applied to go to Italy as an au-pair for the summer break."

How to explain it? While my fellow students are back-packing around Europe on Inter-rail, I'll be wiping snotty noses and reading nursery rhymes. I'm inspired by the idea of brilliant, rebellious governesses after reading Jane Eyre. And I'm used to being an outsider in different families. I learn a lot. But au-pairing is not cool, so I keep quiet about it in the Students' Union.

"Well, at least you'll get the chance to see lots of wonderful art there, I expect—you lucky thing! All the old Masters."

"They weren't all men, you know, those painters. My history teacher at school told me about Artemisia Gentileschi, the female Renaissance painter. Mind you, 'Old Mistress' doesn't have the same ring to it as Old Master, does it?" I muse. "I have seen one or two sixteenth-century paintings that feature Black people—usually servants or slaves—but they don't always seem to get the skin tone right, somehow. Even the relatively modern ones don't quite get it—matt black, all one colour—Manet's *Olympia*, for example. I have even seen one painting with a Black boy's hands painted with black palms—by a French artist, I think."

"I never thought of that," Sam peers round the easel at me. "Your skin is beautiful. I hope I am doing it justice. It has so many different tones and colours in it—ochre, red, blue—and it's glossy where it catches the light."

"That's because I oil it every day, otherwise it looks dry. My Caribbean albino hairdresser taught me that trick. When I was a kid I had permanently dry skin—patches of scabs on my back that they told me off for scratching. White people didn't realise Black skin needs moisturising every day—how were they to know? All we had in the 1950s was talc and calamine lotion, which left weird white chalky patches on my skin."

"Well, now it looks lovely. A couple more sessions should do it," says Sam. "We'll have to finish it after the summer, when you're back from Italy, before the light starts fading into Autumn."

*****

Bologna 21ˢᵗ May 1973

Dear Miss Jane,

I have received your application for summer work and I thank you for all news.

We live in Bologna and we will stay here for the first two weeks after you arrive. From here you can easily visit Florence, Milano and Venice by train.

We shall go to spend our holidays as usual, July and August, in Marina Romea where there is a nice and peaceful beach. My mother-in-law will also come with us for beach holiday. Marina Romea is on the Adriatic Sea, very close to Ravenna where you can also visit and see the most beautiful mosaics of Byzantine times. We shall return to Bologna for the last two weeks of your stay here.

Our family has three children. Three boys very alive and active, Giorgio, seven, Alfredo, six, and Emilio, nearly four. The two oldest know very little of English, the youngest does not speak a word. So, I think important for you to know some Italian.

Your work should be to look after them, to play with them and to put in order, possibly in cooperation with the children, their toys, dresses and all the things. While you are staying with them you ought to teach them some English.

The most important thing I want to say is that you have to be part of the family, and not a guest. In other words, your presence has not to increase the house works routine, but I'm sure you can be of some help to me and, in the same time, to enjoy your stay with us here in Italy.

The weekly pocket money will be of 10,000 Italian lire, and you will be so kind as to let me know how you wish to organise your free time. If you want to visit Roma you will have some time on the way home to London at the end of September.

*My husband Fabio and I will be there to meet you at the
station when you arrive in Bologna.*

*I look forwards to hearing from you and send my best
regards to you and your family.*

Yours faithfully Giulietta Olivieri

Via Del Cocomero, Bologna, Italia

Sounds great, but there is a snag. I don't speak a word of
Italian. So far, I only have schoolgirl French, a smattering
of Finnish, and I can do a war chant in Latin. On the plane
I learn the numbers one to ten in Italian and how to say
Buongiorno and a handful of random nouns—*formaggio,
spiaggia, letto,* and of course, I already know *spaghetti* and
pizza. What a gorgeous language! Thank God I remembered a bit of my Latin from school. Some of the words
are still exactly the same as the Romans used. *Venite
ignoramus!* I just hope I can get away with it.

At the au-pair agency headquarters in Milan, Marina
is giving the new au-pairs a few days' orientation before
sending us off to our postings. "And if you want to avoid
unwanted attention from macho men," she advises us,
"walk confidently as if you know where you're going, don't
make eye contact, don't stop or 'esitate, or look at a map."
How are we supposed to achieve this air of purposeful
nonchalance, when it's our first time in Italy, and we look
exactly like tourists, struggling beneath a pile of suitcases?

If only I could attach myself to another single woman... At the station I look around for a woman to latch on to, or even ask for directions, but there aren't any around. The place is full of men, and the men in uniform are especially infuriating. They are the Official Gropers, they see it as a perk of the job.

My desperate efforts to consult my Italian phrasebook are sabotaged by wandering hands and leering looks. I am getting a first-hand experience of Italian machismo. At first, I am flattered by all the attention. I feel like a goddess. But it rapidly gets beyond endurance. Younger men grope, older men rub their hard-ons up against me on the bus. Every small service demands a tariff. Two pats on the bum for helping you into a taxi, arm around the shoulder and squeeze of the breast for pointing out the way, full-blown snog with tongues required for carrying suitcases or escorting me to the telephone box.

By the time I get to Bologna I'm black and blue and pinched all over. I sit on my suitcase and cry. I do not want another hand fondling my breasts or lugging my luggage. Lamentably, my basic Italian phrase book does not list the phrase for *Fuck off and leave me alone!* The problem is, my suitcases are impossibly heavy. I need help to lift them, they are so full of hair dryers and straighteners and Afro-hair products that I am convinced can't be found in Italy.

"Miss Jane?"

Thankfully the Signori Olivieri are there to welcome

me at the ticket barriers. Signora is tall, elegant, attractive, with light brown wavy hair and a warm smile. Her husband is quietly spoken, dark-haired, slightly shorter and older. They are a charming, gracious couple, and both speak excellent English. I take to them at once.

We sweep through the imposing stone portico and up the gravel driveway to their magnificent home—a converted medieval convent, overlooking the hills of Bologna, a stone's throw from the three-mile-long arched walkway leading up to the seventeenth-century basilica of San Luca, at the top of the hill. The place is surrounded by orchards of pomegranate and apricot trees. I feel as if I have stepped back in time.

"We don't own this place," Signora Olivieri explains, seeing the look of wonderment on my face. "We rent it on a long-term basis from the owners."

A huge Alsatian dog bounds up to us as we arrive. I'm terrified of dogs, especially big ones. "Don't worry," Signor Olivieri reassures me, "his name is Lupo, he's very friendly and you will soon get used to him. He will be by your side constantly while you are outside with the children. There are sometimes kidnappings so it's for security." I'm not reassured by any of this, remembering that 'Lupo' is Latin for 'Wolf'. And did he say kidnapping?

In the cool interior, there are tall stained-glass windows and a sweeping curved double staircase leading up to the family bedrooms. In the hallway, two African girls about my age are polishing the exquisite grain on the parquet floor. They look up and smile at me in recognition. Aatifa and Fatimah help me settle into my small cosy bedroom in the basement. It takes three of us to struggle down the narrow twisting staircase with my luggage. I like the idea of sleeping in a room that was once a nun's cell.

Eavesdropping is really difficult in a foreign language. Soon after my arrival, Signora is entertaining friends for morning coffee in the vast sitting room, its magnificent windows dressed with heavy brocade drapes, exquisite fringed pelmets, ornate lamps and chandeliers, elegant antique occasional tables and Persian rugs. Her guests remark upon how many Black and Brown people she has in the house—even her au-pair from England! The Signora tilts her head to one side, considers a moment, and says she loves lots of different people in her house from all over the world. I think I heard it right. It's maddening. Some of the words I can't make out, but when I get back to my room I consult my dictionary and piece it together.

At the dinner table I teach the children to ask for 'some water please' in English, though the boys are reluctant to respond and would rather I spoke Italian instead. I sit with the family and the children for meals, though the rest of the staff eat in the kitchen. I can hear them laughing and enjoying themselves over their meal after we have eaten. It is Friday evening so we are celebrating Kiddush. The branched candlestick is lit, and there is a chorus of *Baruch atah Adonai* from the family round the table, and then there's a special cake for dessert. It has a strange synchronicity, a Jewish family living in a converted convent.

Cutting the cake and serving everyone in turn, the Signora says, "I thought you were Jewish when I picked you out from the list of possible candidates they sent me from the agency. In the black-and-white photo, I was looking at your hair and your colouring, and also your name, Goldsmit, that's a common surname for English Jews isn't it?" I nod. It's not the first time I've been mistaken for Jewish. "And then, when you put your religion as 'none'— it made me think you must be a non-practising Jew." We all laugh. Even without a photograph, people are apt to form preconceptions. People do a double-take when they see me. My name doesn't match my skin.

"My father is African, and my Mum is British," I attempt to explain.

"How wonderful," Signora exclaims, "Has your father taken you to Africa?"

I still don't know how to reply to these kinds of questions. *No, I have never been to Africa, I am not planning to go there, I don't know my father, I have never met him, he has never contacted me, I don't know anything about my African family, I have never tried to find him, no, I don't know what he looks like…*

I should be used to this by now, but I always feel as if I am raking about in the bottom of a vast empty barrel, trying desperately to grasp the words to describe what is not there. She means the questions kindly, and I can feel she is genuinely interested in me. I don't want to disappoint her by not being able to answer. I would really like to have a conversation with people about who I am, and where I come from, instead of "don't know, pass." It's such an ordinary conversation, people take it for granted, but I can't do it, I don't have the information. I feel inadequate somehow. I fall at the first hurdle, and then I feel I have to spend the rest of the time making up for it.

I need to brush up my Italian fast. When I put the kids to bed and turn out the lights, to plaintive cries of "*E buio!*"—"It's dark!" I surreptitiously borrow their books. I start with the alphabet picture book—a picture of a horse with the word '*Cavallo*' underneath, a picture of a dog with '*Cano*' underneath. Easy enough. Now I'm on to my first reader.

The littlest one, Emilio, takes particular exception to my borrowing his books, even though I promise faithfully to bring them back the next morning. I bribe the boys for a library loan by singing English nursery rhymes to them when I tuck them in to sleep at night—avoiding 'Baa Baa Black Sheep'—always hated that one as a child. There is no equivalent to nursery rhymes in Italian, and the boys really love them—the music, the language, the rhythm and the tune—even though they have no idea what the words mean. Come to think of it, the meaning of some of these nursery rhymes is quite obscure even for English-speaking children—mostly political satire from a bygone era, not written for children at all. So I guess the meaning doesn't really matter.

Signora gives me Italian lessons for half an hour or so every day. She's not impressed with my level of fluency and she can see I need the practice. Finally, she says to me, "I think your Italian has really improved in the last few weeks. Your professors will be very pleased with you at the university."

I feel brave enough now to confess that I'm not actually studying Italian at university, as she had assumed. "I do history, but I'm sure Italian will come in handy, especially for the ancient history tutorials. And I love the language, it's like opera."

She's taken aback. "Oh, I just thought that's because of bad teaching in England—they only teach you how to read Italian, and not to speak it! Well, in that case, you have done even better than I thought, if you came with so little Italiano."

Even though I've been found out, there seem to be no hard feelings. We have really bonded. When the kids are in bed, Giulietta likes to practise her English conversation, so we talk about all sorts of things—Italian politics, history and culture, the Risorgimento, women's liberation, racism, Judaism.

"We would love you to come back and stay with us again next year, and continue your Italian lessons," she smiles. "And the children love your nursery rhymes—such a good way for them to learn English."

Definitely. I'll be back.

Tonight, we're taking the boys on a family outing to the cinema to see '*Willy Wonka and the Chocolate Factory*'—the dubbed version—which will be good for my language skills.

After the film, we take a *passaggiata*, to buy ice creams. The streets are full of families and lovers going for a midnight stroll through the mediaeval colonnades in downtown Bologna, before the summer exodus. We amble along the covered walkways past the fancy shops selling upmarket clothes and local delicacies—great hams hanging from the ceiling above magnificent displays of Parmesan cheese, local wines, and bottles of truffle oils. Emilio is riding high on Papa's shoulders. Giorgio and Alfredo are weaving in and out of our family group and then racing off ahead through the crowds. Refreshed from their afternoon siesta and after a good dinner, all the kids on the street are excitable and full of beans.

When we finally get back to the car, about midnight, there is consternation. Someone has scraped a great gouge along the side of the Mercedes from boot to bonnet. Fabio and Giulietta are having an intense discussion about whether to call the police, but in the end decide against it. I asked Giulietta why. She says the Carabinieri have a negative attitude towards Jews. "It's a waste of time calling them, I doubt they would do anything about it, we will just get the car repaired," she says, shrugging her shoulders. I'm shocked that these attitudes are still prevalent so long after the war. I feel for them. They may be well-off but they are liberal, kind, welcoming, intelligent people. Why

should they be subjected to this?
*****

Marina Romea is a pretty seaside village on the Adriatic where the Olivieris take their summer holidays for two months every year. The kids are pestering me to play 'What's the Time Mister Wolf?' again in the garden, but it's siesta time and they are due for their nap. I have a couple of hours off in the afternoons while everyone is snoozing, and this afternoon, having had a lie-down for half an hour after lunch, I'm keen to try out the bike. I haven't ridden a bike in years, and there are cars and pedestrians everywhere, some slowing down to stare at me. I'm wobbling down the sun-baked avenue concentrating hard, trying not to fall off. I take a short-cut through the market, soaking up the hot sun's rays on my arms and the back of my neck, enjoying the vibrant colours of holidaymakers' paraphernalia displayed in the sunshine. Flip-flops, sun hats, stripy parasols, sunglasses, sun-cream, neon-pink rubber rings and water wings, and those skimpy halter-neck summer tops in rainbow colours, flimsy as two hankies tied together with matching string. Everywhere the lilting sounds of Italian, rising and falling like a never-ending operetta.

I have just under an hour before I need to be back at the house to get the children bathed and clear up the toys before dinner, so I'm going to savour every minute of this. There's a stall selling home-made ice-creams in mouth-watering flavours—peach, pear, tutti fruiti, pistachio, chocolate crunch, caramel crisp. I've got a double scoop of today's special, melon and apricot, made with chunks of fresh fruit. Too late, I discover it's almost impossible to wheel a bike through the throng with one hand, and at the same time lick furiously at my ice cream before it melts in the heat and runs in sticky rivulets down my wrist.

"Sista, sista!"

A voice, high-pitched, sing-song, excited—sounds almost African. Suddenly there's a beautiful young chestnut-skinned woman running up behind me, breathless with excitement, spinning me around, practically lifting me off my feet, runny ice cream and all.

"*Eritrea, Eritrea!*" followed by a torrent of words I don't understand. Finally, she calms down, and I can see the confusion on her face: "Eritrea! Eritrea?"

I shake my head, "No, English."

She looks disappointed, taken aback, and reverts again into broken Italian.

"*Mi chiama Tikri. Tu?*"

"*Mi chiama Jane.*"

"*Mia bella nuova amica!*" she says, and she clasps me to her chest again.

We link arms and walk down the Boulevard together, excited and delighted, steering the bike between us, communicating in a mixture of gestures and laughter, in two different languages.

"*Eritrea,*" Tikri repeats, this time pointing to herself.

"Work in Italian family with bambini."

I nod frantically, "Me too!"

"War Eritrea—Ethiopia—very bad—guns." Tikri shakes her head, pointing two fingers to her temple, her thumb an imaginary trigger. I try and convey sympathy through frowns and gestures. We amble down the main boulevard by the forest fringing the sea where the air is suffused with the sharp scent of pine and seaweed.

We jump out of our skins at the sudden screeching of a car full of young Italian men, bare-chested and bronzed. They lean out of the open windows and the sunroof, shouting and tooting the horn. "Che belle negresse! Che magnifica tinta!" We giggle, and then shrug at the attention we are receiving.

We chain up my bike to the railings near the bus stop, and saunter arm in arm down the shady path through the pines to the beach. We do this every afternoon during siesta time until finally we're beginning to understand each other. She tries to tell me about her experience of the war in Eritrea, but it's hard to follow. Signora Olivieri told me that many Eritrean girls are sent to Italy as house-maids and nannies to escape the war.

"Miss my family, miss my mama." Tikri's eyes fill with tears. "Where *you* from?" she asks me.

This is going to be complicated.

"London," I reply tentatively. I can see the complete incomprehension in her eyes. Impossible to explain in English, let alone my limited Italian.

"My friends!" Tikri exclaims, and soon we are running across the beach to join two more Eritrean girls, Negisti and Mariam. Mariam is educated and speaks good English, so she acts as our translator.

"In Eritrea we are fighting a war for independence from Ethiopia," she explains, "The Italians have been in our country for more than a hundred years, and then Mussolini invaded during the second world war, so that's why so many Eritreans speak Italian. Our families send us here to keep us out of danger, and find work, because we know the language."

She tells me that in Eritrea, most girls are never taught to swim, even though they have lots of beaches by the Red Sea. But it is easy to float in the Adriatic because it is warm and salty, and we are soon lying on our backs gently floating, chatting, forgetting about the time.

"You study history? They talk about the ancient civilisations here in Italy," Mariam tells me. "But in Eritrea we have ancient kingdoms centuries older—more than 3,000 years old, but no-one has heard about them here, they do not want to believe that there were many civilisations in Africa, long before the White man came."

We gradually get used to the excited shouts of 'Le Belle Negresse!' that follow us wherever we go, cars slowing down to hoot, young men and boys leaning out of vans and lorries on the road as we pass, sunbathers lifting their sunglasses in astonishment as four Black girls stroll along the beach together arm-in-arm. After a few weeks in the sun my skin is as dark as theirs. I am thrilled to be part of this group, Tikri, Mariam, Negisti and Jane. But Jane doesn't sound right, so I tell them my African name is Kumba—like the little girl I saw on Clapham Common when I was a kid, barely four years old.

I'm not alone now, I have friends with whom I can share the stares we get, laugh off the comments, hurl back the occasional Italian swear-word we have learned from Mariam. My very first African girlfriends, and I have come all the way to Italy to find them. Sadly, their country is at war with the homeland of the two Ethiopians I met in Moscow.

When I get back to the Olivieris', Maria is sculpting the evening meal in the kitchen—tiny delicate ravioli stuffed with ricotta cheese and spinach, made from handmade pasta using a special intricate cutter, so the edges form a frill as if they have been cut out with pinking shears.

"The Signora likes you because you come from England," Maria smiles. "She was a babysitter, the Signora, an au-pair, just like you, in Londra. She wasn't born a Jew, she was born a Catholic. She ran away to England, when she was only nineteen, around the same age as you... How old are you?"

"I was twenty this March."

"There you are then, not much younger than you, she was, a babysitter in London. She studied English and did a secretarial course, and she got a job in the office of a big oil company."

Maria pauses to wipe her forehead with the back of her hand and sweep back a stray curl of light brown hair that escapes from under her headscarf.

"...The boss, the Signor, of course he falls in love with her, because she is a young and beautiful, and intelligent. So he wants to marry her and bring her back to Italia, but his *Famiglia* are not so 'appy because she is a Catholic girl... in their religion, it all comes down through the mother, they all want a their sons to marry Jewish girls. *La Nonna* agrees, if only the Signora will agree to change her religion. So now, she knows a lot about it. She had to study hard."

So that explains the openness in this family, their willingness to see beyond the stereotypes and be genuinely welcoming to people and ideas. Giulietta understands what it's like to be an outsider in the family too. What it means to have to prove yourself.

Maria is probably in her mid-twenties herself—she has a young child at home. She is a big woman, the weather is sweltering, and she spends many hours in the kitchen cooking over a hot stove. She continues her delicate work with the ravioli whilst I consult my dictionary so that I can keep up with the story.

"I love your cooking!" I say to her in my best Italian.

"I was born here in Emilia Romagna, we have the very best food in Italy—*parmigiano*, vinegar from Modena, *prosciutto di Parma*—so of course you like my food, *e Buonissimo!*"

La Nonna, Fabio's mother, is staying with us for the holidays at Marina Romea. She's a tiny grey-haired woman, serious and reflective as if she has experienced traumas in life she couldn't possibly explain. She invites me to take a walk with her down to the valley in the evening before it gets dark. She doesn't speak a word of English, so I take my dictionary. We set off at sunset, following the forest path, which eventually opens out onto a vast area of brackish water, sandflats and fishermen's huts, with a fringe of pine forest beyond. The fishermen's huts are half the size of a small box room, with a small jetty jutting out into the water for line-fishing and launching small boats.

The tide is low when we arrive, the sun is skimming the horizon. It's peaceful and magical in the orange twilight. She points to the fishermen's huts and says, in Italian, "During the war I was hiding in one of those huts for three years, with three children under five. We could not make a sound in case we were discovered. The only way we survived is because every two days, one of the fishermen came over and brought us bread." I'm shocked by her story. How can people survive under such unspeakable conditions, with tiny children? I'm amazed and humbled at the resilience of the human spirit; *her* spirit.

Signor is also telling me his memories of the war and his childhood experiences of Fascism under Mussolini, this time in English, so it is easier to follow. "All dictatorships have a weakness, you just have to find it," he explains. "In the case of the Fascists in Italy, that weakness is corruption. The Fascisti wrote everything down, they had systems for everything. But at the same time, individuals were greedy, so they could be bribed, corrupted…"

He tells me that in Bologna, where his family lived, they were rounding up Jews to take them to the concentration camps. His father managed to rescue the family from the fisherman's hut where they were hiding. "E was a businessman, he ran the petrol storage station near here, which I'm running now. I took over the management from him after the war. He was able to bribe the German soldiers to take our familia to Roma, where there were friends who could help us. But when we finally arrived there, the soldiers lined my whole family up against a wall…"

They were going to shoot the whole family. He was only nine years old at the time. He pauses and swallows hard. It is difficult for him to continue. My heart is in my mouth, I don't know what to say. The thought of the moment he is describing, and the effect it would have on such a young child, is horrifying.

"My father persuaded them not to shoot. The war was over. Germany had lost. He had heard on the BBC that the Allies were coming. They were going to march into Roma within twenty-four hours. He bribed the soldiers to go while they still had the chance…

The next day, sure enough, the Allied troops marched into Rome.

"I felt the whole world was coming to save us, people

of every colour, Brown, Black and White. It was a multi-cultural force. I thought it was a new dawn. The world united. And on that day at least, I believe it was."

I feel so moved by his story, by the whole family's story. The fact that people can live through that kind of trauma astounds me, it puts life into perspective. But what lifts my spirits most is hearing that the whole world was together for once, Black, Brown and White, in liberating people from Fascist dictatorship. That aspect is never mentioned. It has been airbrushed out of history—we always see White soldiers liberating a White Europe.

"That bribe saved my life," says Mr Olivieri finally. "But after the war I thought, there must be another way of doing things. I vowed never to engage in corruption in my own business. That's often difficult to do in Italy even today, when corruption is part of the system and the culture. But I have to live differently. I made a promise to myself. I have to stand up for what I believe in."

*****

It's my evening out, the sun is going down over the horizon, and we're sitting in a bar on the beach with a few of the local young people. My Eritrean sisters are sadly not allowed out after dark, but the Olivieris are much more liberal, and I have complete freedom after work. The waiter presents us with a giant cocktail—striped bands of different rainbow-coloured liquids served up in a glass bowl as big as a tea tray, spiked with eight brightly coloured straws. The liquor is strong, there's a babble of Italian going on. I'm enjoying myself, feeling the warm breeze from the sea on my bare shoulders, trying to keep up with the conversation. Eduardo, the boy next to me, knows some English. "We like people your colour in Italy—for us, you are very beautiful. It's the Jews we don't like. They are full of shit and they are taking over Italy."

I am consumed with confusion and rage that he assumes I should be flattered by what he says. My lovely Olivieri family picked me because they thought I was Jewish. But this man is telling me he likes me because I'm *not* Jewish. The Olivieri's have truly inspired me and filled me with admiration for their courage.

Eduardo has jet black hair, olive skin and wears an earring. His looks suddenly bring back memories of my experience of the 'Gypsies' in Finland. The Finns say how much they appreciate my difference, and then they call 'Gypsies' 'Blacks'—*Mustalainen*—and drive them out of the local dance. In Finland, maybe Eduardo would be considered 'Black'. People aren't aware of their own contradictions, and they're not aware of how it reflects on me. I'm still *'the Other'*, just not *their* 'Other'. I'm the other Other.

Thank God, Roberto rescues me from Eduardo. Brown-haired, good-looking, moustachioed, a few years older than me, I've been eyeing Roberto up for a while. He's charming, mature and much more liberal in his thinking. I often see him in the evenings down at the beach, after he has finished work at the travel agency in Ravenna. I persuaded him to teach me some Italian phrases. He's very knowledgeable about Italian history, politics and culture, and I'm sure he's flirting with me. Since Calvin went back to the navy, I'm a free woman.

Roberto invites me to join him on a day out to San Marino on Saturday. It's only a few miles away, but it's a separate country in the middle of Italy.

"I think you will like it, it's one of the smallest countries in the world, with lots of mountains," he explains, "and we'll see the Guard of the Rock—those soldiers with the red-and-white headdresses."

I have the whole day off on Saturday. I don't have to be back till late. Signora says she doesn't want to give me a key, but she doesn't mind what time I ring the bell, even if it's the early hours of the morning. She would rather get out of bed and let me in herself, so that she knows I am home safe and sound.

*****

Boiling sun, cooling breeze, racing along the coast road in Roberto's open-topped car, seat tilted back, listening to Boz Scagg's *Lido* on the radio. I hoist my orange-and-white patterned maxi-skirt above my knees, feeling the hot sun burn my legs. Roberto smiles at me and puts a warm strong hand on my upper thigh, shooting electric sparks through my body.

We spend the rest of the day on foreplay, visiting medieval castles, watching quaint strutting soldiers in lampshade hats. We lunch on garlic langoustine, licked and sucked between salty, sticky, buttery fingers. The vocabulary of the nursery is exchanged for the language of *amore*—just for today. This beats "Old MacDonald Had a Farm." If only the Students' Union could see me now. The IS and the CP and the CPBML and the WRP. I long to taste *all* of life, buckets full of it—politics and pain, liberation and revolution, heat and romance. Shed my masks and try on others for size, delight in being unpredictable, true to no stereotype, one-of-a-kind.

On the way back to Marina Romea, we park the car and go down to the deserted beach to watch the sunset, the horizon ablaze with gold and crimson. As darkness falls, the sky is crammed with stars. We shed our clothes among the pine trees and race naked across the cool soft sand, laughing with delight and exhilaration.

As we plunge into the warm shallow water, something happens that stops me in my tracks. I am too afraid to go any further. Our pathway glitters with a million tiny green-gold shining specks, giving off an eerie light with every move we make.

"It's called sea-sparkle, it won't harma you, it's beautiful, it only shines when you move," Roberto reassures me. "This doesn't happen very often—we are so lucky! I have only seen this a couple of times before in my life. It is a miracle of nature, just for us."

He takes my hand and leads me deeper into the water, and then we lie on our backs, look up at the stars, wafting our arms gently back and forth, glittering algae cascading between our fingers, a whole constellation reflected in the inky waters. Memories of Finland drift through my head. Lying naked on the beach by the lake after the heat of the sauna, watching the shooting stars, awakening an intense longing for something I can't explain, something missing, beyond reach.

This man, Roberto, embraces me as a person, not a mistaken identity. For once I don't have to be anything, just go with the flow. He pulls me to him and kisses me hard on the mouth, pricking my top lip with his moustache. I wrap my legs around his waist. This is surely the most beautiful way to make love, on an alien blue-green phosphorescent planet, sea sparkle pulsing with every move we make. But as we pull away from each other, the salty sparkly water gushes up between my legs, and I'm in agony. I race out of the sea clutching my nether regions, screaming with pain. Soon we are both hopping around on the shore, full of sand and fury, legs akimbo, like a pair of electrocuted frogs.

Our romantic assignation has suddenly taken a disastrous turn. How the best-planned lays can go wrong.

"It's okay for boys, external plumbing," I yell at him.

"It's sore a for me too! And I forgotta to bring the towel… " He is sympathetic and apologetic. "Next time, we make love at my place in Ravenna, *Tesoro*. I must take you home now, it's not safe to be on the beach at night. A couple were discovered in the woods a few weeks ago not far from 'ere—I read about it in the paper—the man was murdered and the girl… well, even worse happened to her…"

Now he tells me. I don't know why men think rape is worse than being murdered. The whole episode sounds utterly horrific. But it's high time to go home anyway, sit in a bath of warm water, rinse off the salt and soothe my still-smarting sensitive spots.

We managed to escape being murdered and raped on the beach, and my vagina got pickled in green algae and sea-salt. But it was worth it. Him in me, lips on mine, soul on fire, the world tipped upside down, the stars spilled into the velvety-black Adriatic.

"Ma cosa successo, alora? Tutti bagnati!" Signora exclaims, opening the front door. "What happened to you? You're all wet!"

*****

Upon my return to Leicester in September, Sam the artist is far from pleased.

"You look as if you're wearing a beige bikini! The skin on your legs and arms—and your face!—you're at least three shades darker!"

"I get suntanned, like White people do, only faster and deeper—lots of melanin in my skin, tans easily."

"Oh dear, I suppose I just never thought of that. How long does it take to fade?"

"A few weeks, I guess."

Sam is aghast. *A few weeks!* But the light starts to fade at this time of year... I'll never finish it at this rate..."

"Sorry Sam. I did enjoy the Italian art, though."

Chapter 10
Women's Trouble

"Nurse, that kid is cryin', it sounds like she needs help."

"Leave 'er be, she knows what she's done," the nurse replies.

I'm lying on my side in the hospital bed, head under the covers, knees drawn up to my abdomen, sobbing my heart out. My body is wracked with pain, searing through my insides up to my ribs. I feel ashamed, despairing, wrung out, torn apart.

After a while, my sobbing subsides to a whimper, my breath still catching every now and then at the back of my throat, like an exhausted two-year-old post-meltdown. Random scenes float in and out of my mind unbidden, merging into each other... that red-haired boy calling me woggie at school dinners; dancing with Georgie Blaine at the party in Stafford; struggling through a snowdrift in Norfolk; sipping "ponch" in the hairdresser's on Lavender Hill; thwacking fish in Finland; letting my hands drift through a sea of glittering algae in Italy. Auntie Bel telling Mum and Dad I'm pregnant at just seventeen, while I hide my head under the bedcovers…

I am dimly aware that there are people around my bed, but I can't face anyone—not more doctors and nurses. Finally, I lift my face above the sheet, relieved to see two women, clad in hospital gowns, looking down at me with a mixture of concern and compassion.

"We don't care what you dun love, you don't deserve to be talked to like that," says a friendly voice, patting my hand. "You're all right, we're your friends anyway… My name's Irene Wigston—they call me Wiggie—and this 'ere is Samantha. That's Ariadne in the bed next to you. And Martha's over there opposite, the bed in the corner— she's still knocked out with the anaesthetic, just had a hysterectomy, sleeps all the time…"

I am so moved that Irene—Wiggie—and Samantha have actually got out of bed to come and comfort me, both still attached to the drips they have wheeled over with them. Ariadne lifts her head slightly from the pillow to smile at me faintly and wave.

Next morning, the consultant is doing his rounds. He starts with Samantha, blonde-haired with a strong jawline and aquiline nose. Her husband is there with her to hear his verdict. The couple sound very posh. There is much conspiratorial nudging and winking between the consult-ant and the husband about the joys of trying even harder for a baby, now that Samantha has only one fallopian tube working after an ectopic pregnancy.

The consultant moves to Wiggie in the bed opposite.

"Doc, this op has given me the most terrible painful wind. I'm in agony 'ere. Is there anything you can do for me?"

"I'm afraid you'll have to put up with it for a while, Mrs Wigston. It's an unfortunate side effect, but it will gradually subside. As I explained, it's part of the procedure. We inflate the area internally so we can perform the operation."

Now it's my turn.

"So, you collapsed in the Students' Union, did you? One of those student activists, eh?"

The nurse draws the curtains around my bed, but it is too painful for the doctor to examine me internally. I cry out in agony, and he gives up.

"Well, you've contracted a pelvic infection as a result of your termination, and I see from your notes it's your second abortion. You'll find it very difficult to conceive again. Your fallopian tubes are likely to be permanently blocked with scar tissue this time around. Perhaps that'll be just as well. It will solve your problem, put paid to all your activities," he admonishes me.

I feel utterly crushed by what he says. I really do want babies when the time is right. It feels like a devastating blow, a life sentence, I can't even begin to think what it means for me. At the same time, I am struck by the contradiction. If it's my so-called 'promiscuity' he wants to cure, surely my being freed from the threat of pregnancy may do the opposite.

"I notice her skin is abnormally dry, doctor. There's a

white bloom all over 'er body, like talcum powder."

"I just haven't oiled it today, I was in too much pain, doctor. It's normal for Black skin," I interject.

The doctor perfunctorily inspects my arms, legs and the back of my hands. "Let's treat it with aqueous cream and keep an eye on it," he says to the nurse, ignoring my explanation, and removing his gloves.

A few months ago, I was an artist's muse, posing on the couch, naked, Brown and beautiful, being painted in oils. That's when I fell in love with my own skin colour for the first time—tones of caramel, hints of ochre, red and blue. Now I'm a medical anomaly, in need of skin treatment and lectures about my lifestyle.

The Consultant moves to Ariadne's bed.

"I'm so sorry you've lost the baby, Miss Kostopoulos. We did all we could to save it. But we will work hard in the next few days to get you fixed up and well enough to go back to your friends."

After the ward round, we swap notes, all of us women in different sorts of pain, flat on our backs, or curled up on our sides, sharing our indignation at being talked down to by a male Consultant full of his own sense of importance and superiority, pronouncing on our way of life and our futures without any idea of what we want or feel.

"I s'pose we should be grateful. Our lives in their 'ands—and don't they know it!" Wiggie observes wryly.

"I don't know why all the doctors and nurses think I'm sorry about losing the baby, given my situation," says

Ariadne, in her strong Greek accent.

"How do you mean, love?" asks Wiggie.

"Well, I didn't want this pregnancy. I'm studying law at Athens polytechnic, I'm a student activist like Jane. Have you heard about the regime of the Colonels? They seized power six years ago, causing terrrible sufferrring. The Colonels are supported by your Government, and the US Government as well. They thought the Russians would invade if they didn't support Papadopoulos. But he's an evil, vicious dictator," she says with passion. "He rounded up all the opposition, took away our rights, forced students to join the army, put thousands in prison—ordinary innocent people—and lots of Greeks have fled the country…

"It's terrrible, it's no life. We can't hold meetings or have a free press. When the students protested, the Government drove a tank through the gates of the Polytechnic. They sent the police in, and lots of us were arrrested, and they beat us, tortured us, did unspeakable things. They made me stand in a room for hours and hours on my own, with no food or waterrr, no toilet… bright lights and loud music blaring in my ears. When it stopped I could hear the scrims of the others echoing around the prison…"

Ariadne swallows, she has been speaking fast, the words tumbling out. But now she struggles to hold back tears and express what happened next.

"… And then the soldiers raped me, and that's how I got pregnant."

There's a stunned silence while we try to make sense of the sheer enormity of what we have just heard. I think of the parallels with the experience of the Chilean students we heard from at the NUS conference.

Finally, Wiggie says, "Oh my God, I am so *sorry*, love. What can we say? I never knew what was going on in your country. My sister went there on holiday just last year. We had no idea. How did you get out of there?"

"My friends in Athens got me out, they bribed the prison wardens. I have friends in Leicester. I have claimed asylum here because I'm still on the wanted list in Greece."

"I saw something about the Greek students' strike on the news," says Samantha. "It's despicable that the Americans and the British support governments like that. I can't imagine what you've been through, Ariadne. And then losing your baby..."

"I don't know how to fil about losing the baby... it's probably for the best. I am numb inside, I fil empty, I fil nothing, I can hardly even cry. My whole world has collapsed. I've left everything behind me, my family, my friends, my home... everrrything..."

Everything is quiet on the ward this evening. Ariadne' story has put life in perspective; her suffering, her courage. It makes my stupid little problems and my stupid little mistakes seem as nothing in comparison. There's something far more important at stake. The fight for freedom.

*****

Lunchtime. Hospital food. Lumpy mashed potatoes, cold gravy, gristle stew. School dinners, minus the frogspawn pudding.

"How come you speak such good English, Ariadne?" Samantha asks.

"I learned it from rock music and American films. Anyway, it's easy for me. You have so many Greek words in Englis , especially the language of politics—even the word 'politics' itself. The saddest thing for me is that Greeks invented democracy, but it's the last place on earth you will find it today. But at least Greek food is betterrr," she observes, eyeing her plate with distaste.

After the meal it's visiting time. Mary-Ann and Tiggy from the Women's Lib Group, and Sylvia—the post-grad nurse who runs the 'Our Bodies Ourselves' sessions—are here to see me, bringing a copy of *Spare Rib* and some Granny Smith apples. "Forbidden fruit," laughs Tiggy.

"You poor thing, we were so worried about you when we heard," exclaims Mary-Ann, hugging me. "We couldn't get a thing out of that nurse—nobody would tell us anything!"

"If Leicester Hospital wasn't so full of anti-abortion Catholic doctors and nurses you wouldn't be in this predicament," Sylvia declares angrily, squeezing my hand.

"—Hey, don't forget, Oim from a Catholic family, and I support women's roight to choose," Mary-Ann cuts in.

"Well anyway, you shouldn't have had to go all the way to Birmingham to have it done," Sylvia continues, "And they discharged you far too early. I could see you weren't fit to travel home—your temperature was still too high. I bet if they'd kept you in there just one more night they'd have caught the infection early and treated it on the spot, not let it fester for a week. It's a bloody scandal. It's a conveyor belt, that place."

"Anyways, we just heard they're going to close down that clinic in Birmingham, did you know that? At least they provided a service, even if there was room for improvement. *Now* where will women go? If a good abortion service was available locally, we wouldn't have to travel. There's the National Abortion Campaign March on Saturday. We'll campaign for proper services and a clinic here in Leicester."

"I still feel so bad, though. It was such a stupid mistake."

"Oh God, don't be daft, Jane. Thousands of women are going through this, all over the world, and always have done, throughout history. It's our *right* to choose—remember? The personal is political. And what about the blokes? When do they ever get told off?"

Yes I know, I know. And yet I get a sense that I am re-enacting something, playing something out, that I can't fathom. Beyond guilt and shame, resentment and frustration. Something about how I got here, who I am.

A couple of people from the International Socialists and the Communist Party are also dropping in to see me tonight.

"You're lucky you've got lights in 'ere. We 'ad to get candles for our Miner's Solidarity meeting last night—bloody Heath and his three-day week. Anyway, we had a whip-round for you and your, whaddaya call it—predicament—while we were about it. Twenty quid. Help with your expenses…"

"Mary-Ann will have to do your speech about the nursery campaign at the Union Council tomorrow, it'll be fine."

"… And don't worry, we'll remind your sisters from Clare Hall to bring you in a clean nightie and some underwear when they come tomorrow…"

Revolutionaries have the human touch. I really don't mind them eating all my apples.

The little ward is getting crowded. Ariadne's friends, and Samantha, Martha and Wiggie's husbands are visiting too. Wiggie's four kids have come along, looking very sheepish, as mischievous kids do when they are not sure how much they can get away with in an unfamiliar environment. They are told off by the nurse just for sitting quietly on the end of the bed, good as gold.

Nurse reminds us sternly of the rules. Visitors are not allowed to sit on the beds, and only two visitors at any one time. Socialist student caucuses and Women's Lib meetings are not permitted—too disturbing for the other patients.

"So you're one of these Women's Libbers are ya?" Wiggie remarks, when visiting time is over. "Thought so… What ya gonna do for working-class women like me?"

I consider a moment. "Hopefully we will unite and

fight together, support each other, whatever women need, whoever we are," I venture. "I was brought up on a White working-class estate. We all need equal pay, good childcare, good jobs, the right to choose, men sharing the housework, and to be treated with respect. That's got to be right for *all* women."

"Nowt wrong wi' that," Wiggie smiles. "And who was that handsome Adonis, that vision of loveliness with the long wavy blond locks and the ginger beard, who came in at the end? Is he your boyfriend?"

At the mention of Adonis, Ariadne arches her eyebrows quizzically, but I reassure her, "Not Greek, he's a Geordie; more of a Viking, but gentler. Haven't been going out with him long, though we met two years ago when I first started Uni…"

"Is he the one who—you know—is responsible for your—?"

I nod in answer to Wiggie's question. "It was an accident."

"You wanna keep hold of him, though, chuck. He looks like a good catch."

Yes. Ben stood by me.

"I went to the student health centre when I suspected I was pregnant again. Saw an Asian doctor, quite traditional I suppose. And he says 'You've done it again, you *silly* little girl. You'll just have to get rid of it and carry on with your studies. Girls like you get pregnant all the time, I've seen your sort before.'

"And I thought, that's totally unfair, it's not just me, it takes two. But still, I feel stupid and angry with myself, because I've made the same mistake again, I've learnt nothing since I got pregnant before, when I was seventeen and still at school doing my A-levels. My parents were so good to me and really supported me then. I've let everyone down, including myself."

"Well, everyone makes mistakes love, and some of us are unlucky enough to make the same mistake twice—it ain't a hanging offence, you're only human," says Martha weakly from the corner, revived a little from the anaesthetic.

"Thanks, but I feel so guilty, though. I can't face telling my parents, they'll be so disappointed. The thing is, I sort of want to get pregnant and I sort of don't. I think if I had a baby, it would be my colour, so I wouldn't be alone in the world any more. I was brought up in a White family so I always feel I'm alone, the only one. But when I do get pregnant I realise it's a colossal mistake. I'm not ready to be a mother yet, because I don't know who I am, and don't know who my Dad is either. Can't describe it really. A kind of longing, an emptiness inside..."

I have no sense of my father as a real person. He is reduced to a small dash on my birth certificate, the rest of the column left entirely blank. Mum said she met him at a party when they were both students, but when I try to imagine him, I can't see his face. I wonder if I'm like him, if we'd like each other, and whether he's alive or dead. What would he think of me, if he knew I was here now, going through this? I wonder if he has any other children—and whether he has told them about me. He may have forgotten me altogether. He can do that. He doesn't wear me on his skin. There is no visible sign of me in his life.

There's a reflective silence. Then Wiggie says, "You're a good person chuck, you're searchin' for somethin' important to you, that's what it is. This is the right choice for you right now. You will have those lovely little Brown babies one day when the time is right, you'll see."

"But the doctor says I won't be able to get pregnant again after this, and I just—"

"Oh, what does 'e know?" Wiggie interrupts impatiently. "It takes more 'n that to stop babies coming once they start, believe me. You're probably like me, super fertile. People think we're at it all the time, but we just blink, and that's it, up the spout again. And that doctor said it would be *difficult*, not impossible, for you to get pregnant again. I 'eard him speaking to ya. He's just trying to scare ya, I'm sure of it. Don't let those bastards grind you down."

She leans over painfully and retrieves a large bottle of gin from a fluffy pink hot water bottle cover secreted in her bedside cabinet.

"Anyway, come on girls, bring yer cups over, it's nearly Christmas. Who fancies a Lucozade cocktail? A drop of Mother's Ruin will do us all the world of good."

Soon we are all sipping the strong neon-coloured brew—gin with a dash of Lucozade and Ribena. All, that is, except Martha, who says thanks but no thanks—she's already drugged up to the eyeballs and can't make it out of bed. "But for God's sake Wiggie, give that nurse some of your cocktail. Lighten 'er up a bit."

"And we'll ask 'er to put some in your drip," quips Wiggie.

"Of course, the colour of your baby is going to depend on the colour of the Dad to some extent," observes Samantha, taking up the conversation again. "Mind you, I did read in a magazine about a woman in South Africa who had twins, one Black and one White, so you never know…"

"One of each—I think I would quite like that, provided I wasn't living under the Apartheid regime," I remark, "because all three of us would have to live in separate communities over there. Brown, White and Black."

We are all immensely cheered, enjoying the company, topping up the gin-and-Lucozade in our white plastic medicine cups, marvelling at the possibilities of life and birth. Our laughter brings on an explosion of flatulence for poor Wiggie.

"Excuse the wind," she says apologetically. The sound of hilarity brings the nurse scurrying back into the ward.

"Will you ladies *please* get back into bed! I told you before, there are sick people in this 'ospital and you are keeping them awake with all your raucousness. And what's that smell? Is that Gin?"

"Smell? Errr—must be my wind, nurse, sorry."

We hobble painfully back to our beds, sore, bleeding

and shaking with suppressed laughter, like naughty girls at boarding school discovered by matron whilst enjoying a midnight feast. As the lights go out, poor Wiggie explodes with a tremendous fart which lasts fully five seconds.

"Nobody could trump *that*!" she whispers out of the darkness.

*****

Breakfast time, day four. They wake us up ridiculously early, at six thirty, as soon as the nurses arrive for morning shift, only minutes after I've drifted off after a sleepless night. I'm woken in the middle of one of my recurring nightmares. I'm driving a car in the dark on a busy road, and then suddenly realise I can't drive, I've never passed my test, I'm racing downhill at breakneck speed and I have no idea how to apply the brake. People think I'm tough and confident but in reality I'm faking it. All the time.

Awake so early, there's a whole day stretching ahead, drifting in and out of sleep, to ponder on the meaning of my dreams and confront my continuous failure to come to terms with my own body. I'm not in control of my life. I'm not even in control of my fertility. Or my identity. Somehow, all these things are linked.

My relationship with my Blackness is evolving along with everyone else's. When I was a kid, and my skin was a stigma, my skin was literally darker in colour. Now that Black is beautiful in some quarters, my skin has become visibly lighter. I've done nothing to it, no skin-lightening creams, no bleach. It seems to be a natural process. In any case, in the fifties and sixties there was no consciousness of shade. In the middle of rural Norfolk, with nobody to compare with me, folks thought I was as Black as they come.

As a child, my colour was an anomaly in my family that had to be explained and accounted for. Now it has become a badge of honour. Auntie Bel says they asked her in her job interview how, as a White middle-class woman, she would be able to deal sensitively with multi-ethnic clients in her new social work job. She said she had a Black niece. She got the job. She's well-qualified, she deserved it, but it helped. Having a Black sister helps my blond blue-eyed brother not to get bullied by the big Black boys in the neighbourhood. My sister was quizzed about me at primary school about whether I was her 'real' sister; now she's the only White girl in her anti-racism group at her new secondary school. My White friends are 'colour-blind'. "*You're just Jane,*" they tell me, "*you're one of us, we don't see your colour.*" That's the problem. It's not their fault. They all love me. I love them. But I'm either an asset, or I'm invisible. They don't have to see my colour, because they don't have to live in this skin. They are not mis-taken every day. Everyone has taken ownership of my identity except me. As for me, I am at war with my own body, battling out the contradictions from within. If I'm not careful, I won't survive it.

I remember being at an anti-racist meeting recently, and a Black guy got up to speak about his experience of racism as a child. I was so relieved to hear someone talk about the kind of attitudes I had endured when I was a kid. I got up to speak next, in solidarity with my comrade, and a White woman at the back stopped me in my tracks. "You should be quiet. We need to hear from people like him," she said. White people have the right to say which Black people are allowed to speak, and to decide whose is the authentic voice. I so rarely hear about experiences similar to my own in this country. Most of what I read about race comes from America—where one drop of Black blood makes you Black, visible or not; and South Africa, where they have a different community for every colour, including in-between like me.

Here in the UK it's different. We are being graded by shades these days, despite the philosophy that Black is about political consciousness. In a Black-and-White world, where does that leave rare half-breeds like me? An albino Caribbean hairdresser in Battersea taught me to love my hair. A painter in Leicester helped me to love my skin. All my life, until now, I have suffered from being not White enough. Now I know I am not Black enough either, in some people's eyes.

*****

Over cornflakes, lukewarm porridge and soggy toast, Samantha is reflecting on the conversation of the night before.

"Isn't it ironic? Quentin and I have been trying to have kids for ages and I don't know if we'll ever get lucky. But just because it's expected that women are supposed to have babies, I have to pretend to be devastated, when I'm not really that bothered. I'm just not very maternal. In fact, it's put me off the whole sex thing. I'm getting fed up with the regime—doing it when I don't feel like it and not doing it when I want to. Quite honestly, I'd rather be out riding my horses."

Wiggie snorts with laughter at this, and we all join in, including Samantha, although I'm not sure she quite gets the joke.

Undaunted, she continues, "I have just had an ectopic pregnancy, my third miscarriage. I can't face the family, especially my husband's family. Everyone's talking about it. We've only been married two-and-a-half years, but they think it's a catastrophe because I haven't produced a sprog yet. It seems to me—looking at us all here, and our different stories—that there's so much pressure on women one way or another, to have a baby, not have a baby, get pregnant, not get pregnant. It's ridiculous. I've got a lovely farm in Quorn, beautiful horses, I'm very lucky, I'm really quite happy with my life."

I'm impressed with these feminist insights coming from the likes of Samantha, of all people. It seems I've misjudged her. I'm relieved that she feels this way, because otherwise it would be the height of insensitivity to put abortions, hysterectomies and rape cases in the same ward as women who are desperate to have a baby. But I don't suppose this hospital has even thought about that.

"Well, I can see what you mean, love," says Wiggie, in response to Samantha's comments. "I've got all the kids I need, all four of them. Don't get me wrong, I love 'em to bits, I wouldn't swap 'em for the world. But they're doin' my fookin' 'ead in. I've 'ad a baby every other year since I got married. Two of each is enough for me, but Stan just wants to keep going. It's all right for 'im. He works 'ard, but he gets out of the 'ouse every day, he sees his mates at work, he goes round the pub for his darts matches on Saturdays. But sometimes I don't get out the 'ouse from one week to the next, except to the shops and round the park with Timmy. I had a scare the other week, thought I was pregnant again, and I says to Stan, that's it, I'm going in for the sterilisation."

"Couldn't Stan have gone in for the snip, Wiggie?" queries Martha. "It's much less of a big deal for men. I've 'eard they do it in outpatients these days, and it's even reversible."

"Oh, my Stan wouldn't go for an operation, no matter 'ow reversible," says Wiggie, rolling her eyes and shaking her head. "'E's no good wi' pain. But I didn't reckon on this. Pumping loads of gas into me and now I can't stop fartin'. I've blown up like a balloon. That's the worst thing about it, really."

We all laugh and nod sympathetically, thinking about the night before.

"But for God's sake, don't start us off again, Wiggie," says Martha. "It really 'urts when I laugh."

"What about you, Martha?" asks Samantha. "Why did you have a hysterectomy—if you don't mind me asking?"

"Oh, I don't know, mysterious *Women's Trouble* I suppose," says Martha, resignedly. "'Eavy bleeding, 'eadaches, aches and pains... If in doubt they whip your womb out these days—'it's what we do in these situations' they says to me."

*****

It must be gone midnight and I can't sleep. I can hear Ariadne stirring. "Are you okay, Ariadne? Are you in pain?"

"Yes, okay. The nurse has given me some painkillers, they will start working in a minute."

"Thank you for telling us your story, Ariadne. You are an amazing woman, so brave and inspiring. I'll never forget you."

"I was just thinking about *you*, Jane, how strrrong you are, and how unjust it is that they should make you feel so ashamed, as if you have let everyone down. I heard how the doctor spoke to you when you first came in. I didn't think women would be treated like that in England. We all have accidents sometimes. The real shame is that women should be made to pay so harshly for it. If I hadn't had a miscarriage, I would have made the same choice as you did. Don't give up. We must go on fighting for the right to choose."

The Christmas decorations are up, and the atmosphere on the ward has changed. We are a strong team, Ariadne, Wiggie, Samantha, Martha and me, united in adversity, standing up to the patriarchy, even though we are lying down most of the time. Wiggie calls us the 'Famous Five'. We are notorious in the hospital for being noisy, boisterous and out-of-control, for talking politics and having too much fun, fortified by alcoholic Lucozade. We can no longer be terrorised by doctors and nurses. The hospital staff have ceased to pass judgement on our choices and our way of life. The nurse even laughs at some of Wiggie's jokes.

I remember Mum telling me how happy she was in the unmarried mothers' home, when she was having me. I didn't believe her at the time. I thought she was in denial, trying to be positive about a traumatic situation. I had read so much about the cruelty and stigma meted out to young women in those homes; how they were forced to give up their babies for adoption. But Mum told me her experience wasn't like that at all. It wasn't a religious establishment, but a small home in a converted house for only eight residents, run by the Labour Council, so perhaps that explains why there was less moral judgement and less pressure. My mother was adamant that she wanted to keep me from day one. Although it was less easy to have a Mixed-Race child adopted, she told me they even managed to find a couple in a mixed marriage in Manchester, who were willing to adopt me. But still my mother refused.

At only twenty years old, a disabled single mother with a Brown child, my Mum had been ready to go it alone. In the end, my Grandad visited, looked into the cot where I was sleeping, and said "Let's have her 'ome," in spite of my Grandmother's reluctance. And now I understand that Mum may well have been sad to leave the unmarried mothers' home. When you are surrounded by loving, understanding women with a shared experience, who accept you, and support you, and hear your story without judgement or censure, you can help each other to heal.

*****

On day five, they tell me I'm to be discharged.

I knew this day would come, but now it's arrived, I don't want to leave. I don't want to be discharged from these wonderful women on the ward. I feel safe in here. We are all in the same boat. I don't trust people on the outside. I don't know what box they are going to put me in next, how I will be seen, from moment to moment—negated, stripped of validity and authenticity.

I hug them all in turn—Ariadne, Samantha, Martha, promising to keep in touch. Samantha is going home too. She's waiting for Quentin to collect her.

"Good luck, keep fighting."

"It won't be the same without you."

I say goodbye to Wiggie last. She is a philosopher, a wise woman. We all look to her.

"Listen, you," she says earnestly, gripping my hand tightly, drawing me close to her, "Every time I didn't know what to do wi' me life, I had another baby. Tek me mind off it, you know. But you... you got choices I never 'ad. You got the chance of an education and a career. Go on, you go out an' grab it with both hands...

And don't *sabotage* yerself, girl—because that's what you're doin'. No excuses. Promise me."

Chapter 11

Mis-Taken

Will Dylan has an idea. "Why don't you stand for President? You've definitely got what it takes. Up 'ere—" He taps his forehead, "and in 'ere..." He pats his chest. I'm doubtful, disbelieving. Will is an ex-President himself, a mature student, knows what he's doing, confident, assured.

"The thing is, everyone on the Left has been talking," Richard Martin joins in. "International Socialists, Labour students, Young Liberals, Communists, Communist Party Great Britain Marxist Leninist, Workers' Revolutionary Party," he checks them all off on his fingers. "And we all reckon you're the one with the best chance of seeing off Chris Duggans. We can't afford to split the Left and let that Fascist in. So we are all withdrawing our candidates and backing you."

I can hardly contain myself. "Why me? Why not you? Or Eric? Or Aaron?"

"Not Left enough. Plus, you're well known among students in general, not just among us student activists... You've got the people in halls and the women's libbers behind you, and you could probably even get the apolitical ones out to vote. Also… well, you're a woman and you're Black. More people would vote for you when they know what that Fascist Duggans stands for, because you are literally the exact opposite."

I don't usually like the way some people on the Left bandy the word Fascist about—basically against anyone to the right of the Labour Party. To my mind, Fascism is a real and fundamental evil, and shouldn't be used as a general epithet for anybody's politics you don't like. But on this occasion, it's the right word. This young man Chris Duggans purports to be a National Front sympathiser and scarcely a word comes out of his mouth that is not racist, sexist or otherwise offensive.

"It's a big responsibility… I'm not sure I can deliver all that."

"You can, we know you can. Please say you'll stand," Mary-Ann urges.

Inside I feel triumphant, validated, ecstatic, terrified. I want to laugh out loud! After all the separatism, the put-downs, the political posturing—*I'm* the one they think will bring everyone together!

"What about Politics-not-Personalities, Mr Martin?"

"Yeah, well, we still gotta unite against Fascism, haven't we?" he says with a sheepish grin. "When it comes to it, I mean, we're all on the same side."

Too right.

There are two names on the nominations list: mine

and Chris Duggan's. After my nine o'clock lecture I go over to the Percy Gee building to down multiple mugs of tepid coffee and wait it out, alternating between the Women's Table, where all the Women's Libbers gather; the 'Black Table', all male, where a handful of African and Caribbean students congregate, plus Amun, who is Sikh; and the Socialists table, just next to them. Two hours to go. Nominations close at midday.

Ten-thirty.

Eleven o'clock.

Eleven-thirty.

At ten minutes to twelve we go down to the Queen's Hall for the announcement at the close of nominations and the start of fierce campaigning.

And then the word goes out. Chris Duggans has withdrawn his name at the last minute. I am the only candidate. No opposition. Suddenly, I am in. I feel cheated, unreal. A Pyrrhic victory.

But I am in!

Does it really mean anything? Do I have a mandate? Or a womandate? Should we call another election—call for nominations to open again?

"The rules are very clear," says Aaron, who has taken over as Union Speaker. "If there is only one name on the list at close of nominations, that person is elected unopposed, fair and square."

"What if I withdraw my name as well? Wouldn't that force an election?"

Mary-Ann counsels against it. "Nah, he would only do the same again, Jane. There's nothing to stop him. He will play cat-and-mouse with us the whole year."

As if to prove the point, Chris Duggans laughs as he walks by our little huddle in the foyer outside the Queen's Hall, unsure of our next steps.

"You can have it, Goldsmith, I was never really interested in being President anyway. I just wanted to see you Lefties running scared. It'll be fun watching you make a complete mess of it, Jane—let's face it, you ladies are always bleating on about Liberation, but ask yourself, honestly, are you really up to the job?"

He gives me that sneering look of contempt that I have come to know well, as if I am a small insect that has just crawled over his sandwich. He knows just where to find my Achilles heel, that big angry sore spot of self-doubt, and launch the attack to reach right inside me.

I'm confounded by this unexpected turn of events. Even in my moments of success, I'm never quite good enough. Chris Duggans has robbed me of a real election. I am accidentally President. He's taken away my trophy, handed me a poisoned chalice in its place. My life is ambiguous, divergent, complex—never black and white. I can't just win outright like the White boys.

"Don't be daft. It's not unusual for Students' Union elections to be unopposed sometimes. It was *obvious* you were going to win. Who else is there, apart from you?" says Mary-Ann, putting an arm around me. "First woman! Go on, go and phone yer Mum, she'll be thrilled."

Back at Elms Road, everyone congratulates me. My Clare Hall sisters are mystified by my glum face.

"You won fair and square. They all withdrew because they couldn't bear to be beaten by a short brown woman from Clare Hall!"

"You stick up for women—you know, like the campaign for the nursery, something practical for *us* for once. And who else could take on the Rugby Club and win?"

"We're not even interested in politics—all that squabbling among the Lefties, what's the point? But we would've come out to vote for you, because you made it fun."

"First woman President! We're all proud of you."

*****

Under the desk in the President's Office, brushing hot tears away with the back of my hand, I can hear Fran push open the office door, tea cups clinking gently on the tray. The President's office has real china cups with saucers.

"Where's she gone *now*!" Fran mutters exasperatedly under her breath. She walks around to the other side of the desk, nearest the window. "There you are! What the hell are you doing down there under the desk?"

"Hiding."

"What on earth for? You're the President! Everyone's nervous on their first day, it's natural. Come and sit at your desk and enjoy it, have some tea."

I shake my head. "I can't, Fran, I've just seen Ben coming across the campus, heading this way. I just can't face seeing him. He broke my heart, went off with another woman, another *Black* woman! And there aren't many of us around here!"

"Gosh, I thought you were the *only* one on Campus, apart from the new first-year, Tara, Brown like you."

"No, there are one or two others, I'm sure, but they just don't hang around the Students' Union. Anyway, I don't think Ben's new girlfriend is a student here. I haven't seen her around. Maybe she's at the Poly."

"Awww, you poor love. I know exactly how it feels, we've all had our hearts broken, more than once… " She parts the Venetian blind a little and glances out of the window, her eyes rapidly scanning the campus. My new office is right in the centre, where there's a good view of all the buildings and everything that's going on. "There's no sign of him. Anyway, come on, you're an important person. He's only a man, after all. I've brought your post."

She hands me a paper hanky, holds out a hand to help me up, and gives me one of those beaming, understanding smiles of hers that shows off her dimples, lights up her face and my spirits.

"Thanks, Fran, it's going to be great working with you."

"Well, I can't tell you how excited I am—the first woman President I have ever worked for in all my years here! We'll make a great team."

She consults the diary.

"This afternoon after the staff meeting, you've got Joan, a journalist, coming in with a photographer to do an interview for the *Leicester Mercury* about being the first woman president. Then there's your first Exec meeting at five, and in the evening, Ivan Illych is coming to speak in the Queen's Hall—the guy who wrote *De-schooling Society*. Very busy first day…"

I pick up an envelope on top of the pile of mail, addressed to "Jane Goldsmith, The President, Leicester University Students' Union."

I study it for a few moments, turning it over in my hands. I still can't quite believe it. Me, the little skinny brown kid with no Dad, from the Shaftesbury Estate—the first Black woman president of Leicester University Students' Union, in charge of the Percy Gee building, with twenty staff, my own secretary, a budget of £75,000, and a Student Union of three and a half thousand members. Formal duties—attending Senate meetings—where I plan to wear my banana yellow outfit to shock the mortar boards off the professors; discussing important issues over tea with the Vice Chancellor, looking after student welfare, organising grants demos and sit-ins, proposing resolutions on all the serious political issues of the day, addressing Union Council meetings, attending black-tie dinners.

I know I'm not supposed to feel pride. It's positively counter-revolutionary. Women's Liberation and Socialist revolution is anti-leadership, anti-privilege, anti-careerism.

But I can't help it, a little bit. I wish Grandad could see me now. Maybe the other students take it for granted that they will be accepted for who they are—important, entitled, equal, *belonging*. For me, always feeling second best, an outsider and a misfit, this is a completely new experience. I was afraid I wasn't even good enough to make it to University, and now here I am in the President's Office.

"Oh, by the way, good news, there's a letter somewhere in that pile with twenty complementary tickets to the Stones concert at de Montefort Hall, for Union members. You just have to sell programmes before it starts, and then you get to keep the money and you get front row seats."

This job is going to be fantastic.

*****

In my office, it's a full turnout for the first meeting of the Executive Committee—Eric the Deputy, Phil M., and Phil W., the two Vice Presidents, Pete, our Campaigns officer, Aaron, the Union Speaker who knows the constitution backwards, he claims (although as I point out, we need it going forwards), and Mandy, student welfare. The key issues will be the grants campaign, fighting the rise in rents for student housing and the library cuts, and creating a permanent university nursery for students' children. And we want a woman nominee for Honorary Doctorate this year, instead of the usual men—Doris

Lessing, my heroine, being the favourite. Then, locally, there will be demonstrations against fascism where National Front Candidates are standing for the Leicester City Council elections.

In the external world there is much to preoccupy us too—the fight for Equal Pay and Anti-Discrimination Laws, the solidarity campaigns for the Miners' Strike, the war in Angola, and against the dictatorship in Chile; the Anti-Apartheid Campaign, solidarity with the Irish Nationalist movement, and with the students in Portugal... all that will keep us going. And I must find out if there's anything we can do to support the Greek Student Movement. I haven't forgotten Ariadne's story in the women's ward.

"Oh, and also, I have an idea. I'm thinking about organising the first ever multicultural week on Campus in the autumn... We could do an exhibition, invite a Caribbean band, Indian dancers and get one of those restaurants on the Belgrave Road to supply chicken vindaloo, along with the solidarity campaigns and some guest speakers. Politics and partying—that should be popular—help us draw in a student crowd that's not all the usual suspects, for a change."

*****

In the Queen's Hall, tension is palpable. The vote is going to be very close. We have to be ready to swing into action—or just go and sit in the coffee bar for the afternoon and work out what went wrong, depending on which way it goes.

"All those in favour."

"Against."

"Absentions?"

"Carried."

Too close. The Liberals demand a recount.

The International Socialists are itching to get to the barricades. The recount settles it, just.

We march across the campus to the Fielding Johnson building at the head of two hundred students. This is big stuff. Much bigger than organising a sit-in about long white socks at Stafford High School for Girls. I am disappointed the vote has only been narrowly carried, too close for comfort. Not a huge mandate for direct action if there's any trouble.

The administrative staff don their coats and hurriedly leave by the back door when they see us coming. We are soon settled inside, making ourselves comfortable, setting up coffee stands, leaflet stalls and an impromptu bar, while Phil and Phil lug the heavy speakers over from the Queen's Hall to get the music going. It looks like a home-from-home in no time, apart from the chandeliers. Several students rush home to get their sleeping bags—it's going to be an all-nighter.

I stand on a chair to address the sitters-in.

"Comrades, we shall overcome! They have to listen to

us! We students are at the heart of this University, there would be no university if we weren't here. Students and workers shouldn't be bearing the brunt of austerity—the rent rises, the student grants' cuts, the cut in real wages. Right now, this sit-in is about our library services, our direct line to study. Save our library!"

"Save our library!"

A hundred clenched fists shoot up in the air.

"They aren't going to close the library, just reduce the hours," Eric points out, helping me down from my chair. "Ok yeah, well... good point, but it's a slippery slope... Anyway, it sounded good, didn't it? Hold the fort for me, would you? I'm going back to Clare Hall to fetch my sleeping bag."

Back at Clare Hall, Grayson is in her armchair in the drawing room, enjoying her early evening schooner of sherry.

"Back so soon?"

She has invited me to live with her this year and share her grand Warden's residence and garden. There's only Grayson and Dan, one of the lecturers, living in the big old house. "Come and stay with me, you'll need a bolt-hole while you're President," she advises me. "Somewhere to relax and be at home, a refuge where no-one will think of looking for you when you want to get away from it all."

"Grayson, I'm sorry I can't stop," I say breathlessly. "We're having a sit-in over the library cuts, we've stormed the Fielding Johnson. I've just come back for my sleeping bag and tampons."

"How exciting! Got time for a sherry?"

I hesitate, hand already on the door-handle on my way out. "Oh, go on then, just a quick one, Grayson!" I never can resist a sherry with Grayson. She brings me up to speed with the inside information.

"Did I tell you, I got such a lot of stick at the Wardens' meeting when the other hall wardens found out you were coming to live with me," she giggles, handing me a large schooner of amber liquid. "They told me I was opting to live with the enemy! You wait till they discover you've organised a sit-in. What a hoot!"

"Where the hell have you *been*!" Eric demands on my return. "And what's in the bottle?"

"Sherry. Donation to the cause from Grayson. Hide the label. Not really a revolutionary tipple, is it? Got any cups?"

The following afternoon, Sir Fraser Noble, Vice Chancellor, knocks on the front door to his own building. Richard Martin from the International Socialists goes to answer it, standing in the doorway and blocking his way. Having been up all night, bleary-eyed, my heart is in my mouth. I have no idea what to do. I politely ask Richard to stand aside and let the Vice Chancellor in, as I have an appointment with him in his office to conduct important talks about the Library.

"Then I will stand aside—for our President, " says Richard Martin.

"I see you have authority, well handled," Sir Fraser remarks out of earshot, on the way upstairs. "Let's go up and have some tea and discuss tactics."

Sir Fraser is a grey-haired, avuncular man in his sixties with a warm smile, imposing presence, and a rich deep Edinburgh accent. If it came to a punch-up between him and Richard Martin, I suspect the Vice Chancellor would win with a knock-out punch. He's a serious tea-drinker too—bone china cups and saucers with matching teapot and real leaf tea.

"Now let's see, evidently the Students' Union want to flex their muscles. And you, as the first woman President, naturally want to demonstrate your ability to make things happen, and your undoubted leadership qualities. And I do sympathise with your opposition to the cuts. To be honest, students sitting in on campus do no harm to my argument with the University Grants Committee that we need more funds. Don't tell anyone I said that. But on the other hand, I need to show the Senate that I haven't gone soft on students and their protests. So, we need to come up with something that leaves us both in a position of strength at the end of all this, don't you think? Should be possible..." He smiles. "Morre tea?"

"Yes please, and reinstatement of the library opening hours would help."

Fraser Noble is an okay guy, I reckon. He has his constituency to represent and fight for, and I have mine. He is not the enemy. It's the Government that's the enemy.

"Let's meet on a rregular basis for a catch-up session, President to Vice Chancellor," he suggests as I leave, shaking my hand warmly. "And you did say it was a 24-hour sit-in, didn't you?" He consults his watch. "Just about time to wind it up, I think."

The sit-in is a moderate success. Peaceful, orderly, fun, we get library opening hours reinstated, we show the University we mean business, we are part of the national—no, make that international—movement for student rights and solidarity. The Young Liberal students stay behind and hoover and dust the Fielding Johnson Building so thoroughly after the sit-in that the Students' Union is only charged for a broken strip light in the ceiling. It had been accidentally smashed while erecting a big screen in the pavilion room to show all-night movies and keep the sitters-in entertained, along with endless cups of coffee and sandwiches supplied by the Union canteen.

Not everyone is so happy with the outcome. The Senate is outraged, and the receptionist in the Fielding Johnson is decidedly frosty with me. "You have no right to come storming into our building like that, scaring us all half to death."

*****

In the President's office, getting ready for the big grants demo in London, the coaches have been ordered, Phil and Phil are bringing in the placards, while Aaron and I are working on witty slogans.

I complain about the lack of innovation in demo chants. "If I hear *What do we want, when do we want it, out, out out!*" again, I'm going to scream. I hear those chants in my dreams, I've been on so many demos. I wonder who invents them—it can't be *that* hard to think up a new one."

"Well if you think it's so easy, why don't *you* do it," Aaron suggests with his usual sarcasm.

All right, I will. I think for a moment. Something catchy that rhymes and scans properly, that can be chanted, but is short enough to write on a placard as well.

"How about this: "No ifs, no buts, we intend to fight the cuts."

"We intend? That's a bit wishy washy."

"Ok, how about, "*No ifs, no buts, we are **gonna** fight the cuts.*"

That's it! Not half bad.

Aaron wrinkles his nose. "What *are* all these ifs and buts? It will never catch on."

But it will. Five coach-loads of Leicester students, from the University, the Poly, and Scraptoft Technical College, join the march at the assembly point. At first just a handful join in with my new chant—Mary-Ann, Phil and Phil, and the reluctant Aaron. But soon it has spread to hundreds, all bellowing in unison at the top of their voices behind me, marching along the route to the rally in Hyde Park, clenched fists and placards held aloft. There is nothing like that feeling—the exhilaration, excitement and sheer power of collective action, walking with our comrades in common cause, with one voice:

No Ifs, No Buts,

We are gonna fight the cuts.

"Simple, but effective... you should've taken out a copyright on that," says Aaron. "No-one will know who invented it now."

"Then it will have to be my anonymous legacy." I laughed. "Listen—can you hear that? All the stragglers coming into the park are singing it too, from the other Universities and Colleges. it's caught on right the way down the line." I'm delighted. "I will probably get sick of it soon, though. I'll have to think of another one."

*****

I loved all that stuff. Politics, passion, policy, ideological argument deep into the night. After a year as President, life is an anti-climax. I'm not sure what to do next. But everyone knows, if you can't decide, train as a teacher.

Leicester School of Education is a hotbed of revolution. Marxist lecturers, educational radicals, followers of Paulo Freire's Liberation Pedagogy. In the School of Education lecture hall, there are more than a hundred students tightly packed in, and as usual I'm the only Black student in the room. The Student Union children's nursery is housed in this building, thanks to one of the campaigns I'm most proud of supporting during my time as President.

The late September sun's rays slant through the window of the lecture hall directly into my eyes, half blinding me, making my head pound. After a late night in the gay bars of Nottingham last night, with my friends from the Leicester Students' Union Gay Society, I am feeling the worse for wear. The only woman in the group, I love their company, dancing to Soul and Motown until the early hours, revelling in the music I have always loved since my teenage years.

It's good to be with people who are on the outside, like me, struggling to figure out our place in the world when we don't fit into the usual models of femininity and masculinity. I don't want to be put into a box. I am drawn to people who live in the 'space between'. The connection suddenly strikes me. The drag queens are not modelling their image on White women, who never dress like that—it infuriates White feminists—but on Black women singers like Shirley Bassey, Aretha Franklin, Gloria Gaynor, Diana Ross—all sequins and tight dresses. Black women with big curves and afros, challenging the female 'norm'—blonde, blue-eyed and fragile. Black women look invincible, no matter what we may be feeling inside. In the gay clubs, Black women are role models, heroines, appreciated and adored for challenging the status quo. And I lap it up, being the centre of attention, indulging my taste for extravagant dance moves and dressing-up—a complete contrast to the dress-down shabby-chic of the Students' Union.

But now, the excesses of the night before are taking

their toll. It's uncomfortably warm and stuffy in this lecture theatre. My eyelids begin to droop. Mr Burns, our Lecturer, is exploring the challenges of teaching in a multicultural environment like Leicester. This group of all-White student teachers—myself excepted—are about to go on teaching practice in Leicester city schools, many of them with predominantly non-White pupils of Asian descent. I really want to listen, the subject is dear to my heart. I can hear Mr Burns' voice from far away. Must. Keep. Awake. I drift into that delicious state between sleep and wakefulness, my body tingling, my head lolling forward and then jerking upright every now and then, startling me back to consciousness for a few seconds before I drift off again into half-dreaming.

Suddenly I am aware of a hundred pairs of eyes upon me. Mr Burns has posed a question to someone in the room and is waiting for an answer. I look around anxiously, hoping it's been directed at one of my neighbours. But he has evidently addressed the question to me, because Adrian digs me painfully in the ribs.

"Can you think of any particular ways in which West Indian culture is different from ours—some memories from your childhood, perhaps, or your primary school days?"

There's an expectant hush, awaiting my response. Still groggy, I try to collect my thoughts.

"Umm... I'm not West Indian, actually, Mr Burns. I was born here."

"Well, as I was saying, a starting-point in multicultural education is to learn from the experience of people like yourself or immigrants in your school class, when you're teaching. What about your parents' stories, Jane? Anything you can tell us about them?"

"I don't have a background like that. All my family is White—my early childhood was White working class."

"Are you in touch with your West Indian family at all?"

"No... I told you, I'm not West Indian, My father is African. I... I haven't actually ever met him..."

"Oh, I see, what a pity... and we don't have any other Black students this year so I was hoping you could give us some personal examples from your own experience..."

His voice trails off. As his intended special exhibit for livening up his lecture, I have turned out to be a real flop, a disappointment. And yet there are so many things I could tell them all, about how different my life experience has been from all the students sitting around me in this hall, or from White people in general for that matter... how often I have been the victim of racist taunts as a child and mistaken identity as an adult, how irritated people get when they can't categorise me, and I fail to live up to their expectations.

Yes, I know lots of things about how it feels to be in a minority of one. I don't have the experience of a White person brought up in a White society, or a Black person brought up in a Black community. It doesn't make me a non-person. And it doesn't give people the right to place me in the box of their choice and say *that's who you are, we have decided, and you have no say in the matter... and you have to be prepared to speak up whenever we want to use you as an example, and we don't even need to ask your permission...*

I spend the rest of the lecture cringing with shame, anger and embarrassment. People don't want to hear about the racism and discrimination that I have been exposed to from people like themselves, since the day I was born; it's too close for comfort. They want to hear about the exotic and the far away, and I can't help them with that. They don't want to hear what it's like to be singled out from a hundred students, and publicly required to give a personal account of myself, my unknown origins, and my relationship with my unknown father.

As ex-President, I'm still a well-known figure around campus, but I rarely ever talk about my background. After the lecture, there's the fall-out—a torrent of questions about what just happened, from my friends and from new students joining the College of Education. I can't answer their enquiries, because I don't know anything. I feel wounded, publicly exposed as a fraud.

I am fed up with this. Fed up with having no personal history, geography, no map of me, no words to explain, nobody to share it with. It is getting on top of me, like it did in Stafford. I wake up every morning and feel like screaming.

I need help.

*****

In the consulting room at the student health centre, I'm trying vainly to explain. The therapist, Elaine Rutherford, looks disconcerted. A dark-haired, warm-hearted, softly spoken woman in her late thirties, married with three children, she seems at a loss to be able to understand how I see the world.

"Uncertainty and pain is what I'm used to—being an outsider. When I was eight I wrote a play about it. At fourteen, I wrote novelettes about famous White girls and their Beatle boyfriends for my school-friends. When I was fifteen I became a women's libber. At seventeen I got pregnant, and then again when I was twenty. Then I got elected as President of the Students' Union. I always think of something to get me out of it, to make me feel real, to help me fight back, prove myself. But right now, I can't think of anything—I've run out of ideas…"

"But you're just in the middle of your teaching practice. You'll make an excellent teacher, and you'll be inspiring a new generation."

"But I don't really want to be a teacher. I signed up for the course because I couldn't think of anything else to do, like a lot of other students. But I always hated school, and I dread the thought of going back there, even if I'll be behind the teacher's desk this time, tormenting all those poor students who don't want to be at school either."

"Well… what would you do instead?"

I pause to consider. When Joan from the *Leicester Mercury* came to interview me as the first woman President of the Students' Union, I told her I wanted to be Secretary General of the United Nations. When I met Doris Lessing at her honorary degree ceremony, I told her I wanted to be a writer. What happened to all those great ambitions? In reality, it's far more difficult. I wouldn't know where to start. I need to think of something I can do right now, something adventurous, glamorous, something at least as exciting and impressive as being President of the Students' Union.

"I have always wanted to go on VSO—you know, a volunteer overseas—ever since I was about fourteen, and we read *A Pattern of Islands* at school—the book written by that guy who goes off to the Pacific islands and wrestles with a giant octopus. It was a bit colonialist, his background, but it inspired me all the same. I want to do something practical, political, and worthwhile. You know, learn about different people, places, different cultures…"

Elaine is unconvinced.

"How long do you have to commit to VSO these days?"

"Two years minimum I think. Some people go for three."

"Two years is a long time, Jane, and just when you might be getting adjusted over there you will have to come back home again and face whatever it is you're running away from. You've already had so much change for someone of your age…" She glances down at her notes.

"Battersea, Surbiton, Stafford, Norfolk, Wandsworth, Finland, Leicester..."

"... and Italy..."

"... and Italy. Are you *sure* you want to separate yourself from everything you know again? Isn't that your problem, moving around, putting yourself into unfamiliar environments and having to explain who you are? Your life seems to have involved constant change, trying to fit in with new situations, new families, and different people's reactions to you. I think you've tested yourself enough. Why don't you get your teaching qualification, find a good teaching job with a decent salary, security and stability? That's what seems to have been missing in your life all this time. You're twenty-four now, the age most people think of settling down. Why not give yourself some time and space to build a permanent base?"

I'm cringing, curling up inside with anger and frustration. Why can't this woman understand me, help me deal with my issues? Why does she keep supplying me with solutions that fit someone like herself?

"I don't *want* stability, it's not for me; it sounds absolutely ghastly. I need excitement and change. I need to feel I'm doing something important and positive with my life, I want to change the world—for women, for working-class people, for poor people, for people in the 'Third World'... for me."

*****

Rage against the monstrous regiment of men! They're everywhere! That Dan Wilkinson, my successor as President of the Students' Union—he doesn't miss any opportunity to put me down, every time he sees me. Now he's just taken over as President, he is even more insufferable.

"I had to give a list of your achievements last year to the University inspectors," he sneered at me last night. "There!" He flung a scrappy bit of paper at me across the table, with a list of four or five short items scrawled on it.

"There," he repeated, "anything missing?" and he whisked it away before I'd even had a chance to look properly. "Thought not... Not much to show for a year's work, though, is it?"

I was seething with rage and embarrassment. "Well, let me see the list again, there's the student nursery, I didn't see the nursery on the list..."

"The nursery. Well that doesn't really benefit the whole student body, just a handful of women, but okay, I'll add it if you insist." He scribbled the word 'creche' untidily at the end of his list, and then stuffed it back into his pocket.

I don't feel good about myself. There are so many more things I could add to that list. He gave me no warning, no time to think. The campaigns on the Library, student rents, anti-apartheid, the multicultural week—which turned out to be a great success—the strengthened links between the Students' Union and the University and between the Union and the Halls of Residence—that must all count for something. During my year a whole lot of motions were passed on women's rights, gay rights, overseas students, from people who felt marginalised before, and now felt they could speak out.

Dan seems to be all about claiming stuff for himself. Leadership isn't just about what you do—it's about creating the space for other people to find a voice. I was feeling my way—I didn't have any role models for how to be a Black woman leader. People like Dan Wilkinson just tear it all down with their own sense of entitlement. He didn't give me a chance to think. He just put me in a position where I couldn't retaliate.

Back in Elaine's therapy room, I'm still smarting from the experience. "Some guys have a real problem with me. Not all of them, some are my mates. But a few of them start to attack me, undermine me every time I walk into a room, and the others just watch them tear me apart. It's personal. It used to happen sometimes, even before I became President. Now they're saying I never did anything while I was President, I didn't achieve anything at all. Is it just me? Am I paranoid or is everyone ignoring me?"

"Everyone knows how much you did for the Students' Union, Jane. When you give up such a prominent role—and you being the first woman as well—it's very difficult for you to adjust, especially if you're still on the campus. It's not easy going back to being just another student again. It's a natural reaction, it's not just you."

"Good point, I see that. But I can't understand why

they are so nasty to me. What do they get out of it? I can see the look of contempt and disdain in their eyes. Dan looks at me like that. So does Richard Martin. The way I talk, the way I dress, what I believe in. They belittle everything about me. They don't treat other guys like that, even if they are at opposite ends of the political spectrum."

"Well you could try fitting in, support what they are doing. Tone down the wardrobe, you know—the sari—if you feel out of place…"

"You don't understand—this is politics. Dan Wilkinson is a Tory. Why would I ever agree with him? It's about being seen as an equal, that's what I'm on about. And why shouldn't I wear what I want?"

The sari is not just about clothes. It's cross-dressing—*cross-cultural* dressing in my case. I know it's not African, it's not even my Dad's culture. Sometimes I wear a Dashiki—a short-sleeved top made of African cloth that Remi, my Nigerian Overseas Student friend, gave me. I *need* to dress in non-Western clothes some-times, to be in touch with the part of me that's non-European. In Stafford, I used to go downtown on a Saturday afternoon dressed as a Native American, complete with bare feet, fringed jacket and headband with a feather. It was an outfit inspired by a costumed doll I was given when I was eight.

Why brave all those incredulous stares? I needed to, that's why. It felt good, even if I looked stupid. I got stared at anyway, but at least this was within my control. It was

1966, I was fourteen, dressed as a painful stereotype of another culture. I was looking for something I couldn't find, and still can't find. It's all I had, the nearest I could get to my other Self. It was meant to be an act of solidarity, of connection. Men get away with wearing women's clothes, I thought—they even get their own TV shows. But people just thought I was weird. Look at me now. 1977. At twenty-four, still battling with the same issues.

Out of the Health Centre window, the same trees fringe the courtyard. This was the place I came to see the Indian Doctor, who told me I was a silly little girl for getting myself pregnant again. People don't realise that I am grappling with a serious identity deficit, and there is no-one who can help me manage it, or even recognise it.

"To be honest, Elaine, it's all getting on top of me. It makes me feel eight years old again, being called woggie, Blackie, you're-the-colour-of-dog-shit, that kind of thing. I feel... kind of... powerless again, as if I'm not good enough, that no-one will stick up for me."

"I think a lot of people would be really surprised to hear you say that. You come across as so confident—belligerent, even. You know your problem—you try too hard. You're always out to prove yourself. Why don't you just let go, relax a bit, just let it all wash over you? Ignore them, pretend you don't care."

That's exactly what the teacher said to me in Surbiton when the red-headed boy called me names. *Ignore him, or you will only make it worse.* If I ignore it, nothing will ever change.

"You'll feel fulfilled one day, when you meet a nice man, settle down, get married, you'll see."

There she goes again. *Get married. Settle down. Find a nice man.*

Wrong thing to say to a feminist.

Chapter 12

Strange Fruit

Iringa market is packed with shoppers. The stall-holders wear brightly-coloured wrappers—kangas—around their waists and shoulders, offering their usual produce; small mounds of tomatoes, onions, potatoes. Round fruits are piled up in great green pyramids on wooden trestles. They all look the same, but inside, they are all different. The stall-holder cuts one open on top of each pile to reveal orange, green or yellow flesh—a clue to whether they are oranges, limes, lemons, grapefruits, or tangerines.

Real tangerines! I remember eating them at Christmas as a kid, but they are hard to come by in London these days—full of pips but exquisite flavour. I am perplexed when the stallholder turns her back and refuses to serve me—is my Swahili that bad? I try again in English, without success. An older man standing by the stall asks me where I'm from—and refuses to believe me when I say I'm from Britain.

"There are no Blacks in England. You must be Black American. We don't like you people, you're not welcome here—you are spies."

A little crowd gathers, eager to discuss my origins. Chinese? Zanzibari? Black American? Chagga? I'm a good fit for a Chagga—light-Brown people from the Kilimanjaro region who like to wear Western clothes and speak English—behaviour regarded with deep suspicion. I look as if I am from a deeply suspect tribe. Lawrence, my fellow volunteer, comes over to see what's going on.

"What trouble have you got yourself into now?"

He clears up the issue instantly, insisting I am with the British volunteers' group.

Yes. English.

White men still appear to be the final arbiters around here, even though it's nearly twenty years since Tanzania gained independence. At least I got my tangerines.

*****

It's six months since my interview in London. I'd rehearsed my answer many times about why I wanted to be a volunteer. I'm an internationalist, I believe people should be treated equally, I am angry about poverty and injustice in the world. I want to do something practical, immerse myself in a different culture. I will gain at least as much as I give, bring back an understanding about the 'Third World' that will last a lifetime—whatever I do in the future.

My answer seemed to go down well with my two interviewers—a big grey-haired man in a striped suit a size too small, and a severe-looking woman with gold-rimmed glasses.

"And your background? Where are you from—originally?"

That word again; *originally*.

"Born in Kingston. Not Jamaica—Kingston, Surrey. England."

I could see by the look on their faces that my answer would not do. My hands were clammy with sweat.

"Mother English, father Ghanaian."

"You were brought up here or in Ghana?"

"Here. Never met my father."

They exchange a sideways glance. Let's get it over with.

"So, you'd like to be posted to Ghana?"

"Ummm yes... no... I don't mind..."

"So you definitely don't want to be posted to Ghana?"

I was flummoxed by this line of questioning. I honestly couldn't work out what the right answer was supposed to be. Should I be desperate to go to Ghana in particular, or was it the last place on earth I should want a posting? They could detect the look of rising panic on my face.

"I'll go anywhere... where I'm needed..."

"Well, thank you for that, Miss Goldsmith, and for being open with us. We did need to ask, you understand. We can't have people going off on VSO with a free ticket to trace their lost parents. Wouldn't do at all," he shook his head and smiled simultaneously. "We'll let you know in a few weeks."

That was gruelling. I wondered whether my White counterparts were quizzed so intensively about their motives. Everyone has complex reasons for wanting to leave everything to go volunteering for two or three years—guilty conscience, compensating for parents' colonial past, gone-wrong love affairs... or running away from their own fathers, perhaps?

Next, I was lined up for the 'personal chat' with Susanna, dressed all in black, tall and slim with short dark close-cropped hair. She had a distinctive gentle smoky voice and a much more empathetic personal style. Her accent sounded very upper-crust, but she told me she was brought up in India. She asked me how I felt about having no contact with home for such a long time, leaving family, friends and lovers behind; managing out in the bush with no access to tampons.

"I think I've blown it already," I confided in her. "I had no idea how to handle the questions about my father. What was I supposed to say?"

"Don't worry, you're the first Black volunteer they've ever interviewed, I think. One of the first, anyway. They're just not used to it. You're doing fine."

*****

I got the message from the interview that I wasn't a standard volunteer; my motives were suspect and I had to be carefully checked out. They sent me off to Africa all the same.

Mufundi Technical Secondary School has six hundred pupils, all boarders, aged from sixteen to twenty, not much younger than me. Until recently it was an all-boys school, but to my delight, the first intake of girls just arrived this year. The school compound is like a little village in the middle of a eucalyptus forest, a few miles from Iringa, the nearest town. Teachers and workers are housed in little cream-and-brown-painted bungalows dotted among the trees. When you walk through the forest and rub a leaf between your fingers, it smells like a cough drop.

I upset the Black-White dynamic the moment I arrived. At the beginning of my second week, Kamala, Head of the Humanities Department, called in to my bungalow to welcome me and show me around. We visited some of the other teachers and their families, and then dropped in at the staff room. Kamala insisted on holding hands with me all the while. The more I squirmed and tried to extricate my hand from his, the more tightly he held on to me, entwining his arm around mine and pulling me close to his body. At one point he even put his arm around my shoulders, bending close to me, whispering in my ear, watching to make sure people were looking. My discomfiture increased as the afternoon wore on. If he hadn't been my head of department, and my new boss, I'd have said something—but I promised myself I wouldn't lose my cool, I'd try to fit in. It was all so public. I was attracting odd looks from other volunteers and teachers, but

I'm used to being stared at; maybe they had never seen a Black European before.

Hot, stressed, dusty, a bundle of nerves, I was grateful when the introductions were over and Kamala suggested going back to his compound to meet his family.

I immediately took a liking to his wife—young, exquisitely pretty, flawless satiny chestnut skin, huge eyes fringed with long lashes, perfect white teeth, and a shy charm, all of which their two small boys seem to have inherited from her. I imagined a close friendship developing between us, in spite of the awkward beginnings. She served us bottles of orange Fanta and biscuits on the veranda in the shade, whilst Kamala insisted passers-by come up for more elaborate introductions. I was so thankful when the ordeal was finally over. The whole thing felt disastrous. I felt I'd not made a good impression on anybody.

Alexander came in the early evening. I was so glad to have someone to talk to after the awful events of the afternoon. Alex was coming to the end of his two years as a volunteer teacher in Mufundi, and I was his replacement. Having moved out of his own bungalow, I'd been surprised and pleased when he asked if he could come and stay with me for his last few days before he left for home. A real gesture of friendship, I thought, a chance to get to know each other.

Alex and I could not be more different. His father was a diplomat and he had travelled all over the world as a child, with Black servants and villas and what-not. He reminded me of some of the activists in the students' Union—ex-public schoolboy revolutionary Socialists, eschewing their upbringing and their class privilege to join the struggle.

Alex took his political commitment to great lengths, insisting on being housed in the African quarters rather than the accommodation reserved for foreign teachers. He ate only a simple Tanzanian diet and went around in unkempt, tattered clothes and matted hair, with questionable personal hygiene, in odd contrast to his cherry-cheeked, healthy boyish complexion, and his beaming smile. He went for long walks alone in the bush, and made a point of frequently visiting the African teachers in their homes. In the staff room, the European teachers called it 'going native' and some were full of admiration for Alex's principles, especially the teachers from the Soviet Union. "He has shown us how to be a good Socialist," Ivanov observed. Like Kamala, Ivanov also found it hard to keep his wandering hands from me.

Some of the Tanzanian teachers, by contrast, were perplexed by Alex's behaviour. His motives may have been sincere, but the execution seemed to have missed the mark. Tanzanian students and teachers pay particular attention to being well turned out, no matter how little money they have, and no self-respecting African goes out without hair and skin meticulously oiled and shirts immaculately washed and pressed. Even the postman admonished me once for not having properly oiled my skin. "You have African blood," he said, grabbing my hand and inspecting it closely. "Your skin needs moisture." I suspected it was an excuse to hold on to my hand too long; but the next time I went to collect my post and my *Guardian Weekly*, he presented me with a tin of Vaseline.

After he had left, my students told me they thought Alex might be a spy. Why else would a European behave like that, *Mwalimu*? Taking long walks in the bush for many hours alone, visiting Africans in their homes all the time, speaking such fluent Swahili? And not only had he offended the Tanzanian teachers with his poor dress sense, he had also caused a waiting list for housing by taking up accommodation reserved for an African teacher.

We all have our backgrounds to overcome, myself included. Like a lot of the others around here, Alex couldn't quite place me either. He seemed to look down on me, as if I was a fake, when we are all faking it in one way or another. Now he had come to stay with me, I was hoping we'd get to understand each other, become friends. Alex could be very engaging when he relaxed, and I needed to relax a little too. We'd have some good political discussions at any rate. We're both committed socialists and great fans of Nyerere.

As soon as Alex arrived I went to the kitchen to make tea. Six thousand feet above sea level, the air is fresh and thin here. It still makes me feel breathless sometimes, even though they say you get used to it. We are so high up that when water boils it isn't scalding, even though it bubbles. You can drink tea immediately without burning your mouth—fresh-picked and fragrant leaves from the local plantations.

But that afternoon, Alex wouldn't touch his ready-to-drink tea. He sat on the sofa looking distinctly uncomfortable. Finally, he came out with it. He couldn't stay with me after all. He was moving to the empty bungalow next to Kamala's and he had come to collect his things. I was perplexed and hurt. I told him how much I'd been looking forward to his company. I wanted to ask his advice about what had happened with Kamala in the afternoon. Why the sudden change of mind?

"Well that's just it. Kamala. Since you walked around the compound hand-in-hand with him this afternoon, Kamala has been telling everyone he's sleeping with you. I can't condone that—you've upset everyone, especially the women. They all support Kamala's wife, of course."

I was mortified.

"Oh Alex, surely you don't believe him—you can't do! I've only just arrived here, it's a complete lie, you know it is. What was I supposed to do? He's my boss, he wouldn't let go of my hand…"

"That's not the point. Everyone else believes it and they're all talking about it…"

"But you were there when we came into the staff room, you could see how much I was struggling to extricate myself. People told me not to believe a word Kamala says when I first arrived here. He must have set me up for this. What's he got against me, for God's sake? Couldn't you say something to people Alex? It would make all the difference coming from you. They know you, they would listen to you, and you are leaving, you have nothing to lose. I have to live with this, it's awful. What will people think of me if you walk out now? Please…"

"No. I won't side with you against a Tanzanian," said Alex flatly, and with that he picked up his rucksack and left.

Such double standards! Alex doesn't get criticised for moving in with me, nor Kamala for holding my hand. Why hadn't he supported me?

I watched his back disappear up the dusty path, threw myself on the couch and burst into tears. I'm a complete idiot. Of *course*, men and women don't hold hands here in public—I know that. I was so fixated on trying to do the right thing, I ended up doing the wrong thing.

I'm an idiot, but I'm not a fool. Alex is a public school educated White man, and that counts for everything. White men get to say who gets the tangerines around here and who doesn't—I saw it for myself in the market. Alex is an influential figure, no matter how African he thinks he wears his shirts. To be so publicly rejected by him so early after my arrival, and the disaster with Kamala, didn't help my struggle for acceptance. Perhaps Alex and I were both grappling in different ways with the colour of our skin in an unequal Black-and-White world.

I'd only been here a few days, and I already felt so isolated. I needed someone to talk to. I was disappointed that they hadn't put me in a house with other volunteers—I'd always been nervous about living on my own, or even staying overnight in a house alone. To make things worse, the lights go out every evening after ten o'clock. The whole campus is plunged into darkness until dawn, to save generator fuel.

The morning after the hand-holding incident, Jan and Lars, the Dutch volunteers, walked in through my open veranda doors, to get a haircut. I'd forgotten I had promised them when I visited their compound. They noticed my reddened eyes. I had spent a sleepless night worrying about what had happened the day before.

"What's op?"

I told them about Kamala's behaviour, and Alex walking out. Jan said he wasn't surprised.

"Before you arrived, Kamala told us he 'hates these Black people with White passports'. He said he would make them regret sending you here."

"Why didn't you warn me?"

"Er… Forgot… Anyway, he's always bloffing. Didn't think he would do anything aboud it."

"I feel really upset about it. And did you hear that they refused to serve me in the market? They thought I was Black American and wouldn't believe I was British. What's that all about? Why do they hate Black Americans?"

"That would be because they kicked all the Black

Americans out of here in the sixties—suspected them of being CIA agents, I heard. Turned out there was no truth in it—it was just a rumour." Jan seems to know all about everything—history, geography, politics, people.

"Nobody warned me about this... that I would be treated differently from White volunteers..."

"Don't worry, it's all a shtorm in a tea cop," Lars tried to reassure me in his near-perfect English, shrugging his shoulders. "Forgedda 'bout it. Things will settle down when term begins next week and everybody is busy teaching. We'll come later for the haircot."

I wasn't quite sure what to expect when I was posted to East Africa. My VSO interview had been so awkward on the subject of my African heritage, I'm surprised they sent me to Africa at all. I didn't know if I would feel instantly at home here, or whether it would bring up all sorts of long-buried issues about my father and my identity, in the same way that the proposed school trip to Nigeria had done when we lived in Stafford.

Maybe they had been right to quiz me about my origins; but on the other hand, having pointed out my difference, they did nothing to prepare me for its impact. I didn't realise how much trouble my race was going to cause when I came here. The volunteers don't back me up. The Tanzanians probably hate me. Barely two weeks after arrival, I had already unintentionally caused havoc. Not a good start. And still nearly another two years to go. It seems I transgress all sorts of race, class and gender boundaries that ought not to be crossed.

I'm strange fruit. You have to cut me open to find out what I am.

*****

At least my Marxist lecturers at Leicester School of Education were impressed by my going to Tanzania. Nyerere's brave experiment with *Ujamaa* socialism, African style, is admired by the Left all over the world. The Socialist Government had already started implementing a radical programme of nationalisation, taking over industry and banking, offering free education for all, and *Ujamaa* 'villagisation' to provide basic needs and services.

Soon after our arrival, we met President Nyerere in person on the veranda at State House in Dar Es Salaam, peacocks strutting around manicured lawns. The VSO volunteers before us had been campaigning for an audience with the great man himself for more than three years—lucky for me to turn up at just the right time. Nyerere more than lived up to our expectations. A charismatic character with short wiry close-cropped salt-and-pepper hair, twinkly eyes and an engagingly informal style, he slapped his thigh and laughed whenever he made a joke.

He explained that *Ujamaa* meant 'family' in Swahili. Tanzania was a poor rural economy, so they had to improve life at village level, everyone working together for the common good, measuring progress in terms of human wellbeing. He was passionate about education and insisted on being called *Mwalimu*—teacher—having trained as a teacher himself. He wanted to transform the previous elitist colonial-style school system into one based on *Education for Self-Reliance*, in line with the principles in the Arusha declaration which set out the Government programme—equality, human dignity, shared resources, work for everyone, freedom from exploitation, greater unity with all other African countries...

The man had so many ground-breaking ideas. I came away star-struck, thrilled to think I'd have a chance to be even a tiny part of this.

The other volunteers at Mufundi were amazed that I had already met Nyerere after only a few days in the country.

"What did he say about education—and the role of foreign volunteer teachers?" Jan asked. "Don't foreign volunteers just reinforce the old colonial stuff?"

"He said he's expecting us to be part of the transformation—we should be contributing to the process. I was really pleased when he said students should be involved in decision-making, to give them the skills to participate in a democratic society—schools should be a community, like a village, where academic, cultural, political and social education goes on, not just a curriculum based on exams..."

If only we'd had progressive attitudes like that

when I was at school—I remember trying to start some political discussions going in my secondary school in Stafford, with my idea of a topical class notice-board. It only lasted a week before the Deputy Head banned it.

I didn't tell the volunteers at Mufundi much about our traumatic field visit two weeks after the meeting with Nyerere. On our orientation course, our group of new volunteers were taken to an Ujamaa village to see 'villagisation' for ourselves. At the beginning of the trip, the mood was enthusiastic and upbeat about the changing political landscape in Tanzania. And I was flushed with the success of the night before, when I had been invited to give a talk to local activists about the anti-apartheid movement in the UK. The four-hour drive to the Ujamaa village in heat, dust and sweat, over pot-holed dirt roads, miles out into the bush, took the edge off my enthusiasm. For the first time ever, I was sorry I had burnt all my bras. My new-found soulmate Maggie and I were clutching our boobs and screwing up our faces, as we sat shuddering, jolting, and shaking with the movement of the bus on the dirt roads, much to the amusement of the male volunteers.

We were welcomed by the Headman, Ndugu Mbanga—a short, wiry *Chama Cha Mapinduzi* Party member in his fifties, frequently mopping his brow with a frayed, greying cotton handkerchief. All around us were ramshackle huts dotted about on parched red earth. To our consternation, there was an air of gloom and desolation about the place.

Mbanga explained they had all been forced to abandon their tiny homesteads to build this Ujamaa village. Hundreds of people gathered miles from anywhere, out in the bush, with no clean water, no equipment—not even hoes to till the baked barren soil, hard as iron. He confided that it was an uphill task to persuade people to work communally and share produce. "You can't blame them for wanting to provide for their own families first, and the low price the government offers for our crops doesn't make it worthwhile to sell them. Some people are even talking about going back home—although their homes have been destroyed. We were promised a good life here if we left our settlements. But when we got here, there was notin'. They told us we have to dig."

Added to these problems, they are not used to living so close together, so the villagers haven't built up any immunity. Disease spreads quickly and there are no medicines. Fourteen children had died from measles in the last two weeks. The only means of transport they have is the Coca-Cola lorry which comes once a week.

"Today you are locky. The Coca Cola van has just made a delivery, so we can offer you Sprite, Fanta or Cola. Which would you prefer?"

A group of villagers came to wave us off.

"If there's anything you can do to help us, we would appreciate it," Ndugu Mbanga said forlornly. Bewildered and exhausted, our comradely exuberance evaporated on the return journey.

Back at the Morogoro training centre, Maggie and I sat on the veranda over a cold Safari beer before the evening meal, trying to make sense of what we'd seen and heard.

I was still raging about the injustice of the world.

"It doesn't matter how bad things get. You may have absolutely nothing, but you can always get a Coke. That's capitalism for you. Personally, I never drink it. Hate the stuff."

Maggie, five years my senior, has a soft-spoken Galway accent. She is far more pragmatic and worldly-wise than I.

"But don't forget, the headman says they reloiy on the Coca Cola lorry for lifts into town... and they use flat Coke to treat the children's diarrhoea..."

"Okay, that may be true, but he also pointed out that the world trade system is stacked against poor under-developed rural countries like Tanzania. The price of raw materials like sisal and coffee fluctuates wildly—Tanzania is getting poorer, not richer. I bet Western countries are terrified that Ujamaa socialism will succeed, and everyone will want it. America and other foreign powers are doing all they can to sabotage it and campaign against Nyerere's ideas, whereas everyone should get behind it, fund it, help it succeed..."

"Oi do think the *Ujamaa* idea is good in principle, but the villagoisation process seems to be very brutal, don't ya think? People forcibly ejected from their homes, sometoimes violently, and resettled moiles away with no resources, tools, medicines, and no food. Oi really felt for the people we met today."

"Yeah, I know… I know, you're right, Maggie. I dunno know what to think, it's unbearable. The end can't justify the means. But I did get what Nyerere is saying—it's about economy of scale. Unless there are large enough numbers, you can't provide basic amenities like water, electricity, education, transport, all that basic stuff—it's just not viable. That's why the plan is to move people together—"

"To be sure, but before the new system is up and running and starts to make money, even if it eventually succeeds, they have nothing, they are really suffering. I can't get it out of my head, what we've jost seen. It's awful. Catch twenty-two…"

Over dinner of rice and beans, the mood was subdued and reflective among all of us bright new volunteers. Idealism and reality, suddenly face to face.

*****

I am beginning to get used to being by myself in my little self-contained bungalow—bedroom, bathroom, galley kitchen and sitting room—with a veranda overlooking the maize *shamba*. Afia, a Tanzanian from Arusha, is my next-door neighbour, and Hildegard, a German volunteer, has a bungalow just beyond the next maize plot. We are the only women teachers in the school, all about the same age, so we are regular visitors to each other's bungalows. I join Hildegard for lunch every day after school. The day begins early so by two o'clock in the afternoon, we are free. She employs a cook and cleaner called Bwana James, a slow-moving, taciturn, elderly man. He always serves stewed guavas with custard for dessert.

"I was properly trained by the British," he says proudly—one of the few remarks he ever makes.

Afia politely declines to join us for lunch. She heartily detests custard and any other kind of Western food. She explains that she comes from the North where they eat rice—not *ugali* made with maize which is the staple dish around here—so she prefers to cook for herself, unlike most middle-class Tanzanians who rely on help in the house. The European volunteers, on the other hand, agonise over the colonial issue of 'house helps', who are still referred to as 'house boys' and 'house girls' regardless of their age. I decided even before I arrived here that I wouldn't be engaging a house help on principle, no matter how common it is.

But life isn't that simple. Bwana Baraka turned up on my doorstep on my first day, his short skinny wiry frame and greying hair belying his enormous strength and agility. He had worked for the German couple occupying my bungalow before I arrived, and was most put out by my cherished political principles.

"Tanzanians do not like rich foreigners who come

here and don't give us jobs—like Mwalimu Alex who jost went home," he tells me sternly.

Volunteering turns out to be a political economic social and moral minefield.

No use trying to explain I am not that rich. At least I have a job. We volunteers get the same small salary as Tanzanian teachers, because their teachers' union doesn't like the idea of unpaid foreigners coming in and taking their jobs. Same job, equal wage. Fair enough.

So I ask Bwana Baraka to be my guide and help me do things I don't know how to do myself; show me how to survive here as a clueless townie in the mountains, how to work my garden plot, harvest maize, find out where they are selling deer and pork meat, and eggs. He brings me logs for the fire from the forest—it is chilly here at night—and teaches me Swahili and a few phrases in his mother tongue, Kihehe, the local language around here. It amuses him when I call him *Mwalimu*—teacher.

And so now Bwana Baraka and I get on very well, *asante sana*.

*****

Early rising is not my strong point. But now the term has started, I am always lined up at seven-thirty sharp on the veranda outside the staff room for morning Assembly, alongside the other teachers. The students are already standing to attention in the courtyard in the baking sun.

This morning, half a dozen students are lying stretched out on the ground, face down, naked from the waist up, their toned brown and black torsos glistening with oil after early morning exercises and bucket wash. There is an uneasy silence as the Headmaster, Ndugu Batenga, reads out the names of the miscreants due for punishment. I have a queasy feeling in the pit of my stomach. I know what's coming. Mr Chegeni, the Deputy Head, produces a large switch. The first prone victim twitches and grunts in response as Chegeni enthusiastically administers the first blows to his back.

That's enough for me—at the first crack of the cane I'm off, stumbling blindly up the steep rocky path to my little bungalow, fingers in my ears, a thousand horrific images triggered in my head. Students gunned down in Sharpeville and Soweto in South Africa; runaway slaves flogged on plantations in Alex Harvey's Roots; water-canons in race riots in the US; bodies of young Black men swinging from the trees in a lynching. Nina Simone singing of strange fruit—*Black bodies swinging in the Southern breeze/Strange fruit hanging from the poplar trees...*

I know I'm going to be accused of disloyalty. No-one here is impressed by my conscientious objection over the beatings. The volunteers and foreign teachers are keen to demonstrate solidarity with the school—and they are wary of being thought racist. I have already gained a reputation as a misfit after only a few short weeks, by being the wrong colour for a European. I can see the confusion and denial on their faces: *You're either one of them or one of us. Since you're clearly not one of them, you must be one of us. So why do you keep getting into situations that simply never happen to your average White volunteer? There must be something wrong with you.*

Yes, there is something wrong with me. Too light for Black, too Black for light. Caught in the space between Black and White. The *Other* Place. A place that doesn't exist in most people's imagination. A space that has become ever clearer to me since my arrival on African soil.

The Headmaster, Mr Batenga, wants a word with me. It's not an unfamiliar experience for me to be summoned to see the headteacher.

I strain to adjust my eyes to the gloomy office after the bright sunlight outside. Documents and files are stacked up in dusty, untidy piles on every available surface. A rickety fan ticks over ineffectually in the corner. Batenga is a kindly, mild-mannered man with a broad smile, showing perfect white teeth—unlike his fearsome Deputy, Chegeni, who administers the cane with such energetic relish.

"I know you yong women from Europe have tender harts," Batenga begins, motioning me to a chair. Oh dear. He's attributing my moral and political stand to feminine frailty.

"… But don't feel sorry for these boys. They need to be taught a lesson. If we don't beat them severely, they become most unruly, believe you me."

Clearing the chair of papers so that I can sit down, I explain how I feel about corporal punishment. Batenga patiently replies that it's normal in Tanzania, it's an accepted part of the culture. I point out that it was considered normal practice when I was at primary school in England, too, and still is, at private schools.

I remember my eight-year-old self, witnessing a boy being struck in the face by the teacher when I was in Surbiton, feeling powerless to say anything. So many wrongs have been committed in the name of culture, or because people were 'just following the rules'. This is not about culture. It's about human rights. Indivisible and inalienable. Article five, *the right not to be subjected to 'cruel, inhuman or degrading treatment or punishment.'* Applies to every human being. No exceptions.

"But you most understand, Ndugu Goldsmith, that on this occasion the boys were being punished for being disrespectful to the new girl students. You yourself have come to me with Madam Hildegard to complain that some of the boys are harassing the girls and gettin' away with it."

This is an added dimension. I really do support tackling the harassment of girls, but I didn't envisage this would mean thrashing the hell out of the perpetrators. How to resolve this predicament?

It's complicated. It hardly works as a deterrent anyway. Some of my students are against corporal punishment, but others assure me they would prefer a thrashing to being assigned extra work, the advantage being that it is over in minutes. "We men are strong, Mwalimu, we can take it." I suspect there's more than a little *machismo* about this, as there was in my primary school. I've a feeling some of the boys even see it as a chance to get their shirts off and show how tough they are in front of the girls.

"I appreciate I'm a volunteer—a visitor here, Mr Batenga, and I have to respect the school rules. And I'm so glad the harassment of the girls is being taken seriously. But isn't there a more constructive way to punish the boys—extra work on the school farm, maybe? I just can't condone this kind of punishment… Could I stand on the end of the veranda every morning, slip away quietly if there are beatings, and come back in time for my classes?"

Batenga hesitates, considering my request to slip away while the beatings are happening. He kindly agrees to my suggestion—'until I get used to it'. But I won't get used to it. I know I can't stop the beatings on my own. It would need the support of the other teachers. But I'm not going to stand by and watch while it happens. And I will never put forward the names of any of the students I teach for such punishment.

That's the thing about human rights abuse. It debases the punished, the punishers and those who stand by and let it happen.

Chapter 13

Debatable

May 1979, year two of volunteering. Mufundi Technical School and I are becoming accustomed to each other. The BBC World Service Radio tells me that Margaret Thatcher has been elected the first woman Prime Minister in the UK, and Tanzania has won the war with Uganda. How would we know? We are miles from anywhere. News travels slowly. The school will be pleased to know Tanzania is no longer at war. I'd better run down to the staff room and tell them what's going on.

The dry season is just beginning, and the landscape is rapidly changing. Picking my way down the rocky, dusty path to the staff room, I can't help being more preoccupied about the dramatic change in the political climate back home. Some people are hailing Thatcher's victory as a triumph for equality, and there's no question it's a historic first. I wonder what my Women's Lib group are making of it. Radical feminists are deeply suspicious of leadership of any kind, especially aligned with the forces of the Right. I always argued there should be equal numbers of women and men everywhere, at every level in every occupation, bar none. That's only right and fair. But political ideology is a different matter. I have a deep sense of foreboding that back home, the war on everything I stand for is about to intensify. The odd woman leader in the patriarchal system, no matter how powerful, tends to reproduce more Patriarchy in order to survive. And then women get blamed for it far more than men. Thatcher doesn't stand for women anyway. The upshot could be more misogyny, not less. It's the system that needs to go.

I feel too far away from all the action in the UK. I need some political activism here to keep me going. At least I am in a Socialist oasis here. What Nyerere said at the meeting when I first arrived has stayed with me— that we should be encouraging the students to participate in the democratic process and learn to become active citizens. They don't get much chance to do that in class— the teaching style here remains very formal. It's hard to shift the colonial legacy when most of the teachers have been educated and trained that way themselves. But I have an idea—a school debating society, run by and for the students, to whet their democratic appetite, develop their communication and planning skills and get them thinking on their feet in English. At the very least, it will inject some energy into the usual monotony of school.

A hundred rowdy excitable students are gathered in the hall for the first debate: *This house believes that African culture leads the world.* The Proposer, Gabriel Botango, is a tall, good-looking boy with ebony skin and fine eyes. He has prepared his arguments well and speaks articulately and with passion. He's proud of African history and the ancient Kingdoms of Mali, Ethiopia and Greater Zimbabwe, and disparaging about Western culture. "All these useless Western gadgets—they have even invented an electric brush to clean their teeth!"

The audience is in hysterics, squealing with laughter. An electric toothbrush—who'd have thought! The very epitome of Western decadence, when all you need to do is simply pluck a twig from a toothbrush tree, good for the teeth and healthy for the gums.

But the next speaker has a much more uncomfortable message, arguing that European and African races should remain separate.

"Look at these half-breeds, half African, half European. They are untrostworthy, their brains are feeble, their bodies weak, they are always sick. Mixin' the races dilutes our African heritage and colture."

I have an uneasy feeling he's talking about me; but his words are greeted with an enthusiastic round of applause. My heart hammers, I am screwed up inside, attacked as a person and as a teacher.

Sam Shayo, a short, enthusiastic brown-skinned student, comes to my rescue.

"We are all one race, the human race; mixin' is good. Look at Mwalimu Goldsmith here. She is half African, half European, exactly what we are talking about. But she is clever, wise and kind. She has taught us the importance of communication. And she always turns up on time to classes to teach us. Not all the teachas here do that." To my relief, his intervention is greeted with laughter and applause. Good for Sam. But I'm glad we have got to the end of it.

I had no idea my identity was to become the subject of the debate. That's the trouble with democracy. You have to listen to things you don't want to hear.

Making our way back to our bungalows through the eucalyptus trees, the bright full moon lights up the forest path like a silver-white searchlight. Walking between the two of them, I can finally spill out my distress to Hildegard and Afia.

"I can see how angry the students must feel about colonialism, but keeping Africans and Europeans separate is like arguing for some kind of Apartheid, surely. I don't understand... when Tanzania is at the forefront of the anti-apartheid struggle, sheltering so many freedom fighters from South Africa. I didn't know what to say."

Afia and Hildegard are very different characters, and I'm not sure they know what to make of my activism and the scrapes I get into. But they turn up to support me all the same.

"There are still quite a few Tanzanians who have negative views about interracial mixing," Afia, explains. Tall and slim, she wears her hair in the latest sputnik style, named after the Russian space-craft, her natural hair twisted so that it stands up in spikes all over her head, which makes her appear somewhat startled against the moonlight. But she has a gentle earnest way of explaining things, without making me feel stupid or ignorant. "The students are not used to givin' their opinions, they are testin' the boundaries. Perhaps we should have given them more guidance from the start…"

Hildegard agrees. Short, dark-haired and stocky, wearing frameless glasses, she is a more cautious character than me, preferring to stand back and scrutinise things from a distance. "Ya, the punishment for disrespecting teachers is usually a beating—but zey know you are against that on principle, so zey sink they can get away with saying ferry bad sings about you, to your face. Maybe the hol sing was too risky…"

I spend a sleepless night, disappointed, dispirited, imagining the whole thing is a colossal mistake. I have bitten off far more than I can chew as usual. The students get so few extra-curricular activities here—I so wanted the evening to be a success. I'm always taken by surprise at the confusion and hostility my identity causes.

The next day I am thrilled when I walk into class to a round of applause. My students say the debate was brilliant, they are making plans for the next one—on Polygamy. What could possibly go wrong? Now I just need to encourage some of the girls to speak out.

And success has fired me up for my next big idea.

Nyerere said schools should be about social and cultural learning and building a community—a challenge in this technical secondary school, surrounded as I am by mechanical, electrical and civil engineers, most of whom don't see themselves as artistic or creative. English language is the only 'arts' subject. But to my delight, in addition to grammar, the curriculum I teach includes the wonderful African writers series—Ngugi wa Thiongo, Chinua Achebe, Buchi Emecheta, Nuruddin Farah. I can see how much pleasure and inspiration some of my budding engineers are getting from these books. But how to inject more of this inspiring creativity into school life? We need to create a space where arts and science meet. Remembering the first Black cultural week we organised in Leicester Students' Union, I'm inspired by the fact that we have teachers here from all over the world—Tanzanians, English, Germans, Dutch, Russians, Ukrainians, Georgians. Why not organise an international cultural evening, offering performances in our own languages from our own cultures—dancing, singing, music, poetry...

To my surprise, the idea has gained traction among students and teachers alike—although I don't think they have ever experienced anything like it before. Perhaps they are willing to give it a try since the debating society has proved so popular. On the night of the show, everybody lends a hand, setting up the lighting, handing out the programmes and setting out the chairs. I am sick with nerves. The Dutch clog dancers have pulled out at the last minute for technical reasons. No clogs. The excitement among the audience before the show causes a near-riot. But we have discovered some unexpected talent on campus. The girl students have made their own costumes and choreographed a spectacular dance routine. Batenga's Swahili poem and Ivanov's Balalaika ballad move us all to tears. And so does Lawrence's rendition of 'Jake the Peg,' but in a different way.

The evening is a success. There are calls for it to be repeated next year. I'm more complicated than your average volunteer. But maybe I do know how to get people together.

*****

Lessons are suspended once a week during growing and harvesting season so that teachers and students can work together on the school *shamba*—the farm—to grow maize and beans, the staple for school dinners. It's more than a mile to the *shamba* through the forest carrying our heavy *jembes*—hoes—over our shoulders. I'm already lagging behind. Among the trees it's cool and green, muffled sounds and dappled light. Sometimes you can glimpse small deer running through the trees when it's quiet—villagers hunt them to supplement their diet. I am anxious about losing sight of my students—fear of being alone in a forest has never left me. In a clearing I notice a woman struggling with a huge log she has just felled with her axe. Her tiny baby is bundled up in a wrapper on her back, securely tied with a knot at the front. Two big bags of brushwood lie on the ground at her feet.

I call out a greeting and ask if she needs help. She nods. *"Ndio, asante Mama"*—"Yes, thank you." The two of us grapple with the giant log, struggling to hoist it onto her head. It must be nearly ten inches in diameter and as tall as me. She has a length of cloth twisted into a circle around her head to prevent the load from slipping. Her knees buckle slightly and her face screws up with effort and pain under the weight of it. She steadies herself, then sets off down the path at a trot, tree on her head, axe at her waist, baby on her back, a bag of brushwood in either hand, the muscles of her calves straining as her tiny frame almost disappears under her impossible load. A Tanzanian man calls out *"Jambo Mama"* pleasantly in greeting as he cycles slowly past her.

I sit on a tree stump, head in my hands, not quite believing what I have just seen. One of my students, Jumaa— always late—comes up to console me.

"Pole sana; very sorry *Mwalimu,* are you tired?"

Yes, I am tired—of seeing injustice and inequality and unfairness, sheer grinding poverty, women treated like pack horses and second-class citizens, and being powerless to change it—and even finding myself unwittingly aiding and abetting it by trying to help. Nobody talks about this, here or at home. It's just seen as women's unpaid role, to

347

fetch the firewood and the water and have the babies. It's not even counted as work. Women are strong, they say, they are used to it. They are lifting the kind of loads no human being—or even animal, smaller than an elephant—should be required to lift; putting such strain on the spine, the limbs, the skull, and so recently after having given birth. When I get home, I'm going to get an international campaign going about this. We have to do something. It's a scandal.

As she disappears along the path, I realise I have forgotten to ask her name.

*****

At least the girls at our school have the chance to escape the kind of hard labour endured by the woman I met in the forest. They will be the first young women in Tanzania to be qualified in mechanical and electrical engineering. I plucked up the courage to ask a question about this at our meeting with Nyerere. I told him that in the UK we have so few women doing these subjects, it's a brilliant initiative—did he think the girls would encounter any challenges, and how could we support them?

"Good question, they will need to beware of the boys for a start!" He laughed uproariously at his own joke, with that wheezy infectious giggle that punctuates everything he says. He said the girls would be pioneers, like the Suffragettes in the UK. They have a big responsibility, to show others the way, and women teachers like us should be encouraging them.

I was impressed that he knew about the Suffragettes, but his quip about the boys didn't turn out to be such a good joke. At the end of the first year, two of our girls were sent home pregnant, although the boys responsible remained unpunished and stayed on at school. Hildegard, Afia and I, the only three women teachers, had visited the girls' dorm to talk to them about it, and warn them to be on their guard—not to get pressurised by the boys into having sex, and not to get caught out, to use contraceptives. (And who am I to talk, with my history?!) We should be telling the boys to be responsible too. But Mr Chegeni, the Deputy Head, says it's not necessary, boys will be boys... and apparently that's allowed. The same double standards can be found the world over, from rural Norfolk to East Africa.

I feel for our girls here. It's a tough male environment, not easy for them to thrive in. Some of the girls told us they never wanted to do engineering anyway. They were selected to come here to a technical school because they were good at maths, but they were homesick and wanted to go home. I told them how much I admired their proficiency with numbers; columns of figures made me tremble in fear. At least that made them laugh. We tried to encourage them with Nyerere's message—they are pioneers, role models, they should be proud of themselves.

I was relieved to see that not all of them were so

downhearted. Two of the keenest ones, Busara and Zuwena, are emerging as leaders of our group of girls, and they could already see possibilities for their future opening up. They had big plans. "*Mwalimu*, we are going to set up a business, a garage for women, with female mechanics, because men think we women know nothing about cars. We will treat our lady customers well, so they keep coming back to us."

*****

Lawrence is tall, slim, olive-skinned, bearded and handsome, with a cupid's bow mouth and fine eyes. I feel drawn to him. His quiet energy, his sense of fun, speak to me in some way I can't place. He is a complex mix of elegance and awkwardness, spirituality and schoolboy antics, introvert and extrovert. I can't make him out. Is he shy, deep, or just not interested? He seems a bit lost. Not sure of himself. Like me. I'm attracted to relationships that make me more confused. He fills me with longing and infuriates me in equal measure.

When we first met he persuaded me to eat a raw Scotch bonnet pepper—one of the fieriest chilies in the world— by insisting that, unlike the red ones, the green ones aren't hot. Two seconds later I knew I had bitten off more than I could chew again. It was as if I had been struck over the back of the head with a mallet—mouth on fire, I spat, choked and gasped, and my eyes ran until I thought I was going to die. I was so angry that I had fallen for it. He thought it was funny. I have been addicted to chilies ever since.

Lawrence had already been in Mufundi for nearly three years when I arrived, having extended his contract by a year. My students didn't share our mutual ambivalence about our relationship. They already had the two of us paired up long before we had decided. "Madame, when are you and *Mwalimu* Cane going to get married?"

When Lawrence accepted another posting to Zanzibar at the end of the school year, I thought that would be the end of us, so I started a relationship with Steve in Dodoma—and one or two others besides. I even met up again with the gorgeous Raphael, a Tanzanian I met and fell in love with back in London, although he had since become engaged. But I thought about Lawrence all the time.

We saw each other again at a volunteer meeting in Dar Es Salaam, and then I invited him back to Mufundi for Christmas. Now he has asked me to come and visit him in Zanzibar.

Imagine the most idyllic spice island, the scent of cloves and spices, white sands on palm-fringed beaches, fish plucked fresh from the Indian Ocean cooked in fragrant coconut milk, and you have Zanzibar. Anyone could fall in love here.

But Zanzibar has its dark side. It was the heart of

the Arab slave trade, centuries before the slave trade from West Africa to the Americas. You can still see the remnants of the slave market in Stone Town, where the 'human cargo' was bought and sold. The vast majority of Zanzibaris are mixed Arab and African. Their skin tone and their hair are like mine. For the first time in my life I look as if I belong. When we appear in local dress, people think Lawrence and I are a typical Zanzibari couple, he a bearded Arab, myself a mixture of Arab and African. Confusion only begins when we are with other volunteers, or when I speak in broken Swahili and they expect me to speak it like a local. Then they discover we are faking it.

At the British Council reception for volunteers, Lawrence and I slip out for a midnight swim in the warm Indian Ocean. As soon as we wade into the silky moonlit waters, it instantly lights up with blue-green magical phosphorescent sea sparkle. I remember it from Italy, the night Roberto and I made love in the Adriatic.

"They are mostly harmless, but sometimes they can irritate your skin because they give off ammonia," Lawrence warns me. So that explains it. That's what must have caused the sudden burning sensation that brought my amorous encounter with Roberto to such an abrupt and embarrassing end. Lawrence has the technical explanation for this kind of thing. He's an engineer, not a crazy romantic Italian. And he remembered to bring some towels too—'borrowed' from the British Council bathroom.

The next day we lunch on Lobster Thermidor and chilled Safari beer at the Zanzibar hotel. We talk of the deep connection between Lawrence's devotion to Hindu mysticism and his career in electrical engineering. "I can tell you *how* electricity works," he explains, "but I can't tell you *why*. That's the mystery of the universe for you... it's spiritual."

When he arrives with the bill, the waiter asks if we want a room, which I think rather presumptuous of him; and he is stupefied when Lawrence and I split the cost of the meal between us. Noticing the other clientele—mostly older White men with young Zanzibari women—it suddenly dawns on me that the waiter must have assumed I was a local sex worker, and that Lawrence would be footing the bill for the meal as part of the business arrangement. The sign on the toilet wall confirms my suspicions:

'Polite notice to our esteemed customers:
No loud pleasure noises in the bedrooms after midnight.'

Zanzibar is ninety percent Muslim, and full of surprises. Becky and Rosa, two of the British volunteers, have a group of Zanzibari women friends here, who wear glamorous low-necked sequinned outfits beneath their black burqas, which they call bui-buis—'spider webs'. They drive the men crazy, completely covered, wafting about in exquisite clouds of perfume. They concoct their own special recipes, infused in little charcoal pots, standing over them with their legs astride to allow the smoke to permeate the whole body, trapping the perfume clouds in their black spider-webs.

On Zanzibar Island, women volunteers can go where our male counterparts can't. We are let into a wonderful secret world. Bushra, who speaks good English, invites us to one of their all-female soirées, serving delicious food cooked in coconut milk and spices, and sugary sticky confections made with syrup and flavoured with cardamom. The company of these women has a very special kind of energy—a blend of art, culture, glamour, music, fragrance, joy, eroticism. We spend a delightful evening belly-dancing to squeals of laughter, their smooth satin skin the same shade as my own; and the conversation is of fascinating sexual techniques using only toned and flexed vaginal muscles. I have never heard such frank and open talk about sex among women since my student days discovering my inner cervix. Bushra tells us that wearing the burqa is their key to freedom. It is the perfect disguise. Women have only to change their shoes to remain unrecognised when slipping out to a secret rendezvous in the dead of night.

Bushra takes us to local wedding celebrations, where the night before the official ceremony, her friends perform a special simulated sex act for the bride's education, the women playing all the parts—the husband, wife and new-born baby—and positively no men are allowed to watch. It's an open-air performance. An older woman has the special role of driving groups of inquisitive men away, brandishing her heavy switch whilst the performance is in progress.

I can't help feeling that here, it's the Zanzibari men who are sometimes losing out. These women really know how to have fun. I marvel at their creative ingenuity and spirit in a restricted, segregated world, which few outsiders like me get to see. There is always a catch. This is Zanzibar town, among relatively affluent, open, lively women. Life in the rural areas here is as gruelling, unequal, and punishing as it is for any women in the world. Even here in the town there is a sense of real and ever-present danger for women.

"We are enjoyin' life while we can," Bushra says, "But we are all terrified of being married off and sent to Saudi Arabia, where life is much more restricted and we will be kept like prisoners in our own homes. Women don't have half the freedom there that we have here."

Despite their openness about sexual matters, there is one issue that remains unspoken. Reading Nuruddin Farah's book, *From a Crooked Rib* in class with my students back in Mufundi, we came across graphic descriptions of 'female circumcision' in Somalia, a traditional practice in many parts of Africa, including Tanzania, in which young girls have their clitoris sliced off and their vulva sewn up as part of a puberty ritual, a rite of passage. I wondered what my all-male class would make of it. Some had heard of the practice, but others were genuinely shocked.

I had come across reports of 'female circumcision' before at University in my Phenomenology of Religion class, though I didn't think the term adequately described such a brutal practice. When I protested that it was an expression of patriarchal power, control and cruelty at its most extreme, my lecturers urged me to put aside my feminist outrage and avoid such cultural moralism. I had heard it was practised on Zanzibar, and wondered whether it affected Bushra and her friends. But we never discussed it. I was an outsider. There are some places too sensitive to touch.

*****

Back in Mufundi, I awoke this morning from a terrifying dream—being chased through the moonlit eucalyptus forest by a great, black-maned African lion. In the space between sleep and wakefulness, I heard my own voice screaming for help; but as I surfaced I realised the unearthly tortured sounds of wailing and weeping were coming from somewhere on the compound. Hildegard and Afia came to call for me. "A child has died," Afia said simply. "Quickly, get dressed."

All the women in the community are already gathered in the little bungalow in the lane next to the maize *shamba*. Inside, in the heavy, humid darkness, it is crammed with women sitting on the floor, wrappers over their heads, chanting a high-pitched, agonising, mournful dirge, bodies rocking back and forth in grief.

I take my place at the back of the room with Hildegard and Afia, leaning up against the wall under the shuttered window. Adjusting our eyes to the gloom, we see the tiny frail body of a girl stretched out on a bed in the corner, covered in a cloth, only her head visible, eyes closed. I guess she must be about six or seven—with village children it is difficult to tell.

But Afia whispers that the girl was actually ten years old when she passed away. "We never knew this child even existed until now. They have kept her hidden away at home. Her mother tells me she's never walked in her life, and she never wanted to go outside. A few weeks ago, she said goodbye to all her brothers and sisters, refused to eat or speak, turned her face to the wall… and waited to die."

In the afternoon, two women come to take the body away for washing. As soon as they lift her, disturbing her bedding, we are overpowered by the putrid stench of death. Her little legs are like matchsticks, from Polio—an entirely preventable disease.

We leave as the sun goes down, having had nothing to eat or drink all day except a few sips of water. Queasy, weak, bereft, overwhelmingly sad for the loss of this child, so young and accepting—an old soul. How differently people manage death and disability in different cultures, and how differently we face it as individual human beings.

There's a letter from Mum waiting for me, telling me

Uncle Chas died of lung cancer two weeks ago. He was a lifelong heavy smoker. The last time I saw him we were doing a drunken dance to 'Hey Jude' at my farewell party before I left for Tanzania. "Janie, you are going off on your big adventure," he said. "As for me, I 'ave no worries, no regrets. I've had a good life. If I die tomorrow, I will die a happy man."

Uncle Chas was a coalman in the family business. He spent his leisure time in the pub playing shove ha'penny with his in-laws whilst Auntie Molly ran the house, and looked after the kids and the extended family. He played the piano by ear and always accompanied our raucous rendering of cockney musical-hall songs at family parties. It seems a world away from this one. I will miss him.

I feel a sudden surge of homesickness; a visceral ache that gnaws at my insides and presses against my ribcage. I sometimes wish I had Uncle Chas's contented approach to life. He was at home in his own skin. He wasn't born with a sense of isolation and longing for adventure like me. I am always searching for something just out of reach, wanting my life, society, the world, to be different, especially for women, for Brown and Black people, gay people, disabled people, people in poverty, people who are alone and abandoned. I can never just accept things the way they are. The world doesn't accept me the way I am.

*****

Hildegard the German volunteer has gone home and we are joined by Angela, a big, bold, lively red-headed volunteer from Durham. 'Angie' is a breath of fresh air, full of the energy and enthusiasm of a new volunteer. Nothing fazes her. She speaks her mind, and she is immediately at home.

"I used to get hung up about my weight all the time at hoome," she beams. "But they seem to like big women around 'ere. And I like a bit o' Black."

Angie wears tight straight-legged figure-hugging jeans, to the amusement of my students. At weekends, out of school uniform, they sport big baggy trousers and platform shoes.

"Where did you get those terousas from, Madam? Zanzibar?" Zanzibar being a byword for un-cool.

"These are the latest fashion in London, believe me. Baggies and flares are out. Soon you'll all be wearing these, you'll see."

I am mortified. Flares snuffed out, just like that. My entire wardrobe rendered obsolete at a stroke. I will be a laughing-stock when I get home.

It's been a gruelling term. We are in need of some light relief. Angie proposes a weekend of fun in Dar Es Salaam. Luckily, Ahmed and Rashid—who supply the school with fruit every few weeks—have dropped into the school office to firm up the orders for next term. They offer us a lift on their return journey to Dar, followed by a party in the evening.

Halfway there, we stop off at the upmarket Morogoro Game Lodge for refreshments and a comfort break. Rashid and Ahmed seem to know the owner of the place well, and they are ordering drinks and food on the house. We gorge ourselves on sizzling Zebra steaks, washed down with red wine from Dodoma—a rare luxury compared to our monotonous Mufundi diet of *ugali*—maize—and beans. Soon the *Konyagi*—the local gin—is flowing, along with imported whiskey. It's obvious that neither Rashid nor Ahmed is in a fit state to drive, and now the owner is offering us rooms for the night.

It is pretty clear this is a set-up, and as usual, the pairing has not gone in my favour. Angie, the White girl, is the prize for the tall, handsome and charming Ahmed, and she evidently feels she has bagged herself a prince. Rashid may be a very nice man when sober, but I don't find him remotely attractive in that way. Now he's attempting to kiss me, and he has wandering hands, it's time to make a break for it.

On the pretext of visiting the ladies' room yet again, I race out of the back door of the lodge, unsure what to do next. If I can get to the main road and flag down a car, perhaps I can secure a lift to Dar Es Salaam and persuade Angie to come with me—although it's debatable whether she would want to tear herself away from the delightful Ahmed.

Skirting the side of the building, past the dustbins by the kitchen wall, I am stopped in my tracks. I have come face-to-face with the biggest, scariest-looking bird I have ever seen. It is fully five feet tall, my own height, standing upright like a stork, its motley vulture-like feathers unkempt and bedraggled. It has a bald head and a revolting dirty-pink, bulbous wattle protruding the length of its throat. It blinks its beady eyes at me suspiciously. Beyond, there are six or seven more of them, monstrous shadows in the dark, circling the bins. I scream and race back into the dining room, terrified witless.

"Marabou storks—scavengers—ugly as sin," the owner laughs. "They fly over from the game park every evening to rummage through my dustbins. What the hell were you doing out there anyway?"

"I want to go to Dar—we'll miss the party..." I protest feebly.

"Good time girl, eh?"

"Of course, the party, let's go!" Angie enthuses. She has finally read the discomfiture in my expression.

The others get up unsteadily, making ready to leave.

I have had just enough to drink to be fully conscious that what I am about to do is madness, and still do it anyway—take a long-distance ride in a car with a driver who is drunk, to escape having to share a bed with his friend. But at this moment, it seems like the lesser of two evils.

We screech off along the empty road in the pitch black, the others laughing and shrieking while I screw up my eyes tight and silently pray. This is a real-life re-play of my recurring nightmare—careering along in the dark in an out-of-control vehicle. I am terrified of speeding cars. That's why I never wanted to learn to drive.

After a while my head starts to nod forward.

Suddenly the car stops again. We have arrived. I must have fallen asleep.

"Told you we'd get you here okay!" Ahmed boasts. "So, ready for the party?"

I hate to be a party-pooper, though my heart really isn't in it. I am wrung out by scary giant flea-bitten birds and the death-defying car ride. But I tore my companions away from a luxury night at the Lodge on the pretext of this party, so I have to show willing. The gathering is an intriguing multicultural mix of African, Tanzanian-Asian and Ex-pats. I spend most of the time trying to avoid the disappointed Rashid. I feel sorry for him, but he is intent on misinterpreting any attempts I make just to be friendly.

I end up having a flaming argument with an Aid Worker from the Netherlands about foreign men and aid workers visiting 'prostitutes' here. As usual I'm told that I am inappropriately bringing my Western Feminism into a completely different culture where it doesn't belong. The Patriarchy, on the other hand, belongs everywhere, apparently. After an hour or so, worn out, I manage to get a lift with a couple who are heading in my direction. Angie promises to follow soon, but I've a feeling she and Ahmed are planning to make a night of it.

It's after one o'clock in the morning when I finally

retrieve the keys from the upturned flower-pot under the bougainvillea. Jenny and Colin, the VSO field officers, are away up country, and they always leave their apartment available for visiting volunteers wanting to take a break in Dar Es Salaam. I switch on the lights—a luxury after the lights-out curfew at ten o'clock every night in Mufundi.

Nice place. Colourful wall hangings, cushions in local fabrics, Makonde carvings, and a collection of giant seashells from Zanzibar. Near the French windows leading onto the garden, an unusual mottled salmon-coloured shell the size of a saucer catches my eye. I hadn't noticed it before when we dropped in briefly to change for the party. As I reach out to investigate, eight long legs uncurl from underneath. It's alive. I recognise it. I have seen pictures. It's a giant crab spider. As it lumbers sideways towards me, I scream the place down, hurtling to the nearest safe space—the toilet—where I lock myself in.

On the toilet seat I collapse into meltdown, body shaking, teeth chattering, every pore in my skin invaded, defiled and disgusted, blood pounding in my head, as if I am about to have a heart attack. I am an extreme arachnophobe. Even a photograph of a spider propels me into panic. This is my *1984* room 101—trapped in an unfamiliar apartment, alone in the middle of the night with a giant spider.

My hysteria gradually abates to gentle sobbing. Spiders and snakes, heights, columns of figures, speeding cars, being alone in the dark or lost in the woods. I will cross the

street to avoid a strange dog. There is a rabid canine somewhere out there with a killer bite reserved solely for me. I
can't remember a time I wasn't afraid of all these things.
After tonight's experience, I must add oversized ugly
birds to my catalogue of horrors. My mother is afraid of
things that fly, especially moths. I am petrified by
everything else. The world seems such a hostile place, full
of sinister forces out to get me, known and unknown. I can't
anticipate how creatures—or people—are going to react
to me, scrutinise me, attack me. My portfolio of phobias
is becoming harder to manage and more difficult to
hide. Nowhere is safe. Nothing to fear except fear itself.
Terrifying.

It isn't just the spider bite I'm afraid of—although that
is unbearable enough. It's the spider entity itself. Too many
eyes, too many legs, too many dark and dreadful secrets.
That *Thing* is still lurking somewhere in this apartment,
assuming ever greater proportions in my imagination.
Now it's the size of a tea-tray…

I try to make myself comfortable enough on the toilet
seat to sit it out until Angie's return. Angie is afraid of
nothing. I'd be ashamed to confess to her that I've been
hiding in the toilet all night. I'm debating whether to lie
and tell her I've had an upset stomach brought on by too
much zebra steak. Angie will wonder why I didn't just
confront the *Thing* and smash it with a frying pan. Show it
who's boss. But I couldn't even contemplate getting close
enough to kill it. That would be worse. It belongs here, it's

a Tanzanian spider. I'm the one who's out of place.

The next thing I feel is a sickening blow to my head.

Dozing off, I've fallen forward off the toilet seat and smacked my forehead up against the sink. Everything is pitch dark. A power cut—not unusual in this city. The toilet is stiflingly hot, smelly and airless. I am bathed in sweat and bitten to death by mosquitoes. The apartment is open-plan. That *Thing* could be anywhere. But if I can make a dash for it up the narrow passageway I can retreat into the bedroom and shut myself in. I reach for the torch, which I spotted beside the toilet brush before the lights went out.

This is it. Sooner or later I have to face my fears. As dawn breaks, I unlock the door and open it cautiously, just a crack, sweeping the torchlight across the floor. No sign of the giant spider. Suddenly something jumps and I slam the door shut. Opening it again after a few moments, heart hammering, my torch beam picks out a tiny frog in the middle of the corridor. A frog. The one creature I am not afraid of. It blinks at me. Relief floods over me, tears course down my cheeks.

They say you have to kiss a lot of frogs before you find a prince.

I'll stick with the frog.

Chapter 14

Culture Shocks

I hate school. I have recurring nightmares that I'm still in the fourth form, sitting at the back of the Latin class in Stafford, endlessly repeating that stupid Roman war chant: *Bloom bloom bloom, Blee blow blow, Bla bla bla, Borum Bliss Bliss.*

I have to do a probationary year at the local secondary school in Wandsworth to qualify as a teacher in the UK. Two years' teaching in Africa doesn't count, even if it was Nyerere's *Education for Self-Reliance*.

"Poor you. The newest teacher always gets lumbered with the notorious 4B," Maisie says sympathetically, handing me the timetable. 4B. Twenty fourteen-year-old girls of all sizes, races, colours and creeds. So different from my time at school, when I was the only Black kid in class. Some have barely entered puberty. Others are coping with things that even the average adult would find a challenge.

Take Elaine, for instance. Tall, gangly, pony-tailed rebel, with that look of defiance in her eyes. Bolshie troublemaker, unreliable, cheeky, exasperating and disre-spectful, a regular pain in the arse. She reminds me of me at that age. This morning she came to me to explain why she was late yet again. She has five younger brothers and sisters, and she has to get them up, breakfasted and ready for school every morning. Her mother is a single parent, working night shifts as a nurse, arriving home soon after they have all left for school in the mornings. Her youngest sibling, five-year-old Jordan, was running a fever during the night. If any of the kids are sick, it's down to Elaine to be nurse. A fourteen-year-old surrogate mother of five.

"I 'ad to wait for me Nan to arrive to look after Jordan 'cos 'e's too sick to go in today." So she was ten minutes late for school.

You learn a lot from people's stories.

The weather is as rainy, cold and miserable as any wet Friday afternoon in November could be. We should all be at home by the fire, or better still, in Tanzania, ambling through the shady eucalyptus forest in Mufundi. Today 4B is in uproar as usual. How can I possibly entertain such a diverse audience in form-time on a dismal Friday afternoon?

Left to themselves, 4B are an excitable, engaged, ener-getic class. There are occasional fights, bullying, name-calling, ostracism, racism, as in any group of volatile, hormonal teenagers. But on a good day they can be a perfectly charming bunch—articulate, interested and interesting. That atmosphere changes completely, to one of resentment and hostility, whenever a teacher intervenes.

If I just sneak out now and go home they probably won't notice, and they'd have a thoroughly riotous and stimulating afternoon without me, until the bell goes. They are perfectly capable of entertaining themselves, teaching and learning from each other. There must be at least half-a-dozen different languages spoken in this room. At least that's a start.

"Okay, 4B, let's have some quiet now. Who's going to teach us to count up to ten in the language they speak at home?"

"Why, Miss? Wass the point?" I fear this idea is dead in the water.

"Because everybody counts," I counter feebly.

But suddenly it takes off. The two Roma girls are counting in the same numbers as the Hindi speakers. There are stunned looks.

"It's practically the same Miss! *Ik, du, tin, car, panch!* How come?"

These girls have made a discovery. "That's because Roma originally came from Rajasthan," I explain. "That's a region in northern India. I'm going there on holiday this summer to visit Leyla, a friend of mine. I read up about it. The red skirts the women wear there are just like the traditional dress that Roma wear in Europe. The Rajastanis travelled all the way across India to Egypt. Some say that's where we get the word '*Gypsy*', from the word 'Egypt'. They call themselves Roma, that means 'people', I think—"

"—My Grandad is proud to call himself a Gypsy, Miss. He says it's traditional," Rosa interrupts.

"Good point, Rosa, we should respect what people want to call themselves... I think they came into Europe through Spain, where they started that fantastic flamenco dancing. The flamenco costumes look pretty similar too, all those frills and flounces and the bright colours..."

I wonder whether this is going to provoke some racist comments from some of the White girls.

But Maria nods in agreement.

"I learnt Flamenco as a little kid!" She gives us an expert twirl, stamping her feet and clicking her fingers in the air above her head, to laughter and clapping from her audience. She reminds me of Vicky, the 'Gypsy' girl I admired on the Shaftesbury Estate when I was a kid.

"I even saw Roma in Finland," I point to the globe on the desk, spinning it around with the tips of my fingers. "Rajasthan's here, Egypt's here, Finland's here—look how far they travelled—and you know, the Roma I saw in Finland were wearing pretty much the same clothes as they do in Rajasthan, come to think of it, doing the same kind of dances as they do in Spain. Gorgeous long red skirts spangled with golden sequins, swirling around when they moved. It was fantastic to watch..."

"You've been to a lotta places, Miss."

"You learn a lot when you're travelling. Everything's connected. Let's see how many connections we all have here between us when we count to ten. One at a time, girls, *one at a time…"*

I had envisaged an orderly performance, each girl coming up to the front of the class to count out loud to a silent and respectful audience. But the whole exercise instantly erupts into pandemonium. Everyone is swapping stories, the Scots with the Irish, the Italians with the Spanish, Africans with the Caribbeans, the Hindi speakers are still talking to the Roma girls. I'm counting to ten in Swahili with Rupa, whose family are Ugandan Asians. Rupa tells me her mother speaks fluent Swahili—but it's hard to hear above the hubbub. There's not enough room around the globe for everyone's jabbing fingers to trace journeys across oceans and seas. I can't keep up. We need a bigger map.

"Elaine, run to the geography room and ask Miss Rainer if we can borrow the big world map. And ask *politely.*"

It crosses my mind, fleetingly, that Elaine might not return. I wouldn't blame her. But within a few moments she has reappeared, breathless and grinning.

"Miss Rainer asked me if I was plannin' my escape when I asked her for the map, Miss!"

We unfurl the big map carefully across three desks pushed together, and soon we are all poring over it, tracing journeys across continents, following the paths of ancient and recent migrations. It's creating a chaotic, excited and noisy discussion. Everyone is talking at the tops of their voices about where they went on holiday and where their grandmas were born, discovering how exciting it is to find out where you come from and uncover shared roots.

There's a sudden obedient hush as Miss Rainer pokes her head around the door, with that severe teacher's look on her face, the one that haunts my dreams.

"What's going on here? Everything okay?"

"Yes, yes, fine, everything is *fine*," I reassure her. "We are just learning Finnish."

"Well, please keep the noise down. You are disturbing other classes who are actually trying to learn."

"*Finnish*, Miss?" they all query as Miss Rainer's head disappears.

"Yes, Finnish," I repeat. I've got to get back in charge somehow. "We are all going to learn how to count up to ten in Finnish. It's one of the most difficult languages in the world. I should know. I tried to learn it when I was an au-pair. That would be a very challenging 'finish' to the afternoon if you'll pardon the pun."

Undeterred by the groans, I persevere.

"I bet you can't learn to count to ten in Finnish in twenty minutes before this lesson ends."

There's a moment's hesitation, when I imagine they're going to say, *what's-the-point-Miss* again. But then, they must be used to it. The school curriculum is full of mystifying things that don't seem remotely relevant to later life for the average fourteen-year-old. And they are right—most of them aren't relevant.

"I bet we can do it, Miss," says Elaine. Elaine the class

rebel. If she is up for it, then it must be okay. So they're off, stuttering and laughing as they try to get their tongues around those rhythmic, seductive and seemingly unpronounceable sounds, a mysterious magic spell...

"Uksi, Kuksi, Colme, Nelya, Viisi..."

They are pretty much word-perfect by the time the bell goes. A completely useless exercise, but a highly successful lesson. Fourteen-year-olds learn so fast. We have all had about as much fun as it is possible to have in school, and 4B look pleased as punch. And I have sustained a whole lesson based on numbers, which usually scare me to death. Not bad for a rainy Friday. I will teach them that Latin war chant next week, *Bloom bloom bloom, Blee blow blow...* You never know when it might come in handy.

Thank God it's Friday. I collapse into an easy chair in the staff room, exhausted by the international counting exercise. I've earned the nickname 'Buzzer' among my teaching colleagues, apparently because I'm constantly charging up and down corridors bearing armfuls of felt-tip pens, scissors and multi-coloured sugar paper. *Buzzer.* I'm not sure if I appreciate the name. It's reminiscent of an angry flying insect—a Tanzanian locust, perhaps.

I still feel queasy from lunchtime. When the bell went, Pattie and Maisie from the English Department disappeared down the road in Maisie's car, and returned to the staff room triumphantly bearing small boxes smelling of cheap greasy meat.

"A cultural revolution took place here while you were

on VSO in Tanzania, Buzzer," Pattie said grandly. "Friday lunch, you're in for a treat."

"Once bitten, forever smitten," Maisie beams, handing me a small warm red-and-white cardboard box. I open it cautiously. The contents look suspiciously like Wimpey and chips.

"Where's the vinegar? To put on the chips?"

"You don't have vinegar with it, silly, it's a *McDonald's*!" says Maisie, and they're all roaring with laughter, the word *McDonald's* uttered as if it is self-evidently sacred. I take a cautious bite and my suspicions are confirmed.

"Well it's bloody disgusting! The box looks more edible than the contents. You can have the rest of it—I shall never eat it again. Sorry, no Coke for me either—never drink the stuff. I'll stick to my Marmite sandwich."

I had already stunned them today with my peculiar gastronomic tastes. As the other teachers stagger into the staff room at the end of the day, I realise opinion is also divided as to the effectiveness of my unusual pedagogical approach.

"What was all that racket coming from your class? From now on, you must make them do their homework, or get them to read quietly in Friday form time," says Miss Rainer, Head of Geography and Deputy Head. Miss Rainer says what goes around here. "They're making far too much noise, it's too disruptive. Those girls in 4B are hyper by the end of the week."

"Well, I think Buzzer got them going," says Maisie,

sticking up for me. "They've never shown that much excitement in my English class…"

"True," Pattie agrees, "4B are always a tricky bunch. Not clever enough to pass exams, not dim enough to do as they're told. It's amazing to get them all focused on anything at all…"

"Well, look at the séance you did with them last week," says Miss Rainer, ignoring my colleagues' support and peering at me over her reading glasses. "One or two Christian parents have already written in to complain about it."

"But we have different faiths in the class, not just Christian, Miss Rainer… I was trying to explain to them about the roots of religion, where the ideas come from. It's a serious philosophical discussion. I studied all that at University…" I'm warming to my theme. "Spirituality, death, loss, psychic experience, wanting to be connected with those you have loved. All fourteen-year-olds are interested in that sort of stuff…"

Miss Rainer rolls her eyes in despair.

There's no chance of educating anybody in school. I've got to get out of here. The trouble is, I came back from Tanzania without a plan. The Labour Party's torn apart, the Yorkshire Ripper's on the loose, Thatcher's not for turning, John Lennon has been shot dead, the world's in chaos. And I am stuck in school, not doing anything about any of it. I don't want to teach for the rest of my life. But what else to do? What happened to all those grand ambitions I had as a student to be Secretary General of the United Nations?

I have to get to Sainsbury's on my way home. I have run out of Marmite. How I longed for Marmite when I was in Africa! Black Gold. I don't know what they put in it, but I used to dream about it. And I need to shop for my dinner party tomorrow—Mike Wooldridge and his wife are coming over. Mike interviewed me in Tanzania for BBC Radio 4 about my experience of being on VSO.

"You ought to go into Radio, you're a natural!" he told me. He gave me his card. "Look me up when you get back home. We'll do a few demo tapes. I'll help you."

Radio. There's an idea.

But what to cook?

Shopping in Wandsworth is an assault on the system. I'm overwhelmed with thousands of products, hundreds of varieties, lined up in immaculate antiseptic rows, the illusion of choice and abundance. You can get anything you like, whenever you like; there are no seasons. The world will never run out, plenty of everything in a standard size, shape and colour—dairy, poultry, meat and fish, vegetables, cakes, bread, pasta, rice, tins, jars, frozen chips and pizza, cleaning products and toiletries—produce from every country in the world. Just take your pick from the dizzying array. Impossible to decide.

It's a complete culture shock after shopping in Mufundi, which was admittedly a hit-and-miss affair. The village shop was a shack next to the bar, the size of a box bedroom. Sometimes there was almost nothing to buy. The wooden shelves would be empty, save for a lonely bag of salt and a few tins of *tanbond*—a bright yellow margarine the texture of axle grease, very much sought after for spreading on white fluffy cotton-wool bread— if you could get the bread. The golden vat of maize cooking oil was particularly prized, but you had to bring your own container. Empty plastic bottles were almost as valuable as full ones. Clothes-washing soap was sold by the yard, in a long bar the colour of cream toffee. Customers could walk away with the whole bar, or buy a lump expertly sliced off with a wicked-looking machete. On a good day there was *Africafe*, coffee powder from Kilimanjaro, and *konyagi*, the local gin in a clear round glass bottle. Occasionally *kanga* would appear, the colourful wrappers the women wear. They came in pairs, one for a wraparound skirt, the other for your head and shoulders. Every item was scarce, coveted, transported home in a wicker basket like a trophy, because shortages of any basic commodity could suddenly occur—salt, toothpaste, soap, cooking oil.

When word went out that there'd been a delivery, there was always a long, excitable queue. The rule was to get in line anyway, even if you weren't sure what was on offer. If I turned up on my own, wearing local dress, I took my place at the end of the queue, whilst shoppers glanced at me sideways, wondering. But when I came with White volunteers we were often served first, despite our insistence that we should take our turn with the other customers. Even if there was nothing to buy, the village shop in Mufundi was a great place to meet and chat, see what was going on in the village, and find out when the next delivery was expected.

Here in the Wandsworth Sainsburys, no-one talks to strangers, except perhaps to enquire whether they have come across the pesto. It's a kind of time-warp. No clocks or windows, no distractions, just the aroma of half-baked bread, and the occasional piercing shrieks of a toddler in meltdown.

The items I want are out of reach on the top shelves— one of the many disadvantages of being only five foot tall. Everything is constantly being moved around the shelves to different areas of the store each time I come, and I get lost among the aisles. I can't find what I came here for, and I can't remember what it was anyway—I have mislaid my shopping list.

Lined up at the tills, the trollies in front of me are laden with packets of edibles, piled on top of each other, some of which will be thrown out within a week or so, unopened and mouldy. I have come away with all sorts of special offers I don't need. And I forgot the Marmite.

In Mufundi, once the shopping was completed, the village beggar was always there to wave us goodbye. A tall, skeletal figure dressed in tattered shirt and shorts, leaning on a wooden crutch, his right leg missing below the knee, his nose and lips completely eaten away by leprosy. He dribbled from the gaping red sore where his mouth should be, making inarticulate sounds, thrusting out a scabby stump, devoid of fingers, begging for *fedha*—just a few coins. They called him 'the *Fedha* man'. Whenever I saw him, I was filled with a mixture of revulsion, compassion and frustration at not being able to help him in any way, other than giving him money.

Outside our Wandsworth supermarket, a bedraggled beggar sits on the pavement with his dog, his belongings around him in plastic bags, by his side a polystyrene cup containing a few coins, and a sign that says 'hungry'— the *Fedha* man of Wandsworth. I can't do anything for him either, apart from give him money. Does that even help? Anywhere you go in the world it seems there is no shortage of inequality.

*****

Belgrave Square. I remember walking into this building two-and-a-half years ago for my interview. The big guy with the striped suit a size too small, the woman with the gold-rimmed glasses, sizing me up, both wondering whether I was too Black and too fatherless to be a suitable candidate for VSO. I keep thinking about Lawrence, still out there in Zanzibar—what he's doing, whether he ever thinks of me. He hasn't been in touch since I left six months ago. The thought of him still makes my heart sore. Angie's latest letter offered me her characteristically blunt relationship advice. "If I were you I'd stop floggin' a dead 'orse. I've 'eard rumours that Lawrence 'as been spotted with a Zanzibari girl in a Burqa."

I have come back to the VSO office to talk to Suzanna about my experiences in Tanzania—excluding my love affairs. Suzanna is still dressed all in black.

"Black volunteers need support," I tell her. "I was harassed and rejected sometimes because of being Black British. They don't even know we exist. People mistook me for a Chagga, a 'prostitute', a Zanzibari, a Black American. Some people even objected to my being two races, mixed up. I just wasn't prepared for it. I sometimes felt isolated and bewildered, way out of my depth."

Suzanna is supportive and empathetic. She says she'll talk to Colin about it. "You know Colin, he was the field officer in Tanzania when you were out there. He's the Head of Department here now. Maybe we can get some special training designed for Black volunteers. But there aren't many of you, and it would have to be quite specialised for each country. In the meantime, would you be prepared to have a chat with the Black volunteers we send out? We could give them your phone number. And we could get you to do a talk for all the volunteers about women and development. What about the idea you had for a returned volunteer women and development group? That sounds exciting."

"Yes, I keep thinking about the woman with the tree on her head. The one I wrote to you about—the woman I saw in the forest. I didn't even ask her name. We have to do something, Suzanna."

The woman with the tree is always on my mind. The giant log on her head, baby on her back, axe at her waist, a bag of brushwood in each hand, the wince of pain on her face and the working of the lean muscles of her calves, as she steadied herself and headed at a trot down the dirt path. The casual way the man on the bike greeted her, as he passed her by. "Jambo Mama." All grown women are called 'mother' in Swahili, whether they have children or not.

Colin puts his head around the door.

"Jane Goldsmith! They told me you were back, causing trouble as usual. You'll be pleased to know I have put your name forward for the VSO Board as a new Trustee. You'll be one of our first elected ex-volunteer representatives. We need rabble-rousers like you to shake them up a bit. Not that I ever agree with a word you say, of course."

"Good idea to have volunteer reps on the Board at last. We've been campaigning for that for ages. But how do you know I'll get elected, Colin?"

"Oh, you will. Believe me, you will. For some unaccountable reason, you have many supporters."

The VSO Board meetings are formal affairs, held in the high-ceilinged board room around a vast polished mahogany table. I am one of only three women Board members, the only Black person, and at twenty-eight, the youngest person in the room. It is like being a student again, outnumbered on the Senate, the room stuffed with peers of the realm and 'the Great and the Good'—and I am neither. The agenda includes a stack of closely-typed documents for approval, which mostly go through on the nod. Undeterred, wearing my banana yellow outfit accessorised with a man's tie to add gravitas, I make spirited speeches about Black volunteers, women in development, equality and sexual harassment. I can see their eyes glazing over.

"Don't resign," says Mum encouragingly. "You've been elected to go in there and shake them up."

But I am bored to tears with the Board. I'm a fish out of water and I'm getting nowhere. I'm an activist, not a paper-shuffler.

Frank Judd, ex junior Labour Minister and Chief Executive of VSO, instructs his secretary to call me at work. The great man wishes to see me. I am terrified. You don't get called to see the Headmaster unless you've done something disastrous.

"You are frightening the Lords and Ladies on the Board!" says Frank. "I really need you to say what you have to say, but couldn't you just tone it down? Just a little bit?"

"Frank, I honestly thought I wasn't having any impact at all. I had no idea I was making such an impression. I thought they were terrifying *me*. Now I know I am frightening them too, I'll stay."

*****

Cousin Vic introduced me to his new girlfriend Leyla before I went on VSO. She is a little younger than me, clever, fun, vivacious, exquisitely pretty, with cascades of dark wavy hair. She is Anglo-Indian, my first friend who is mixed, like me. She and Vic are now just friends. She's invited me and Auntie Bel for a visit to India in the summer holidays, where she's been working for several months in Rajasthan, where the Roma come from.

Leyla's been working in the Maharaja's palace for a year, still the home of the Maharaja himself, a tall, elegant, handsome man in his mid-forties. He has recently converted the palace into a guesthouse—a magnificent, shabby, crumbling old edifice, in need of renovation and a good clean. "… And that's just me, never mind the hotel!" he jokes.

Dun-coloured geckos slither down the peeling walls, great long-legged spiders lurk silently among the cobwebs in dark corners of high ceilings, heavy faded red-and-blue tapestries of Maharajas on horseback adorn the walls.

After a leaky shower and copious application of insect repellent, the best place to sit in the evenings is up on the flat roof-terrace, with a view across Udaipur to the lake palace and the mountains beyond. Lounging on battered sofas on the rooftop, we watch the sun go down, sipping iced gin-and-tonic with wedges of fresh lime from the tree in the kitchen garden.

Leyla and I stay up until the small hours, doing 'the Bump' to Sister Sledge's 'We are Family'. Everyone falls for Leyla, she's a magnet for both sexes. She brings romance and glamour into people's lives. Ultra-feminine, sweetly seductive, she sashays down the street, hips swaying beneath full skirts, oblivious to her own charms. Later, we go travelling together around India for a month by train, visiting Delhi, Calcutta and Madras (where Leyla's family come from), and ending up in Bombay to catch the flight home.

The locals think Leyla and I are Indian sisters, especially when we wear our Salwa Kameez, brightly coloured outfits with tunic, loose trousers and scarf—perfect travel wear. Some Southern Indians even have soft Afro-looking hair like mine. To his utter confusion, we persuade our rickshaw driver to get in his carriage so that we can take him for a ride.

"We feel so guilty," Leyla explains, eyeing his thin spindly legs. "You need a rest. We'll pay you just the same."

But we are hopeless at the job. Within a few minutes we collapse exhausted, in fits of giggles.

In Varanasi we hire a boat to see the sunrise on the Ganges. A twelve-foot-long alligator joins us for the ride, diving repeatedly under our boat and resurfacing either side of us by turns, a row of spines clearly visible along its shiny black arched back, as it breaks the surface and plunges again into the red-brown murky waters. We lie on the bottom of the rowing-boat as dawn breaks, laughing in sheer terror until we cry, clinging to each other for dear life as the boat races along, low in the water, carried away by the powerful current.

"Don't vorry!" our boatman reassures us, grinning, shaking his head from side to side. "They von't eat us. They only eat the dead bodies thrown in after funerals. They like the cooked food best."

On the 24-hour train journey from Calcutta to Madras, travelling in the 'ladies' carriage', Leyla and I have plenty of time to exchange life stories, as the paddy fields roll by outside the window. Leyla is 'different', like me. That is why we have become so close. Her Anglo-Indian parents gave up their family and community in Madras to come to England, with the sole purpose of giving their girls what they believed was a 'good education'.

"The first thing I remember about coming to England is that my bedroom door handle felt cold. I had never experienced that before. Funny what sticks in your mind as a kid."

Without a family support network, Leyla's parents became very isolated, whilst Leyla and her sister spent most of their childhood at boarding school, and then in the rarefied atmosphere of Oxford University, surrounded by students who had experienced a privileged and insulated upbringing.

"This is the first time I've been back to Madras since I was seven."

I am envious that Leyla has family here in India. She knows where her roots are and can return to them. I wouldn't know where to start.

Our Indian adventure is a bonding experience. I have found my soul-mate. There is no-one I would rather be with than Leyla. She radiates warmth, light, energy and fun. Back home, we become flatmates in Tooting.

Lawrence is back from Tanzania now. He has a teaching job in the technical college in Wolverhampton and comes down to stay at weekends. If I hadn't managed to get to the VSO volunteer reunion, we would never have got together again. It was a close thing. The train was delayed at Paddington because of heavy snowfall, and I had been waiting nearly one-and-a-half hours on the freezing platform. I was about to give up and go home when it pulled into the station and I jumped on board. A near miss. It's the story of our relationship, somehow.

*****

I have some big news for Miss Rainer, Head of Geography. I am leaving teaching for a new job in the voluntary sector, with the World Education Services.

"Leaving teaching! I am so disappointed!" Miss Rainer exclaims, to my complete surprise. "But why? You are so good at it!"

Elaine is leaving too. "I'm pregnant, Miss. I 'ave to look after all the kids anyway. Now I'll have one o' me own. I can still count up to ten in Finnish though. I won't forget, and I'll teach my kid."

"I won't forget you either, Elaine. We'll leave together,

heads held high."

Two rebels checking out of school at the same time.

This new job is the life for me. Touring the UK visiting university campuses, to persuade student unions to fundraise for scholarships for refugee students from Chile, South Africa, Uganda, and Palestine. I didn't get into radio. But now I'm *on* the radio, and on platforms, giving speeches around the country about all the things I care about—student activism, refugees, internationalism, solidarity, women's rights. All my passions and experience rolled into one. I'm having the time of my life.

The World Education Services offices at Compton Terrace, Highbury, are in a handsome converted four-storey Georgian double-fronted townhouse, with wide steps up to the front door, white-painted sash windows, and high ceilings embellished with ornate ceiling roses. Twenty of us are working there—a large, boisterous, loyal, dysfunctional family of politicos and activists. My desk is at the front, on the ground floor, overlooking the carefully-tended gated garden that runs along the length of the terrace, where we eat our lunchtime sandwiches when it's sunny. In the evenings after work we pile into the Hope and Anchor for a pint and some politicking.

There are very few refugee women being awarded degree scholarships at World Education Services—a mere two percent of the hundreds of student refugees arriving from Chile and Uganda. I invent my own job as Women's Officer, apply for funding from the European Union, and establish a women's campaign for women's adult education in 'Third World' countries, and lobby for more scholarships for refugee women to study in the UK.

On one of my first field trips I'm off to Liverpool University, where I am shown into the students' union office. There's a young woman on the floor on her hands and knees, writing out posters for the grants' demo in coloured felt markers. She's strikingly good-looking, with startling blue eyes and short raven hair. I notice she's wearing a little black dress and pearls—unusually posh for a student activist.

"I'm from WES. I'm here about raising funds for a refugee student scholarship."

"Valerie, Deputy President. Come on in."

Val and I form an instant rapport. Originally from Manchester, her elegant dress sense belies her working-class down-to-earth origins. Her father was a left-wing egalitarian trade unionist like my grandfather, and we share the experience of working-class extended family values and culture. When Val gets a job in London working with WES's sister organisation, she comes to live with Leyla and me in our flat.

As part of our Women's Campaign, Val and I are writing a book, based on our research about women overseas students.

"What we need is a witty title, Val—something eye-catching that's really going to jazz up our report. How about *It Ain't Half Sexist Mum*"?! You know, based on that

TV series about the British Raj."

Val is sceptical. "Isn't that a bit racist?"

"Well that's the point. We all know that TV programme presents a very stereotyped racist view of the British Raj—all in the name of jolly tongue-in-cheek harmless British sitcom humour. I had enough of that when I was a kid. Our title would be a spoof. I can just see it now. On the front cover we could have a design of a life-sized airmail envelope containing a letter with *"It Ain't Half Sexist Mum"* written on it—as if it's a letter from a young female overseas student here, writing to her mother back home, complaining about sexism in overseas student recruitment and services in the UK. I think it would work, turn the whole thing on its head, get people talking at least. Something a bit different from the usual dry reports. We won't get anywhere if we don't take a few risks along the way."

There's great excitement at the news that the Shadow Minister for Overseas Development, Judith Hart, is going to launch our report at the press conference. But my sense of humour is not going down well with the senior civil servants at the Ministry. "You can't have that title, *It Ain't Half Sexist Mum*—they won't take you seriously," one of the friendly civil servants advises. "You could print some extra copies with plain covers for the launch with the Shadow Minister and the press."

We decide on a plain white shiny laminated cover for the formal launch, "Like the Beatles' *White Album*," I reason. "White on the outside and full of colour inside."

The launch is a great success. We even get a mention in the *Guardian*. One of the ODA staff comes up to congratulate us. "You have highlighted a real issue, well done. Between you and me, there are lots of feminists here in the Overseas Development Administration, trying to escape from the worst excesses of the Tories. You can count on our support from behind the scenes. By the way, can I have a few copies with the designer cover to give my colleagues? The ones that say *It Ain't Half Sexist Mum?* Such a witty title—great fun."

*****

Our Returned Volunteer Women's group is organising a national two-day residential conference in Wolverhampton, with over a hundred delegates already registered, one of the first conferences in the UK dedicated to a discussion of women and development.

I'm leading the steering committee, with my best friends, Marilyn, Katy, Efua and Val. Barbara Rogers is going to make a keynote speech on Development and the Domestication of women, based on her new book. Efua is delivering a speech about her campaign against female 'circumcision' in Africa. Val is the treasurer and my flatmate Leyla is doing a grand job on creative communications and entertainment. She has concocted an impressive line-up already—an all-female rock band,

Indian classical dance, and the highlight of Saturday evening will be an up-and-coming comedienne called Meera Syal, who has promised to perform a sketch featuring a waitress on roller skates, sporting a gigantic prawn on her head. Lawrence is working hard for the event. He has secured the venue, and he's organising some of the men to run the creche and do all the catering. On day two it's my thirtieth birthday and Lawrence has organised a giant cake.

My mother is the mainstay of the whole thing—administrative officer in charge of registration, crises, complaints and complications. We are a formidable mother-and-daughter team. This is going to be the conference of the year, bang in the middle of the United Nations Decade for Women, putting women on the world map. We are trailblazers, campaigners, world-changers. We'll send a message to the Overseas Development Administration, to the Women's Movement, to the Development organisations, to the press. I wish I could tell the woman carrying that huge log in Tanzania that I have never forgotten her, even though I forgot to ask her name. In my head I call her Kumba—like the little girl who first awakened me, on Clapham Common, when I was four years old.

*****

We are all going to Nairobi—Val, Katy, Marilyn and

me—to the United Nations Third World Conference on Women. Thirty thousand feminists from all over the world are gathered in the campaigners' forum, attending workshops, rallies, meetings, caucuses, or sitting on the grass outside in the sun, arguing earnestly, drinking in the atmosphere. If there really is a worldwide women's movement, this must be our coming together.

Women from the UK have an axe to grind. More than a hundred UK non-governmental organisations are represented here in Nairobi, and we are unhappy about the way the British Government is largely ignoring us. NGOs are not allowed into the official conference where the Government delegations from around the world are writing a plan for equality, development and peace that will affect millions of women around the world. We want daily briefings from the British Government, just like the Americans give their NGOs, an opportunity for them to tell us what's going on, and put our position to them. Instead, the British Government invites us all to a tea party on the lawn at the British High Commission. There will be cucumber sandwiches with the crusts cut off. No lobbying, no campaigning, and positively no political speeches allowed. We have been warned.

We have written a speech anyway. I draw the short straw and have to read it out on the manicured lawn at the British High Commission, in front of Baroness Young and increasingly sour-faced civil servants and dignitaries, on behalf of all the UK campaigning and development organisations, expecting to get thrown out at any moment. We want business, not tea parties.

This feels like making a difference.

We come home via field trips to women's groups in Tanzania and Zimbabwe, to be greeted by news of more riots in Brixton. The first half of this decade has been rocked by events that have shattered the Black Community—the Brixton Riots, riots across the country, the New Cross Fire.

The few Black and Asian members of staff at WES are not political activists, and my colleagues in the humanitarian aid and development sector are mostly White. My women friends in the community movements are Africans and Latin Americans. The women I campaign with in the local government women's committees in Tower Hamlets and Islington are multicultural. Meanwhile Black Britons are sending so much money home to their communities to help in their development—more money than all the Aid programmes put together. It's exciting—but disorientating—for me to be moving constantly between these different groups. Worlds with different political cultures, languages and social class, talking about the same things—inequality, racism, solidarity, social change. There is a kind of solidarity-in-silos going on.

When my friend Mia and I were volunteers as part of the support team preparing for Angela Davis's visit to Hackney Town Hall, I realised how charismatic leaders like Angela have the rare ability to bring so many of these diverse communities and groups together. On the day, the Hall was packed with heroine-worshippers, the excitement palpable, the audience composition demonstrating the cross-over between feminists, local activists, the Black movement and internationalists. Angela brings the magic with her whenever she steps onto the platform. A prolonged, ecstatic standing ovation greets her, electrifying the room. She sounds as if she were incanting poetry, not political polemic, dissecting and intersecting race, class and gender in her inimitable authoritative, mellifluous, lilting voice, calling for capitalism, prisons—and housework—to be abolished. What a wonderful world that would be.

In the early hours of that morning, we found ourselves on the edge of the 'red light' district, in a first-floor flat in Kings Cross, drinking neat high-proof Jamaican rum— Mia's friend Roy, our host, having run out of mixers. With the lights of Kings Cross winking outside, there were just seven of us in the dimly-lit room: Roy, Mia and me, Diane Abbott and Janet Boateng, and Angela's partner, listening enthralled to Angela expounding on the way the White feminist movement has failed to recognise the struggles of Black women, and that you can't have Feminism without getting rid of capitalism. Diane and Janet regaled us with tales of the trials of Black women in local UK politics. All our struggles are inextricably linked. All a consequence of the colonial legacy and patriarchy—poverty, exploitation, racism, sexism, exclusion.

*****

Back in the offices of World Education Service in Compton Terrace, things are fragmenting again. The staff meeting is the usual turbulent, highly-charged affair. Communists, Trotskyists, Labour stalwarts are all vying for position. Tensions are running high, like raging counter-currents in the Ganges.

There are still some things we can agree on in the full agenda. The miner's strike and the miners' wives are an inspiration. The anti-apartheid movement, and the campaign against the banks and big corporations bring us all together. And we are all behind the solidarity movements for Chile and Central America, even if there are still endless rows about who caused what fascist takeover and how to organise a *proper* revolution.

But the cracks soon begin to surface. We are split between supporting the Eritrean movement for independence and supporting the socialist state in Ethiopia. Likewise, the Palestine and Israel issue is fraught with tension. We are all against Thatcherism, but the feminists among us, myself included, despise the misogyny her worst policies is engendering among our male colleagues. Right-wing male politicians don't get blamed for their gender, along with their agenda, in the media and the press. All the same, it's a travesty that our first female prime minister has had such a disastrous effect on the social, political and economic fabric of our nation. Be careful what you wish for. Fresh from the excitement and inspiration of the Nairobi world women's conference, we feminists are determined to get women's rights centre-stage on the agenda in every campaign, regardless—Southern Africa, Latin America, the Palestinian cause.

After the meeting closes, exhilarated by the heady debate, and daunted by the work we still have to do in the women's campaign, I am dismayed to discover Katy in the women's toilets, on the verge of tears.

"I absolutely support the Palestinian cause. But there was so much anti-Semitism going on in that room—did you hear what they were actually saying about Jews, Jane? I can't stand it. Just because I'm Jewish doesn't mean I support Zionism. I felt totally silenced in there."

The images of the Holocaust I saw on television in the 1960s have remained with me since I was a fourteen-year-old. It was the first time I became conscious of injustice, and those pictures led to my personal and political awakening as a teenager, and set me on the path to becoming a lifelong activist and campaigner.

Why didn't I speak out just now?

"I'm so sorry Katy, I should have said something. I was so focused on getting the boys to support the Palestinian women's campaign, I just didn't think."

"Why is it that a room full of people who live their lives claiming to be fighting inequality and injustice can think it's okay to be racist against Jews? How come they can distinguish between the Pinochet regime and the Chilean people, but not the Israeli Government and ordinary Jewish people, people like me—who want peace and justice, and hate the treatment the Palestinians are suffering?"

I put my arms around Katy, and she rests her head on my shoulder. How often I have been in her situation, when my identity has been mistaken, attacked or simply ignored. As if I don't exist. As if the political is not personal.

Politics is a constant balancing act, not to forget one oppressed group in the passion and intensity of supporting another. To distinguish between Governments and the people, and empathise with people's fear and historical trauma, without necessarily supporting their politics. To do away with solidarity-in-silos, and take other people's struggles for freedom into your own heart.

*****

Leyla is going to have a baby! It's decided. We are all going to live together in an alternative kind of family. Lawrence is moving to London from Wolverhampton, and we are house-hunting for a home large enough for a family of five and more, where we can establish a new life for all of us. Finally, maybe I can think about becoming a mother too.

It is a radical change from our life together as two sociable, politically active, fun-loving singles. Despite our grand plans to re-invent the notion of the conventional family, the arrival of Leyla's baby inevitably alters the dynamics in our friendship. Suddenly we each have different priorities and perspectives. There are tensions we should have anticipated, but never really imagined or prepared for. Differences between us are amplified, now that we are leading different lives. Leyla's a mother, while I'm still living the life of an independent woman. I feel jealous that she has had the courage to go through with her pregnancy. And yet I am torn between the freedom of my exciting career, and the idea of being a parent and living together in a big family. But I am thirty-three, going on thirty-four. If not now, then when?

I can see that motherhood is taking its toll on Leyla. Having lost both her parents in the last two years, maybe she's looking to me as someone from an extended family who can help fill the gap in her life, now that she has become a mother herself. I've applied for a week's parental leave from work, so that I can help her. But Leyla is now in a family of three, recovering from a difficult birth, with the baby and her boyfriend living in our flat. I am the outsider, not sure of my role, awaiting Lawrence's arrival.

I suddenly feel alone in my own home, a failure, agonising over dark issues re-surfacing from my past—my abortions, my own longing for a child, all the old feelings of loss, separation, and uncertain identity. I realise I can't give Leyla the help she needs right now, much as I want to. I have lost my place, lost my bearings. I don't feel ready to be a third parent to this child. I know I'm not really helping the new parents, who are going through their own transformation. But I have something missing of my own. I haven't yet been a daughter to my own father.

Leyla finally plucks up the courage to express her disappointment. I have let her down. She doesn't want to go ahead any more, with us all living together, as we'd planned. She needs space, time, to get away, find herself, be her own woman, create her own family.

Everything has changed. Lives colliding, falling apart.

Chapter 15
There is No Body

1986

Friday 11 April, 5pm, Ranmore Street

I reach the blue front door and knock, trembling with exhaustion and anxiety. As it opens, I stumble upstairs, throwing off coat, umbrella and shoes as I go, and fling myself, soaking wet and gasping, onto the white sofa. I weep as if my heart would break. When my sobs subside, I'm conscious that Ray has followed me silently into the room and is sitting in the low chair opposite me, waiting, his long slim legs crossed under him. I'm making a whimpering noise like a little frightened cat. The sound reaches me as if it is coming from somewhere else. Eventually I turn my head to look at him. I want to go on lying face down, to protect my chest and stomach.

"Sorry about your sofa, Ray. It's all wet and muddy."

"It's okay."

"I can't sit up."

"That's okay. Stay as you are."

I give him a wry smile, despite myself, and then my body starts to shake with laughter as it shook with sobs before. This is utterly absurd.

But Ray is still sitting there, waiting for me to begin. So I begin.

"Last night, I had a dream.

I'm feeling very happy in the dream. I'm on a train to Holland, going on holiday with a group of friends. It all starts to go wrong—one of those jumbled up dreams where I'm leaping on and off trains, going in the wrong direction, until finally I have lost all my companions and I'm left all alone on a deserted platform, at twilight.

The next train is leaving from the platform on the opposite side of the tracks. I can see the headlights approaching in the distance. I have to cross a tiny rickety old bridge, high above the ground, with no rails or sides, to get to the platform in time. I feel waves of vertigo-induced panic rising in me—I'm not going to make it. I screw up all my courage, race across the bridge and leap onto the train just as the doors close and the bridge collapses behind me. I still have a strong feeling this train is going the wrong way.

I unfold my Ordnance Survey map, to find out where I'm going. I am useless at reading maps, especially detailed ones. The background of the map is a deep midnight blue. As I study it, the blue expands, takes up the entire carriage, and then the whole of the sky. In the centre is the gigantic shape of the Circle Line, suspended in outer space—no stations, no place names, just the bright yellow outline against the inky sky. I haven't a clue where I'm going and I've lost all hope of seeing my friends again. In my peripheral vision I can just make out stars twinkling at the furthest edges of the map, light years away. But I can't be sure."

Ray is impressed with the dream. "It's fantastic! That's a very powerful image, the yellow Circle line against the blue-black sky. How does it make you feel?"

Empty, abandoned, lonely, lost, directionless. No map of me.

"Even in real life I have no sense of direction, Ray. I'm always afraid of getting lost. The wrong way becomes so familiar, I take it every time."

I pick at a tiny loose white thread on the white sofa.

"Can you really understand what I'm getting at Ray? Your life experience is so different from mine."

"If you mean gay, White, male, yes, it is different from yours. But that makes me a good listener. I don't have your experience so I have no preconceived ideas. You are an amazing person. It's really exciting to work with you. Would you mind if I tape-record you telling your dream about the Circle Line? I want to use it for my group therapy class—it was brilliant."

"I guess so." I'm flattered. But that's not the point.

"Great. Same time next week then."

Outside, the rain has stopped and the sky is beginning

to clear. With the money I have spent on counselling, I could have bought a ticket to Ghana.

Thursday 15 May, 2am, in bed

I'm still being plagued by vivid, ghastly dreams. I'm appalled at the horror emerging from my subconscious. I lie here in the dark, heart hammering, trying to convince myself I'm not warped and sick, just hurt. I don't really want to eat babies, or be mauled by wild animals or get stuck on the Circle Line forever, in outer space, with no reference points, no place names, going round and round in circles. These things are symbols. They must mean something. I feel better now I've written them down.

8.25am

My palms are sweating, there's a knot in my stomach, I feel anxious and irritated and angry, especially with all these people sitting in the carriage, crowding me out. I can't write because the tube train is swaying and jerking, and I'm afraid people will look over my shoulder and try to see what I'm writing. My heart is pounding like crazy. I want to scream and cry—but I don't have the energy. How can I possibly cope with work today?

Lawrence is going to Ghana at the end of August. The pain of it! I have been trying to get to Ghana all my life. (Correction: I have been avoiding going to Ghana all my life.) And he gets a free ticket, just like that.

Monday 30 June, hottest day of the year so far, 30 degrees

I ended up at the Ghana High Commission in Highgate this afternoon, miles away from Highbury and Islington where I work. God knows how I got there. I don't remember making a decision about it. I was on my way to the office, and then suddenly I was there, at the High Commission, enquiring about my father. We were seated at opposite ends of the room, the other three people behind desks, surrounded by piles of paper, erected like barriers between us. I had to shout above the noise of the electric typewriters and the telex machine. Shout to strangers about things I haven't even come to terms with myself.

"I am searching for my father."

When I started asking questions about Ghana, they assumed I was going there on a visit. I told them I wanted information about my Dad and they said, "Doesn't your mother have a letter from him? Or a photograph?" I said, I think the letters got lost, or she sent them back. And I've never seen any photographs. *We can't help you,* they said. *We don't know him.*

Yes, I was on my way to work and then I ended up there at the Ghana High Commission. I still can't remember quite how it happened. I woke up this morning at about 11am after more bad dreams. Mornings are my worst time. I couldn't move. Leyla had already left for work. I crawled to the bathroom and got into the bath.

I must have left the house and walked down our road, but I don't remember it. On the corner next to the tube station, I do remember passing our two local down-and-outs, already boozing by mid-morning, as usual. They are always so cheerful, not a care in the world. To my shame, although I pass them every day, I still don't know their names.

"What's up, darlin'? It can't be that bad."

The one with the grizzly beard offered me a slug of something tepid from his can. "'Ere, 'ave summa this, cheer you up, put 'airs on yer chest!" I sat down beside them on the pavement and sipped it cautiously.

"It *is* lager you're drinking!"

He seemed mildly offended. "What did yer think it was—meths?"

I seemed to be chatting to them for ages. I staggered a little as I got up, and the one with the hat held out his hand to steady me. "Dronk at this time of the day!" he quipped. "And to be sure, now you've spoiled yer noice whoite trewsers."

I was irritated that one of the worst-dressed men in Tooting had cause to criticise my appearance. A black patch of oily grime had smeared itself across the seat of my pants where I had been sitting on the pavement. I tried to dust it off with my hand, but that just spread the stain and made it worse. It was nearly midday. I should have been at work for several hours by now, but I'd only just made it to the corner of my street. Even our local street-dwellers manage to start their day earlier than I do.

I finally made it to work by about 5pm, via Highgate. I can't think why I didn't just take the day off sick and go home. I was in the middle of explaining to Kate about ending up at the Ghana High Commission, when I suddenly jumped up and started screaming and hurling paper from my desk, shouting "I hate it, I hate it!"

Then I raced out of the front door, hurtled down the steps and into the gated garden. The flower beds were ablaze with midsummer blooms—orange and yellow marigolds and blousy chrysanthemums. I wasn't in control of what was happening. I went mad. I could hear someone howling in the distance, an animal in pain. Looking down, I could see a figure sprawled, distraught, face down on the parched grass, clad in white trousers, a black grimy patch clearly visible on the seat. It occurred to me that they would be covered in grass stains and dry dust at the front when she got up from the ground.

I jolted back to earth, just as everyone came running from the office into the garden—Kate, Marilyn, Val, all of them. I recognised immediately what had happened. Another out-of-body experience, like the one I had as a child in Surbiton, just after Mum got married.

I was so angry with everyone looking down upon me, teary and blinking, as I lay prostrate on the grass in the baking sun. Angry with Lawrence for going away. Angry with Leyla for going away. Angry with my father for going away. Angry with myself for feeling so angry.

They told me I had to take sick leave, go home, get some rest, go and see a doctor, take my trousers to the cleaners, don't come back for at least a week.

I am so ashamed.

Northern Line, Stockwell, 7pm

This carriage is like an oven—baking, humid, sweaty, crammed with tourists and commuters. It's been a very, very long hot day. I can't go on like this. Thank God they told me to take the week off.

I rest my notebook on my lap and close my eyes. It's a long way from Highbury to Tooting. Five more stops. The down-and-outs will probably be gone by now. I will ask them their names when I pass by tomorrow, and present them with a six-pack of lager, nicely chilled.

Overcome with drowsiness, my head lolls sideways, nearly touching the passenger next to me. He touches me on the shoulder. I mumble an apology before discovering it's Ben, my old boyfriend from Leicester when I was a student. I don't want him to see me like this, half asleep, my trousers muddied, my face bloated with tears.

All the same, it's an amazing coincidence to see him again after almost a decade, sitting right next to me on the tube. Last time I saw him I hid under the desk in the Student Union President's office, broken-hearted when he left me. I did love him. We talk about old times, lazy loving weekends in his room at Beaumont Hall at University, listening to Stevie Wonder's *Inner Visions*.

He invites me back to his flat for a drink. We get off at the next stop, and he shows me up to his penthouse suite on the tenth floor.

"Sit yourself down and admire the view while I fix you a long cold one," he smiles, disappearing into the kitchen. His voice is so comforting. Slow deep tones with that slight Geordie lilt I have missed for so long.

Ben tells me he has qualified as a psychotherapist. He's evidently doing very well for himself.

"Nice flat, Ben!" I call to him. Modern, air-conditioned, beautifully furnished.

"Only the one bedroom, though," he calls back. "Won't be a tick. Ice?"

This is wonderful, just what I need. Cool and peaceful. I collapse gratefully onto the plump white sofa, looking around the room at the hangings and tasteful bric-a-brac, beginning to relax. I'm exhausted. I still feel a little self-conscious about my filthy trousers.

There's a panoramic view from Ben's window. Even though we are ten floors from street level, I am disconcerted to see a dense tropical forest outside. A playful lion cub comes bounding through the foliage, leaps through the open window and onto the sofa beside me. I am dismayed to see it pulling threads in the white sofa with its sharp claws. It's unusual to see a lion cub on its own like this. It must be lost. Where there are lion cubs, the parents aren't far behind. Our guide told us that, while I was touring the Tanzanian game park. Now I'm afraid, really afraid. I run in panic into the dingy ill-lit kitchen, where my mother and stepfather are sitting at the table, feeding the baby in the high chair. I tell Dad about the lion cub and he gets up to deal with it, just like he used to if there was a spider in the bath when I was a kid.

I warn my mother there could be an adult lion around looking for its cub, and sure enough, there is a huge male lion with a magnificent black mane, sitting at the table with us, its enormous paws resting on the table-mat. My baby brother Tom is standing precariously on the edge of the high-chair tray, his arms outstretched, tottering towards me. My mother screams with fright and I bound forward to catch the baby. The lion shakes his mane and slips silently away in search of his cub. I suddenly remember we are still in Ben's flat.

"Mum, have you seen Ben?"

"Ben? I thought you finished with him years ago," she says, comforting baby Tom in her arms.

My head lolls forward again, and I'm dimly aware that the man beside me has got up from the seat next to mine and is moving toward the exit. A complete stranger, not Ben after all. He looks nothing like him.

Mouth parched, head throbbing, I glimpse the platform at Tooting Bec slipping away as the doors close and we accelerate into blackness. Missed my stop. Another long dark tunnel. What the hell is happening to me? I can't tell whether I'm hallucinating or dreaming. It is all equally frightening, bizarre, unreal, mixed up in my head—my mother, my father, Ben, Leyla, Lawrence, African lions, dark-holed memories of toddlers falling off the table... My baby cousin Vic fell off the table when I was a child, when I was supposed to be looking after him. Everyone said I must have pushed him.

My inner visions seem more vivid than life.

Friday 25 July, 5pm, Ranmore Street

I'm going through some kind of mental breakdown, melting inside, disintegrating, pieces detaching from my body and my life and floating away. No wonder I'm shaky and tearful. No wonder people are afraid of me. I've been to hell and back. I'm unlovable and unliveable with. Leyla wants to move out. Lawrence has a ticket to Ghana. I've met lots of Ghanaians, I have Ghanaian friends—Efua, Nana, Adua. But Lawrence going there, without me, it's too painful.

"Tell me what you know about your father," says Ray.

"Not much really. I've tried to piece it all together over the years. Mum and I have very fragmented conversations. We both find it difficult to talk about him, and difficult to listen to each other. We are going through very different kinds of pain about the same person, we have lost track of whether we are protecting ourselves or each other."

"So tell me what you *do* know. It may be more than you think."

I hesitate. My heart is pumping. I hardly ever get a

chance to really talk about my Dad—put all the pieces together, say what I feel. I am so used to this being a no-go area, forbidden territory. I find it difficult even to say his name out loud.

"His name is Samuel Kofie. I don't know how you spell it exactly. I have never seen it written down. He came from Ghana—which used to be called the Gold Coast—from a town called Takoradi. Bright, clever, outgoing; an extrovert, like me apparently. A bit of a show-off, Mum says, liked an audience. Studied Geology at London University. Active in the Pan African Movement and the Independence Movement. Lived at number 13 Castlenau, West London. He and Mum met at a party. Auntie Bel says he was invited to Sunday tea once to meet the family, but at the last minute my Nan put a stop to it. She didn't want a Black man in the house.

My father knew Mum was pregnant with me, but he left the UK six weeks before I was born, so he never saw me. After he left London, he went to Borneo to work for Shell Petroleum as an oil driller. Mum couldn't go with him because of her bad leg. She's had it since she was a kid. She has had such a traumatic life herself…"

When I think about her life, her disability, being alone in the unmarried mothers' home with a Brown baby, I want to weep.

"…and your father—we were talking about your father?"

"I don't know much more, Ray. I think he was rather

short and stocky, though I have never seen a photo of him. But I think of him as a huge, ferocious African lion with a black shaggy mane. I keep dreaming about African lions.

That's about it. That's all I have."

"Perhaps you are seeking answers outside, when the problem and the solution are inside yourself."

"How do you mean?"

"You are thinking about who your father is, when the important thing is who *you* are."

"I don't have anything to go on, Ray. I don't know who I am. I'm a fake. A fraud."

"You cannot imagine how many people have sat on that couch and told me that. Brain surgeons. Directors of stockbroker companies. Child prodigies. All afraid of being found out."

"But they are *fake* frauds, they're just pretending. I'm a *real* fraud, Ray. Everyone tells me so. Not just me."

"Does it matter what other people think?

"You don't get it, do you? I am suffering from a serious accumulated identity deficit here, and it's not all in my head. Let me give you an example. I went to visit some volunteers in Tanzania. They were driving me to the next village in their car, and one of their Tanzanian neighbours waved and looked stunned as we passed. 'He's looking at you,' they said, 'wondering why we've got a strange Black woman in our car. Little does he know, you're not a *real* one.' Not a real what? Not a real person? Not a real Black? Not a real White? What am I? I am a *real* fraud, I tell you,

I get found out every day. The other people you've had on your couch here are a bunch of rank amateurs in the fraud stakes. They've got a crisis of confidence. I have a crisis of *identity*, which is an entirely different thing. You look inside of me, and *there is nobody*."

"I don't think they meant to insult you."

"No, of course not, they're my friends. That's not the point. Everyone sees the one incident. They hardly notice it. It's of no significance to them. But I've had it day after day since I was born. Nobody recognises me. I mean *re-cognises*—understands who I am and where I fit in. How am I supposed to find my compass, when everyone says I don't fit, I'm not real? When I don't have a personal story or geography or history or even a language to describe myself, except by describing who my father is—and I don't *know* who he is."

"I think we are back where we started this conversation. You need to look deep inside yourself for the answers. This is your child-self responding."

"But Ray, this is not only about me, and it's not only about who I think I am. It can't be personalised away like that. It's not just distant childhood memories. It's about stereotypes, assumptions, discrimination, power. Negative connotations about Black people and women are *real*—sexism and racism and prejudice against illegitimacy exist out there in the real world, they are happening *now*, every day. You don't feel it so you don't see it, you're a White man. It's part of the system, it's a weapon used deliberately by the powerful to keep the *Other* down. I am not responsible for all that, it is coming at me from outside, every single day, and those messages get internalised—so I end up feeling that I'm *abnormal, inferior, hyper-visible, invisible, not standard, an aberration, not good enough. Borderline.* You must at least know that much, being gay. You are oppressed by the patriarchy too."

"I think you can choose how you respond to it. You don't need to hide behind your politics. You can choose your identity. You can take control."

"I *can't* hide it!" I can feel the anger rising up inside me. "Your difference isn't as visible as mine. My politics are Black, but my identity is neither Black nor White. People see it as soon as I walk in the room, people puzzle over it. The words people use to describe me are all negative: half-caste, half breed, Black bastard… I'm half a person, I don't exist, I am in no category. When I fill in the Equal Opportunities forms I have to tick *Other*. That poses particular problems for people like me, on top of the 'Fraudulism' that your average brain surgeon feels, or whatever you want to call it. At least they have an option to tick a box labelled Brain Surgeon. There is no box for me. It's not me that needs fixing, it's society's attitudes. We have to be empowered to fight it. The personal is political. You have to understand that, otherwise how can you help people like me—if you don't recognise me either?"

12 September, 11am, at home in the flat

Lawrence is back from Ghana, suntanned and enthusiastic. He says there are lots of people out there who look just like me. We should go, take a holiday, I would love it.

I still have too much to do and not enough time to do it. And this is on my week off sick with stress. I'm under pressure to go shopping and cooking for my cousins who are coming round for dinner tonight. Why did I invite them? I love seeing them, but I don't want them to see me like this. Why can't I lie down and die quietly, without dinner guests? At least my sister Molly is coming back from Uni to stay with me for the weekend. She's a light at the end of my dark tunnel. Molly says Mum is so worried about me. "She can see you're struggling, but she doesn't know how to help."

Leyla gave me this notebook for my 30th birthday. I didn't write in it for three years. It seemed too beautiful to make a mark in it. I sometimes stroke the silky Chinese fabric cover with my hand, my eyes half closed. Dark green, with turquoise and red birds in flight, flowers and ornamental trees on the cover, a maroon gold-embossed leather spine, the dark-red leather repeated at each of the corners. It soothes me just to pass my fingertips over it, feel the contrasting texture of silk and leather. Sometimes I put it to my face and sniff its musty papery smell. You would never think, to look at it, that it could contain so much pain. It's like Doris Lessing's *Golden Notebook*, only it's a work of grief and anger rather than genius.

I'm afraid of losing my Chinese notebook, so I keep it under my pillow at night. I ought to burn it. I can't stop writing. The mindless tortured ramblings of a distorted psyche. If anyone got their hands on it and read it, I would be so ashamed. I have no excuses really. This is all nonsense. Why do I make so much of it? Why can't I just live my life and forget all this stuff? Why is that so hard?

Tuesday 14 October, 3am again, in bed

I need to talk to someone. Sitting here in semi-darkness, writing in my Chinese notebook, I feel so lonely. Even with three other people in the house. My friends are fed up with me. I'm fed up with me.

I'm going to ring the Samaritans. I just dial directory enquiries, get the number, pick up the phone, and speak. What am I going to say? I haven't been beaten. Mugged? No. Survivor from a concentration camp? Divorced? Suicidal? Poor and in debt? Someone I love has just died? Been made redundant then? Car crash? Fatal disease? Nope. What then? I just don't know my Dad, that's all. And I miss him.

Oh God, this can't be real. Get the number, pick up the phone, speak. Will they say, *Sorry no time-wasters?* Will they say, *This is the Chinese takeaway, can I take your order please?*

Got the number. Okay. Pick up the phone. Go on. Pick

up the phone.

"Hello. Is that the Samaritans? I'm sorry to ring you in the middle of the night. I just badly need to talk to someone."

"Go right ahead, I'm listening. That's what I'm here for."

"I don't know how to begin. I don't know what's wrong with me. Why do I feel so bad?"

I can hear myself sobbing again, sobbing into the phone, with a complete stranger on the other end. I have to get a grip.

"I just feel as if everything I've done, everything I am, is bad, worthless. I bet you've heard that a million times. But I feel not real, a fraud, an impostor, half a person, the wrong half of the wrong person that I am, even... sorry... that doesn't make any sense..."

"What makes you feel that way?"

"Why? Well I feel so alone."

"Are you alone in the house?"

"No, my friend Leyla is still here, in the next room, asleep. But she's moving out. And I feel bereft."

"Did she say why?"

"She doesn't want to live with me anymore."

"How do you feel about it?"

"Desperate, rejected. I feel as if I'm getting a divorce, with a child involved."

"She has a child, or you?"

"It's hers... and she's going to live nearby with her

boyfriend and the baby."

"But does that mean your friendship is entirely lost? Won't you be able to see them?"

"Yes, I think we'll still see each other. I'll be moving into a flat with Lawrence, my boyfriend, near here. But we all planned to live together, me and my boyfriend, her and her family. All of us in one big house. She is mixed like me. Anglo-Indian. And I'm half African and half White. We would have been a family."

"Won't you still feel like a family if you're living nearby, with... sorry I've forgotten his name—?"

"—Lawrence. But I still feel alone. I can't explain." Difficult to explain to a stranger on the phone. I need a woman and a man in my life to feel complete, I guess.

I love people who are unattainable.

I am lost, detached from my own body.

"Do you know *why* you feel so alone? Is there something—some*one*—you might be missing?"

Good question.

"I'm missing *myself*. My Dad was Ghanaian and he left before I was born—he didn't even see me... I was brought up in a White family so I didn't quite fit... and I got called woggie and bastard at school... and I got pregnant and I had two abortions... and everyone asks me where I come from and I don't know... and I have never met anyone else who has been through all that... so that's why... that's why I feel alone... " I'm breathless.

My Dad, I never met my Dad. And whenever anyone

leaves me, whenever a relationship breaks up, it reminds me of him. And there's no-one I can talk to about him, no-one who knew him, except Mum.

30 November, 3am, in bed

I can't phone the Samaritans again. It's embarrassing. "Yes, hello, remember me? I'm still in bed, it's three in the morning again, I'm still crying, I'm still afraid of the dark. Can you help?"

I have to get out of here. Dial a mini cab. *Just get out of here.*

I throw on a coat over my nightdress, my heart thumping as I try to shut the front door noiselessly behind me and avoid waking anyone. As the cab passes through Croydon, there are still a few people on the streets, hanging around the bus station and all-night cafes. What am I doing here at half-past three in the morning?

The third pebble finally taps at the casement window, and it opens.

"Val, it's me. Jane."

"Janie, for God's sake, you gave me such a fright. What's wrong? What the hell are you doing here in the middle of the night?"

"I'm sorry, I can't sleep, I can't stay home. Can I come in?"

Val runs down in pyjamas and bare feet to let me in, and I fall through the door onto the doormat and scream and scream and scream, curled in a tight little ball at her feet.

Val sits on the floor beside me, stroking my back.

"Don't you want to get up from the doormat, Janie? You're shivering. Let me put you to bed, or at least come into the living room where I can get you warm."

"I can't move, Val, I just can't… I feel like a doormat… I can't open my eyes."

The stiff bristles of the doormat are chafing my cheek. My feet are ice-cold, my face is burning, my head is splitting. I feel exhausted, yet strangely not sleepy. I'll get up in a minute and go and sit by the gas fire. Val covers me with her blue dressing-gown over the top of my nightdress and coat, and brings me hot, sweet tea in a white mug with the face of a whiskery cat on it. She loves cats.

Through my teary eyelashes I can see the steaming mug of tea, the inscrutable cat's face, and beyond it, more cylindrical white shapes appear, gigantic, like the pillars of an Ancient Greek temple. Inside the temple it's cool and white, derelict, fallen pillars lying on top of each other, candles flicker in the alcoves, a pungent smell of incense wafts in the silence. I pick my way through the ancient debris strewn about the floor towards the far end of the shrine. A white marble colossus of an ancient Greek god towers above me, carrying a golden trident, a wreath of laurel leaves encircling his head.

The god opens his eyes, and slowly, majestically, bends down towards me, so low that his long whiskery beard brushes my cheek. He is going to speak to me, to give me a message that will help me, guide me. His lips are moving slowly, deliberately. I wait breathlessly for the word of God.

"Leave it out, Duck!" he says, in Grandad's great booming cockney voice, echoing around the ancient walls.

"Why don't you come up to bed now?" says Val gently. "You can't stay on that doormat all night. I've put a hot water bottle in the spare bed for you." She helps me to my feet. "Come on, finish your tea, try and get some sleep."

I climb the stairs, leaning heavily on her. Leave it out. *Leave it out.* What on earth could that possibly mean? Is this all a colossal waste of time?

1 December, 9.30am, Val's place

"You know how much I loved my Dad, he died when I was only twenty-one. He meant the world to me. I can't bear to see you so unhappy, Janie. Dads are so important. You need to find him... There must be *something* we can do. We know your Dad went to London University, that's a start. They will help me search, I'm sure. I did my post-grad teaching course there and they know me through my work with overseas students. I'll look in their records around the time you were born, see if I can find your Dad's name... when he left the country, where he went next. Would that help?"

"Would you really do that for me? Would you? I'd be so grateful."

But I'm not sure how to spell his name. Coffee? Kofi? Koffey? Kofie? I've never seen it written down.

"Ask your Mum. She'll know."

But I feel awkward asking her. My heart thumps and I can't speak. When I finally pluck up the courage, I'm so anxious, I can't listen to the answer. She's reluctant to repeat it, and she often says it very quickly. Or is it just that I can't listen, I can't hear it, I can't remember it? I don't know... I'm so screwed up. It must be so hard for her, too. Neither of us can handle it.

"I'll take the afternoon off on Monday anyway and go up there and look through the registers. There must be some record of him somewhere. Why don't you write to the head office at Shell, too, see if they know of him, where he worked in Borneo? And the National Council for One Parent Families—you used to know the Director, Sue Slipman, didn't you? Wasn't she one of the first women Presidents of NUS in the 70s? There's loads we can do... We're on the case, we've got a plan!"

"Val you are so good to me. I don't deserve a friend like you."

"*Leave it out!*" she laughs, on her way to the kitchen to make the breakfast.

"What did you put in that tea last night Val? It gave me hallucinations..."

1987

Sunday 4 January, 4.30 pm, at home

Leyla moved out. Lawrence has moved in temporarily before we move to our new place.

"Shell says they've never heard of Samuel Kofi. And Sue Slipman can't help. She says the National Council for One Parent Families only deals with UK, not foreign nationals. And Val hasn't found any trace of him in the London University records, it's mystifying. We've drawn a blank, Lawrence. I feel as if he is a figment of my imagination, doesn't exist, *never* existed."

"Tell you what. Let's drive over to Castlenau. Let's go visit number 13. It might give us inspiration."

"What, right now?"

"Yeah, c'mon. Right now, to Castlenau. What have you got to lose? Put your coat and hat on."

Lawrence parks the car, and we walk down the busy street, away from Hammersmith Bridge. It's already dark. The houses along Castlenau are huge, handsome detached five-storey buildings, many converted into flats, some white-painted, with bay windows, spacious tiled porches and double front doors.

Number thirteen, Castlenau. His student digs. This is the closest I may ever get to walking in my father's footsteps. We crunch up the gravel drive and approach the black-painted front door. There are six doorbells and an intercom in the porch. Two young women open the door, on their way out.

"Can we help? Looking for anyone in particular?"

"I—I knew someone who used to live here," I reply uncertainly. That's a lie. I never knew him.

As they close the door, I glimpse a tiled hallway, telephone table, neat letter racks. My Dad walked up those stairs. Maybe I was even conceived in this house.

Sunday 15 February, 4pm, Everville Road, Wandsworth

"It's K-o-f-i-e," Mum says. "I told you that ages ago. He had lodgings at number 26, Castelnau, on the second floor. I've told you everything I know. It was a very brief relationship—six months at most."

"Number 26? I thought you said number 13!"

"No, 26, definitely number 26. He was a geologist studying at Imperial College."

"Why didn't you tell me you knew which college? We've been looking at the records all over London University."

"Why didn't you ask me first? I did tell you. Imperial isn't part of London University. I told you years ago. You just forget things."

"Well what about Shell, then. Can you remember anything about him going off to Borneo?"

"Shell? Borneo? What are you talking about, Jane?"

"You said he had a scholarship from Shell Petroleum, and so when he finished his studies he was sent to Borneo to work for them as an oil driller..."

"Well, I can't imagine where you got all that from. I haven't a clue where he went after he left here. I think he may have gone back to Ghana. I'm not sure."

"Mum, I can't have made all this up, it's too detailed. How could I have invented it all? I don't even know where Borneo is and I can't see how—"

"—Well it was a long time ago and I can't remember everything. I certainly don't remember that. Maybe it was one of your crazy dreams."

It wasn't a dream. I only have about half a dozen facts to hold on to and now it looks like most of those were false.

I can feel the hysteria rising in my throat again.

Friday 20 March, 5pm, Ranmore Street

I tell Ray about the conversation I had with my mother.

"And then what happened?" asks Ray, after a pause.

"Dad came into the room—I mean my Stepdad—and that was more or less the end of the conversation. But I felt angry, betrayed. She says she can talk to anyone about anything, I have only to ask. Yet there is a chasm between us at the moment and the fragments of this story just don't add up. It's not her fault, she was betrayed and abandoned too... I do love her and we have so much in common, so much friendship and shared interests and passions. We used to organise Women's Conferences together, we were a team, much closer than most mothers and daughters…"

"You can't expect miracles of people, Jane. Your mother. Leyla. Lawrence. They are only human beings. Irrational. Contradictory. They have their own stories to come to terms with. They can't always help you. You expect a lot from the people in your life. You want to depend on them completely and you can't always. You are repeating patterns with relationships because of your very first loss, the father-daughter relationship, which under normal circumstances would have been one of the first, closest and most important relationships in your life."

I must sound selfish and neurotic. But I just can't let it go.

"It's *my* story, Ray. I have a right to it. I love my Stepdad. And I love my Mum…"

My Mum is one of the bravest, most intelligent and interesting women I have ever known, my greatest influence, my inspiration, my friend. I have not lacked for strong father or mother figures in my life. My Great-Grandmother, who said "I don't care what colour you are, blood is thicker than water," and called me her little brownie; my Grandad, who looked into my cot in the unmarried mothers' home and said, "Let's have her home." My Auntie Bel who asked what was wrong and straightened my hair; my Auntie Lucy who made me a pink mini-skirt and told me I should never have been born. My Stepdad, who hugged me while I cried.

But it's my African Dad I am aching for, the one I

carry with me wherever I go, in my skin and my hair. The one everyone sees when they look at me.

I am disloyal, ungrateful. And angry.

"Anyway, Ray, I didn't lose my Dad. He just wasn't there."

"But it was *like* a loss, like a death that no-one would talk about. So every time you have a crisis, you return to your very first loss. It's becoming an obsession."

"But I can't get away from him, Ray, I can't avoid him. He defines me, whether I like it or not... every time I look in a mirror... every time anyone looks into my face. When people ask me where I come from, which they do, all the time, I can't explain my existence without reference to him. What am I doing in an all-White family with brown skin and fuzzy hair? People demand to know. I am forced to talk about him. I can't escape it. No other explanation makes any sense."

"But this stops you from being in the here and now. You need to be able to move on, without reference to this man. He is having far too big an influence on your life and your relationships, for a person you never met and never will. You have to accept that."

There's a pause, while I try and digest what he's just said. A lifetime's-worth of dark-holed, desperate, unarticulated thoughts swarm about in my head. Before I can think of a response, Ray continues. He has an idea.

"What I'd like to do next week is have a little ceremony—a ritual, as it were. You can bring anything you like—flowers, candles, music, a letter to your father, which we can read out loud—anything you want to say to him. We'll both be here, in this room, and we'll say goodbye to your father and let go of him. Bury him."

I'm stunned.

"*Bury* him! But where's the body, Ray? I'm not going to bury someone when *there is no body*. I came to you to try and find myself. You're doing your best to kill part of me off. Thanks for the invitation, but I'm not coming to your funeral."

"The point is, Jane, he's dead to *you*. You need to live your life without him, and be happy, and not expect other relationships to compensate for this first loss. You won't be able to move on with your life, if you can't say goodbye."

Goodbye?

Wrong thing to say to an abandoned child.

And *this* child within, I will love, cherish, nurture and adore, always.

"I'm pregnant, Ray."

Chapter 16

Lost and Found

Browsing among the *Ladybird* children's-wear in Woolworths, wondering if I can afford to buy anything, I'm dimly aware of someone calling *Miss, Miss!* Someone looking for their teacher. I'm so glad I have left all that behind. I fought for years to be called *Ms* and then ended up in one of the few remaining professions where *Miss* became my official title.

A young woman in her early twenties runs up to me between the aisles, interrupting my reverie.

"Miss, don't you recognise me?"

I frown. Nobody calls me 'Miss' these days.

"Burntwood School! Elaine, class 4B, the trouble-maker, don't you remember?!"

Of course! "Great to see you! How are you doing, Elaine?" Hugging her over my bump, I'm wondering whether she has had her baby adopted after all.

"So, you've gone and got yourself pregnant too, Miss! I work here part-time now—Mum's looking after my little boy. You remember that wet Friday afternoon in form-time? I can still count up to ten in Finnish."

And she recounts it for me there and then, in the middle of the aisle, sing-song at the top of her voice— and almost word perfect as far as I can tell—to the astonishment of her colleagues.

"Elaine, we didn't know you could speak Finnish!"

At least I have left some useful lasting legacy behind me in my teaching career. Woolworths is lucky indeed to have found such an employee.

It's not the first time my past has revisited me lately, and not always in such a good way. When I went for my last scan, the consulting room was crowded with student doctors. I was beginning to regret having said yes when the Consultant asked me if I minded some of his students joining us to observe the consultation. There must have been at least fifteen of them crammed in there. I had imagined there would be four or five at most. I lay on the couch like a beached whale, a prize exhibit, bump exposed, legs akimbo.

"What do we notice about this patient's history?"

"On her records it says she has had two pregnancy terminations, the second leading to a pelvic infection."

"Excellent. And what is the danger with pelvic infections? Anyone?"

"Infertility."

"Doesn't seem to be the problem in this case."

A dutiful ripple of laughter.

I was back to being treated like an exhibit, robbed of

dignity, with no feelings, a specimen to be analysed and humiliated.

I bet they hadn't even thought about the possible repercussions of such a public disclosure. I glanced over at Lawrence standing awkwardly by the door. Thank God I had been open and honest with him from the start. But supposing I hadn't told him? This could have ruined our relationship, caused tension between us at a vulnerable time—the birth of our first baby. How could they be so insensitive, without checking if I am okay with exposing confidential information about my past?

I could feel the anger rising inside me.

When I walked out of the hospital, I made up my mind to make a formal complaint about it. But then I had a sudden flashback to my time in hospital in Leicester, the disdain of the consultant, Wiggie gripping my hand when we said goodbye.

You will have lovely Brown babies one day when the time is right. But don't sabotage yerself. Because that's what you're doin'.

I told my raging heart to be still, for once. This baby doesn't need to feel my humiliation, my fury and pain. I don't regret the choices I have made, just their medicalisation. I feel so lucky to have this little one inside me.

*****

Vic is sitting at the kitchen table at Everville Road,

nursing a mug of tea. Perhaps now's the time to bring it up.

"What was it like when you met your Dad for the first time, Vic? What did you say to him? What did he look like?"

"Well…" Vic hesitates, tracing the rim of his mug with his finger. "It's funny, I was quite keen about it at first, but when I finally met him, I didn't connect with him as much as I thought I would. He took me to a restaurant in Chelsea, bought me lunch. And he offered to buy me some expensive kit for my holiday…"

"But did he look like you, Vic? Tell me what he looked like."

"Similar nose and chin, maybe…"

I wonder how I would react if my Dad ever contacted me.

"Did he tell you why he had got in touch after all these years?"

"He says he's had only daughters and I'm the only son he'll ever have. So he wanted to make contact. I was more interested in knowing my siblings—all my life I've thought I was an only child."

I feel happy for him. And jealous.

"Oh my God, that must have been so difficult—what did you say to him Vic? How did you handle it? Are you going to see him again?"

"The thing is, it's complicated—when there's family on the other side who don't even know you exist. It's not that easy. Once you meet your Dad, you kinda want to know the rest of the family too…"

He pauses, uncertain, fighting back the emotion.

Vic has siblings. Maybe I have more sisters. And brothers. And African Grandparents. Family who don't know about me.

"Oh Vic, I know, I know how it feels, I'm sorry. Not knowing tears you to pieces. It's like a big chasm inside. At least you have met him. That's a big step. I know that's not even possible for me. Where would I start? I was wondering… what did my Mum say when you told her you met your Dad?"

"Ummm… I think she was all for it, really. Said her own Dad meant such a lot to her when she was a kid… She said she was much closer to her Dad than she was to her Mum—as you know. She reckons every son has a right to know his father."

Every son. And daughter? And what do I tell my baby about their Grandad?

*****

Jake was born on the Ides of November, 1987. An auspicious date, a month after the great storm. Trees went down like matchsticks, roofs blew off, windows rattled, dustbins clanged down the street in the middle of the night. The worst hurricane on record, and Mr Fish just didn't see it coming. A month later, Jake stormed into the world after a 24-hour labour and mid-forceps delivery, and we finally brought him home.

Our new flat is a spacious, airy, homely maisonette in Tooting, a minute from the tube station, occupying two upper floors. The sitting room is light and sunny, full of windows, running the whole width of the house. The drawback is that there are stairs everywhere: a long flight up from the front door, steps up and down between the bathroom, the kitchen, and the sitting room, and another long flight up to the two attic bedrooms. Not an ideal arrangement for a baby on the move. He will have to learn to be a mountaineer.

Baby Jake is an instant success—good-looking, smiley and sociable, popular with friends and family alike. Mum, Dad, Lawrence, Auntie Bel, Cousin Vic, Nan, Sister Molly, Brother Tom, Auntie Molly, and my best friend Val—a whole retinue of admirers turn up every day to bathe him, coo over him, take him for walks. Even Lawrence's parents take to him, though they made a special trip to Wolverhampton to try to persuade Lawrence not to move in with me. They feared that brown grandchildren would be permanently disadvantaged in life.

Everyone gets to know Jake before I do. Exhausted by the birth, half asleep, I lost my footing and tumbled down the full flight of stairs on my way to let the midwife in, badly spraining my ankle. I lay at the bottom of the stairs writhing in pain—I could not bear any more suffering after the agony of my long labour.

"Good job I was here to strap up your ankle!" the midwife remarked authoritatively. "That's ten days' bed-rest for you."

If she hadn't called so early I wouldn't have fallen downstairs. But she also advised me to drink a bottle of Guinness before my six o'clock feed every evening. "Relaxes the mother, improves the quality of the breast milk." Best advice I ever had.

When Jake is ten months old, I go off to Peru for a women's conference with World Education Services. "You go," says Mum. "It's the opportunity of a lifetime. We'll look after Jake." I return with a toy llama, but to my dismay, Jake doesn't recognise me. Three weeks is a long time in a baby's life.

I am happy. I have my own family, a supportive partner, and a Brown baby. I am no longer the 'only one'.

And now I have been offered my dream job!

I am to be the campaigner and outreach officer of *WomenGrow*, a new organisation set up to support and fundraise for rural women in developing countries. After eight years at WES, this is a golden opportunity to move on, to work exclusively on my deepest passion.

I've known Beverly Hunter and Norma Sackville for years, and we've worked together many times on different gender projects. They are not part of my usual activist networks, but I'm so thrilled that they encouraged me to apply for this post. Beverly is a senior researcher at an international development research institute, and

Norma is a director of the charitable wing of an international development bank, both committed Feminists, well-known and respected in the field of Women's Rights. They've given up their high-profile jobs to work together as joint Chief Executives of *WomenGrow*.

This is a ground-breaking venture in so many ways—not only the idea of job-sharing Chief Executives, but also what the organisation is setting out to do. It's not your usual old-colonial-charitable-aid approach. It's about solidarity—an active response to the United Nations Decade for Women's stark and unjust world statistics—*Women are half the world's population, grow 80% of the world's food, earn 10% of the world's income, and own 1% of the world's property*. WomenGrow is based on the idea of growing *LIFE*—growing Leadership, Income, Food and Empowerment, starting from where women are, seeing them as leaders and potential leaders, supporting them to make their own choices, run their own programmes, develop practical solutions, enabling them to lead the change.

Eventually we will have partners co-ordinating in every world region, collective decisions about where the money goes, and hopefully even programmes for low-income rural women in the UK too. The idea is to avoid being London-centric and develop feminist solidarity and campaigning hubs all over the UK, starting with Bristol and Manchester. A consortium of wealthy, high profile women and men have put up the money to set us up. Best of all, Tanzania is to be one of the first countries where we will be testing out the ideas. The woman I met in the forest all those years ago, tree balanced on her head and baby on her back, is exactly who we want to support.

*****

I crawl into bed and sob my soul out, like I did on Ray's couch in the consulting room. Eighteen-month-old Jake is bemused. It's usually his job to cry.

I feel as if I have been run over by a train, crushed, obliterated by wheels of steel. I haven't been so low since my last nervous breakdown. Angry, inadequate, a failure at everything. I knew I was struggling. But this bites deep into my divided self, the part of me that feels worthless, that doesn't know who I am or where I belong. The part that wanted to make a difference in the world.

A few months into the job, it was clear that things were already beginning to fall apart. Norma and Beverly, from two different worlds, research and banking, couldn't find a way to communicate or work together. They presented an odd couple, little and large. Norma in her early fifties, almost six feet tall, thin and angular, always smartly dressed and in full make-up for the office, her face framed with short straight greying hair; and Beverly, ten years younger, rounder and about my height, White South African, with a strong South African accent, peering at everyone over half-moon spectacles. She reminded me of Miss Rainer,

Deputy Head of my old school in Stafford, who broke up our sit-in and refused to let us wear long white socks.

I arrived at work one morning to find Beverly standing at my desk having a conversation on the telephone.

"Why do you want her to be your speaker?" she challenged the person on the other end of the line. "She's not Efrican, she's Brritish."

My friend Efua called me later that morning. "I tried to explain to Norma that your father is African, you are our sister, and you are the best speaker we know. And you've lived in Africa, you know what you are talking about. It's up to us who we invite to our own meetings. This is a big conference, a really good opportunity for you to represent WomenGrow. That's supposed to be your job, isn't it, to represent the organisation? You will bring a lot of credibility. What's the problem?"

Bemused, I shared the incident—one of many—with Anthea in the pub after work. Anthea runs our North of England WomenGrow campaign. She has soft, wispy, blonde hair and speaks with a gentle Manchester accent. She's a fitness fanatic—running, skiing, cycling. Her right leg was in plaster, propped up on a stool, after a recent skiing accident. Anthea understands what it's like to struggle with a demanding job and a baby, having had her little girl around the same time as I had Jake. She filled me in on the Manchester feminist scene, and the recent successful campaign to open the Pankhurst Centre, where she has set up her office. The pub was getting noisy, filling up with commuters dropping in for a quick one after work.

"Anthea, I don't know where I'm going wrong," I confided in her. "It's all going bad between me and Beverly, after only a few months in the job... We used to get on so well, we were such good friends."

Anthea was pensive, concerned. "Yeah, I can see things are getting really strained between you two. It's puzzling. Maybe it's because Beverly was brought up in South Africa, under the Apartheid Regime. She rebelled against it of course—the life of privilege. But she can't place you. You're not African, not Caribbean, not White, and you're an activist, not a researcher. Maybe she was expecting to be invited to be the speaker at all the African Women's conferences. She might see you as some kind of threat... it's weird..."

"But she and Norma *asked* me to apply for this job. They chose me. And I worked with both of them such a lot before I joined WomenGrow... We always connected, we admired each other. At least I thought so. When we had a one-to-one last Friday, Beverly actually asked me how I identified—as Black or White. What a strange question— why do I have to choose? I said Black of course. It's a political choice. But that's really only the half of it. Talking of which—another half?"

"No thanks, you're all right, I have to get goin' soon. With this leg, it takes me ages to hobble to the station. Anyway, I've got a feeling Beverly assumed you were Caribbean, and hired you without really understanding what you have to offer. Jane, to be honest, I didn't know myself that you were brought up in a White family until you told me when we started working together," Anthea confessed. "Listen, you are really good at being you. You are a great communicator—look at how you can hold an audience. A storyteller, a powerful woman. The things you have told me about, the racism you suffered when you were a kid, and your experiences in Tanzania—it's amazing, it's given you so much insight. I don't think you realise how well you are regarded in the movement, honestly. Don't let them destroy your confidence, ignore them, don't let it get to you, keep doing what you do well..."

I was so glad I talked to Anthea. She is thoughtful, empathetic, and she gets to the heart of things. But it was hard for me to ignore the situation when I was in the middle of it. I learnt that as a kid.

Every day I dreaded going into the office. It was stressful and energy-sapping. I was struggling with new motherhood, breastfeeding, and full-time work, with a two-hour commute in the rush hour on top. I had no idea it was going to be so hard. I started having bad dreams again, leaping on and off trains, going in the wrong direction. I was supposed to be doing a four-day week, so I could spend more time with Jake, but I often ended up going in on a Friday anyway, because I couldn't finish my work in four days. I was exhausted. In the end I wasn't doing my best at work, and I didn't have enough energy left to be a good Mum when I got home to Jake. I knew something had to give.

Being a first-time mother at thirty-five has its draw-backs. An *Elderly Prima Gravida*, that's what they called me in the hospital. The teenage mother in the maternity ward in the bed next to mine sprang out of bed within hours of giving birth. She was told off by the nurse for dancing around the ward with her school-friends in her tight-fitting ski pants, whilst I was still exhausted, sore and wounded, hobbling to the bathroom, nursing my stitches. Ironically, *I* would probably have had the same kind of energy if I'd gone through with my accidental pregnancy at seventeen. In my efforts to avoid emulating my mother, a 20-year-old single Mum, I fear I may have left it a bit too long.

Back home, Lawrence listened patiently to my well-worn rant.

"It's so unfair that a woman's best chance of getting on in her career coincides with her ticking biological clock. It's an entirely artificial and unnecessary problem thrown up by a system which is really designed for working men. We are all living so much longer, so we have a much longer working life. Why can't society be organised around both parents looking after, raising and nurturing children together, when we are young enough to do it?"

Lawrence could not be a more involved father, fitting in the domestic chores, the shopping, and the baby around his teaching career. He does everything any parent could do, he takes charge, and he's good at it. I can go travelling for my job, stay late at meetings, knowing he has it covered.

He could see I wasn't happy at work.

"Don't give up," he said. "We need two salaries coming in. It's bound to get better."

But it went from bad to worse. The stress finally got to me. I was off sick from work with a nasty virus which laid me up in bed for three weeks and left me drained, weak and demoralised.

When I got back to work, still not completely recovered, one thing Norma and Beverly could agree on was that they were not happy with me. My writing wasn't up to scratch, I wasn't keeping up, I was behind with the admin and filing, I was just not pulling my weight. I knew I was having problems. I just wish they hadn't said it at the staff meeting in front of the rest of the staff.

It was becoming a nightmare of a dream job. I had lost my way, lost my spirit.

"But Jane is a campaigner, a networker, a powerful speaker," Anthea defended me. "She's got loads of experience, she knows so much about women and development. She lived in Tanzania for two years, she has experience on the ground."

"But we don't see that," says Norma.

What doesn't she see? She doesn't see *me*. The Brown girl cowering at school dinners, *Blackie, woggie, nig-nog, golliwog*, good for nothing but rolling in dog-shit. It always seems to come back to that, no matter how hard I try to prove myself, no matter how hard I try to hide it. People don't know who I am, so they guess, and then expect things of me that I can't possibly deliver. If they ask me who I am, I can't tell them anyway. There are no words to describe me. I always have to resort to describing my mother and father's race.

"I think Beverly might have some kind of problem with you working with us. I don't know why; we are proud of you," says Efua, when I turn up to speak at her African Women's Conference. Here at least, I'm in a safe space, empowered, respected, comforted by my African sisters.

Serina, the administrative officer at WomenGrow, had also picked up on the worsening dynamics. "I have the feeling they might want to get rid of you, be careful," she whispered when I went to pick up my post from the front desk. Serina is Caribbean, uncomplicated. But she felt for me. "I overheard Norma and Beverly talking—seems like they were expecting you to be doing more fondraising among the Caribbean Community or something—"

"But I'm not—that's not—but this is my dream job." I burst into tears. Why was this happening to me in an organisation run by feminists?

Don't resign, stand and fight, my friends advised me. *Defend your reputation.*

What reputation? It was already in shreds.

Finally, I was summoned to a formal meeting at the Holborn office of the WomenGrow treasurer, Peter Barker, an influential lawyer. Anthea came with me, as my friend and union representative.

"Don't let it get to you," she counselled, as we waited anxiously to be called in. "They may have been hoping you'd get scared and resign before it got to this, who knows. But why should you? You haven't done anything wrong. The same thing happened to me at my last job at World Rights Alliance. It's gut-wrenching when you are made to feel in the wrong in an organisation you really believe in."

How had it got that bad? Maybe I *should* have resigned. It was all too stressful for everyone involved. Sometimes I don't know when to give up.

"But you can't give up now!" Anthea urged me. "They're saying you brought the organisation into disrepute, and that's a hell of a serious charge, complete overkill, it seems way over the top to me. They could sack you on the spot for that, with no severance pay and no references—so they bloody well better produce some good evidence..."

We were shown into a plush-carpeted office with exquisite drapes and serious-looking legal tomes displayed in glass-fronted bookcases. There is nothing like a high ceiling and a heavy mahogany desk to strike the fear of God into me. I remember feeling so small and guilty, and scared, and I didn't even know what I was supposed to have done. A rabbit frozen in the headlights.

"Keep your cool, it'll be okay," Anthea whispered. Thank heavens she was with me. With a PhD in women's employment rights, she was a formidable champion.

Norma, Beverly and Peter Barker sat behind the desk, waiting for us.

"We have received a letter of complaint against Ms. Goldsmith," Peter began.

"Well, we need to see the evidence," Anthea countered.

"Not possible, it's confidential. It might identify the sender."

Anthea was shocked. "My friend knows absolutely nothing about this. Why should the sender have the right to anonymity? If you're accused of something, you're entitled to see the evidence. Natural justice, surely."

That went down well with the lawyer, at least. Peter Barker was almost looking sorry for me. The case had collapsed almost as soon as it began.

I couldn't face going back to work after that. I felt devastated. And it had upset everyone—my colleagues, my friends, my family. It was distracting everyone from the real work of fighting for Women's Rights.

An agonising week later, a letter arrived offering me constructive dismissal 'because of childcare issues'. I have never had 'childcare issues'. Lawrence, my mother and my grandmother were as involved and supportive as any father, grandmother and great-grandmother could be. It broke my heart, as if I wasn't acknowledging all they did to help me get back to work after having Jake.

But it was a way out, so I signed the letter anyway.

There must be better ways of working things out than this. People invest so much time deciding what an organisation is going to do, but hardly any time thinking about how it's going to *be*. And then it all unravels.

"We'll all miss you, it's hard," Anthea wrote to me afterwards. "But you'll bounce back, you'll get another job just as good, you'll see. You'll find a way of going on working for the cause. We all need to move on now."

But jobs like this are hard to come by. Losing this one feels like a bereavement. I had such high hopes. If I can't do this, what *can* I do? At thirty-five, I still haven't figured out what I've got to offer. How to be me. I disappoint people. I can't live up to their expectations.

*****

1990, the beginning of a new decade, and I'm without a job, wondering what to do with my life. The experience at WomenGrow has shaken my confidence, left me adrift. I have a young family and a mortgage, and I need an income.

My friend Valerie has recommended me to a Member of the European Parliament, Diana Truman. She urgently needs to commission some research on the impact of *Fortress Europe* on Black Women in the European Union. I am delighted. At least now I have some paid work, so soon after being ejected from WomenGrow. At home with my brand-new Amstrad computer installed in the back bedroom, which serves as a makeshift office, I can do some interesting research, look for another job, see more of Jake.

The research is going well. It's exciting and absorbing, and it's new territory to be focusing on Europe for a change, instead of the rest of the world.

Efua calls me at home. "Jane, Diana Truman has asked me to present your research to the European Parliament. I thought, that's Jane's research, isn't it? Why can't *she* present it? She's done all the work and written the report. I called Diana Truman to check, and she said, 'Yes, Jane's a great speaker, she has done a very good job on the report, but she's Jewish, I need a Black woman'."

"I told her, no, she's not Jewish, she's half Ghanaian. I know her well, she's a good friend of mine. Jane, you had betta call her and talk to her, see if you can sort it out."

Mistaken identity is getting me down. I'm constantly sidelined, misrepresented, unplaceable.

Diana Truman is contrite when I call her. "I'm so sorry, Jane, I just assumed. Your name, Goldsmith, sounded Jewish. I'm an Aussie. I'm trying to get my head around the minorities landscape 'ere in the UK. So complicated. It's different back 'ome. We mostly just have Aborigines…"

She can hear my silence at the other end of the phone.

"Oh dear… I don't think I'm making this any better, am I?" The way she pronounces it, it sounds like 'bitter'. "… But unfortunately, it's too late to change it now. I've already put Efua's name on the programme and booked her ticket. Tell you what, I have to present the findings to the European Commission in June. Why don't you present your report for me there instead?"

*****

446

Free-lance work is complicated and unpredictable. I need something more permanent. I have an interview for a job at the Association of Women's Organisations. On the interview panel, Pat, one of the Trustees, explains that they are recruiting someone to work on two key projects—on rural women, and women with low incomes.

"With your Caribbean background, and your interest in International Development, I'm wondering if this is the right job for you, Jane. How will you handle working-class White women's issues, and connect with women living in the countryside in the UK?"

An easy question to answer.

"I was brought up in a White working-class family in Battersea, and I spent six months in rural Norfolk with my cousins as a fifteen-year-old, doing my O-levels. And I'm not Caribbean. I'm half African."

I have life experiences people would never guess at, just by looking at me.

I got the job. This dream job has to be better than the last one. Jane Graham, my new boss, is full of warmth, energy and ideas. As there are two Janes in our small office, I adopt the nickname Goldie—Goldie Goldsmith—to distinguish us. I am used to collecting a new name wherever I go. Not as good as Kumba. But better than 'Buzzer'.

I am delighted with my new position, working with the feminist movement in the UK, and building a feminist women's lobby throughout the European Union. The only drawback is that the office is in East London, in the same building as my old job at WomenGrow. I have been issued with the identical key again. Beverly seems to have decided to forget all about my existence. She calls me 'Sarah' when I meet her in the corridor. Norma and I sometimes have to squeeze past each other on the narrow stairway on my way up to my new office on the third floor. It's a small world. Two steps backward, one step forward.

In the last few months I have been mistaken for Jewish and Caribbean, and assumed to know nothing about White working-class or rural women—even though I was brought up by them. People don't ask about my background. Maybe they are afraid to, or don't know how to, or they think it will cause offence. I'm too complicated. I can't be put in a box. It eats away at my sense of self—if I ever had any. And it's damaging my career.

"This won't go away, will it? This mistaken identity thing," says Lawrence.

He hands me an envelope. Inside are two British Airways tickets to Ghana for a holiday in July. Mum has offered to look after Jake while we are away.

"It'll be too hot for him out there," she says. "He'll be fine with me and his Grandad."

I wonder whether Jake will find the world a different place when he grows up, one which will embrace him and not constantly mistake him.

Efua is as excited as I am about my trip. "At last you will be going home to Ghana! You will love it. Next time

I will come with you and introduce you to all my family. I will give you some names and addresses. You must call on my Mum who lives near Cape Coast."

A few days later, Efua calls me again, just after I have arrived at the office. Efua and I are working together on a conference against female genital mutilation. Her distinctive Black-velvet voice, usually smooth and lilting, is now uncharacteristically full of urgency.

"Jane, are you ready for this? You betta sit down. Are you sittin' down?"

I thought she was calling to give me some information about my upcoming trip to Ghana. But she clearly has some astonishing news. A conference in Africa? A new project? More funding?

"Yes, yes, I'm sitting down, I'm ready, what is it? Tell me!"

Chapter 17
Amazing Trace

"Where are we going?"

"To meet someone who can talk to you about what you need to know," Mrs Quah smiles.

A diminutive brown woman in her fifties, about my height and skin-tone, Mrs Quah has close cropped salt-and-pepper afro hair, twinkling eyes and a captivating sing-song voice.

"My family is mixed Lebanese and Ghanaian," she explains. "But I was born here in Ghana. There's been a big settled Lebanese community in Accra for years, business people mostly."

So that explains why I have been mistaken for Lebanese in the shops around here.

Mrs Quah is at the wheel, pointing out the landmarks to Lawrence as we drive down 'Oxford Street', jammed with heavy traffic, and around Danquah Circle.

We pass shops, mosques, and small booths spilling out their wares onto uneven pavements. A tiny boy covered in white soapy lather from head to toe is bending over a tin bucket by a standpipe.

My hands are cold and clammy, even in this stifling heat, and panic is gnawing at my guts, but my senses are on fire with blasts of colour, noise, smells.

I keep thinking, this is wrong, I shouldn't be doing this. I'm not ready.

Suddenly it's dark.

"These pipple! They don't even *look*!" Mrs Quah throws her hands up in despair, slowing to a crawl as death-defying hawkers weave amongst the cars, selling bananas, peanuts, toilet rolls and chewing gum on trays balanced at impossible angles on their heads.

. Pungent aromas of grilled meat mingle with the putrid smell of drains, turning my stomach. We pass streets teeming with people cooking, eating, shopping, chatting, laughing, criss-crossing the street, wearing vibrant patterned cloth in red, gold, blue and green that stands out radiant in our headlights, like a flock of brightly coloured birds.

We have left Osu and the Green Leaf Hotel far behind. We seem to have been driving for hours.

We sweep at breakneck speed down a wide, busy dual carriageway, some sections still under construction. A pall of dust thrown up from the roadworks still hangs in the air, suspended by the heat.

"Achimota Road—we call it the Airport Road. It will be the best road in Accra when it's finished," Mrs Quah enthuses.

I wind down the window and try to gulp in air, but the dust chokes me. I don't know where we are going or what's going to happen next.

"Hold onto your hats!" Mrs Quah advises Lawrence in the back seat, as we make a right turn at the traffic lights, bumping along a dirt road, weaving precariously around potholes. It is much quieter here. There are a few big houses and buildings interspersed with wooden shacks, lit with oil lamps and candles, selling roasted maize and torch batteries.

I'm wearing my yellow dress with the dark brown Makonde figures on it, the one I bought in Dar Es Salaam to woo Lawrence the night he left for England. It's more than ten years old now, but it's kept its vivid colour and it is usually the coolest and most comfortable thing to wear in the heat. But right now, my whole body is bathed in sweat. My glasses keep slipping down my nose. I wipe the beads of sweat from my top lip with the back of my hand again. Pointless, as they re-form instantly.

I had a feeling something was going to happen. It came to me in the dream I had last night at the Green Leaf Hotel. In the dream, I was alone in a forest—a tropical forest. It was pitch dark, but I could just about make out the shadowy outline of trees and bushes. I was startled by rustling in the undergrowth in front of me. There was a wild animal thrashing about in there! And then out of the bushes emerged a fabulous peacock, feathers erect. It turned around slowly, majestically, displaying its plumage, back and front, like a slow-moving rotating fan. Only, the peacock was completely black—shiny jet-black all over, no other colours at all, apart from the faint blue-green petrol sheen on the eyes at the tips of its feathers. It was astonishingly beautiful.

That dream. I knew the meaning of it instantly. Why are messages from the subconscious so embarrassingly obvious, so unsubtle? Why do I patronise myself even in my dreams? Yet it haunts me now because I know it is going to happen.

Mrs Quah stops to inquire at each house. We are getting closer. Each time she disappears, that feeling of dread starts up in the pit of my stomach again. "This is wrong," I repeat again in my head, like a mantra. "I'm not ready."

"I was dreaming about this last night. I feel as if we've been set up," I say to Lawrence, breaking the nervous silence. "I just don't feel ready for this. What the hell is she *doing* in there?"

"We can't go back now," Lawrence speaks out of the darkness of the back seat, leaning forward to gently squeeze my shoulder. "We just have to trust her, go with the flow. It will be okay. She seems like a nice woman to me. What's the worst that could happen?"

I don't know. Rejection? Denial? Shock? Abandonment? Mistaken identity? Failure?

Mrs Quah appears again, drives a bit further, gets out of the car once more. "Sorry about this. Not exactly sure which house…"

This time she disappears for longer. At last she's back.

"Now don't say *anything*," she instructs us. "Leave all the talkin' to me."

Oh my God. This must be it. We enter the gate and follow the path single-file in the darkness around the side of the house, past outhouses, trees, and a stack of plastic buckets by the standpipe at the back door.

"Watch your feet on the paving stones, they're uneven," Lawrence warns me. I want to hold onto his hand for safety, but my palms are too wet with sweat. Finally, we turn into an immaculately tended garden. A White plaster statue of the Virgin Mary stands on a plinth in the centre. Neat rows of garden lights edge the lawn, illuminating mango and avocado trees and spiky flaming bird of paradise flowers. The air is cooler here, scented with jasmine. A man and woman relax on the open veranda, listening to Catholic hymns playing on a tape recorder. As we draw near, I recognise the man instantly, although I've never seen him before—not even in a photograph. My mind is racing. Where are we? Who is he? I know who he is. At least, I think I know.

We are invited to sit around the table. Mrs Quah motions me to sit beside the man and I obey her instructions to say nothing. But I stare. That face! So familiar. The dread is giving way to panic. Mrs Quah is speaking in Fanti. She's explaining something. The man looks from me to her and back again, his eyes widening in astonishment, his deep rich voice rising with incredulity. I understand nothing. Then in the middle of a sentence he says "Nineteen-fifty-three" in English. The year I was born. It *is* him.

There's a pause. Should I say something?

"Could someone translate this for me, please?"

"Well Jane, this is Mr Sam Kodjo. You've been waiting to meet him all your life. What have you got to say to him?" For once in my life I am speechless—though I have often rehearsed this moment. He speaks first.

"What did you say your name is?"

"Jane Goldsmith." Another pause. And then I go and say something unrehearsed and embarrassing. "I believe you knew my mother?"

As clichéd as *Doctor Livingstone I presume?*

But he doesn't laugh. Instead there's a heavy, unbearable silence, punctuated by cicadas calling to one another through the mango trees. He is going to say he doesn't know me, he has never heard of me, I have the wrong person.

And then he breaks into impeccable English and says: "Oh yes, I knew your mother. And you are my daughta. Welcome home."

We both stand up and embrace each other. I can feel his warmth, his solidity. Over his shoulder, through the window, I glimpse a spacious lamp-lit room with heavy, chintz-covered wooden furniture, framed batiks on the walls, and patterned rugs on the floor. A window on the life he has been living apart from me.

I am thirty-seven years old. I have been without this Dad all my life. And now he has his arms around me, holding me. I am shocked and amazed by the instant feeling of recognition and connection to this man I have never met before. This moment is real, yet unreal; both strange and familiar, unbelievable, yet inevitable. It is happening right now, but it is already in the past. It is my future and it is history. *My* history.

Now the woman stands up and embraces me too, a tall, handsome woman, perhaps a little taller than my father. "I have always wanted a daughta," she tells me. "I'm Faith, Sam's wife. If I had known about you I would have sent for you years ago. But I didn't know. Don't cry. It's not your fault." She glances at my father meaningfully. "I'll deal with him lata."

It's only then that I realise I'm crying, as well as laughing, and I can't stop.

"It's not your fault, don't cry," she repeats. "You must call us Mom and Dad."

But tears of joy and relief are still flooding down my face, mingled with the sweat on my lip.

Lawrence is taking photographs of me and my new Dad, posing with our arms around each other.

"They look so like each other. He couldn't possibly deny she's his daughta, it's obvious!" Faith exclaims to Mrs Quah.

We sip cold beers on the veranda, marvelling about

what has just happened.

"But tell me, how did you finally track me down? It can't have been easy. Tell us the story."

Where to begin?

"Well… the search went on for at least three years, on and off. My friend Val was looking through the records at London University…"

"But I was at Imperial College, studying for an MSc in Geophysics when I met your Mum. We met at a party…"

"Yes I know, Dad, we were looking for you in all the wrong places! I asked all my Ghanaian friends if they knew of you, and I went to the Ghana High Commission too. We tried everything… and Lawrence had been saying for such a long time we should come to Ghana…"

"I thought it would do her good," Lawrence explains. "I came for a conference here a few years ago—I told Jane there were all these wonderful people here, looking just like her, she would love it. Jane and I actually met in Africa, while we were volunteers in Tanzania. Africa is such a strong link between us. I just *knew* we had to come."

"I had got to the point where I couldn't live my life without finding you, Dad. I became obsessed with it, I got really depressed. So Lawrence just booked us a holiday here…"

"I am so sorry it has been so painful for you. How long had you been here in Accra before you found us?"

"Only a few days. But it all started before we left. I was at work one day and my friend Efua Dorkenoo, who is a Ghanaian, rang me up. I told her my story years ago, and she knew I was about to come here for the first time, so I thought she was calling me to give me some contacts to visit while I was here. But just out of the blue, she said 'I know who your Dad is.' It was such a shock, a lightning bolt. I didn't believe her at first."

"You must have been shell-shocked! How did your friend—Efua, you say her name is?—how did Efua find out about me?"

"She had apparently been talking to an old family friend of hers called Frank, who was studying in the UK in the 1950s, around the time you were in London. She asked Frank if he knew you, and he said 'Of course I knew Sam, he was a good friend of mine. There were only about half a dozen Ghanaian students in London at that time and we all knew each other!'"

"Oh my goodness, yes my old friend Frank. We travelled back home on the boat together from London. We have lost toch these last few years... I can't believe it. I must thank him—"

"—well, I spoke to Frank on the telephone before I left. He told me you were really good friends in those days. Honestly Dad, I was so thrilled to speak to someone who knew you and could tell me about you. I thought that would be enough, really, after all these years. I was afraid to go any further. But Frank said he was sure you would want to meet me. He told me a Ghanaian father never rejects his own child."

"That is true…"

"Frank told me you were a big Chief and a political figure in Ghana, so he warned me there was a bit of protocol involved, it would have to be managed properly. But he said, leave it to me and I'll see what I can do. He's still in Manchester, so he sent me a letter which I was to give to someone called Mrs Quah who would meet us at the airport…"

"—So that's where I come in," Mrs Quah beamed. "Frank and I are good friends, we go to the same Chuch. When they arrived, I took Lawrence and Jane to the Green Leaf Hotel in Osu. Frank told me roughly where to find you, Nana, but I had to do a bit of research. It took me a while to find the right house at first…"

"What a story! It must have taken a lot of courage!" Dad raises his glass of beer in a toast, "Here's to Frank and Mrs Quah, and your friend Efua, for bringin' you home to us."

"And to Lawrence for booking the tickets," adds Mom Faith. "Your Dad is a Chief, you know. That makes you a Fanti Princess."

"A princess? But—I used to pretend my Dad was an African Chief and I was a princess when I was a little girl at school! I even wrote a play about it when I was only eight years old. I made it up to make myself feel better, but of course no-one really believed me…"

"Well, now you know—it's true…"

My new-found Mom and Dad go inside a moment to

confer. They emerge again a few minutes later to make an announcement.

"We have decided you must move in here with us, we will get your room ready. It's our weddin' anniversary tomorrow, so the priest will be here. You can join us for our celebration mass. And all the family will be comin'—so we can introduce you. You are a gift from God, coming at this time, on this date."

This is all happening so fast. Suddenly, a whole new family, a whole new self.

Chapter 18

Call Me Names

The Green Leaf Hotel is just as we left it—battered old furniture, peeling paint, holes in the netting at the window letting in the mosquitoes. The fat, shiny, russet-brown cockroach waves its feelers warily at us from its usual station in the chipped enamel bath. A world away from what has just happened to me.

Lawrence always falls asleep before his head hits the pillow, no matter what, whilst I lie here in semi-darkness, listening to the ineffectual fan whirring wonkily in the ceiling, and two men arguing loudly in Twi in the stair-well outside the door. Was it real, did it happen? Did I just meet my Dad? I finger the corner of the photo he gave me as we said goodnight, now carefully placed under my pillow, the only tangible evidence that it isn't one of my hallucinations. I have waited a long time for this photograph. Every now and then I slide it out and peer at the picture in the dim light seeping through the gap at the bottom of the door. In the semi-darkness I can just make out my father, resplendent in his Chief's robes, against a backdrop of crushed blue velvet curtains. On his head is a black velvet crown, decorated with golden stars and moons, the royal fly-whisk and sword in either hand, and his feet clad in ornate sandals planted firmly on the Axminster carpet. This is the Dad I refused to bury that day in my therapist's consulting room.

The morning after, we breakfast in the sunshine outside on the terrace looking out onto the street. While Lawrence is away at the Forex bureau getting more cedis, I sit at the table and sip my tea, doling out coins to every passing hawker and beggar. Word has got around about my reckless generosity, and by the time Lawrence comes back I have attracted quite a lively, eager crowd, some in wheelchairs, on crutches, and kneeling on skateboards.

"What the hell are you doing? You're distorting the local economy! They will follow us everywhere—we'll never get rid of them. And how many more of those bracelets do you actually need to buy?"

I don't care. These are my new friends. I am so happy, happier than I have ever been in my life. I want to share my good fortune with the world.

*****

Later in the afternoon, when we turn up with our suitcases at my new-found parents' home, there is already a stream of visitors arriving for the wedding anniversary party, excited to meet Dad's new daughter. Once settled into our room,

Mom shows us around the house before joining the guests downstairs. Upstairs there are four spacious bedrooms with ensuite bathrooms, Dad's study stuffed with dusty old papers stacked untidily on the shelves, and a large TV room with a balcony overlooking the garden, the TV permanently switched on even though the room is empty.

"Your Dad designed this place. He's don everything out in granite and concrete, with rosewood on the floors and ceilings... He's a geologist, so everythin' has to be solid, just so, built to last..."

Downstairs there's a huge kitchen, another bedroom, and the vast reception room I had glimpsed the night before from the veranda, where all the guests are now assembling. After the Priest has said Mass, there is time to discuss the big news. Dad is constantly repeating the story of my homecoming to newly arrived guests. They are wide-eyed with wonder and full of questions. Nobody seems the least bit disapproving or judgemental. In fact, they all look delighted.

"He can't deny it!" they all insist. "You look exactly like him, and you talk like him too. You even walk like him. The same personality, enthusiasm, energy... You are a Ghanaian. Not quiet, like most British people."

This is startling news for me as a feminist. I have always strongly believed in nurture over nature, but if you can inherit eye colour, then why not personality, temperament, tastes and mannerisms? It doesn't mean we have to accept the world as it is. We still have choices. We are also and equally the product of our environment. To be human is to learn, change, adapt.

I'm sure there are as many differences between me and Dad as there are connections, but all the same, the similarities between us are uncanny.

"That pink wine they have in London—what's it called? Rosé, Mateus Rosé. That's it. In the famous round bottle. I love the taste of that. And the colour."

It turns out we both drink the pink stuff, even though it is unfashionable and hard to come by. And we wear our shoes down at the heels in the same place. We both love performing, teaching, making speeches. I always felt the odd one out in my nuclear family of introverts, my temperament regarded with suspicion: over-emotional and indiscreet, prone to exaggeration. My new-found Dad and I are both passionate about politics, pan-Africanism, performing, and international travel. Dad and Mom Faith both lived in Canada for a few years, and came to Britain too. Dad travelled the world when he was a high-ranking civil servant during the Nkrumah era, negotiating trade deals for mining equipment and mineral exports. He's now a member of the Council of State (which is a bit like the House of Lords), representing the Chiefs of Ghana.

"You wait till you meet your first cousin Tima!" says Auntie Annie, my Dad's vivacious sister-in-law. "She's your Uncle Patrick's eldest daughta. You are two peas in a pod! Same smile. She's lively and outgoing, like you."

When Tima joins the party half an hour later, I feel I

have known her all my life, a darling sister. She did a degree in Italy, and to everyone's astonishment we immediately start chatting away to each other in fluent Italian. As the beers, Fanta, plantain chips and plates of fried guinea-fowl are passed around, Tima tells me Dad is planning to take me to Cape Coast, about 100 miles away, and introduce me to the family there.

"My Mum and Dad live there, in Cape Coast, in the house our grandfather built," Tima explains. "My Dad is your Dad's youngest brother. You have thirty-one first cousins, you know. You'll meet some of them down there. It is different from European culture, we have a big extended family system here."

"I do at home too, that's how we live…"

"Then you will fit right in. We have the city-dwelling family like us, living in Cape Coast, Accra, Takoradi and Kumasi—we are mostly teachas, doctas, office-workas—and of course your Dad is a politician. My Dad, your Oncle Patrick, is a businessman. He runs the Kingsway stores, the biggest shop in Cape Coast. Our village is a few miles from there, just a few hondred people, very traditional, no running water, no paved roads. They are mainly subsistence farmas and the women also smoke fish the traditional way and grow palm oil. You'll see when you go there, it's quite different. You will see rural Ghana, the real Ghana."

*****

It's mid-evening, the guests have gone, and Dad and I relax on the veranda, sipping Club beer, talking way into the night, catching up on our separated lives—decades of missed events, adventures, emotions—while the other members of the household look on, staring and giggling from behind the door onto the veranda, until Mom Faith ushers them off to bed.

"Why didn't you come and find *me*?" I ask him.

"Because I was waitin' for you."

Waiting. It makes me angry. For what? For me to forgive him for leaving me and my mother?

"Waitin' for you to want to see me. I had no right to see you, unless you wanted it." He pauses. "And why did *you* wait so long?"

Hard question to answer.

Maybe fury, or pride. But mostly fear. Fear of betraying those who brought me up. Fear of abandonment all over again. *Fear of the unknown. If we meet, will we get along? Will we even like each other?* And fear of rewriting my life's script—*the girl who never knew her father*, transformed into *the daughter who knows her father and has his address*. From the known to the unknown to knowing.

"I was scared, Dad. I thought it might be very tricky to suddenly introduce myself to a whole new family who maybe didn't even know about me. And what if you denied it, rejected me all over again? What if I'd got the wrong person? And my family who brought me up, how will they feel? My Mum, especially, and my Stepdad. I didn't want them to feel hurt, you know. They have all done so much for me..."

"I understand... I understand... But why *now*, dear daughta ? Why now, after all these years? How did you conquer your fears?"

"I think one of the things that really spurred me on was... we have a son Jacob Kwesi. He's two-and-a-half, your grandson. I didn't want that to happen to our boy, you know, that he would also be asked *where do you come from?* and he wouldn't know either. I needed to know my story, for his sake, because it's his story too. It belongs to the next generation. Lots of things have happened to me in my life, sometimes painful things. I felt out of place, I got called names, people always assumed I was a foreigner. That made me think of you constantly, Dad— even when I tried to put you out of my mind. In the end I just *had* to do it."

"I am so sorry you had so much pain. But I thank God you came before it was too late. I am sixty-seven, not young anymore. You have come to light up my old age, and Faith's too. I had to make sure she was happy with it first. But she said to me, this daughta is my daughta too. And now we discova we have a grandchild! We are sooo blessed, we really are. You must bring your little one to see us. Where is he now?"

"My Mum is looking after him."

"That's good. So she knows you are coming to find me. I was wonderin'..."

"Actually, Mum doesn't know exactly. I didn't even know whether we would find you. She knows we have come on holiday here and she offered to look after Jake, so that was her way of saying she knew the trip was important to me... What about your family, Dad? Did you tell anyone about me when you got back here from England?"

"Yes, I told my mother and my brothers. Your Grandmother and your oncles all knew about you. Your Grandmother has sadly passed on now, but all four of your oncles are still livin'. I'm going to take you to Cape Coast to meet them. That is where we come from."

"My Mum said you mentioned a place called Takoradi."

"Takoradi is not far from Cape Coast. That's where your Grandfather, my father, was born."

"What did my Grandmother say when you told her about me?"

"She told me I had to go back to London and bring you here. Your Grandmother was a wonderful lady, a Queen Mother. Our sister, her only daughta, died very young in childbirth with her first child... she was such a beautiful young woman, our only sister. Our mother was devastated. I don't think she ever really recovered after that, it broke her heart to lose her only girl. Girls are very precious in our clan—they carry the bloodline of the family. Your Grandmother was desperate for a grand-daughta. It is traditional here for grandmothers to bring up their grand-children, so she really wanted me to go and fetch you, and bring you home so that she could look after you."

Dad trails off, full of emotion. And so am I. I had so much wanted to meet my African Grandmother.

"What did you say to your Mum, about why you didn't come to fetch me?"

"Well, I explained that two social workas turned up at my flat in Castlenau and told me I had to get out, leave the country, as soon as I finished my studies. They told me your Mum was in an unmarried mothers' home and you were to be adopted, it was all arranged—"

"—but Mum said you were angry when you heard she was pregnant, that you refused to meet my Grandad."

He looks a little uneasy at this. I suspect I have hit a nerve.

"Well, the social workas warned me never to contact you. They said it would disturb you. I wanted to see you, but unmarried fathers had no right to see their children. That was the law then—I checked. I know your Mum's parents were very upset, especially her mother. I heard she didn't want a Black person in the house. And things were happening sooo fast here in Ghana… We were about to become the first independent post-colonial African country. I wanted to be home, be part of it, be part of history. I was torn, it was very difficult…"

I'm perplexed at all this. "But Dad, I wasn't even born when you left, you left six weeks before I was born, you couldn't have—"

"—No, six weeks *afta* you were born. I paid maintenance for you, ten shillings a week, until I left the country…"

This is a revelation. "I wish I had known that. It would have reassured me that you cared about me, acknowledged me in some way, at least. Did you ever think of me in all these years, Dad?"

"Many times. We even adopted a little girl from the orphanage, her name is Adwoa. I thought that if someone else was looking after my daughta , the least I could do was adopt a baby girl here. And I thought about you, especially when I was in London in the 1980s. I wondered what had happened to you, my little girl. Every young Black woman I passed, I thought, could she be you?"

"You were in London in the '80s! But that's when I was looking for you!"

"Yes, I was a refugee then. It was a very turbulent time in Ghana in the 1980s. I was head of bauxite and diamond mining, and the workers captured the mines and took me hostage. The Government sent the army in to rescue me and escort me to Accra 'for my own safety'. That's what they said... but when the soldiers came I soon realised they were puttin' me under arrest. Rawlings, the President, had taken over and he didn't want any opposition. He distrusted other powerful men. Many of us were being rounded up. So, as soon as I got back to Accra, I used my contacts to get the first plane out to Nigeria, and then to the UK."

"How long were you in the UK?"

"About eight years. Things had got so bad in Ghana I went to the World Education Services to try and get your brother, Sam, a scholarship, so he could join me. Do you know it? Their offices are in Islington."

I am stunned.

"But Dad… that's where I worked, in the 1980s! What year did you go there?"

"It would have been about 1986, I suppose. I spoke to Sarah and Sarah, who were running the scholarship programmes there."

"What? But they were my colleagues, my friends! I worked with them, I was there then!"

"That's extraordinary! I remember them because they both had the same name and I got confused. They told me they only did scholarships for South Africans, Ugandans and Chileans, so I had no luck…"

I can't believe it. My blood is running cold. At the very time I was having my nervous breakdown, wearing my smeared white trousers, I could have been in the same building as my Dad. I could have passed him in the corridor. The grants department was in the office adjacent to mine on the ground floor. All those missed opportunities. All that lost time when we could have been together…

"Perhups it was meant to be," says Dad. "You were meant to come to Africa to find me. To come home. It is not just me you needed to find, it's also your family, your country, your tribe, your people, your culture."

*****

Next day, Mom Faith promises to make us a traditional Ghanaian dish for dinner—fufu and groundnut soup with chicken and fish. "We will eat it late afternoon. It's too heavy for an evening dish, it will lie on your stomach and give you the tummy ache."

"Don't forget Lawrence is vegetarian, Mum."

"Yes, that will be okay. He can just eat the chicken gravy. It's very tasty."

We go outside into the yard at the side of the house to witness the pounding of the fufu. Agostina, the cook, thumps the over-sized wooden pestle rhythmically in the mortar, making a hypnotic *thock, thock* sound. Faith sits on a low stool, expertly turning the dough with her hand as the pestle rises and falls with split-second timing. One small mistake would result in smashed fingers.

"It's made with yam and I've mixed in some ripe plantain too, to make it soft and yellow, and then we will steam it."

As she works, she fills us in on more of the family stories.

"My mother-in-law, your grandmother, used to tell our adopted daughta Adwoa I was not her real mother," Faith confides, bending forward to knead the dough. "The old lady told Adwoa she had a twin sister living in London with her real mother. What a thing to say to such a small child! She was barely four years old. She hadn't been told she was adopted. I was sooo upset, I told your father his mother was telling tall tales and upsetting our little girl.

The true story is that Adwoa's natural mother died in childbirth along with her twin sista."

So my Grandmother really did know about me. And she wanted me.

"I thought the old lady was making it all up, raving, losin' her mind. I didn't realise she was mixing up two stories together—yours and Adwoa's. Adwoa even used to write letters to this mythical mother and sister in London when she got older. As soon as you came, it aaall started to make sense, it aaall fell into place. All the half-truths and mixed up stories. Your Grandmother was evidently missin' you, and she needed to share her sadness with someone, though she had sworn not to tell. Your adopted sister Adwoa is very confused by your arrival, as you can imagine. Her 'twin' can't be ten years older than her! But at least now we know the truth."

Two little girls on either side of the world, Adwoa and me, connected by the myths the grown-ups wove for the children, to cope with their own grief. Myths survive when the truth has long since evaporated. What is the truth anyway? I came here to seek it, but what I have found is myriad interwoven versions of the same shadowy events.

The kneading of the fufu complete, Mom Faith straightens up and stretches her back. "You know your Dad told you we have a son too. You have a half-brother, livin' in Golders Green. When you go back home I will fly to London and introduce you to him."

*****

Dad and I are making up for lost time in our father-daughter relationship, fast-forwarding through baby-hood, childhood and adolescence like a speeded-up home movie. On Monday I follow him around the house begging him not to go to work and asking when he will be home. I am in love with my Daddy, handsome and regal in his chief's robes, his gleaming chestnut skin, his rich laugh, his eyes widening as I tell him of my exploits in London.

By Friday I have reached adolescence, and I am in full rebellion.

"He's met his match" says my new Mom approvingly. "You're the only person who has ever challenged him."

Lawrence is laid up in bed with the runs.

"That hot pepper sauce, so delicious, what do they call it? Shitto—it works! That's exactly what it does… " he moans.

"… and you've been drinking the water straight from the tap too, against all travellers' advice. I'm sure that hasn't helped."

Lawrence's unfortunate confinement leaves me plenty of time to argue with my new Dad.

"I am going to a meeting today, supporting a charity to stop all these boys who make girls pregnant and then abandon them—such irresponsible behaviour," Dad tells me over breakfast.

"Like you did with my mother?"

He looks startled, as if he genuinely has not made that connection.

"Have you come here to try and make me feel bad?"

"No, no, honestly, Dad. I didn't mean to upset you, I just thought that's why you were mentioning it."

"Well while you are mentionin' it, *you* ought to marry Lawrence. I can't understand why you are not married. You should stick to the rules of the country you are living in."

I bite my tongue and resist the temptation to say 'Like you did with my mother' again. He notices the look I have given him, but he perseveres.

"I will perform a traditional ceremony for the two of you to be married before you go home."

"But I'm a feminist, Dad. I don't believe in marriage. Men and women should be equals. Relationships should be based on trust."

"Is that why you are down here arguing with me and not upstairs looking after your poor sick hosband?"

"He's not my husband, Dad. I just *told* you, we are not married… and Lawrence is fine, he doesn't like being fussed over when he's sick. He just likes to sleep it off and not be disturbed."

"You should take him some of this soup I am having for breakfast—turkey with giant ground snails. It will do him good, make him strong. He is probably getting sick because he is a vegetarian. He needs meat."

"Anyway, am I the only one, Dad? Are there any more like me—I mean illegitimate children that you haven't talked about before?"

"You are the only one," he says solemnly, even though I have heard rumours of others from my new-found cousins, who have dared me to try and find out the truth. "And anyway," Dad continues, "there are some things you should not know. They are only for me to know…"

"Why?"

*****

"Honestly, can you believe it, I have been without this Dad for thirty-seven years, and now he's telling me how to live my life. We should leave!"

"Why do you always have to be so tactless and fiery?" says Lawrence weakly, still prostrate on his sick bed. "I'm not going anywhere more than five feet from this loo. You will just have to go downstairs and make up with him and apologise."

But Dad seems to be getting quite used to me, and he is making more plans.

In the evening, he announces, "Faith and I have been discussing between us… We are going to give you a new name, your African name.

"We have decided on Esuantsiwa, after our Ancestress, who became our first Queen Mother… Long ago, more than a hundred and fifty years past, she saved the tribe from Ashanti attack, so they enstooled her as Queen of our people, and all her descendants are members of the Royal

Family and can be chosen as Chiefs and Queen Mothers in their own right, through the maternal line. That's why I have been made a Chief. But Chiefs are chosen, not born. You have to earn the title as you have earned this name. What you did was very brave, coming here, not knowing what you would find."

I can't think that it's remotely equivalent to what this original Esuantsiwa did, but all the same, I'm thrilled. This history is so exciting. What luck for a feminist like me to find out I am from a matrilineal line! And I have my African name at last, even though I can't spell it or pronounce it.

"We are taking you to Cape Coast to introduce you to your family, and we'll have the official naming ceremony there for you."

Mom Faith takes me to the tailor around the corner, to sew me some new outfits for the trip to Cape Coast.

"The tailor doesn't like rosh jobs. She always grombles that she is too busy and there's not enough time, but don't mind her, she'll do it, and she'll do a good job. And I have asked the hairdressers to come to us tomorrow to fix the style you want, the small braids with extensions, isn't it? Chinese style, that's what they call it. That will take a long time, about eight hours for two of them to do it. I better make them some fufu while they are workin', they will get hungry. They can fix your hair out on the veranda where it's cooler."

*****

We start the drive to Cape Coast in the early morning, in Dad's car. I'm already stiff from sitting for so long the day before, having my hair done for the trip. Mom Faith and I sit in the back seat, munching groundnuts. There's time to catch up with her, now that Dad isn't here. Lawrence sits up front with King, the driver, getting a running commentary on the places we are passing.

Small fishing boats are out on the vast picturesque lake, in the relative cool of the early morning. "That's where Accra gets its water supply," King explains to Lawrence.

At Kasua Junction, the market is teeming with people. Hawkers swarm around the buses in the terminus, their round trays piled high with fat white loaves of bread.

"What are those things that look like round cheeses wrapped in leaves, stacked up on the stalls?" Lawrence asks.

"*Kenke*. It's a local dish made from fermented corn, wrapped in banana leaves. We eat it with fish or vegetable soup and hot peppa . It's good, you must try it."

Lawrence winces. "Maybe later... I'm still a bit delicate in the stomach area at the moment."

The names of the places are so evocative—Kasua, Saltpond, Winneba roundabout with colourful painted figures of a whale, a bird, and three men in bowler hats.

"We'll stop at Holy Child, my old secondary school, along the way to Cape Coast," says Mom Faith. "We are famous for our secondary schools around here. They are set up by different Christian groups—Wesleyan, Catholic, Methodist—most of them more than one hondred years old. It's a very strong tradition. I loved studying English at school, especially the poems. Wordsworth's golden daffodils—so exotic. I was entranced to see my first golden daffodils when I went to the UK."

That poem again. I remember my class reading it while I was secretly writing novelettes about the Beatles under my desk.

I am to be introduced to Faith's family first, before meeting Dad's family, so Dad has time to go ahead to Cape Coast and prepare the naming ceremony. This trip is also to give Faith the space to introduce me to her family in her own time, in her own way. I am impressed by the way they have swung into action, about how I am to be introduced and in what order, and when. A few days ago, Faith had no idea I existed.

"When your Dad had to flee to the UK during the 1980s, I was alone in the house in Accra," she explains. "The night he left, soldiers came to the house and broke down the door. They came into the bedroom where I was lying in bed, pointin' their guns at me. I told them, you can shoot me if you like. I am a Christian, I am not afraid of death. But as for my hosband, you will not find him here, he is long gone..."

My admiration for Faith grows with every moment we spend together. Her dignity, bravery, compassion. The way she accepted me immediately as her daughter.

"It is never the child's fault," she says. "It is for the adolts to explain."

*****

My first sight of the coast road makes me cry. The stretch between Cape Coast and Elmina—coconut palms, windswept beaches, ocean waves crashing onto the rocky shoreline, fishermen mending nets, women tending earthen fish-smoking ovens that look like neat red anthills among the pine forests fringing the beach. It feels timeless, as if I remember it from somewhere, deep in my past. It is my favourite place on earth.

When we reach Cape Coast Castle, Mom Faith urges us to go in with the tourist party. "I have been here many times. I want to rest my legs, they are swelling up in this heat. I will stay in the car with King."

Beyond the whitewashed castle walls, the magnificent panorama of the ocean extends to the horizon. Fearsome waves dash the rocky coastline, dotted with palm trees and fishing boats—a scene that can hardly have changed since the days of slavery. This was the last glimpse the captured slaves ever saw of Africa before beginning the horrific six-week Middle Passage across the Atlantic.

Our tour guide shows us the magnificent courtyard with grand white-painted staircases sweeping upward to the Governor's quarters, and the rows of cannons pointing out to sea. He shows us the ball and chain where the women slaves who refused to sleep with the White slavers were stripped and tethered and exposed for hours in the searing sun, the suffocating low-ceilinged dungeons where thousands of slaves were packed in the stench and the darkness, the thin shallow gullies in the concrete floor for collecting human waste, and finally the Gate of No Return, through which the slaves passed on their last journey, chained and beaten, bound for the slave ships to America.

"A third did not make it," explains the guide. "Some even jomped into the ocean on the way out to the ships to drown themselves…"

I expected to be moved and appalled by the history of this place. But I am not in the least prepared to be engulfed by the wave of unexpected, uncontrollable grief and terror which seems to emanate from the walls of the dungeons, as if the ghosts are still present. It's visceral, turns my guts to stew, grabs me by the throat, chokes and nauseates me… I have to get out, I need air or I will collapse.

I stagger back through the crowd of mostly White tourists, out into the vast courtyard, empty save for two African-American women sitting on a stone wall, similarly affected. With no introductions, we cling together, reeling from the sheer force and enormity of the horror, weeping as if we have just lost our nearest and dearest, relieved that we can grieve together. Gradually emotion subsides enough for us to speak. Susanna and Mariam, my new-found companions, have come to trace their lost roots through slavery. I feel a survivor's guilt, mixed with my joy in my recently-discovered African family, and culpability because I am also half White, and I bear the genes of the oppressor.

"But coastal people in Ghana also helped to go on slave raids in the interior, and they traded with the slavers," says Mariam. "And so many of us are descendants of slaves and owners, most of us are Bi-Racial. One drop of Black blood and you are classed as Black in America. Slavery is humanity's shame, not just one race's. It's so complex—it's not just Black and White."

Our party of tourists finally emerges from the dungeons.

"What the hell happened to you?" demands Lawrence, looking concerned. "You suddenly took off. I didn't know where you'd gone…"

"You have the sickness," our guide observes. "Soo many African-Americans like you are afflicted when they pass through the dungeons. It must be your ancestors callin' to you…"

I explain to him that I am from the UK, and I have just met my Ghanaian Father who is a Fanti Divisional Chief from Cape Coast.

"Then you are our sista," he says. "Welcome home."

*****

My Dad and my four Uncles—Patrick, Frederick, Steven

and James—are there to welcome me in the courtyard of my Grandfather's home. There's a strong family likeness among the brothers.

"Your Dad told us about you when he came back from England in the '50s," says Uncle Patrick. "Where did you say you live in Tooting? I went to South London College to study management. I lived there for many years, in Foulser Road."

It's a stone's throw from where we live now. So many connections with family I have only just met.

Uncle James has tears in his eyes as he takes both my hands in his. "Anna Richter has come back to us."

Who is Anna Richter?

"She was your paternal Great-Grandmother. She was the daughta of a Dutch trader and Ghanaian mother, and she was much loved," says my Uncle James. "She was the same colour as you—light brown skin." He pats my arm affectionately.

I wonder how someone of Mixed-Race would have felt living under a colonial regime; what life would have been like for people like us.

"You see the big white building at the top of the hill? That's the lighthouse. It was built by your grandfather, he was the lighthouse keeper. We spent our childhood livin' in that house. You can see the whole of Cape Coast town from up there," my Dad explains. "Come inside now and meet your aunties."

Inside the house, I am taken to my father's room for

my aunties and Mom Faith to dress me: a strip of black-and-white adinkra cloth under a red and gold *kente* robe, a plaited headdress, sword and fly-whisk in either hand, gold-plated jewellery, ornate sandals. These were the clothes I was meant to wear—the colours, the patterns, the texture and flow of the heavy double-weave fabric. I feel right in them. I feel at home. I feel me.

"This is a special dish called Oto," says Auntie Esi, handing me a plate. "Pounded yam and eggs with *Shitto*, the hot peppa sauce. This is what we eat on ceremonial occasions."

I follow them into the reception room, with blue-painted walls, and a low table in the middle of the room bearing Fanta, Cola and Sprite, and an unopened bottle of Old Geneva Schnapps. My Dad, his brothers and the other elders, dressed in their *kente* robes, are seated on a line of stools at the back of the room, their bare shoulders glistening with oil. A bank of televisions is stacked in the corner—status symbols. "Although not all of them work," whispers Auntie Esi. She notices me staring at an old framed black-and-white photograph of a Queen Mother, surrounded by her sons, mounted on the wall ahead of us.

"Your grandmother, your father and your oncles," Auntie Esi explains. I feel a sudden sharp pang of loss, for the grandmother who wanted me to be here with her. Auntie Esi guides me to the empty stool directly in front of my father, ornately carved with a *Gye Nyame* adinkra symbol that means 'Accept God,' or 'Except God', depending on your interpretation.

More and more guests arrive as word gets round. They sit on chairs around the room and on the floor in front of us, dressed in black-and-white patterned cloth—the colours of celebration. Each new arrival goes round the room, shaking hands with everyone in turn, in the Ghanaian style. Soon the whole room is packed, joyous, smiling, full of energy. We have run out of space, so late-comers are crowding in at the doorway.

The ceremony is called to order. My Father, the Chief, does not speak. Kwesi Tobias the linguist, the *Okyeame*, speaks on his behalf.

Kwesi Tobias explains in Fanti why I am here, and then translates into English for me.

"The villagers demand to know why they have been summoned, so we have told them that your father has brought his lost daughta to meet them. Your name will be Nana Eruefua Esuantsiwa. You are a princess so you will be called Nana. You were born on Friday so your name will be the Lady Efua; and you will be known as Esuantsiwa because you have the spirit of the Warrior Queen, our ancestress who saved our village from destruction. You are brave because you came here on a plane on a long journey to find us."

I've been called a lot of names in my time. *Woggie, darkie, Blackie, golliwog, nig nog, the-colour-of-dogshit*. But I have finally got my African name, the one I've always wanted.

"We welcome you as a daughta into our clan, the *Anona*."

At the word Anona, the whole crowd suddenly erupts into a noisy spirited chanting in English—*"Who are we, why are we, how are we, what are we!"*—at the tops of their voices, clearly enjoying the whole spectacle.

"The Anona are one of the Akan clans," Kwesi Tobias continues. "Our emblem is the parrot. We are well known for being intelligent, well educated, great travellers, speaking many different languages. You are one of us. Welcome home."

Kwesi Tobias breaks open a bottle of Schnapps and pours libation onto the ground outside in the courtyard to invite the ancestresses to come and bear witness, reciting the names of the Queen Mothers—my Grandmothers—since the original Esuantsiwa's time. He pours a little of the strong colourless liquor into a glass, dips his forefinger, and dabs it onto my tongue to complete the naming ceremony.

"Like a baby, eight days old," he explains. "That is when we normally do the ceremony—that is why I am giving you the Schnapps with my finga ."

I could do with a good slug of that stuff right now to calm my nerves.

The formal ceremony over, the guests are full of excited questions, and demanding explanations. The eldest Queen Mother rises unsteadily to her feet, her skin wrinkled like a walnut, and wags her finger at my father, berating him in the most energetic terms in spite of her bent, fragile frame. "Why have you hidden this beautiful daughta from us all these years? If you have any more daughtas like her, you better bring them out now, or you will be in trouble..."

Addressing me and pointing at Lawrence, she adds, "Nana Esuantsiwa, bring me a handsome White hosband like him from England next time you come," to roars of appreciation from the audience.

Lawrence has a sudden thought. "If Esuantsiwa is a princess, what does that make me?"

"Prince Philip, of course!" quips Auntie Esi.

They drag me from the stool and whirl me around, black-and-white wrappers twirled above my head, women ululating, men clapping, children laughing. My aunties treat me like a baby, passing me from lap to lap, and then whisk me up onto the floor again to dance.

When everyone congratulates me, I respond in Fanti.

"We didn't know you could speak the language!"

I can't. It's coming from somewhere inside me, a powerful energy. I just *know* how to respond, like speaking in tongues. The next morning, I can't speak a word of it.

"And tomorrow we will take you to our village to meet the rest of the family," says my Dad.

I am living through an extraordinary time in my life. Taken in, embraced and cared for in this new family, with genuine affection and human warmth. The ritual and traditions are not solemn or staid, but joyous, chaotic, full of spirit, full of meaning. Everything happens in the right order. Everyone knows what to do and sees it is done properly.

Sometimes magic happens. You can't explain.

Chapter 19

Double Vision

"It could have been handled differently, I know," Mum says hesitantly. We clasp hands across the bright yellow plastic gingham tablecloth in the kitchen in our flat in Tooting. In that moment, Mum and I have come together again. The laughs, loss, pain, politics, feminism; the friendship, solidarity, admiration and the love we have always had for each other.

"This is the conversation we probably should have had years ago. But I felt abandoned. Only nineteen. People said we wouldn't amount to anything, you and I. And now look at us…"

We are all human, with hearts that get broken. And it's hard to forgive men who abandon women and leave single mothers to do all the explaining, pick up the pieces, answer the questions. But as the child of the secret—the unmentionable and unforgivable secret—I needed to know. It's *my* story, even when it is so painful.

We got through it. The most difficult thing is forgiving

ourselves.

"Thanks for looking after Jake, Mum. We really missed him."

*****

Within the space of six months, the political and personal framework of my life has been torn apart. In November 1989 the Berlin Wall came down. In January 1990, Nelson Mandela was released after a lifetime in prison. In July 1990 I met my Dad. Nothing is as it was. Everywhere I go, I carry the photos of meeting Dad for the first time. Strangers used to ask me where I'm from. Now I go up to total strangers on the tube, at bus stops and in meetings to tell them what happened to me, show them the pictures. I can think and talk about nothing else. It's like being Born Again. People must think I'm mad.

Faith has flown to London as promised to introduce me to my brother who lives in Golders Green. *My brother*, who has been living a few miles from me in the same city for more than a decade. He's ten years younger than me, about the same age as Molly and Tom. He is good-looking, charming, welcoming and affectionate. I am as instantly and deeply taken with Sam Junior as I was with my father when we first met, a physical force drawing me towards him. I'm embarrassed that I want to stare at him, drink him in, reach out and touch him and hold him and tell him how much I love him.

We crack open a bottle of champagne to toast our new-found siblinghood. I ask him how he feels about suddenly finding out he has a big sister, living a few miles away from him in London all this time—discovering that he's not the eldest child any more.

"To be honest, it's a relief, it's excitin'," he beams. "In some ways I felt a bit like an only child all this time. Of course, I am fond of my adopted sister, Adwoa, you met her while you were out there, I think? She's a very private person, a bit shy—not like you! You are so like our Dad, much more so than I am. Talkin' to you is like talkin' to him. Your energy, enthusiasm, the way you talk and even the way you walk. I can't get over it!" He nods and smiles again. "And I like your outfit, green suits you. Did you have it made in Ghana?"

Mum and Dad Ernest are coming to meet Mom Faith and my new brother, Sam, at our flat. I feel anxious about the meeting, unsure how to address them in front of each other, how the meeting will go, how to open up the conversation. But I needn't have worried. As soon as they walk in, Mom Faith moves towards them, scooping them both up in her arms, pressing them to her bosom, dwarfing them in a warm embrace.

"You have done a wonderful job bringing Esuantsiwa up. We are so lucky to have her as our daughta, she is a gift to light up our later life. Thank you both sooo much, we are all so blessed."

Watching the three of them hugging each other in

front of me, right here in our front room, Sam Junior looking on, I am flooded with relief, love and affection for all of them. It has taken a lot for them to do this. I can see there is instant, mutual admiration and respect, the beginning of a lasting friendship.

*****

I meet up with Melanie in the Reubens Hotel in Victoria for lunch. She wants to do an interview about my story for *Marie Claire*.

She tells me they will call the story '*I found out I was a Princess*'.

I'm doubtful about the title. A tad counter-revolutionary.

"That's the hook, that's what our readers are interested in, trust me," Melanie counters eagerly. "They like rags-to-riches fairy-tales. Working-class girl on Council estate, born in an unmarried mother's home, only Black kid on the block, traces her African Dad in her thirties and finds out she's a Princess. Brilliant! To be honest, you're a little bit old for our readership, at thirty-seven, but I persuaded the editors it's such a good story we should publish it anyway."

"But my story is about finding out who I am. It's about identity, belonging, prejudice, racism and sexism and single motherhood…"

"Yes, yes, I know all that stuff is important. We'll try

and do it justice," Melanie attempts to reassure me. "But our readers will like the Princess bit, believe me. The human story, that's the draw: meeting your father for the first time, what you said to him, what his wife thought about you turning up, your birth mother's reactions to you finding your Dad, how you—"

"—I dunno, it all gets very difficult when it involves saying what people who are close to you think and feel," I interrupt, "I'm really not sure about this Melanie… I don't want to upset anyone."

I'm squirming with dread. I wish I'd never agreed to this. What will my socialist republican comrades make of the princess angle? Sounds like a total sell-out. They won't understand what it means to me, to my sense of African-ness and belonging in my Ghanaian family. Something happened to me on a deep level, like a rebirth, when I went through the naming ceremony in Ghana. Speaking in tongues, feeling in the right place for the first time after a lifetime's searching. It's impossible to explain in words to anyone who has never been there.

"Look, I can see how you feel. It's not easy talking about the personal stuff, family secrets and all that. Why don't you just tell me what happened and I'll turn it into a great story," says Melanie brightly, breaking into my thoughts, "… and you'll see it before it goes to print, promise. I don't usually do that, but I can see how much it means to you. I don't have the final say, mind you. That's down to the editor."

The spiritual transformation and the politics don't seem to have made it into the final copy, despite Melanie's best intentions. Only ten days to go until publication date, and I'm panicking. Nobody is going to like it. In the newsagent's, buying the *Guardian* on Saturday morning, the front cover of the latest edition of *Marie Claire* catches my eye. *'I found out I was a Princess,'* complete with a picture of me inside in regal robes accompanying the article.

"The latest *Marie Claire* always arrives a couple of weeks early—increases the shelf life," my newsagent explains. It may make good business sense to him, but for me it's a personal PR disaster. I buy up every copy in the shop, regardless of the newsagent's complaints—"Hey, I've got regular customers coming in for their copies... you can't take all of 'em!"

I have campaigned all my life to see more Black and Brown women's faces in public life and in the media. I know how much it would have meant when I was a teenager to have seen images that looked like me, images that celebrated black hair and dark skin as beautiful, not an aberration. But where does celebration of beauty stop and objectification begin? I am beset by the same contradictions that plagued me when I saw photo shots of Black beauty queens in the sixties, and when I posed naked on the couch as an artist's model. I raged then at the oft-repeated excuse that Black women were never featured on the covers of magazines, because 'they don't sell'. But why should any woman want to be sold?

Now that it's *my* face in this month's *Marie Claire*, I dash home to hide it.

Jake, only three-and-a-half, is thrilled to see a picture of himself in the magazine. He thinks it's the Argos catalogue. We took him out to Ghana, the year after first meeting Dad, to see his new Grandad, and they bonded immediately.

At the family gathering at Everton Road, reaction is mixed.

"You got yourself published in a very sexy magazine!" says Auntie Molly, in her seventies, clearly impressed.

"You're thinking of *Cosmo*, Auntie," says Auntie Bel. "Although they *are* similar."

"It's good, so exciting!" says my sister Molly.

"Well I think it's *dreadful*!" says Auntie Lucy, "Absolute rubbish. Why did you let 'em do this? You should never talk to journalists, they always get all the facts wrong. Shaftesbury Park isn't even a council estate, it's a housin' estate. And why should *that man* get all the publicity and all the credit? 'E abandoned yer Mum. We're the ones who brought you up and we 'ardly get a mention. Think how yer Mum feels…"

This remark seems to meet with general agreement. I can see Mum looking pained. She hasn't said much. She left the room to read the article on her own. She hates publicity.

I feel bad. I have not earned the status of official *Abandonee* in my own right, I am more of an accidental by-product. I should be supporting Mum, not demanding all this attention on my own account, talking about how I feel, opening up to strangers...

That old feeling. I've let everyone down again. But it's not every day a Black woman gets a story published in a national magazine like this. It's not a bad article, really, all things considered. I want to say to them, 'I didn't mean to hurt anyone, this doesn't change anything. I still love you all, I appreciate what you've done for me, I really do. Mum is the bravest woman in the world—she fought to keep me against all the odds.'

Instead I sit in awkward silence, listening to them combing the article for inaccuracies, longing for the conversation to turn to something else. I can see how unfair they think it is. Do I have the right to tell this story, is it mine to tell? Does it belong to the tribe—my London tribe, or my Cape Coast tribe?

It's hard for everyone to come to terms with. I have just had a shattering experience, I have rewritten my identity from the ground up and people are interested in it. But it's not that easy to talk about it without upsetting people. I feel guilty. There's no blueprint for what's happening to me. I wish I could learn to deal with this better. It seems as if it's my responsibility to manage my own and everyone else's emotions, to protect everyone, but I don't know how, I just haven't got the hang of it. I haven't a clue where to start.

If this is how my UK family feels, what about my

African family? I have no idea of the protocol. Ghana Dad is a public figure. What if it ruins his career? I should have asked everyone's permission before I did this, in both families—and I imagine they would all have said no.

I usually telephone Ghana every few weeks. I can't put it off any longer, or they will worry. Perhaps I just won't mention it. What are the odds of them ever seeing a UK-published young women's magazine in Accra?

But Ghana Dad telephones *me*.

"Esuantsiwa! Why didn't you tell me you were in the magazine?"

"Oh dear, I am so sorry Dad. I meant to ask your permission, it all happened so fast…"

"It's *marvellous*. I wish I'd known about it in advance! I was astonished when the Vice President's wife came up to me at the Council of State reception. She said, 'Congratulations on your beautiful new daughta, Councillor Kofie!' She has *Marie Claire* sent out to her from UK every month!"

"Dad, I can't believe you liked it!"

"Of course, Esuantsiwa. I'm so proud of you. Send me more copies to give to my colleagues—all their wives want to read it."

*****

I'm knocking on the blue front door again after all these years. Ray welcomes me, smiling.

"You found him! What an extraordinary story! You know that in Gestalt therapy, they say there is a prince or princess in every one of us. It's what Jung would call *synchronicity*. I can't wait to tell them your story in my group therapy session. I wouldn't mention your name of course."

"It's okay, Ray, public knowledge, they can read all about it in *Marie Claire* magazine. It *sounds* like a fairy-tale ending, but really it's brought up more issues than it's solved. No-one ever asks how Cinderella gets on after the wedding. 'Happy-ever-after' is a bit more complicated, in spite of feeling absolute joy in finding my Dad and my Ghanaian family of course..."

"So how do you feel about it all now?"

"I still feel split and conflicted, sometimes, to be honest. I'm in the middle of it, and I just don't feel up to the job. How do I manage two separate sets of parents and siblings? How do I introduce them to each other? How do I refer to them and what do they call each other? My half-sister's-found-family's half-brother? There's no language for this, no guidelines, no rulebook. I'm trying to juggle it all, with my own feelings in turmoil—excited, elated, ecstatic, guilty, confused, overwhelmed—trying not to hurt anyone or make anyone feel left out. Sometimes it all gets too much."

"Too much?"

"Yeah, it's like living in a constant state of tension, on the edge, Ray. I don't know how else to describe it. That's how it's been all my life. There is still no one else in my position. Not wanting to say anything, in case it causes offence. And then I explode, and it spills out all over the place in anger, and hurts everyone—including me. Trying to resolve my own issues has caused chaos."

"What kind of chaos?"

"Well, for example, since I found my Dad, it's prompted the adopted children on both sides of my extended families—Ghanaian and British—to go in search of their birth parents, with mixed results. It doesn't always turn out like my story. It's not so easy to re-invent yourself like this, learning to be a Black woman in a White family and a White woman in a Black family—when really I'm not either of those. I even have a different name in each family. I keep thinking, where *is* this place I have arrived? Do I recognise myself? Does it have a name?"

"When you walked out of this door, three years ago, I had the feeling you were back in the here-and-now, moving on—your first baby on the way, a new dream job, a new family," says Ray thoughtfully. "But it seems, from what you have told me, the things that happened in your work and in your life, you were born with this issue and it just keeps coming back. You refused to bury your father here in this room with me and say goodbye—"

"—Yes, and what kind of crazy idea was that, Ray? Of course I refused to bury him when I didn't know whether he was alive or dead! Even if your parents are dead and buried, they don't cease to exist for you, you don't cease to love them, do you? You don't stop having a relationship with them."

"I can see how strongly you feel it was the wrong thing for you, but you did seem a bit stuck. I wanted to suggest something that might bring you some closure…"

"But you were asking me to bury a part of me. People like me need help to find our own path—not close it down, but open it up."

"People like you?"

"Yes. Us. Half-caste, cira-scura, sasso-buro, mulatto, touch-of-the-tarbrush, hint-of-a-tint, coconuts, mutts, half-breeds, people of colour, dual heritage, high yellas, Mixed-Race… whatever you call us, whatever we call ourselves. I am probably one of very few Mixed-Race people my age who were brought up in Britain in the 1950s, so it was really important for me to find my Dad. Not all of us want to trace or embrace our heritage—not every Mixed-Race person even wants to define themselves as such. But there are many more of us out there now, trying to find our own way. Therapists like you need to recognise that. We need to be empowered to find ourselves in ourselves. That's what I came back here to tell you."

*****

Building the connections between my two worlds. Every year we take friends and family with us from the UK to visit Ghana. Auntie Bel, Leyla and family, my friend

Valerie, Cousin Vic and his family, my sister Molly and her husband and kids. They are keen to discover the delights, the history and the people of Ghana. The sights and sounds—Kakum Park and the canopy walkway above the rainforest, the slave forts and the Gate of No Return, the *Afeyshe* festival with all the Chiefs parading in their Palanquins through the streets, the vibrant cloth sewn into any design you desire by expert tailors, freshly caught lobster and yam chips served up on the beach with an ice-cold beer...

For my city-dwelling Ghanaian family, life is not easy. They are struggling with the daily challenges of professionals in a developing country—cuts in water and electricity supplies, poor roads and transport, lack of supplies and equipment, frequent attacks of malaria and other health challenges, and the poverty of their service-users; and often having to do several other jobs, like keeping chickens or shop-keeping, because the pay is so bad.

The visit to the village is the most special, the welcome, the warmth, the energy—even though every visit is never easy and always takes complicated organising, planning and protocol. The villagers are mostly subsistence farmers and fishermen, with a sprinkling of teachers, technicians and other professionals. The women smoke fish and grind palm nuts for oil to sell in the market. The huts dotted among the mango and banana trees are built with local bricks topped with tin or grass roofs. A patch of ground serves as a football pitch and a parade ground for festivals.

On every visit I get a sense of renewal and inspiration which is hard to describe. It's a powerful kind of spiritual nourishment, a real sense of 'coming home', that keeps me hungering for this connection, returning year after year.

*****

It's a golden September afternoon, season of 'mellow fruitfulness', warm light flooding our garden full of autumn flowers, a full crop of crisp red-blushed apples on the tree, ripe for picking. A rural idyll in Tooting. We moved in here when Jake was three. I'm in the deckchair on the lawn, propped up with cushions, breathing hard. Mum times my contractions.

"You better go to the hospital right now, the second one just pops out!" my neighbour Louise advises, looking over the fence. She already has two boys of her own, so she is speaking from experience. But I know for a fact that my babies aren't going to 'pop out'. They like to take their time. Jake took twenty-four hours to come, and even then, he had to be delivered by forceps. I have already been to the hospital every day this week with Braxton Hicks, each time a false alarm. I am not going to waste this lovely weather sitting in the maternity ward at St George's hospital, being told yet again that I'm in fake labour.

My mother shakes her head in disbelief. "Can't understand it. All three of my babies came in an hour or two, almost no pain."

"Thanks for that, Mum—good to know," I gasp.

By six o'clock the sun is going down, Lawrence is back from work, things are speeding up. All the neighbours are on the doorstep to wave us off. Jake is standing beside his grandma, desperate for the new baby to arrive. What a weird and wonderful thing it must seem to a child, when Mum goes off to hospital and comes back with a baby, who will be here to stay, regardless of whether you take to it or not. You can't send it back. The story of the goose-berry bush or the stork must seem more plausible than the reality. Within five minutes we are back. Forgot the sand-wiches and the nursing pillow.

As I predicted, my babies like to take their time. Eleven hours later, I'm disappointed and exhausted, ready to throw in the towel.

"You have a kink in the birt canal!" explains the Jamaican midwife. "Clearly you don't take after your mother with her instant painless birts."

It must be from my paternal side. I remember my Ghana Dad saying his younger sister died in childbirth. Important to know the health history from the other side of my family, the missing pieces. If it wasn't for modern medicine, I would surely be a goner by now. I have to accept that I have run out of time on this one. I am all prepped up ready for Caesarean section, numbed up to the eyeballs, cracking jokes with the friendly Consultant, about to be wheeled down to theatre.

The midwife checks once more. "You're ready!" she

proclaims triumphantly. "And jost in the nick of time! It says on your birt plan 'ere that you wan' a natural birt. Let's push!"

Push? I think not. To hell with the birth plan—too late for all that! Give me more drugs. I cannot bear another ounce of pain. Take me down to theatre, I beg you!

But Midwife is determined. She shoos the doctors out of the room and closes the door, with Lawrence looking on uncertainly, and then she sits by my bed, holding my hand, to deliver me a pep talk.

"I know all about you feminists from the NCT," she says. "You'll thank mi in the end, trost me. I'm here, you won't feel a thing. I'll be with you all de way. It'll be wort it, jost wait till the anaestetic wears off enough so you can feel to push."

"*Promise* me I won't feel any more pain…"

"Promise."

An hour later, I am holding our daughter in my arms. Her eyes, like dark liquid pools, hold me with intense concentration, knowing, understanding, recognising me in some deep place. The two of us close-bound together, mesmerised, the world shrunk to the space between each other's gaze. The magic of our daughter's first hour on earth. I am thanking the midwife with all my soul.

"I told you you'd thank me!" she beams. "She's gorgeous. By the way, those big dark patches on 'er spine that look like bruises—that's Mongolian blue spot. We have to point those out to all parents of Mixed-Race babies these days and note it down in the file. In the past they've been mistaken for real bruises and the parents have had to endure totally unfounded claims of child abuse. Disastrous! And you have a rare blood group, A-negative, more common in West Africa. That's why you needed a hinjection. Otherwise your babies would be even more blue! Very dangerous."

This Midwife is on the ball.

Jake is overawed. A little sister!

And Mum is thrilled with her first grand-daughter. She peeps into the cot and says, "We have our girl! Let's take her home!"

Later she mentions casually that there was a telephone call from Ghana for me.

"From Sam Kofie, asking for news about the baby."

"What did you say?"

"I told him you were still in labour, it was taking its time."

"Oh, Mum, he must have known it was you... Did you tell him it was you?"

"No. He didn't ask either. He sent you his love and I just told him I would pass on the message and someone will call when there's any news."

I have never seen my birth parents in the same room, never seen a photo of them together, never seen them interacting. My Ghanaian family say I am just like my father. My British family say I am just like my mother. A fusion of both. My two parents have just become grand-parents to the same beautiful grand-daughter, separated by a profound connection and thousands of miles, unable to say, unable to share that delight.

*****

Despite being a bit of a patriarch, Ghana Dad is proud of my adventures in Beijing attending the United Nations Fourth World Conference on Women. "So you were part of the official UK Government delegation there, Esuantsiwa?"

"Yes, but I was representing INGOs, not part of the Tory Government, Dad."

"I was in China myself in the 1960s, on a trade mission." He shows me the photograph with himself and Chairman Mao, and calls me his *Beijing Girl*.

He invites me to have tea with his friend Mary, the Ghanaian Minister for Overseas Development, who led the Ghana Government's delegation to Beijing.

"The *Platform for Action* that came out of the conference was printed in full in all the Ghanaian newspapers," the Minister says proudly. "It will form the basis of our development strategy for women."

I wish the British government would do the same. We pored over every word of that *Platform for Action*, disappointed at what was left out. We didn't know we were making history.

There was barely any mention of the World Conference in the British press. What little coverage there was focused mainly on China's poor human rights record and the mud in Huairou, where the biggest NGO Forum in the world was being held. It was my job as representative of the NGOs to escort the Minister, Lynda Chalker, around the site with her party of civil servants. I spent most of my time going to and fro, reporting back from each of the two conferences—government and NGO—which were nearly ten miles apart. I spent so much time on the road, I nearly missed Hillary Clinton's speech. By the time I arrived, the room was packed. I only just got in. The atmosphere was electric. I was just in time to hear her utter the immortal words, "Women's Rights are Human Rights."

There were intense security precautions everywhere we went. One of the taxi drivers told me they had all been advised to carry a sheet in the boot of their vehicles, because Western women like to stage protests by taking all their clothes off. In that eventuality they were to throw a sheet over us immediately. The Chinese people were so friendly and welcoming, despite warnings of our impending nudity, and they were desperate for news of the outside world. The lesbian and gay rights tent was a big draw, packed out with young Chinese women. "We never heard of such a thing before! So exciting!" one of the Chinese delegates told me. Many of my sisters were invited home to meet Chinese families, although sadly I never seemed to be in one place long enough to accept an invitation.

The Beijing Conference had a life-changing effect on many of us who went. Some got married, others divorced, changed jobs, moved house, kept in touch with Chinese friends. As for me, I missed my baby girl, and my boy, and I couldn't wait to get home to them.

I decided to take the momentous step of giving up my job to go freelance and set up business on my own. Even feminist organisations can end up behaving like patriarchal ones. I am too much of a revolutionary. I want to change everything. An Outside Child.

My new consultancy as a facilitator and strategic planner will be called *Anona Development Consultancy*, after our Ghanaian clan, the Anona. The parrot will make an intriguing, eye-catching logo. I know it will go down well in Ghana—a vibrant, clever, colourful, showy bird that speaks many languages. On the other hand, in Western culture, the parrot is known for repeating empty phrases without knowing the meaning of what it is saying.

Perfect. Double vision.

Chapter 20

Through the Mill

My consultancy was supposed to be a short-term arrangement, while I looked at other options; but it seems to have turned into a permanent career. I have trouble explaining exactly what I do.

"Facilitator? What the hell is that—some kind of engineer?" Auntie Molly asks. I suppose it is. Knowing what can go wrong. Using some of the tools I've learnt along the way. Helping people to make connections with each other.

I hit the big time within a few weeks of starting. I am Chair and facilitator of the Oxfam Assembly, a three-day residential conference, with nearly four hundred delegates attending—tea planters, coffee growers, craft makers from developing countries, Oxfam workers, aid agency representatives, civil servants, activists, campaigners, volunteers from Oxfam shops, people from all over the world, exploring the big issues. What is poverty? Why does it happen? And how can we get rid of it?

"Our Gender Team insist we have to have a Black

woman chairing this new initiative—and they think it should be you," said the interviewer from Oxfam.

The participants were excited, eager, full of anticipation. Simon had done this sort of thing before; we would be co-facilitating.

"Facilitation works best the moment people forget you are in the room," he advised. "When the energies go low, you go low; high, you go high. Dress like the group, blend in, follow their lead… "

Oh dear.

"I'm not sure I can deliver on that, Simon. I think I'm more at the showbiz end of facilitation—stories, gags, fun and games, music and dancing, infotainment, razzamatazz, marker pens and sugar paper. I used to be a teacher. I'm terrified of losing my audience. I go in for total participatory engagement—mind, body, spirit and stand-up comedy. And you should see my outfits—tailor-made in Ghana… not subtle."

Simon looked taken aback. "Did you tell them about this at the interview?"

"Yep. And I wore one of my outfits. So I think they know what they are getting. Let's put on a show."

"Well we'll give it a try then, it's certainly original. We can always tone it down if it's not working."

And it *did* work.

"Look, it's obvious the participants want to see *you* onstage, not me. I'll back you up," Simon said.

He was my champion, checking the timing and the

programme, troubleshooting, supplying me with gags and one-liners and gin-and-tonics at the end of the day. Good for Simon. I haven't met many White men in my time who will give up their space to let a Black woman shine.

On day two, the African women delegates came up to the platform at the end of the session.

"We are so proud of you—up on the platform there, running the show, wearing our cloth, doing such a good job. You are showing what African women can do. We can be the best, better than anybody."

This is the best thing anyone has ever said to me, apart from "You are my daughter. Welcome home." I can talk to the African delegates about Africa, about my Dad, Ghana, my village, my heritage—all those things that used to be a mystery to me. Now I have my own story.

On day three, I introduce our star guest, Sam Theka from India. Dressed in starched white trousers, tunic and sandals, with nut-brown skin, sparkling eyes and full black beard, he is handsome, charismatic and compelling, commanding the stage, speaking from the heart.

"I was invited by Oxfam to leave my village project in India and take a trip to the UK to investigate powerty here," he begins. The way he pronounces the word, it sounds like 'Power T' to my ears, giving it a whole new meaning. "This was a most unusual assignment," he continued. "My brief was to visit some of the poorest and most troubled areas in the UK—Brixton in London, Toxteth in Liverpool and Chapeltown in Leeds—and report back to Oxfam and to my communities in India.

"They tell me these places have been in the grip of turmoil—riots, poverty, racism, crime, stop-and-search—in short, fractured communities. But, to be honest, at first I couldn't see anything that looked like powerty to me, compared with India. Even the poorest people here have social security and cars and TVs…

"But then I came across one story that had a big impact on me. I heard of a man in Leeds who was what you call a 'hoarder'. He died alone in his flat, and his body was not discovered for three months. When I reported this back to my village, they were so moved by his story, they had a collection for this unknown man's funeral… and don't forget, they are living in extreme powerty themselves. 'But this is *true* powerty,' they told me. 'A man dying alone, a soul abandoned, undiscovered for months…

"So, what is powerty?" Sam challenges us. "It must be more than lack of jobs, money, housing, health services. Powerty is also loneliness, isolation, alienation, not belonging. It is when a community loses its soul, its connection, its humanity—and its compassion."

What a speech! Challenge the ubiquitous Western view of the world; see the world through others' eyes. Power should be in the hands of people like Sam and his community. My cousins in Accra are exasperated by the negative portrayal of developing countries like Ghana in the UK. Western development organisations have to understand that they are part of the problem if they want to be part of the solution.

The participants rose as one—a standing ovation, stomping, clapping, shouting. I felt a sudden surge of crazy Utopian optimism, everything turned on its head, a vision of the future brought on by the energy in the room. Aid agencies joined in the movement for international solidarity, patriarchy smashed, capitalism faded away, money a thing of the past, equality reigning, every human being *belonging*...

"Hey Jane, wake up, you're on!" Simon nudges me, pushing the order paper across the table. "Summing up, vote of thanks, coffee break..."

I have proved I can do this job, do it well and do it differently. I'm best when I get my creative juices going, bring people together and then shake them up.

*****

When I get home, reality kicks in again. Jake comes back from school in tears.

"I *hate* being Brown!" he wails.

"Why, what happened love? Tell me."

"Because... because none of the super-heroes are Brown. Batman, Superman, Spider-man. They're all White. It's not *fair*."

It's a devastating revelation for an eight-year-old. The world doesn't include him. I came to live in Tooting to give my kids the multicultural environment I never had. After all these years, these stereotypes carry on, even in a diverse community. The revolution hasn't even started.

*****

The year after the Labour Government landslide in 1997, the Department for International Development wants to send me to South Africa to be facilitator and co-ordinator for a nationwide programme, Against Violence Against Women, working with the women's movement, the media, the police, politicians, health workers, rape crisis centres and retired nurses to come up with a national plan. It's my kind of job. But I have my doubts. Could this be typical colonialism, sending someone over there from over here?

"Why don't you hire a South African facilitator? There are so many amazing women facilitators out there… "

"Good question. You might think so," said the man from the Department for Overseas Development. "But it's also about the legacy of apartheid. It's about who they trust, after such a history. You have just the right profile. You've got all the skills, plus you are not Black, not White, and not South African. You'll be able to work with everyone. It's a challenging place to work, but one of the best. There's big aid money invested in this. We've got to get it right."

No pressure then. Steve, a young White male assistant, is assigned to accompany me.

"He's in training," the man at the Department for International Development explains. "He'll be supporting you, doing all the documentation and log frames. You'll be leading and designing the whole process, doing your participatory magic. We want him to see how you work."

What a relief. I hate log frames. Can't see the point of them. Steve is a nice enough guy, fresh-faced, around half my age, keen to learn, always sporting a smart grey suit and tie, no matter what the temperature outside. I struggle to establish my leadership and authority at first, in a country in which race is still the key signifier. Wherever we go—Pretoria, Jo'burg, Cape Town, Soweto—everyone approaches him first, welcomes him formally and shakes his hand. They assume he is the guy from DFID, the one who's in charge. Black or White, they often ignore me at first; they think I am his secretary.

"It just prolongs the confusion if you don't say anything, Steve. Can't you tell them at the start you are the administrator, or my assistant or something?"

"I'm a civil servant. It's not my fault if people think I'm in charge."

"But you don't realise that if you're White and male everyone takes you seriously as soon as you walk into a room, regardless. I can spot it a mile off. I'm short, brown and female, and middle-aged. I really have to work at it. No-one ever takes it for granted that I'm in charge. I have to prove it, every time, try twice as hard to be thought only half as good. It gets me off to the wrong start, it's just wearing and energy-sapping… I could use a little help here, Steve…"

He is mystified. No-one has ever questioned who he is or his right to be.

But once I have got the message across, people are delighted—especially the women.

"At last DFID has sent us someone who looks like us!" they beam.

The DFID man in London was right, South Africa is the most extraordinary place to be. I cried when we flew over Robben Island for the first time. I never quite believed I would see the end of Apartheid in my lifetime. The creativity and guts of the women I meet there—battling poverty, oppression and violence every day of their lives— bear testimony to the spirit and power of African women. They should not have to work so hard for it.

*****

My Ghanaian Dad is doing consultancy work too. He has come to the UK to work on a geological survey project with a Canadian company. Having visited Ghana so many times, it's wonderful to see each other in the UK, to welcome him to our home in Tooting for the first time.

He's doing well for a 75-year old, still travelling, still working. But it must be a shock to his system to move from soaring December temperatures in Accra to freezing weather in London. In the gathering dusk and bitter cold, we huddle in a little group in our garden under the bare branches of the apple tree, while Dad cracks open a bottle of Old Geneva Schnapps to pour the customary libation, calling on my Great-Great-Grandmother, Esuantsiwa, Queen Mother and founder of our tribe, to look after me and my family.

I love the rituals of my new-found heritage, marking homecomings, new arrivals, momentous events, rites of passage, connecting the past, present and future, and calling on our ancestors to be with us on the journey. I explain to Dad that we had a naming ceremony for Jake and Araba here in London when they reached their first birthdays, in a Hindu temple, pouring an African libation. "Lawrence has been a Hindu devotee since he was at University," I explain to Dad. "The Hindu Priest said the libation could be a problem. You're not supposed to have alcohol in a temple."

I didn't mention that my friend Efua, now a Ghanaian Queen Mother, also confided that only male Chiefs are normally allowed to pour libation. "But I will do it myself, as a Queen Mother, to welcome Araba into the world, and strike a blow for Equality at the same time," she assured me. Rituals are most powerful when they are a fusion of your whole identity.

Though he is a traditionalist, my new Dad seems pleased to hear about my adaptations, on the whole. Libation-pouring over, time to go inside.

"I'm worried about you getting too cold out here in the

garden, Dad. Your chest sounds very tight and wheezy—come indoors and sit by the fire."

"Oh, don't worry about me, Esuantsiwa, I've had this problem for a while. The doctor says I have cardiac asthma. I will be all right if I keep taking the tablets, and he has given me a spray."

Later, Araba falls asleep in her Grandad's arms in the big armchair by the fire.

*****

The day before he left for Ghana, Dad and I went Christmas shopping in Victoria Street, just the two of us, wandering among the Christmas lights, hand in hand in the freezing cold, choosing presents. The first time I had ever been Christmas shopping with this Dad. Afterwards we enjoyed afternoon tea in the lounge at the Reubens Hotel on Buckingham Palace Road, where the Canadian mining company had booked him a room. The lounge was decked out with festive Christmas trees and baubles, carols playing softly in the background.

"This is where I was interviewed for the *Marie Claire* magazine article, Dad, in this lounge…"

"Esuantsiwa, I could not be prouder of you as a daughta," Dad stirred his tea and added three sugars. "You are doin' sooo well, and you can't imagine how much joy the grandchildren are bringing to me and Faith. I want to buy your mother a present to thank her for doing such a wonderful job of bringing you up."

As we kissed goodbye, he said again, "Esuantsiwa, you have still not told me what gift your mother would like…"

He was trying to reach out, but in his heart, I think he knew it wasn't possible. I ached for both my divided parents. Acceptance and forgiveness have brought me untold riches, but it's been hard. My Mum has embraced my heritage in so many other ways. But sometimes the past can't be undone.

I remember, as I turned around for a final wave at the corner of the street, looking back and seeing Dad's figure still framed by Christmas lights at the revolving doors of the hotel entrance. I felt such a surge of affection and love for him, I wanted to run across the road and hug him one more time, but I stopped myself. I didn't know that was the last goodbye.

*****

The hotel manager assumes we are tourists, and he's anxious to fill us in on the local news.

"You're lucky to get a room," he tells us. "There's a big Chief being buried in town this week, the whole place has been brought to a standstill. Everywhere in Cape Coast and Elmina is fully booked. A thousand people are expected—even the Vice President is coming…"

"Yes, a big man, I know. I'm his daughter…"

The hotel manager is impressed. "My deepest

condolences. It will be televised," he adds. "The TV crews are staying in this hotel. You can come back and watch yourselves on the six o'clock news every evening…"

Dad lies in state in an open coffin, his face caked in heavy make-up and rouge. It doesn't look like him at all.

"He's been in the fridge for three months while we got everything ready," whispers my brother Sam.

The whole funeral is an extraordinary spectacle. I want to drink it all in, absorb every moment: the fusion of ancient and modern, African and Western, animism and Christianity, weeping and dancing, drumming and wailing, light and shade.

Every day we wear an outfit in a different colour. On day one it's the wake-keeping. We sit up all night, wearing dark brown robes in sticky heavy heat. I make a speech about how I came to Ghana to meet my Dad. I only knew him for eight years, our precious time together when we got to know and love each other now cut unbearably short.

On day two, we are all in black, signifying deep mourning, letting go, saying goodbye. May is the hottest time of year. It's been 40 degrees the whole week, and most of the ceremony has been held outdoors under giant awnings. Black robes make it feel even hotter. We are absorbing the heat, sweltering under the canopies all day, mopping brows with crumpled white cotton handkerchiefs.

On day three, the burial, we are dressed in red and black, like the earth. Dad has a tomb dug six metres deep, lined with tiles, his body laid in a grand mahogany sarcophagus with polished brass trim. When the Chief dies, no-one mentions it at first, and people stay indoors. Legend has it that in the old days they would capture people to be buried with the Chief to serve him in the afterlife. Much of this reminds me of the traditions of Ancient Egypt, even the fact that the Queen is often the Chief's mother, or sister, not his wife. Around ten thousand years ago, I've read, there was a trade route from Ancient Ghana, across the Sahara, to Egypt. And along with the trade route came the exchange and influence of customs and traditions.

It is powerful to be amongst all this living ancient history, to see each day marked with a thousand people all dressed in the same colour, to signify the process of death, burial, saying goodbye, and then celebration of his life.

I am only just beginning to recognise who my father really was. Twenty-two Chiefs of the Fanti turned up to mourn the passing of their Divisional Leader and Acting Paramount Chief, processing in their palanquins, wearing magnificent red-and-gold *kente* robes. The Vice President and fellow Councillors of State filed past the coffin to pay their respects to their colleague. The Alumni from Holy Child School, Mom Faith's old schoolmates, were all dressed in elegant, vibrant canary-yellow uniforms to dance with her out on the parade ground—the only time I saw her smile.

On day four we are all assembled in the Catholic cathedral on top of the hill with a magnificent view of

Cape Coast, where the Archbishop conducts the final celebratory mass. It's cool and shady in here, in contrast to the searing heat outside. Today we are dressed in black-and-white or blue-and-white cloth, bright colours symbolising celebration for a life well-lived, for the passing of a great man. The pattern on our cloth has a special meaning: *We have lost someone dear to us.* My brother Sam squeezes my hand, and whispers, "The thing with Ghanaian funerals is that by day four, everyone is so exhausted, they just want to get the guy buried and over with…"

It's true, I am emotionally and physically wrung out, emptied of tears.

I remember Ray's advice to bury my father.

Here I am.

Lost and found, and lost again.

I knew this Dad for only eight precious years. But our meeting will last a lifetime.

*****

The next day I fly to South Africa to resume my work on the DFID project.

My first meeting is at the edge of the Kalahari Desert, working with activists and ex-nurses against violence against women. Some of the participants have journeyed for two days on foot to get here.

"Before we begin, we will hev a minute's silence to pay our rispects to Esuantsiwa's father," says the leader. "We are lucky she has still managed to make it to be here with us, straight after the sorrow of the funerral."

These women are in the middle of nowhere with next to nothing, supporting women suffering unimaginable horrors—violence, rape and murder. And they show instant empathy and care towards me, a complete stranger, over the loss of my father.

After the meeting, as the sun goes down over the Kalahari, we dance and sing around the open fire in the courtyard as sparks fly upwards to the sky.

On the plane home I'm in floods of tears again, showing pictures of Araba, my little girl, to all the air-stewards. I've lost my Dad again, and I miss my kids. I have lost my bearings once more. It's agony being away from home this long.

*****

Now that Dad has gone, the villagers have asked me to go on helping the village as my father did. I am thrilled. This is an opportunity to forge a relationship in my own right, and not only as my father's daughter, to feel I have a real role.

At our first meeting with the village development committee, my cousin Vic and his family are with us, and Vic is taking the minutes.

The idea of a corn mill is gaining traction. It sounds like a good idea, but there is fierce and energetic debate.

"This isn't a corn-growing area. We would have to import the corn, and the supply and the price are always going up and down."

"But a corn mill will give the village an income. We could make money to spend on other development projects."

"But who would own the mill? Who would decide what to charge, and what would the revenues be spent on? And who would maintain it, and pay for fuel to run it? And spare parts are hard to come by... these things are always breakin' down..."

"—and where would we kip it? We would need to build a shed to kip it safe from thieves and protect it from the rain."

I am worried that the budget won't stretch to a building as well. This is all sounding very complicated.

Finally, the women speak up.

"We've been through the corn mill arguments—we women don't want it. We grind palm oil berries by hand. It is soch hard work, and that is our local crop. We should have a palm oil kernel mill."

"No, let's have bathrooms—communal bathrooms. That will be good for everyone. We will all be able to make use of them. We women need somewhere clean and private to wash. It's not dignified, washing behind palm screens."

They take me outside to show me their makeshift, dilapidated washing huts.

I can see there are complex power dynamics playing

out in this small village community with its scarce resources—between different families, the women and the men, subsistence farmers who can't read and write, and the sprinkling of educated professionals who have stayed in the village. It's exciting but at the same time daunting. It's certainly not simple or straightforward. I am used to working on development projects with the backing and experience of big aid agencies and local NGOs. This will be trial and error working within my community. It's a big learning curve.

And I'm worried. Will it change my relationship with the village in ways I don't anticipate and don't want—from mutual family affection and support to the usual colonial-type relationship of foreign donor and beneficiary? And where will I get the funds from anyway?

I needn't have worried on that score. A note in my usual Christmas card, together with some photos of our last visit to the village, brings a tremendous and generous response from my friends and family, although one or two of my aunties are highly sceptical: "Charity begins at 'ome," they say. But the village *is* my other home. It means a lot to me to deepen my relationship and my sense of connection with Akwonsa, now that my Dad is no longer here. My city-dwelling family in Accra are enthusiastic about the idea and offer practical advice about prices and sourcing of materials... and how to make things happen in Ghana, because I have no idea.

My Mum in London has become the village's most

enthusiastic champion. Auntie Bel, Cousin Vic, Sister Molly and my friend Val, see it as one side of the family helping another. My friends Marilyn, Rosie, Maggie, Sheila and Mark and lots of others are keen to give to something directly, through personal connection, and see how it develops.

Most of the money has already been raised, over two years ago, but it is taking forever for the village to agree on priorities. What am I supposed to tell the people who gave so generously? I am losing hope that we can resolve the issue. I have bitten off more than I can chew, as usual, and I am supposedly a professional facilitator with a background in development.

Walking back up the rocky village path between the huts with my family group after the meeting, Fremah approaches me. She has just been elected as Assembly Member on the District Assembly at Saltpond. I congratulate her warmly—how wonderful to see a woman from our village being a successful political leader!

"It's not easy, Nana Esuantsiwa," she tells me. "I am one of only five women, out of seventy-five Assembly Members. The men make it so difficult for women to get elected, and they give us such a hard time. They think we can't do the job. The priority this year is to improve the sanitation facilities in our villages, and I want to prove that we women can deliver. The women in this village really want bathrooms, you heard them say so yourself. It is not so important for the men to have privacy, hygiene and safety as it is for women, so they don't understand. If you help us build the bathrooms, I will get them built in six weeks. I won't let you down. And I can do it within the budget."

Back at the Mango Tree Guest House, where I am staying with Saffia, I feel elated. If bathrooms meet the needs of the women and this project supports women's leadership, and shows the men what women can do, then it will be a triumph all round. And everyone will use the bathrooms—men, women and children. It will upgrade the facilities for the whole village.

Fremah is as good as her word. A few months later, I am back to open the bathrooms officially, cutting the pink satin ribbon fastened around each of the doors.

Fremah has even solved the problem of who will keep the bathrooms clean and maintained.

"I have positioned the bath houses around the village so there is one for each family group to share. Each has a key and a padlock, so the women can have privacy and don't have too far to walk to have their wash, and they will make sure their own bathroom is kept clean." And she has won over the Chief, even though he voted for the corn-mill, by reserving one of the bathrooms for his own use and presenting him with a key. We have brought a suitcase full of sponges, soap and towels donated from my Mum all the way in London. It's quite a celebration. I am full of admiration for Fremah's diplomatic and problem-solving skills. She has broken the deadlock and everyone seems happy for now. Time for a wash and brush-up.

"We need to replace the bulbs in our street lights," says one of the elders, as we leave. "Your Dad put the first ones up twenty years ago and they have all gone out one by one. It is very dangeros to walk around here at night. The paths are slippery and stony."

A lightbulb moment, another project led by the village that will benefit everyone. They are coming up with good ideas now, ideas that we can all manage. It's taken a while, but we are getting the hang of how to make this partnership work.

*****

I have found my place in the village and my home in London. But the space in between? Soon after Barack Obama's election as President of the United States in 2008, I felt elated and brave enough to talk about my Mixed-Race experience for the first time in a public meeting. It was at a celebratory event in London called *Can there ever be a British Obama?* hosted by the Law Activists Association and sponsored by a big corporation in the Barbican. There was a sizeable turnout, more than two hundred people, and a panel of Black and Asian Speakers.

During the question-and-answer time, after the speakers, I raised my hand to say how delighted I was that Obama, by becoming President, had empowered Mixed-Race people and opened up a space for us to find our voice. In the 1970s and '80s, the race dialogue was literally "Black and White." People wanted to know whose side you were on. In the past I'd been reluctant to say I was Mixed-Race or dual heritage. There was no room for nuance in the race discourse. I felt that part of me had been silenced, albeit for a just cause. Because of Obama, I could be out and proud now, feeling sure that I had something real and authentic to contribute, confident that being Mixed-Race was an important part of my Black identity.

Caroline Reynolds, one of the speakers, remained unconvinced. She countered that Mixed-Race could be a distraction. She pointed out that while Obama was running for office they called him a 'Black man' to undermine him. When he won, they called him Mixed-Race because White society could not bear to think that a Black man had won the presidency. "Mixed-Race people don't know how it feels to have really Black skin—to be told how ugly and dark you are as a child," she said.

Caroline is one of my heroines, one of the stars of the Black British movement. I feel her frustration. Colourism and shadism can divide us, when we need solidarity between us. But perception of skin colour is relative. As a 'half-caste' in the 1950s, I had a similar childhood experience of being thought ugly and dark in a White community. There was no-one else around to compare with me. I was considered as Black as they come. People tend to see difference rather than commonality. They see 'otherness'. I am desperate for the space to talk about this, to talk about what it's like to be Mixed-Race, without seeming to betray the cause of anti-racism.

Seb Williams, another of the speakers, whom I'd known for many years, came to my rescue from the platform. "We should listen to the sister here!" he said, gesturing toward me, "She's got a point. We should respect the contribution of Mixed-Race people. It's high time our dialogue was more inclusive…"

Sally, a tall White woman, one of the organisers of the meeting, could not understand my disappointment that the space for exploration of Mixed-Race identity had been closed down. My intervention evidently caused tensions all round.

"Tensions? Well you created them yourself just now, didn't you?" she countered crossly, on our way out of the meeting-room. I didn't mean to. I'd gone and mixed it all up again for the Black and White people, when they wanted to celebrate. I'd let them all down. I felt guilty, stupid, ashamed, a traitor. Stranded in the space between.

This was personal as well as political. I had been an activist in this equality and diversity movement all my life. The only other Mixed-Race person I'd come across, who embraced his mixed-ness and had crossed the miles to find his father in Africa like me, had now become President of the United States. If I couldn't find the space to talk about my mixed-ness now, then when? Where was the space for what I had experienced? To have a voice and know that it is valid, strong, collective, part of the movement for

Equality. What must that be like?

At the reception, things started looking up. Seb confided that, having been adopted by an all-White family, he found it very difficult to speak out about his mixed background in the Black movement here. A couple of White women from the audience joined us to say they were grateful for what I'd said. They both had Mixed-Race children and found it hard to create a space for their kids to explore their dual identities, and to hear from older role models about what the Mixed-Race experience might mean for them.

Another woman came up to join us, a woman around my age, with my skin-tone, and an Irish accent. "Rosanne," she said, raising her glass. "Agree with everything you said. Owning your own lexicon is power. You don't hear all these Whoite people endlessly arguin' about whether they should be called Whoite or not. They don't need to. They're in charge. I'm loike you—I was born in an unmarried mothers' home in Dublin, brought up in the fifties in a children's home, absolutely oisolated, no-one around who was moi colour, no-one to talk to when I got called racist names, no sense of who I was. I went through the mill. Come and join our *Mixed-ness* group, we are all people with Mixed-Race heritage who aren't afraid to say so. Let's talk some more…"

I'm not alone. There are more of us.

Chapter 21
Tales from the Palanquin

Saffia greets me in a flowing orange-and-turquoise robe, her long salt-and-pepper dreadlocks tied up in matching headpiece. She built the Mango Tree Guest-House with her husband Brandon more than a decade ago, part of a growing diaspora of Caribbeans from the UK, along with African Americans, who have come to Ghana to make a new life here. When I visit the family in Cape Coast, I always come and stay at the Mango Tree. It's a little Rastafarian oasis in the middle of Elmina, a taxi ride from our village.

I like the Bob Marley Room best, with the balcony looking out over the eponymous mango tree in the courtyard. I remember what Bob Marley said about having a "heart-home." This must be mine; a fabulous fusion of cultures—Ghanaian, Jamaican, British.

Saffia has been helping me with the school in the village. We share our usual cold beer on the veranda as she updates me on progress at the school. The news is good. More than twenty children have already been enrolled, and plans for refurbishment of the roof, windows and doors are well advanced. They are going to need more bags of cement and tins of paint.

Saffia pauses, taking a sip of Club beer. She has some startling news for me.

"They want to make you Queen of Development in the village—for the work you are doing for the villagers, raising funds for the street lights, the washrooms and the school. They told me not to tell you, it's supposed to be a secret! But I thought I ought to warn you before we go to the village tomorrow, so it's not too much of a shock. You'll have time to think about it…"

I'm stunned. This is not at all what I expected. "But it's not just me, Saffia. I couldn't have done it without all the money and support from my family and friends in the UK, and without your help too. What do you think?"

"Well, it's a huge thing, but it won't happen until next year. They will need months to prepare, so you'll have time to get used to the idea. It's so exciting, you should go for it. How could you refuse? This is your family, they want to honour you. You deserve it, but it will be challenging, for sure."

I don't quite know what to make of the idea of being Queen of Development—*Nkonswa Ohemaa*, the Fanti title. Then I remember that when I first met my Dad he sat me down very formally on the veranda in the house in Accra to recite the story of Esuantsiwa and how she established the royal line.

"It's an oral tradition," he told me. "But it's based on historical events. The colonials wrote it down, I believe. They say there is an account of it among the records in the British Museum…"

*****

Long ago, more than a hundred and fifty years past, Esuantsiwa and her cousins were carrying bowls of oto—pounded yam, eggs and hot pepper—across the village to her sister-in-law's hut for the naming ceremony of the new baby. Esuantsiwa was an 'outside child'; part of the clan, yet different. Her name means "Woman of Ashanti"—she was an Ashanti Princess, lately married into the Fanti tribe, the fisher-people and traders on the coast.

There had been no rain for weeks, and the air was dry and heavy with dust. Although it was still early morning, the sun beat down mercilessly, the hot, red earth burning the soles of Esuantsiwa's bare feet. As she approached the compound, she could see a long-limbed young man racing like the wind towards the centre of the village, head thrust forward, weaving between the low thatched buildings.

Ashanti! Ashanti! The dust-covered messenger arrived, panic-stricken, breathing hard, and collapsed by the gate to her sister-in-law's compound, just ahead of her on the path. In her alarm, she dropped the wooden bowl she was carrying, scattering clumps of yellow pounded yam in the red dust. The messenger had uttered the word they all dreaded most. Through ruthless warfare, the Ashanti Empire had conquered great swathes of the west and central lands south of the Sahara, sacking villages and stealing young people away to serve in the palace of the Asantehene—Chief of Chiefs—in the Ashanti capital of Kumasi.

As soon as they heard the sound of the alarm ringing out on the metal gongon, men, women and children emerged from the huts and stony paths and hurried to the centre of the village. Rapidly, almost silently, the whole village was assembled. Bending low as he emerged from the doorway of his hut, Nana, the Chief, adjusted his kente robe over one shoulder and walked slowly, deliberately, with the elders to the large acacia tree. The stool-carrier placed the royal stool on a level patch of ground, and the Chief sat, his palms resting on his knees, as the umbrella-carrier took his place beside him, bearing an enormous fringed red parasol.

Tension hung in the air, heavy, palpable. The messenger, still breathless, delivered the news that the Ashanti troops had burned down Okonswa village three days earlier, for refusing to pay taxes.

"They have killed the older men, who were unable to escape, and taken the young women, and the men and the gold back to Kumasi," said the messenger. "There are at least one hundred Ashanti warriors only a day's march from here. We are in great danger!"

Nana listened intently, and remained deep in thought after the messenger had finished. The only sound was the swish of the white-haired royal fly-whisk and the hum of the flies in

535

the heat.

Finally, he leaned forward and spoke in a low voice to the elders seated on stools on either side of him. He whispered at length to his Okyeame, his Linguist, his spokesperson. The Okyeame in turn stood up and faithfully relayed Nana's thoughts to the assembled villagers, waiting anxiously in the burning sun.

"Nana has spoken!" the Okyeame announced. "We have tried to bargain before, but these Ashanti warriors are ruthless. If they don't receive their taxes they will raze the village to the ground. Look at Okonswa village—totally destroyed. But the taxes they demand are too heavy for us to bear. It would ruin us and they would steal our young people and take them away to serve in the palace of the Asantahene in Kumasi. Let us take all the gold reserves we have and leave the village until it is safe to return."

*****

Last time I was in Ghana I went to the University Library in East Legon to see if I could find out more about Development Queens. I spent days in the rare books section, sitting at a wooden bench by the open window looking out onto the courtyard. At the information desk they couldn't find anything specifically on Queen Mothers, but they did find me a pile of dusty old manuscripts on the role of Chieftaincy from colonial times, and some more up-to-date academic and political tomes exploring its role in modern democratic Ghana.

Students dozed off next to me in the afternoon torpor as I pored over the records. Apparently, Chiefs were a key focus of resistance to Western invaders in the nineteenth century. They fought with courage and bravery, and some were captured and exiled, like the famous Queen Yaa Asantewa, who was our Esuantsiwa's first cousin. My Grandmother's name is the Fanti version of Yaa Asantewa's name. But later the Chiefs were bought off and became tools of colonial rule. The colonials ignored the Queens because they were only women, but these Queens were clearly a force to be reckoned with. In the 1970s and '80s they were powerful businesswomen (the Tomato Queens, the Yam Queens), controlling prices of key crops and employing hundreds of farm workers, male and female. These Queens were seen as a threat by generations of male rulers.

I was once looking for the room where I was about to facilitate a meeting in Accra, and by mistake came upon a room full of Queen Mothers. There must have been at least fifty, a magnificent sight all dressed up in their *kente* robes and headgear. I asked the doorman what was going on and he explained it was a meeting of the Queen Mothers' Trade Union, discussing their role in development for women. Collective action among women in Ghana clearly has a long tradition. In Western countries we are still waiting for women's political representation to become the norm.

Nowadays Chieftaincy appears to have a somewhat mixed reputation. On the one hand, it's seen as anachronistic and anti-modern—part of the problem rather than the solution, an obstacle to progress. On the other hand, the role still seems to command a lot of respect among many Ghanaians. The Chiefs and Queens have a long tradition in Akan ceremonial culture and they have ritual and moral authority. The basis of their power is enstoolment, and they have a local political and judicial role, including control of lands and resources, and the power to mobilise villages.

They can still be extremely influential locally, and some of them have earned a name for themselves as 'progressive' Chiefs and Queens. They can be catalysts for development, leaders and custodians of culture that can be harnessed at rural level, arguing against harmful traditional practices, raising funds for village amenities like roads, sanitation and water supply. Some of them seem to be quite active, installing street lighting, schools, clinics, community centres. So-called development doesn't have to come from outside. I like the fact that they are all referred to as 'Nana', there is no distinction between male and female, although the men still have the most power.

And like any system of power, it's also open to abuse, exploitation and self-aggrandisement. But the system is not static, it adapts and changes. The flexibility of Chieftaincy seems to have ensured its survival. For instance, my Dad agreed to be a representative of the

Chiefs on the Council of State, despite having been hounded out of Ghana as a refugee in the '80s. He told me what an acute dilemma it was for him. Should he see it as joining the other side, or as an unexpected opportunity to contribute his experience so late in his career?

And what about Development Chiefs and Queens, which would be my role? These positions appear to be relatively modern, created in 1985 by the paramount Chief of the Ashanti at the time, Asantahene Otomfuo Opoku Ware II, who wanted to bring Chieftaincy into the modern age by creating a role in the traditional system that was specifically dedicated to rural development. This was an attempt to speed up the development process while keeping it under village control. The Development Chiefs and Queens are largely from the villages themselves, or they are relatives living in towns who can supply leverage, influence and funds. It wasn't envisaged that it would be a role occupied by foreigners at first.

When I get home to London, my friend Raphael, a Ghanaian studying for a PhD at King's College on the subject of foreign-born Chiefs and Queens of Development, tells me he has traced fifty-four so far, one-third of them women (including Americans, Dutch, British, Australians, Germans, Swiss and Japanese). Raphael assures me I would be in illustrious company: some of them are famous, like Rita Marley, wife of Bob, Michelle Obama, Isaac Hayes, Stevie Wonder, even Bob Geldof... In the Western media, they are portrayed as 'White Chiefs', trophy rulers of exotic tribes, but in reality they are mostly fundraising for development projects like schools and clinics that are often run by the villagers themselves. But so far Raphael hasn't come across anyone in my position, with a Ghanaian father and English mother, who has 'come home'. The people in my village are my direct blood relatives.

My daughter Araba says the greatest fear of young people in her generation is FOMO—*Fear of Missing Out*. In contrast, the greatest fear of my generation, for people who were politically active in the 1970s, is FOSO—*Fear of Selling Out*. And, as a Mixed-Race person, I have an even greater challenge: FOBI—*Fear of Being Inauthentic*. Wherever I am, I seem to be making the wrong choice, being in the *Wrong Place*, not quite belonging.

My lifelong commitment to feminism, socialism and equality, and my lifelong search for identity and belonging—for my African self—has brought me to this crossroads. Do I see it as a threat or an opportunity? I have a choice: either I can reject this honour as being inauthentic, incompatible with my deeply held egalitarian principles, or I can hold on to my principles, and still embrace this as a rare opportunity as a daughter of my village, to work alongside my family and learn from within.

Looking back through my notes from my research in the library in Legon, I come across examples of graffiti I scribbled down in my notebook, copied from those I saw etched into the battered wooden desks in the library. In amongst the usual protestations of love and desire, my scrawled notes said:

> *I miss you, Daddy.*

> *Relax, God is in control.*

> *Stop misreading the world.*

> *You are unique, so be who you are.*

Forgotten graffiti seemed to point the way.

*****

Long ago, more than a hundred and fifty years past, the villagers listened in silence to the Chief's linguist, the Okyeame, telling them they must prepare to escape from imminent Ashanti attack. And then one by one the elders began to speak. Opinion was divided.

"We must stand and fight for the honour of the village and the protection of our children," said one.

"No!" said another, "there are too many warriors! We will never survive an onslaught of one hundred Ashanti warriors armed to the teeth, skilled in battle and triumphant from their recent plunder. They will be in no mood to compromise. Better to take the gold and treasure and go far away from here."

There was a murmur of agreement from the crowd. Then Esuantsiwa spoke up. Her voice was clear and strong and she

541

argued with passion.

"Nana, Father-in-law, we must remain and fight. We women will stand side-by-side with you men. If we run away and do not stand up to them, the Ashanti will return to kill us and steal our treasure when we come back home, no matter how long they have to wait. We have heard that when they find villages empty, the Ashanti burn down the houses and destroy the fields and crops, so when we come back we may find there is nothing left for us."

A ripple of dismay passed among the villagers. Perhaps the village should make ready to fight. The Okyeame stooped once more to hear the Chief's word.

"Nana says the words of his daughter-in-law Esuantsiwa are full of courage," began the Okyeame. "But it is useless to resist. The Ashanti are many, their weapons are more powerful than ours, and their warriors are experienced and disciplined fighters. At least we shall escape with our lives if we flee now."

There was a murmur of assent.

The Okyeame turned to Esuantsiwa.

"Nana says you must be the leader of the women here. Take the food and some of the gold dust from the storeroom and go deep into the forest with the other women and the children, where you cannot be found. Wait there until it is safe to return. The men will take the fishing boats and go out to sea as far as Saltpond. When the messenger tells us it is safe to return we will come into the forest and find you."

Esuantsiwa's face looked like thunder. She was breathing heavily, wiping her palms on her patterned wrapper. She opened her mouth to speak but the Chief made a gesture of silence.

The Okyeame said, "We have only a day to prepare. Nana says we must start immediately!"

The villagers began murmuring again, but Nana held up his hand and stood up to leave, with his entourage of stool carrier, umbrella-carrier, Linguist and Right-and-Left-Hand Elders.

When they had disappeared into the Chief's compound, the villagers began shouting and gesticulating.

Esuantsiwa tried to speak again but Dede, her aunt, intervened.

"Esuantsiwa, you are a young woman. You are not from here. You do not know how much danger we face."

Kwesi said, "Esuantsiwa was an Ashanti before she married the Chief's son. Perhaps she plans to betray us! Even your name means 'Woman of Ashanti!'"

Esuantsiwa had often wondered if they really trusted her. Did they think that because she was an Ashanti by birth, she could not be completely loyal to her new tribe? That she would lead them all into some kind of trap, by insisting that they stand and fight?

Esuantsiwa looked hard at Kwesi. She was not beautiful. She was small and slim, but she was strong. She had gained authority among the people of the village for her courage and intelligence. She had large, raven-black almond-shaped eyes, and she could hold people in a penetrating and fearsome gaze when she was angry or serious. One look was enough to silence

Kwesi.

"My first loyalty is to the Fanti now!" she countered. "And you well know that I have Fanti blood flowing through these veins as well. My Grandmother was a Fanti who married into the Ashanti. And now by marrying the Chief's son I have come home again to my people."

But she knew she had lost the argument about staying to fight. The villagers were still not sure whether to trust her. Is she really one of us or one of them? She went down to the harbour to help organise the carrying of the gold, kente cloth and provisions down to the boats, where the men were stowing everything safely on board. She watched as the Chief's stool, umbrella, fly-whisk, ceremonial sword and staff were carried down to the waiting boats, and then Nana himself, carried in his palanquin by four strong bare-chested young men.

She bade farewell to her husband Kofi, the Chief's son. By early evening, the last of the long fishing boats, piled with gold, food and treasures, slipped silently into the sunset heading towards Saltpond.

*****

It's the night before the big ceremony, and I badly need to get some sleep, but I just keep turning over the events of today in my head, terrified about what will happen tomorrow.

This morning started off well. We went for the pre-enstoolment ceremony at the village and I was all dressed up in my new blue, green and yellow *kente* print robe after spending hours at the guest house while the hairdresser worked on my hair.

At the entrance to the village there was a message for us, proclaiming 'We Welcome you, Friends of Akwonsa from UK', emblazoned on the American stars-and-stripes, probably left over from Obama's visit to Cape Coast last week. It was the wrong flag for us, but a heart-warming message, nonetheless.

In the village square there was music, singing and dancing, and then they carried me shoulder-high around the village. My Sister Molly and Lawrence's cousin Viv formally opened the newly refurbished schoolhouse, funded by donations from our UK family and friends. It was all going smoothly, until they showered a whole tin of talcum powder over me—all over my new dress and my hair-do, accompanied by much cheering and merriment. The talc stuck to my hot damp skin, lodged in the braids in my freshly done hair, and in the embroidery at the neck of my new dress, and went up my nose, causing hilarity amongst my British family members. I tried to brush it off my dress with my hand, but that just made it worse. What the hell was that all about? No-one could tell me. They just shrugged their shoulders. "It's tradition," they laughed. That's their answer to everything. I ended up laughing too.

Then the Chief, Nana, took me aside, away from the crowd, deeper into the village with the elders, to a place

I'd never been before. It was a clearing surrounded by huts, with a small stone circle in the centre shaded by a tree. Inside the circle there were three round smooth stones, the size of goose eggs.

"Queen Mother, these are our village gods. They will protect you, and the village and every one of us. You must tell no-one the whereabouts of our sacred place."

I am awed by the quiet stillness of the place, the depth of the symbolism. I am so privileged to have been welcomed into the heart of the village. I studied phenomenology of religion at university, the tradition of West African animism, the ideas the colonialists dismissed as pagan idolatry that were in fact symbols of oneness and of a supreme being, *Nyame*. Here in the villages the animist traditions have been fused seamlessly and beautifully with Catholicism, without any apparent contradiction.

Fremah told me later that the talc signifies the winner of an election, or of a court case; or who has been chosen to be Chief or Queen.

"It's not automatic," she explained. "You have to be chosen. The Council and the villagers have to agree on you, from a number of candidates. If people can't read, or they weren't there when the decision was made, it's still obvious the one covered in White powder is the chosen one. It signifies victory and joy. In the old days, before we had talcum powder, I think they used to use chalk. And now I must go and see the elders and try to sort out some problems before tomorrow…"

And there certainly *are* problems. Some of the local Chiefs don't want my ceremony to go ahead because there is an interminable land dispute going on between different factions in the village and the town. I'm caught in the cross-fire of a legal argument hundreds of years old, which doesn't look as if it's going to be settled any time soon. Apparently, these disputes are common in villages all over Ghana, especially now the price of land has risen. Some of the elders on one side of the argument think the other side will use my influence as Queen in the battle to resolve the dispute, so they don't want my enstoolment to go ahead until it's settled. The police have been given notice to stop the parade.

Fremah hopes to find a compromise. She wants me to sign a paper saying I will not use my position to intervene in the land dispute in any way. This is fine by me. I admire the way Fremah takes these things in her stride, just another hurdle to be negotiated. But this is all happening at the eleventh hour. Will she be able to pull it off by tomorrow?

She does a great job as my Okyeame, my spokesperson. Nevertheless, I am filled with trepidation. My family members from the UK have spent all their money coming out here for this ceremony, and donated money to the school, and on Fremah's instructions I have spent hundreds of pounds on food, cloth, brass bands, awnings, hire of tables and chairs. Hundreds of people are expected. We are all looking forward to a show. It is a decade since my father died, and this has given me a feeling of belonging, a tangible connection to the village in my own right, now that he is gone.

But what will happen tomorrow? Will we all be arrested? Will the ceremony be stopped? Nobody tells me what's happening or what it all means. There's no written plan or budget. I am just expected to pay up. I had no idea I was in for all this when I accepted this role. It seemed like an honour. Fremah said they sometimes send thugs from neighbouring villages to break the whole thing up. I can imagine falling from my palanquin to the ground, with chaos, fury, shouting all around me...

Lawrence is asleep already, gently snoring. He can sleep through anything. He's had a busy day, arranging transport and accommodation and food for all our guests. And I'm still lying here tossing and turning, listening to the crash of the ocean waves, thoughts about tomorrow cascading through my brain. I told them I didn't want to ride in a palanquin. It looks too precarious, especially if there might be trouble. I saw my father riding in a palanquin in the parade of Chiefs at the annual Afeyshe festival in Cape Coast. Dad looked magnificent in full regalia, wearing his crown, his sword and the royal fly-whisk in either hand, the talking drums pounding, the giant red umbrella whirling above his head as he waved and danced and swayed.

As his eldest daughter, I had to lead the procession, walking in front of him, whilst hundreds lined the route waving and cheering. I was overwhelmed with pride and admiration and excitement—and relief that I was not up there with my father, being borne aloft over the heads of the crowd. I told Fremah categorically if I have to go in a palanquin 'because it's tradition' then they must find the shortest men in the village to carry me. I don't like heights.

Inevitably, they have chosen four of the very tallest men they could find, stationed at each corner of the palanquin. They must be nearly seven feet tall—African albinos with caramel skin, blond Afro hair and eyelashes, reminding me strongly of my old hairdresser Karl, their faces creased with effort as they take the strain and lift me up onto their heads. The procession sets off along the beach, and as they hoist me into the air I can feel myself slipping and falling backwards into the ocean, as I call out desperately and grasp the sides, but to no avail... I slide backwards into deep dark water, drifting soundlessly down, down, in slow motion, holding my breath, like Holly Hunter in the movie, *The Piano*. As soon as I breathe in, I will surely drown.

Dark silhouettes of my ceremonial sword and royal fly-whisk float above me. There are stars in the water, like sea sparkle... in fact, they *are* stars, twinkling in the distance light-years away; and I am in space, doing the breast-stroke. The universe is in deep cosmic silence. More stars appear, until the Blackness is crammed with constellations.

There is a blue-and-green planet in front of me, like a

gigantic bubble. Planet Earth, her continents floating in translucent oceans. And stretched out on top of the planet is a live goldfish, as big as the Arctic, its golden-orange body curved along the disc of the globe, the scales on its back glimmering in starlight. It is a breath-taking sight. I feel a deep sense of peace, harmony, belonging, floating in space...

"Are you awake, Lawrence? I just had the most vivid dream about fish again."

"You and your fish dreams! I remember you said last time they all jumped out of the pond and were flapping about, dying on the garden path."

"No, not like that, only one fish this time, and it was alive, the size of the Arctic continent! It was on top of the world..."

"A really happy fish! Well that makes a change. It's a good omen I'm sure." Lawrence is only half awake.

"Not quite what I meant, but yes, it must be a good omen."

I hope so. When momentous things happen, I step into my out-of-body place of parallel hallucinations. Before breakfast, I go down to the guest house lobby to check my emails for messages from my step-cousins Lizzie and Kevin, who are arriving from the UK today, just in time for the big ceremony. And as I sign in to the internet, there it is: the icon for British Telecom, a green-and-blue transparent bubble with a flash of orange on top, a miniature inspiration for my dream of Planet Earth.

*****

Long ago, more than a hundred and fifty years past, at dawn's light, the two Ashanti envoys appeared in the village. In the dead of night their warriors had already assembled noiselessly in the forest.

"We have surrounded the village," the Envoys announced. "Where is your Chief? We have come to take our dues."

"Our messenger said they were a whole day's march away! How could they have travelled here so soon?" whispered Ama, Esuantsiwa's terrified sister-in-law. "We must run for our lives! If we scatter now, some of us may get away."

Esuantsiwa was also deeply afraid, but she knew they would not survive if they tried to escape. She had to find a way to save them all. She needed a plan.

"Nana is not here. I am Esuantsiwa, daughter-in-law of the Chief," she said. "I am a woman of Ashanti, I am the leader here. I must speak with your General."

The envoys exchanged uncertain glances. They had hoped to terrify the villagers into immediately surrendering all they had, especially if the news of the treatment of Okonswa village had reached them. They had expected fear or resistance at the very least, or that the villagers would try to make their escape.

Reluctantly, discovering that the Chief had already left with the rest of the men, the envoys agreed to take Esuantsiwa to see the General. She took a length of heavy double-weave gold-and-red kente cloth, the cloth of kings, out of one of the baskets in her hut, and wrapped it loosely around her body and over her shoulder. She retrieved one of the two pots of gold dust from the store that she had kept back from the treasures loaded onto the boats. She and her three sisters-in-law, Ama, Efua and Esi, followed the Envoys down the winding path through the shaded forest and beyond the trees, where they came to a large patch of open ground flooded with sunlight. A group of a hundred warriors stood waiting for battle, the red plumes of their headdresses quivering, their bare limbs muscled and oiled, their spears at their sides.

They could hold me hostage here, or kill me and attack the village, she thought. Why would they listen to me, or show any mercy? We should have tried to run away and escape. Ama was right. Surely some of us would have made it into the forest. Her palms were wet with sweat, but she didn't falter. She approached the Ashanti General.

"I am Esuantsiwa, woman of Ashanti," she told him. "I am your kinswoman, married into the Fanti. I beg you not to attack our village. Our men have gone and only we women and children are left, and a few old men. I can offer you a token of one pot of gold dust if you will go and leave your kins-woman's village in peace."

The General hesitated. Then he took a step back and conferred with his lieutenants. He turned to her again. "We will weigh the gold in our own pans," he said. The weighing pans were made ready on level ground. Esuantsiwa's sisters-in-law Efua and Esi poured the gold dust carefully into the pan, weighed against the ornate brass weights carved into designs of animals and birds. But the pan had been deliberately punctured with tiny holes, and the fine dust was running through to the tray beneath.

"More!" the General demanded.

There was a pause. Esuantsiwa felt the anger rising within her. She fixed him with her hard stare. She wanted to call him a cheat, to show her fury and contempt, the bitterness the Fanti villagers felt at being enslaved and impoverished by Ashanti aggression over so many years.

She moved as if to speak to the General. But she checked herself. There was too much at stake. Instead she asked her sisters-in-law Efua and Esi to fetch another pot of gold dust. It was all they had left. If the General insisted on more, she could not deliver. They waited in silence in the burning sun until the two young women returned. Efua and Esi began to pour again. "Pour faster!" Esuantsiwa directed. All eyes were on the golden stream. As it cascaded more rapidly, the holes in the weighing pan became blocked with gold dust, and at last it was filled to the brim and the pans were level.

*****

My Mom Faith helps me dress in the Bob Marley room at Saffia's guest house: a long *kente* robe with gold metallic threads arranged loosely over a snow-white underdress, a plaited *kente* circle around my head, and matching slippers. I am wearing my father's gold chains, bracelets and rings that Mum has brought with her, carefully wrapped in tissue paper and stowed in velvet-covered jewellery boxes. In my hands, I carry my father's golden sword and fly-whisk.

In these clothes, I feel transformed. It means the family wants to show they accept me. I have a role, a part in this clan. I belong. I was afraid that my cousins would feel put out—any one of them could have been chosen, but they say they are very happy for me. "You have earned it, you have done a lot for our village."

In private my brother Sam said they are all very relieved. "We have all got busy lives these days. We don't have so much time for the traditional stuff, like the older generation. Dad was so thrilled when you took such an interest in our culture, and you are so like him, the way you talk, your energy and enthusiasm, your personality, they took to you," he tells me. "It's a lot of responsibility, this role. They expect you to support the village and it can be a lot of work. It is definitely a case of servant leadership!"

"But I keep telling everyone, I couldn't do it without my UK family's and friends' support."

Every part of my family in the UK is represented—Lawrence and our children Araba Grace and Jacob Kwesi, my sister Molly and her family, and Lawrence's cousin Viv and her family, have all flown in for the ceremony. Even my Stepdad's niece and her husband are here.

And they are all looking on encouragingly as I step into the palanquin parked at the back of the school on the outskirts of the neighbouring village.

It's not a dream. This time it's real.

Up close, the palanquin is the shape and size of a

narrow canoe, draped in bright lengths of *kente* cloth and contrasting black-and-white adinkra cloth, stuffed with straw and paper underneath and plump cushions on top for comfort. As soon as I am seated, an oversized *kente*-print cloth is tossed over me, shrouding me inside the palanquin like a tent.

It is stifling, humid, hot and dark in here, muffling the din outside. I can't see anything, but I can hear the ululating women, the shouts and laughter from the crowd. Sitting in front of me is my Spirit Child, a beautiful, small, slim seven-year-old girl, ebony-skinned, dressed in *kente*, a matching plaited circle of cloth on her head, and a pure white handkerchief in each hand. She doesn't say a word, but she turns around to me and flashes me a smile, showing perfect white teeth. She is Fremah's daughter, Aisha. Fremah told me that every Queen or Chief must be accompanied by a Spirit Child, to remind them of the child within every leader—creative, spirited, playful and pure-hearted, lest they become too high-and-mighty and abuse their power.

I can hear the talking drums start up, slender, barrel-shaped, narrowed at one end, carried on the heads of four men, the drummers beating the drum-skins from behind with long slender hammers.

The cloth tent is whisked away, and the palanquin is hoisted up into the air on its wooden frame, like a clumsy camel rising to its feet, back legs first, then front. There's much urging and shouting of instructions as many hands lift us onto the heads of four strong young men, a circle of cloth protecting their heads from the pressure of the wooden frame. And then we are off, skirting the side of the school building, down the slope, onto the main road, emerging into a cacophony of sound amongst the dancing, shouting throng.

It's a spectacular sight from this vantage-point. The Head of the village walks just in front of me in his robes, bearing the village standard, with small carved figures in gold on the top. Flower girls shower petals ahead of us on the path. They are wearing matching outfits, with decorative white chalk stamps on their slender dark brown arms. Hundreds of people are gathered, some from neighbouring villages, sporting T-shirts bearing my stool-name, Nana Efua Esuantsiwa I, with my photo on the front. Others are wearing matching *kente* print cloth, the men in shirts and dashikis and the women in Fanti dresses sewn specially for the occasion, a sea of blue, green and yellow—the colours I have chosen specially for the parade.

A gigantic red umbrella twirls above my head, beating the air in time to the drums. The four giant elongated 'talking drums' just behind me are hammering so hard in my head, I can hardly think. Lawrence, Jake and Araba follow the palanquin, walking in front of the 'talking drums', wearing their *kente*, dancing their way slowly along the road in the procession.

Above the crowds, alone in my separateness, excitement, fragility and fear, it is bewildering, strange, another out-of-body experience. But this time I am up here, actually in my body while it's all going on down below, the untidy parade snaking off into the distance, and hundreds more behind me, making towards the village. I am in their hands. I have to give them my total trust. If they wanted they could drop me at any moment, shovel me into the gutter with the rubbish and the flies. They tell me nothing about what is going to happen next. There is no written plan or programme. I have an intense fear of heights, of not being in control. I'm a strategic planner—for God's sake get me out of here!

Aisha, my seven-year-old 'spirit child', sits in the palanquin in front of me. She doesn't have time to chat or give me reassurances, she is completely engaged in energetically waving her handkerchiefs in the air with rapid rhythmic flicks of her wrist, first left, then right. People are urging me to *Dance! Dance, Nana*! Lifting my sword and fly-whisk into the air, I sway my body from side to side, as I saw my father do. Within minutes, my arms and hands are already stiff and aching. Luckily Spirit Child knows what to do and I follow her lead as she alternately performs her expert hanky-waving, and then rests for a few moments before resuming. She gives me the energy and spirit to carry on.

A tall thin man drifts nonchalantly through the crowd, looking detached and cool, wearing an outsize pair of swimming goggles. Is any of this real? Any minute now I will see a giant goldfish swimming past.

Doubts begin to flood through me again. What am I doing up here? Would anybody recognise me? What right has anyone to be called a Queen? Why should anyone be carried on a palanquin, above everyone else, when we are all equals? I am suddenly reminded of the woman in Tanzania whose name I never knew, the heavy tree on her head, baby on her back, a bag of brushwood in each hand, her face creased with effort as she staggered down the forest path with her load. I wonder how I can possibly square all this with my socialism, feminism, vision of liberation.

I have been disintegrating again these last few years, going through the mother of all menopauses, lashing out at people, verbally and physically. Hurting those I am closest to, those I love and admire most, against all my principles. Guilty of the very behaviour that has given me the most pain in my own life. It's no way to heal. I want to apologise to all of them. I am not even up to being the kind of person I've tried to become. What right do I have to be up here?

I look at other people with envy, the way they wear their 'Selves' so lightly, without thought or hesitation, like a *kente* mantle casually draped over a shoulder. I have spent my life in constant tension, trying to navigate the world, searching for the space between Black and White. People will always look down on me up here. A fake.

*****

Long ago, more than a hundred and fifty years past, Esuantsiwa's sister-in-law Ama had filled the weighing pans to the brim with gold dust, and Esuantsiwa demanded of the Ashanti General, "You have your gold. Now will you leave our village in peace?"

The General hesitated. Should he just capture her now and attack the village anyway? But she caught him off-guard again with her penetrating gaze. There was something about the confidence of this young woman who dared to stand up to him. Besides, his men were tired and hungry. They had sustained some casualties, in spite of their triumphant raids. His envoys had come back with the search party and assured him there were no more treasures to be found in this village, the men had taken them all and gone off in their boats. It would be impossible to catch up with them over land. Finally, he nodded assent, and shouted some orders. The warriors collected the gold dust and the weighing pans, followed him from the clearing with the rest of the battalion, and disappeared into the forest. Esuantsiwa and her sisters-in-law watched them go.

Esuantsiwa and Ama returned to the village triumphant and unharmed, followed by Esi and Efua carrying the two round empty pots.

"Your bravery has saved us, Esuantsiwa," old Aunt Dede said. "No one but you could have faced the General and expect to return with their life. We thought he would kill you instantly."

Esuantsiwa could not believe the Ashanti had gone. She could not sleep that night. She left the lamp burning and jumped with every stir or rustle that came from the forest. The following night she slept fitfully again, disturbed by dreams of faint shadowy figures emerging out of the darkness of the trees.

By the third day she was finally convinced it was not a trick. They would not come back, for now. She sent the messenger to Saltpond to tell the men it was safe to return, and within a few days they were back with the gold and treasures, to hear the story of how Esuantsiwa saved the village.

"She is the second cousin of Yaa Asantewa, the Queen of Ashanti," they said. "She has the blood of a great Warrior Queen flowing through her veins."

And so, they enstooled Esuantsiwa as Queen of the people, and all her descendants have the right to call themselves members of the Royal Family and be chosen as Chiefs and Queen Mothers in their own right, through the maternal line.

*****

All the same, it's thrilling to think I am descended from a Warrior Queen. Who'd have thought it, with my temperament? A matrilineal tradition any self-respecting feminist like me should be proud of, where women have an automatic right to a voice, and to political representation. And Esuantsiwa, my ancestress, didn't even fire a shot. It was all done through negotiation, based on her dual heritage.

There's a battered old cream-and-maroon bus going by, full of passengers waving, cheering, calling out to me. The excitement, the crowds, the energy, the atmosphere—I am getting drunk on it, it is flooding through me. Why do I keep beating myself up? I should go with the flow, follow my inner Spirit Child.

This whole procession is for me, a daughter of this village, daughter of my father, great-grand-daughter of Esuantsiwa. I am at the centre of this beautiful powerful ancient ritual, and it is an extraordinary experience. Some good must come of it. My English sister is chatting to my African brother, my step-cousins and my cousinsin-law from England are dancing with my cousins from the village.

And there's that same battered cream-and-maroonbus again, only minutes later, coming back from the opposite direction. It's slowing down. They must have deliberately decided to turn the bus around to take another look at the parade. They are all waving again, the same passengers, leaning out of the windows, smiling, waving, cheering, taking photos, calling to me, *Nana, Nana!*

I have lost track of time, we seem to have been going for hours. We must surely be nearing the end by now. Turning off the main road on the outskirts of the village, the parade has stopped while the palanquincarriers are replaced with fresh, even more energetic young men, of ill-matching heights and full of vim and vigour—a disastrous combination, as they whirl me wonkily round and round in a circle, and bounce me up and down, the crowd reaching a frenzy and shrieking their approval. It must be the palanquin equivalent of the bumps.

We are on our way again, weaving among the huts towards the centre of the village. Finally, we reach the parade ground where the Chiefs, Queen Mothers, elders, and hundreds of guests are assembled under brightly coloured awnings, and the brass band signals our arrival with a rousing tune. I do love a party! We are only running three hours late. I am plucked from the palanquin, queasy and unsteady, to sit in state with my UK family around me. Spirit Child Aisha sits in front of me, sipping a Coke, while the speeches are read out and we enjoy the dancing by children from the local orphanage, dressed in matching pink. The Paramount Chief of Oguaa, Cape Coast, tells us that progress must involve a joint effort from everyone. He thanks me and my family for supporting the village, and tells me that my professional background and knowledge of development will come in very handy in the future.

From now on, he says, I must drop the name Jane and go by my stool name, Nana Efua Esuantsiwa the First. Imagine signing a cheque with that.

They call me to swear the oath in Fanti in front of the crowd:

"Emi Nana Efua Esuantsiwa, se wofremi anapao se awiabrio, awia muo nsumuo, ma ba."

The Paramount Chief translates for the English guests. "You have now become a Queen Mother, a leader of your people. You have sworn an oath that any time they call on you—rain or shine, morning, noon or night—you will answer their call. And the Chief has sworn an oath to you in return, on behalf of the village—if ever you call on them, they will respond to your call. So, it is a shared responsibility between you and the village, and the village and you, and this should go on, until death do us part…"

And now everyone is dancing. Fremah has done such an excellent job of organising it all, it is her turn to be covered in talc. She is a winner.

I am profoundly moved by this experience. I feel it deep in my bones, as if it were a story already written.

I have my mother to thank for all this, and all of our family. She fought to keep me, she gave me life, inspiration and possibilities that few others have known. She has the spirit of a Warrior Queen. And I have my Ghanaian father and my father's family to thank for all this—for instantly embracing me and welcoming me home.

Epilogue

Chameleon

Accra, early Saturday evening

Fearsome Atlantic waves crash onto the shore on palm-fringed Labadi Beach. It's been a long day. Weary emaciated horses follow their owners up and down the sands, proffering rides to the usual weekend crowd of visitors and locals. Most of the beachgoers prefer to stay prostrate under their beach umbrellas, sipping cold beer and feasting on plates of grilled lobster and shrimps, bargaining with the hawkers selling jewellery, carvings, roasted nuts and cigarettes. Meanwhile, troops of skinny athletic boys work the sands, their extraordinary acrobatic feats—cartwheels in the air, human towers, fire-eating, walking on smashed glass—earning them only a few tossed coins and a desultory ripple of applause. Everything is on offer. You can even get a massage or a pedicure with the sand between your toes. We too are stretched out on the loungers alongside the others, whilst Araba has her picture taken with a real live python.

"Those boys over there keep calling me *obibini oburoni*. What does that mean?" Jake asks the waiter.

"Don't mind them," the waiter replies genially. "It means Black White people. There are a lot more of you around these days... More beers? Club or Star?"

We race into the ocean to enjoy the last of the fun before sundown, joining scores of people in a narrow strip of water, leaping up and down, frolicking in the waves. Either side of us, the water is empty of bathers. Dangerous cross-currents rapidly emerge here. Seawater that is only ankle-deep can suddenly and unexpectedly surge over your head, with waves so strong they can knock you off your feet. The lifeguard on duty blows a whistle from time to time, herding revellers to a different stretch of water further along where it is safe for bathing. Discarded slimy blue plastic supermarket bags and transparent water sachets are caught in the backwash, swirling around us in the shallows—the sad price of development.

Emerging on the sands again, dripping and exhilarated from the surf, I walk a little way along the shoreline, away from the crowds, to dry off and escape the hustle and bustle. A trader approaches me in tattered shorts and dreadlocks, unrolling his frayed bundle of oil paintings of the usual colourful palm-fringed beach scenes at sunset, and women carrying pots on their heads, their voluptuous rounded rears always the focal point of the picture.

"Sista! African American Sista! You got dollars? You

wanna buy pictures? I paint them myself, just look, no charge for looking…" His eyes twinkle and he grins at me broadly through broken teeth. I shake my head vigorously and smile, "No dollars, sorry, only pounds…" and walk on a bit further to enjoy the last rays of sunset before we go home to Dzorwulu for dinner, where Mom Faith will be waiting for us, with dishes of fried grouper, jollof rice and hot pepper sauce.

A young woman in a blue swimsuit races up to me excitedly with her new iPad. Can she take a selfie with me to put on her Facebook page, "to show I have a new White friend"?

"But my Dad was Ghanaian. I have family here…"

A flicker of uncertainty crosses her face. She looks taken aback.

"O. Are you sure?"

"Yes, of course I'm sure. Look, my skin tone, my hair… mixed… like Bob Marley, Barack Obama… *Obibini Oburoni*?"

She looks blank. "Your Dad was Ghanaian? Well then, he did a very good job. I can't see any Black in you at all."

Now it's my turn to be taken aback. "But why should it be a good thing to hide your Black skin? I am proud of being Ghanaian."

"Well, to me, you look White—*shiny* White," she insists.

I am confused and crushed. Is this the legacy of colonialism? How can it be that everything good must be

White, and Blackness is so undesirable that an African father does the best job if he can succeed in leaving no trace of it in his children? I have been on this life-long journey to find my roots, my father, my heart-home, only to find that I can still change from a 'White-Black' to an 'African American' to 'shiny White' in an instant.

An awkward silence follows. We are both perplexed. She hesitates, not quite knowing what to do next. Then she shrugs, and is off again with her iPad, to look for a Facebook friend less complicated than I.

The beach begins to empty before the sun disappears— half-light, half-dark, palm trees dissolving into shadow. Afro-beat blares from the bars as the lights appear in the night-spots strung out along the shore. I pause a moment longer looking out across the ocean, trawling the sand with my toes. I suddenly remember Kumba on Clapham Common at twilight, a lifetime ago when I was less than five years old, how we two small girls saw each other, by the swings, in a moment of complete recognition.

A slimy blue plastic bag washes up and wraps itself around my ankle, like alien blue seaweed. My identity is still everybody's property, up for grabs; flotsam and jetsam tossed about on the waves with the discarded plastic, ebbing and flowing with the tide. A chameleon, magically changing colour in an instant through other people's gaze.

Is this it?

Is it possible just to stick two bits of narrative together and call it "me," like missing pieces of a jigsaw puzzle? Do people ever see the whole picture, or just bits of it?

I've been looking for a place to heal from things I don't speak of. To deal with my rage and fear and depression. I have lived in a state of alert, fending off attack, preparing for attack. I have made decisions I don't want, deciding not to decide, seeking for ideas, hoarding things because I am lost, afraid of losing myself because I'm not found. Still searching for a space to be safe, at home in my own body.

*****

Four years later, I walked into a room full of Mixed-Race activists for the first time.

I cried. And laughed. No need to explain what we are. We argue, fall out, come together, support each other. Family.

Living with ambiguity is an art. Perhaps wholeness consists of holding many contradictory identities in your head at any one time.

It's a life's work.

Acknowledgements

Special thanks to:
My Mother, and all my Mums and Dads for all your love, patience and support.

Our Children, Abena Grace and Joshua Kwesi

My mentor, Dr Rosalind Eyben (Professor Emeritus, Gender and International Development, University of Sussex), for invaluable advice, encouragement and ideas, and being by my side throughout the creative process; and my editor and agent Kelly Davis, without whose continuing support and belief in me, this book would not have been written.

The writers Michael Morpurgo, Hannah Pool, Kate Morrison, and Mark Haysom for helping to find the writer in me.

The people who taught me the craft of writing: The Arvon

Foundation, and the memoir writing course at Morley College London 2015–16.

All my British and Ghanaian family and my friends all over the world, especially:

John Christopher Lawrence Caine, Hugh Goldsmith, Mary Bull, Valerie Shawcross and Naomi Rich for your constant support and generosity; Natalie Jones, Mary Ann Clements, Marion Bowman, Jane Buckley Sanders, Carlis Douglas, Bernadette Vallely, Maureen Stevens, Maggie Baxter, Kate Grosser, Rosemary Adaser, for reading the text and giving me your generous feedback and help with technical issues; and Amy Hughes for copy-editing the final manuscript; Faustina Koomson, Tina Britwaum, Adiki Doe, Akoanso village, Dr Raphael Aidoo, Sonia Lye-Fook, Chandra Bedu, Marilyn Aniwa, Nana Otoo Oyortey MBE, for your invaluable help with our Ghanaian context, language and heritage; Charlotte Wynne-Parry, Sheila and Mark Smith, Charles Bell, Fliss and Sue, Joanna Maycock, Sue Tibballs, Marilyn Thomson, for enduring friendship, and Clare Walters, my 'Wise Woman'; The Ottolenghi family for inspiring stories.

In memoriam: Efua Dorkenoo and Angela Hale, who played such pivotal roles in my story and will never be forgotten.
My networks who gave me memories, insight and

solidarity:

Mixed-Race Peeps, Mixed-Race Irish, Intermix, Mixed-Race Matters and Halu Halo; Phenomenal Women, Powerful Women and the Queen Mothers; Healing Solidarity, The European Women's Lobby, Womankind, Fawcett Society, Gender and Development Network, Women's Resource Centre, Management Development Network, FORWARD, Fawcett Society; Old School Ladies who Lunch, Sisters who Scoff, and the Round Table; University of Leicester Library archives, Leicester University Students' Union and Leicester Mercury for documents and photographs.

Patricia for beautiful Caribbean braids and Barbara for Ghanaian tailoring, to create my Afropean Style.

And thanks to all my family and friends who contributed interviews, memories, stories, advice, encouragement, and waited patiently for this book to appear.

About the Author

Esuantsiwa Jane Goldsmith was born in the UK in 1953 and lives in London. She grew up as Jane Goldsmith but now uses her Ghanaian name, Esuantsiwa. In 1975, while studying at Leicester University, she became the first woman of colour to be elected President of Leicester University Students' Union. She was awarded an Honorary Doctorate of Laws by Leicester University in 2015, in recognition of her work in International Development and Human Rights. In March 2018, Leicester University unveiled a specially commissioned portrait of Esuantsiwa, to celebrate International Women's Day and the centenary of the women's vote.

In 1995, she founded Anona Development Consultancy to work in the not-for-profit sector as an energiser and motivator, offering management development consultancy, facilitation, training, team-building and strategy development. Her clients include over 100 different organisations on five different continents. She was formerly a member of the UK Government Delegation to the United Nations Fourth World Conference on Women, Beijing 1995, Commissioner for the Women's National Commission (Public Appointment), Chair of the Fawcett Society, Chair and Co-founder of the Gender and Development Network, Vice Chair of ActionAid UK, Trustee of VSO, the Equality and Diversity Forum, Akina Mama Wa Africa, and Ambassador for the Women's Resource Centre.

Esua plays a leading role in her local Black Lives Matter group and in the Healing Solidarity Collective